FUNDAMENTAL JUSTICE: SECTION 7 OF THE CANADIAN CHARTER OF RIGHTS AND FREEDOMS

ESSENTIALS OF
CANADIAN LAW

FUNDAMENTAL JUSTICE

SECTION 7 OF THE CANADIAN CHARTER OF RIGHTS AND FREEDOMS

HAMISH STEWART

Faculty of Law, University of Toronto

IRWIN LAW

Fundamental Justice: Section 7 of the Canadian Charter of Rights and Freedoms
© Irwin Law Inc., 2012

Published in 2012 by

Irwin Law Inc.
14 Duncan Street
Suite 206
Toronto, ON
M5H 3G8

www.irwinlaw.com

ISBN: 978-1-55221-225-7
e-book ISBN: 978-1-55221-226-4

Library and Archives Canada Cataloguing in Publication

Stewart, Hamish

Fundamental justice : section 7 of the Canadian Charter of Rights and Freedoms / Hamish Stewart.

(Essentials of Canadian law)

Includes bibliographical references and index.

Issued also in electronic format.

ISBN 978-1-55221-225-7

1. Civil rights—Canada. 2. Canada. Canadian Charter of Rights and Freedoms. I. Title. II. Series: Essentials of Canadian law

KE4381.5.S74 2012   342.7108'5   C2011-908152-0
KF4483.C519S74 2012

The publisher acknowledges the financial support of the Government of Canada through the Canada Book Fund for its publishing activities.

We acknowledge the assistance of the OMDC Book Fund, an initiative of Ontario Media Development Corporation.

Printed and bound in Canada.

1 2 3 4 5   16 15 14 13 12

For my teachers

SUMMARY TABLE OF CONTENTS

DETAILED TABLE OF
CONTENTS

PREFACE

Some years ago, at the end of a class on the *Motor Vehicle Reference*,[1] a student asked me, "What are the principles of fundamental justice?" In response, I quoted Lamer J's holding that these principles are the "basic tenets of our legal system" that lie "in the inherent domain of the judiciary as guardians of the justice system"[2] and defended his justification for judicial review under the *Charter*.[3] The student was not in the least satisfied. "Yes, I understand all that," he continued, "but what *are* the principles of fundamental justice?" What he wanted was not only a general description of the principles, or a methodology for determining what they were, but a specification of the precise legal norms that the Supreme Court of Canada had identified as worthy of constitutional status under section 7. This book is a belated attempt to answer the student's question. I discuss the place of section 7 in the constitutional order (Chapter 1) and I give an account of the Court's method for deciding whether a particular legal principle is so fundamental that it merits recognition under section 7 (Chapter 2). I go on to state, as clearly and positively as the caselaw permits, the conditions under which section 7 will apply to a legal dispute (Chapter 3), the legal norms that have been recognized, or rejected, as principles of fundamental justice under section 7 (Chapters 4 and 5), and the very limited circumstances in

---

1   *Reference re Motor Vehicle Act*, [1985] 2 SCR 486.
2   *Ibid* at 503.
3   *Ibid* at 495–500.

which an infringement of section 7 will be justified under section 1 (Chapter 6). But throughout the book, and in the conclusion (Chapter 7), I return to my original answer to the student's question by trying to show the importance of these principles to the legal order of a free and democratic society.

I have dedicated this book to my teachers. Like most contemporary legal academics, I was formally a student for a very long time, and informally I will always remain one; so I have had many teachers over the years, and I expect to have many more. The dedication is sincerely meant for all of them. Nonetheless, I would like to specifically acknowledge the influence of several teachers from whom I have learned something about the craft of teaching: my parents Ian Stewart and Ella Stewart; Ms Patricia Leuty, formerly head of mathematics at Lawrence Park Collegiate Institute; Professor David K Foot of the Department of Economics, University of Toronto; Professors Benjamin M Friedman and Amartya K Sen of the Department of Economics, Harvard University; the late Dr J Anthony Dawson of the Royal Conservatory of Music, Toronto; and Professor Ernest J Weinrib of the Faculty of Law, University of Toronto. These teachers all have several outstanding qualities in common: a deep belief in the seriousness and importance of their subject; the ability to present their material clearly; respectful responsiveness to all questions raised inside and outside the classroom; and a habit of making their students feel like "partners in the great joint venture of learning."[4] In these ways, they exemplify what Northrop Frye liked to say was the primary function of a teacher: "To help create the structure of the subject in the student's mind."[5] I try to live up to their example.

I am very grateful to Jeffrey Miller of Irwin Law for supporting this book and to Alisa Posesorski for her meticulous editing. I would like to thank, with apologies to anyone I have overlooked, the friends and colleagues who have read portions of this book in draft or who have taken the time to discuss its subject matter with me: Sujit Choudhry, Thomas Cromwell, David Dyzenhaus, Audrey Macklin, Marc Rosenberg, Martha Shaffer, Robert Sharpe, and Gary Trotter. Erica Bussey provided excellent research assistance at an early stage of the project. I am grateful to Michel Troper for forcing me to rethink some of the justifications for judicial review of legislation that I had always taken

---

4   Ernest J Weirnrib, "The Teacher" (2007) 57 UTLJ 131 at 144.
5   Northrop Frye, *On Education* (Markham, ON: Fitzhenry and Whiteside, 1988) at 13; this theme is repeated throughout the book.

for granted. And I thank my students in Criminal Law and Evidence Law, who have helped me explore the structure and content of section 7.

Finally, my wife Susan Taylor and our children Sean, Geoffrey, Matthew, and Colin provided inspiration and support for this work, as always.

Toronto
Remembrance Day 2011

CHAPTER 1

INTRODUCTION

A. INTRODUCTION

Section 7 of the *Canadian Charter of Rights and Freedoms* reads as follows:

> Everyone has the right to life, liberty and security of the person and the right not to be deprived thereof except in accordance with the principles of fundamental justice.

> Chacun a droit à la vie, à la liberté et à la sécurité de sa personne; il ne peut être porté atteinte à ce droit qu'en conformité avec les principes de justice fondamentale.

The subject of this book is the interpretation and application of section 7. In this introductory chapter, I place section 7 in the context of the Constitution of Canada as a whole, and particularly in the context of the *Charter* itself, and I briefly consider its relationship to other rights-protecting instruments.

B. THE *CHARTER* IN ITS CONSTITUTIONAL CONTEXT

The Constitution of Canada consists of a number of texts as well as a number of principles, practices, and conventions that are not expressly stated in the texts.[1] The two central constitutional texts are the *Constitution Act, 1867* (better known to students of history as the *British North America Act, 1867*) and the *Constitution Act, 1982*.[2] Both are statutes of the Parliament of the United Kingdom. The history of the *Constitution Act, 1867* is well beyond the scope of this book. The political process leading up to the enactment of the *Constitution Act, 1982* — the negotiations between federal and provincial governments, the questions referred to the Supreme Court of Canada, the federal/provincial compromise of November 1981 reached without the participation of the government of Quebec, and the legislative process in the United Kingdom — has been described elsewhere and will not be reviewed here.[3]

The purpose of the *Constitution Act, 1982* was two-fold, and both purposes were equally important to the federal government of the day. The first was to provide an amending formula for the Constitution of Canada so that further constitutional change would not require a statute of the United Kingdom enacted in response to a petition to Her Majesty, but could be done in Canada in accordance with the constitution itself. To this end, section 2 of the *Canada Act 1982* provided that "No Act of the Parliament of the United Kingdom passed after the *Constitution Act, 1982* comes into force shall extend to Canada as part of its law." It might be argued that since Parliament cannot bind itself, section 2 cannot prevent Parliament from continuing to amend the Constitution of Canada. But the better view is that any such attempt to amend the Constitution of Canada, regardless of its validity as a matter of UK law and regardless of section 2, would not be valid Canadian law because Canadian political and legal actors, including Canadian courts, would not recognize or give effect to such enactments.[4] Thus, when Queen Elizabeth II gave royal assent to the *Canada Act 1982* on 17 April 1982,

---

1   *Reference re Secession of Quebec*, [1998] 2 SCR 217 at paras 49–52. The principles not expressly stated in the constitutional texts are sometimes called "unwritten" (*ibid* at para 52).

2   *Constitution Act, 1982*, being Schedule B to *Canada Act 1982* (UK), 1982, c 11.

3   See, for instance, Peter H Russell, *Constitutional Odyssey*, 3d ed (Toronto: University of Toronto Press, 2004) ch 8; Edward McWhinney, *Canada and the Constitution 1979–1982* (Toronto: University of Toronto Press, 1982); Roy Romanow et al, *Canada . . . Notwithstanding* (Toronto: Carswell/Methuen, 1984). The main source texts are assembled in Anne Bayefsky, ed, *Canada's Constitution Act 1982 & Amendments: A Documentary History*, 2 vols (Toronto: McGraw-Hill Ryerson, 1989).

4   See, among others, Peter W Hogg, *Constitutional Law of Canada*, 5th ed supplemented, loose-leaf (Scarborough: Thomson Carswell, 2007) ch 3.5(e); Brian Slattery, "The Independence of Canada" (1983) 5 Sup Ct L Rev 369.

the Constitution of Canada was "patriated" in the sense that future amendments would be made in Canada and not in the United Kingdom.

The second purpose of the *Constitution Act, 1982* was to provide a constitutional instrument for the protection of basic human rights and freedoms in Canada. That instrument is the *Canadian Charter of Rights and Freedoms*.[5] Section 7 is part of this *Charter*; in contrast to some other sections of the *Charter*, its final wording was achieved as early as the federal government's proposed draft resolution of 3 September 1980 and remained unchanged in subsequent drafts.[6]

Section 52(1) of the *Constitution Act, 1982* provides:

> The Constitution of Canada is the supreme law of Canada, and any law that is inconsistent with the provisions of the Constitution is, to the extent of the inconsistency, of no force or effect.

Thus, any law that does not comply with section 7 and cannot be justified under section 1 of the *Charter* (see Section C(2), below in this chapter) is, to the extent of its non-compliance, of no force or effect.

Section 24(1) of the *Charter* provides:

> Anyone whose rights or freedoms, as guaranteed by this Charter, have been infringed or denied may apply to a court of competent jurisdiction to obtain such remedy as the court considers appropriate and just in the circumstances.

Where an applicant's rights are violated by state action that is not prescribed by law, the remedy for the violation is to be sought under section 24(1).[7]

C. SECTION 7 IN ITS *CHARTER* CONTEXT

The *Canadian Charter of Rights and Freedoms* guarantees a number of basic rights and freedoms, states the criteria for justifying legislative limits on those rights, provides courts with very broad powers to remedy unjustified violations of rights, and provides a mechanism by which legislatures can override actual or potential judicial determina-

---

5   *Canadian Charter of Rights and Freedoms*, Part I of the Constitution Act, 1982, being Schedule B to the Canada Act 1982 (UK), 1982, c 11 [Charter]; see also RSC 1985, Appendix II, No 44, Schedule B.

6   See Bayefsky, above note 3 at 704.

7   *R v Ferguson*, 2008 SCC 6 at paras 60–61.

tions that legislation does not comply with the *Charter*. I consider each of these aspects of the *Charter* as it relates to section 7.

1) Bilingual Interpretation

Since both the French and the English versions of section 7 are equally authoritative,[8] in principle both versions should be taken into account in its interpretation. Moreover, there are arguably differences between the English and the French versions. There is nothing in the English version corresponding to the stop at the end of the first phrase of the French version; and the French phrase "porté atteinte à" might suggest an English word such as "infringed" or "damaged" rather than "deprived." Thus, there might be nuances of meaning that could be drawn out of the quest to find a common meaning for the French and English versions of section 7.[9] But the principles of bilingual interpretation have had no discernible impact on the meaning of section 7 and the basic structural issues that might have been affected by bilingual interpretation are now well settled. However, I argue in Chapter 2, Section D(1) that the principles of bilingual interpretation support the Supreme Court of Canada's interpretation of the relationship between "life, liberty and security of the person" and "the principles of fundamental justice."

2) Section 7 and Section 1

Section 1 of the *Canadian Charter of Rights and Freedoms* reads as follows:

> The *Canadian Charter of Rights and Freedoms* guarantees the rights and freedoms set out in it subject only to such reasonable limits prescribed by law as can be demonstrably justified in a free and democratic society.

Section 1 has a very important double character: it guarantees *Charter* rights and it provides a criterion for limiting them.[10]

The Supreme Court of Canada has often accepted the argument that a law limiting a *Charter* right is justified under section 1 and is there-

---

8   *Constitution Act, 1982*, above note 2, s 57.

9   On the principles governing the search for the common meaning of a bilingual statute, see *R v Daoust*, 2004 SCC 6; Michel Bastarache et al, *The Law of Bilingual Interpretation* (Markham, ON: LexisNexis Canada, 2008); Ruth Sullivan, *Sullivan & Driedger on the Construction of Statutes*, 4th ed (Markham, ON: Butterworths, 2002) ch 4.

10   *R v Oakes*, [1986] 1 SCR 103 at 135 [*Oakes*].

fore constitutionally valid. Section 7 appears to be somewhat different from other *Charter* rights in this respect because its internal qualifier—the requirement that the state respect the "principles of fundamental justice"—often overlaps with the test for justification of a limit under section 1. The Court has often stated that violations of section 7 are very difficult to justify under section 1; never has a majority of the Court accepted a section 1 justification for an infringement of a section 7 right. Nonetheless, the possibility that a court might recognize a section 1 justification for an infringement of section 7 cannot be ruled out. The relationship between section 7 and section 1 is considered in detail in Chapter 6.

3) Section 7 and Other *Charter* Rights

a) Section 7 and Sections 8 through 14

Sections 7 through 14 of the *Canadian Charter of Rights and Freedoms* appear under the heading "Legal Rights." The characterization of these rights as "legal" and the association between section 7 and the rights enumerated in sections 8 through 14 shed considerable light on the meaning of section 7. Lamer CJC, an influential early interpreter of section 7, was particularly interested in this connection. He saw the sections following section 7 as defining specific principles of fundamental justice; indeed, his view was that "ss. 7 to 14 could have been fused into one section, with inserted between the words of s. 7 and the rest of those sections the oft-utilised provision . . . . 'and, without limiting the generality of the foregoing (s. 7) the following shall be deemed to be in violation of a person's rights under this section.'"[11] This reading of the relationship between section 7 and sections 8 through 14 supported Lamer CJC's (unsuccessful) effort to restrict the scope of the liberty interest to legal proceedings involving the state and the individual (see Chapter 2, Section D(3)(a)).

Certain rights are exhausted by sections 8 through 14 and therefore have no independent content under section 7. For example, section 11(*e*) guarantees an accused person a right not to be denied bail without just cause. In the absence of section 11(*e*), the denial of bail would certainly engage section 7, because it would affect the liberty interest, and courts might recognize an entitlement to reasonable bail as a principle

---

11   *Re BC Motor Vehicle Act*, [1985] 2 SCR 486 at 502–3. The predecessor of s 7 in some early drafts of the *Charter* was structured along these lines: see, for instance, the federal drafts of January and October 1979, reproduced in Bayefsky, above note 3 at 538 and 575. Lamer J did not, of course, hold that ss 8 through 14 exhausted the content of s 7.

of fundamental justice under section 7. But the presence of section 11(e) means that constitutional challenges concerning the reasonableness of bail can be, and are, dealt with entirely as a matter of the content of the section 11(e) right rather than as a matter of fundamental justice. In the context of a claim that a law governing bail is unconstitutional, section 11(e) is exhaustive; a section 7 claim has no additional value.[12]

Similarly, section 11(f) of the *Charter* provides a right to trial by jury in civilian courts "where the maximum punishment for the offence is imprisonment for five years or a more severe punishment." The entitlement to a jury trial in other cases depends on the provisions of the *Criminal Code* and on the Crown's election of the mode of proceeding. In *R v B(S)*,[13] the Saskatchewan Court of Appeal rejected the claim that section 7 can supplement section 11(f), refusing to find a constitutional requirement for a jury trial in cases where the potential punishment is less than five years' imprisonment. Section 7 provides no constitutional entitlement to trial by jury beyond what is contained in section 11(f).

The presence of a right against unreasonable search and seizure in section 8 of the *Charter* means that search and seizure issues can be usually considered entirely under section 8 and do not need to be dealt with under section 7; but it is sometimes necessary to consider the claim that the law is "unreasonable" in section 8 terms because it violates a principle of fundamental justice. The clearest example in the case law is probably *R v B(SA)* (*B(SA)*).[14] The Court considered a constitutional challenge to provisions of the *Criminal Code* permitting warrants to issue for the seizure of bodily samples for forensic DNA analysis. The Court had previously held that such seizures violated section 7 of the *Charter*; in *R v Stillman* (*Stillman*) Cory J described the seizures as "without authorization" but also as "the ultimate invasion of the [accused's] privacy."[15] These reasons could be read as holding that the seizure of a bodily sample for forensic DNA analysis violated section 7 for at least three distinct reasons: the seizure was unauthorized by law; the absence of any legal criteria governing the seizure was procedurally unfair; or the seizure of a bodily sample capable of revealing intimate detail about the person was so intrusive that it would always violate the principles of fundamental justice. In other words, *Stillman* raised the question of whether the taking of DNA samples could be made to comply with the principles of fundamental justice merely by

---

12   Compare *R v Pearson*, [1992] 3 SCR 665 at 688–89.
13   *R v B(S)* (1989), 50 CCC (3d) 34 (Sask CA).
14   *R v B(SA)*, 2003 SCC 60 [*B(SA)*].
15   *R v Stillman*, [1997] 1 SCR 607 at para 51, Cory J.

providing lawful authority (which would itself have to comply with section 8). In *B(SA)*, the Court held in effect that a seizure of bodily samples for forensic DNA analysis had to comply with both sections 7 and 8 of the *Charter*. The Court treated the constitutionality of the DNA warrant provisions of the *Criminal Code* as a section 8 issue, but also expressly considered the relevant principles of fundamental justice in its section 8 analysis.[16] In deciding that the provisions were "reasonable" in section 8 terms, the Court did not limit itself to the *Hunter* criteria for a constitutionally valid search power,[17] which balance privacy and the state's need to investigate offences, but also considered whether the provisions infringed a principle of fundamental justice that was not captured by the *Hunter* balance, and concluded that they did not.[18] If the statutory provisions had violated section 7, they would also have been unreasonable in section 8 terms, even if they had otherwise satisfied the *Hunter* criteria.

Courts have taken a similar approach in other cases involving searches and seizures that intrude on the body. In *R v Rodgers*,[19] the Court considered a constitutional challenge to provisions of the *Criminal Code* authorizing the seizure of bodily samples for forensic DNA analysis from previously convicted sexual offenders. The Court held that it was not necessary to consider the applicant's section 7 challenge and that the issue could be resolved entirely under section 8.[20] The warrant provisions were "reasonable" in section 8 terms because they struck a proper balance between privacy and other interests;[21] given this holding, in this particular context, there were no principles of fundamental justice that could be infringed. In *R v Knight*,[22] the accused argued that a general warrant to search his vehicle had not been validly issued because the police had not told the issuing judge that the manner of search might create a risk of harm to the accused. The Newfoundland and Labrador Court of Appeal held that this issue could be dealt with as a matter of reasonable search and seizure; in this context, the accused's claim that the conduct of the police affected his security

---

16   *B(SA)*, above note 14 at para 35.
17   *Ibid* at paras 36–56; compare *Hunter et al v Southam Inc*, [1984] 2 SCR 145.
18   *B(SA)*, above note 14 at paras 57–60.
19   *R v Rodgers*, 2006 SCC 15.
20   *Ibid* at para 23.
21   As the Court held: *ibid* at paras 25–44.
22   *R v Knight*, 2008 NLCA 67, 241 CCC (3d) 353 [*Knight*]. Compare *R v Tse*, 2008 BCSC 211 at paras 187–92 (claim that *Criminal Code* s 184.4 was overbroad to be dealt with not under s 7 but as a claim of unreasonable search or seizure under s 8).

of the person in a manner that violated the principles of fundamental justice was completely subsumed in his claim that the warrant was not validly issued because it depended on the same fact: the alleged non-disclosure.[23] In other words, because there was no section 7 violation *and* because the warrant was validly issued, the section 8 claim subsumed the section 7 claim.

But the relationship between sections 7 and 8 is not always made as clear as it should be. In *Lavallee, Rackel & Heintz v Canada (AG)*,[24] the Court considered the validity of section 488.1 of the *Criminal Code*, which establishes procedures intended to protect solicitor-client privilege during police searches of law offices. The Court held that the objections to the section did not have to be considered under section 7 and that an analysis under section 8 would be sufficient, for the following reason:

> If the procedure set out in s. 488.1 results in an unreasonable search and seizure contrary to s. 8 of the *Charter*, it follows that s. 488.1 cannot be said to comply with the principles of fundamental justice embodied in s. 7.[25]

The Court then went on to identify several ways in which the section offered inadequate protection to solicitor-client privilege and for that reason found it unreasonable. But the holding that the section 7 violation follows from the section 8 violation is misleading; the section 8 violation—the unreasonableness of the search—is made out only because the statute unreasonably interferes with an interest protected under section 7. That is, the conclusion that section 488.1 violated section 8 follows only because solicitor-client privilege is a principle of fundamental justice.[26] If not, section 488.1 would not be unreasonable. Section 488.1 is unreasonable in section 8 terms because it offends section 7, not the other way around.

b) The Residual Role of Section 7

The Supreme Court of Canada has often recognized that section 7 can play a "residual" role in relation to the specific guarantees in sections 8 through 14. When these specific rights do not apply, the principles they

---

23   *Knight, ibid* at paras 45–48.

24   *Lavallee, Rackel & Heintz v Canada (AG); White, Ottenheimer & Baker v Canada (AG); R v Fink*, 2002 SCC 61.

25   *Ibid* at para 35.

26   The Court expressly identified solicitor-client privilege as a principle of fundamental justice: *ibid* at para 36. See also Hamish Stewart, "The Principles of Fundamental Justice and s 488.1 of the *Criminal Code*" (2001) 45 Crim LQ 233.

express and the interests they protect sometimes support the recognition of principles of fundamental justice under section 7. For example, section 10(*b*) guarantees the right to counsel specifically "on arrest or detention"; the principles of fundamental justice may require the right to counsel in situations other than arrest or detention.[27] Similarly, section 7 plays a well-recognized residual role in the law of self-incrimination. Section 13 of the *Charter* provides:

> A witness who testifies in any proceedings has the right not to have any incriminating evidence so given used to incriminate that witness in any other proceedings, except in a prosecution for perjury or for the giving of contradictory evidence.

This right applies only to an individual in her capacity as an accused person or defendant in proceedings taken with a view to "incriminating" her; it does not apply, for instance, to a person who is being questioned by the police or by other public officials. Yet section 13, together with section 11(*c*), section 5 of the *Canada Evidence Act*,[28] and the traditions of the common law, strongly suggest that there is a general principle against self-incrimination in Canadian law that goes beyond the particular situation envisaged by section 13. And the Court has recognized several principles of fundamental justice under section 7 that are aspects of this wider principle: the section 7 right to silence in criminal investigations and the right to "derivative use immunity" for certain kinds of compelled testimony are two examples.[29]

Similarly, section 7 may play a residual role in relation to the section 11(*b*) right to trial within a reasonable time. The period of time relevant to this right is the interval between the laying of the charge and the completion of the trial; pre-charge delay does not count.[30] However, pre-charge delay may be relevant to the claim that the proceedings amount to an abuse of process, which would violate section 7.[31] Section 11(*b*) also has no application to appellate delay, but excessive appellate delay might make a subsequent trial unfair and so violate section 7, or

---

27 *Delghani v Canada (Minister of Citizenship and Immigration)*, [1993] 1 SCR 1053 at 1076; however, the Court did not recognize a s 7 right to counsel in the applicant's situation. See further Chapter 5, Section B(1).

28 RSC 1985, c C-5.

29 *R v Hebert*, [1990] 2 SCR 151 (right to silence); *R v S(RJ)*, [1995] 1 SCR 451 (derivative use immunity). These cases are discussed in more detail in Chapter 4, Section E.

30 *R v Kalanj*, [1989] 1 SCR 1594. On abuse of process, see Chapter 5, Section A(4).

31 *Ibid* at 1610–11; *R v Perrier* (2000), 152 CCC (3d) 549 (Ct Martial App Ct).

might create some other form of prejudice that entitled the accused to a *Charter* remedy.[32]

c) Section 7 and Sections 2, 6, and 15

In addition to sections 8 through 14, there are other sections of the *Charter* whose content might be matters of fundamental justice. I briefly consider three such possibilities.

The rights and freedoms guaranteed under section 2 of the *Charter* — the rights to freedom of conscience, religion, thought, belief, opinion, expression, peaceful assembly, and association — are so basic to a free and democratic society that a law infringing them might well be said to violate the principles of fundamental justice, particularly since those principles are applicable outside formal legal proceedings. But the case law under section 2 is so well developed and the interpretation of many of the section 2 rights is so generous that section 7 probably has no residual role to play in respect of section 2 claims.

The mobility rights guaranteed to citizens by section 6 of the *Charter* are similarly basic to a free and democratic society, and might well qualify as principles of fundamental justice. As with section 2, it is unlikely that section 7 has any residual role with respect to section 6 claims. But it is possible that section 7 might, in the right case, play a role in defining the beneficiary of the section 6 right. Section 6(1) guarantees certain international mobility rights to "citizens," while section 6(2) guarantees certain interprovincial mobility rights to "citizens and permanent residents." But the Constitution of Canada contains no definition of a "citizen"[33] or of a "permanent resident"; a person acquires citizenship or permanent residency in accordance with statute. Section 7 applies to those statutory definitions, so to the extent that a statutory definition of citizenship or permanent residency affected life, liberty, and security of the person, it would have to comply with all the principles of fundamental justice discussed in Chapters 4 and 5. And to the extent that a law deprived individuals of their citizenship, or prevented the acquisition of citizenship or permanent residency status in violation of the principles of fundamental justice, section 7 might be used indirectly to protect section 6 mobility rights.

---

32 *R v Potvin*, [1993] 2 SCR 880 at 916. See, for example, *R v Williams*, 2009 ONCA 342 at paras 26–32, where the Crown's lengthy and unjustified delay in perfecting its appeal from the accused's acquittal appears to have mitigated the sentence he received when the Court of Appeal set aside the acquittal and entered a finding of guilt.

33 Contrast with the US Const amend XIV, § 1.

Section 15 of the *Charter* guarantees "[e]very individual . . . the right to equal protection and equal benefit of the law without discrimination" on certain enumerated grounds (which have since been judicially expanded to include several analogous grounds). Claims that are essentially concerned with equal treatment are therefore not considered under section 7 but under section 15.[34] In the absence of section 15, it might be arguable that a right to equality was a principle of fundamental justice under section 7. But an equality claim that fails under section 15 will not always fail under section 7, because the content of the rights guaranteed by section 7 is quite distinct from those guaranteed by section 15. It is entirely possible for a law to comply with section 15 but to violate the principles of fundamental justice. In *R v Hess; R v Nguyen,*[35] for example, the majority found a provision of the *Criminal Code* compliant with section 15 but contrary to section 7.

This possibility appears to have been overlooked in *R v Cornell.*[36] The accused was charged with an offence that existed in some provinces but not in others, because the relevant section of the *Criminal Code* allowed the government to declare it in force in different provinces at different times (or never).[37] He argued that the government's decision to declare the offence in force in some provinces and not others was contrary to the principles of fundamental justice. The Court characterized his claim as one of unequal treatment under section 15; since section 15 was not yet in force when he was charged,[38] he could not assert it. The Court concluded that he therefore had no claim under section 7. But the accused's claim was that it was a principle of fundamental justice that the criminal law should be uniform throughout Canada, a point which is quite arguable apart from its success or failure as an equality claim under section 15. A similar issue might arise under section 61 of the *Youth Criminal Justice Act,*[39] which permits provincial variation in the sentencing regime under that Act.

---

34 *R v Edwards Books & Art Ltd,* [1986] 2 SCR 713 at 785.

35 *R v Hess; R v Nguyen,* [1990] 2 SCR 906.

36 *R v Cornell,* [1988] 1 SCR 461.

37 The section (*Criminal Code,* RSC 1970, c C-34, s 234.1) created a new offence of refusing to comply with a demand for a breath sample. The successor of this offence is found in s 254(5) of the *Criminal Code,* RSC 1985, c C-46, and is in force everywhere in Canada.

38 By virtue of s 32(2) of the *Constitution Act, 1982,* above note 2, s 15 came into force three years after the rest of the *Charter;* that is, on 17 April 1985.

39 *Youth Criminal Justice Act,* SC 2002, c 1.

4) Section 7 and Section 33

Section 33 of the *Charter* reads as follows:

(1) Parliament or the legislature of a province may expressly declare in an Act of Parliament or of the legislature . . . that the Act or a provision thereof shall operate notwithstanding a provision included in section 2 or sections 7 to 15 of the *Charter*.

(2) An Act or a provision of an Act in respect of which a declaration made under this section is in effect shall have such operation as it would have but for the provision of this Charter referred to in the declaration.

(3) A declaration made under subsection (1) shall cease to have effect five years after it comes into force or on such earlier date as may be specified in the declaration.

(4) Parliament or the legislature of a province may re-enact a declaration made under subsection (1).

(5) Subsection (3) applies in respect of a re-enactment made under subsection (4).[40]

This section, generally known as the "notwithstanding clause" or the "legislative override," permits a legislature to override the application of certain sections of the *Charter* to its legislation for a renewable, five-year period. The legislature's invocation of the notwithstanding clause is not subject to judicial review on substantive grounds; as long as the declaration is made in the proper form, the override is valid.[41] There is no requirement that the override be used only in response to a judicial declaration of invalidity; it may also be used prospectively to insulate legislation from review for compliance with section 2 and sections 7 through 15 of the *Charter*.[42] However, the override does not insulate legislation from review on other constitutional grounds.

Section 7 rights are subject to the section 33 override. Between 23 June 1982 and 23 June 1987, all the statutes of Quebec operated under a declaration made under section 33, so no claim that a law of Quebec violated section 7 could succeed during that period.[43] Since then, the override has been used from time to time to insulate provincial statutes

---

40   *Charter*, above note 5, s 33.
41   *Ford v Quebec (AG)*, [1988] 2 SCR 712 at 740–1 [*Ford*].
42   *Ibid*.
43   *An Act Respecting the Constitution Act, 1982*, RSQ c L-4.2. See also *Ford*, above note 41 at 742–47; *Gosselin v Quebec*, 2002 SCC 84 at para 15.

from *Charter* review.[44] But it appears that no Canadian legislature has ever enacted a section 33 override directed at preserving a specific violation of section 7.

D. SECTION 7 AND OTHER RIGHTS-PROTECTING INSTRUMENTS

1) Section 7 and the *Bill of Rights*

The *Canadian Bill of Rights*,[45] a federal statute enacted in 1960, provides on its face protection for many of the rights and freedoms that are guaranteed in the *Charter*. But, although it was sometimes said to have "quasi-constitutional" status,[46] the *Bill of Rights* had a limited effect on Canadian law. During the twenty-two years when the *Bill of Rights* was in force and the *Charter* was not, the Supreme Court of Canada declared only one law inoperative for inconsistency with the *Bill of Rights*.[47] There were at least three reasons for this limited impact. First, the *Bill of Rights* applied to federal statutes; it had no impact on provincial statutes. Second, reflecting the doctrine of Parliamentary supremacy, section 2 of the *Bill* provides that Parliament can "expressly declare . . . that [a statute] shall operate notwithstanding the *Canadian Bill of Rights* . . . ." Although express notwithstanding declarations were rare,[48] the doctrine of Parliamentary supremacy also includes the doctrine of implicit repeal; namely, that an inconsistency between an earlier and a later statute should be resolved in favour of the later statute.[49] So, although it was clear that the *Bill of Rights* applied to statutes that had been enacted before it came into force, it was argued that in case of an inconsistency between a subsequent statute and the *Bill of Rights*, the later statute would prevail without the need for a notwith-

---

44   See Tsvi Kahana, "The Notwithstanding Mechanism and Public Discussion: Lessons from the Ignored Practice of Section 33 of the *Charter*" (2001) 44 Can Pub Admin 255.

45   *Canadian Bill of Rights*, SC 1960, c 44; see also RSC 1985, Appendix III.

46   In *Hogan v R*, [1975] 2 SCR 574 at 597, Laskin J dissenting characterized the *Bill of Rights* as a "quasi-constitutional instrument" and would have adopted an exclusionary rule for evidence obtained in violation of the rights it protected. The majority was hesitant to adopt this characterization of the *Bill*, but in any event refused to recognize an exclusionary rule: *ibid* at 583–84, Ritchie J, and at 585, Pigeon J.

47   See *R v Drybones*, [1970] SCR 282 [*Drybones*].

48   The most famous instance of such a notwithstanding declaration may be found in the *Public Order (Temporary Measures) Act*, SC 1970-71-72, c 2, s 12.

49   *Sullivan & Driedger on the Construction of Statutes*, above note 9 at 275–78.

standing declaration under section 2.[50] This line of argument has been rejected in connection with human rights codes[51] and should probably not apply to the *Bill of Rights* either.[52] But the question of whether an inconsistency between the *Bill of Rights* and a subsequently-enacted statute might be construed as amounting to an implicit notwithstanding declaration has never been finally resolved. Third, and most important of all, courts were quite cautious in using the *Bill of Rights*, treating it as a declaration of rights existing at the time of its enactment[53] and construing even those rights quite narrowly.[54] The *Bill of Rights*, though still in force, is rarely invoked today.

It is nevertheless worth noting that the central provisions of the *Bill of Rights* have some affinities with section 7 of the *Charter*. Section 1(*a*) of the *Bill of Rights* provides:

> It is hereby recognized and declared that in Canada there have existed and shall continue to exist without discrimination by reason of race, national origin, colour, religion or sex, the following human rights and fundamental freedoms, namely,
>
> (*a*) the right of the individual to life, liberty, security of the person and enjoyment of property, and the right not to be deprived thereof except by due process of law . . . .

Section 2(*e*) provides:

> . . . no law of Canada shall be so construed and applied so as to . . . deprive a person of the right to a fair hearing in accordance with the principles of fundamental justice for the determination of his rights and obligations . . . .

These sections are both broader and narrower than section 7. Section 1 of the *Bill of Rights* incorporates an equality guarantee, and it protects

---

50   See, for example, Bora Laskin, "An Inquiry Into the Diefenbaker *Bill of Rights*" (1959) 37 Can Bar Rev 77 at 131–32.

51   See *Winnipeg School Division No 1 v Craton*, [1985] 2 SCR 150 at 156, McIntyre J.

52   See also *Authorson v Canada (AG)*, 2003 SCC 39 at para 10 [*Authorson*]; Walter Surma Tarnopolsky, *The Canadian Bill of Rights*, 2d ed (Toronto: McClelland & Stewart, 1975) at 138–43.

53   See, for example, *R v Burnshine*, [1975] 1 SCR 693 at 705; *Canada (AG) v Lavell*, [1974] SCR 1349 at 1365; *R v Miller*, [1977] 2 SCR 680. This position was reaffirmed in the *Charter* era: *Authorson*, *ibid* at para 10.

54   See, most notoriously, *Bliss v Canada (AG)*, [1979] 1 SCR 183, treating an unemployment regulation that had an adverse effect on pregnant women as not discriminating on the ground of gender because the inequality in question was "not created by legislation but by nature" (at 190).

the right to enjoyment of property; section 7 of the *Charter* has neither of these features. Section 2(*e*) applies to all hearings, while section 7 of the *Charter* applies to a hearing only if the proceedings affect life, liberty and security of the person. But under section 1(*a*), a person can be deprived of a right "by due process of law" rather than "in accordance with the principles of fundamental justice." The phrase "due process of law" was generally understood to provide only procedural protections and not to permit any consideration of the substantive justice of the statute in issue,[55] though a few post-*Charter* cases leave open the possibility that the phrase could have been construed more generously.[56] Similarly, it is quite clear that section 2(*e*) of the *Bill of Rights* applies only in hearings and does not provide any substantive grounds for judicial review of legislation. But, as discussed in Chapter 3, the principles of fundamental justice under section 7 of the *Charter* include substantive as well as procedural principles of justice.

These similarities and differences mean that in some cases a law can be challenged under either the *Charter* or the *Canadian Bill of Rights*. Specifically, a federal statute that deprives a person of a fair hearing; that affects life, liberty, and security of the person; and that does not comply with procedural principles of fundamental justice would violate section 7 of the *Charter* because it deprived a person of life, liberty, and security of the person without complying with the principles of fundamental justice; but it could also be challenged under section 2(*e*) of the *Bill of Rights* because it deprived a person of a fair hearing without complying with the principles of fundamental justice. The leading example of such a double challenge is *Singh v Canada (Minister of Employment and Immigration)*,[57] where the Supreme Court of Canada held unanimously that the provisions of the *Immigration Act* governing refugee hearings were inoperative, but divided evenly on the question of whether those provisions violated the *Charter* or were inconsistent with the *Bill of Rights*.

---

55   See in particular *R v Curr*, [1972] SCR 889.

56   See, for instance, *Authorson*, above note 52 at para 51 (leaving open the possibility of substantive protections for property rights under the *Bill of Rights*); *R v Cembella*, 2002 BCSC 1129 (holding that conviction for an absolute liability offence was a deprivation of liberty without due process of law). These possibilities appear inconsistent with Dickson CJC's comment, in 1986, that it was too late to reconsider the early cases emphasizing "the merely statutory status of the *Canadian Bill of Rights* and the declaratory nature of the rights it conferred": *R v Beauregard*, [1986] 2 SCR 56 at 90.

57   [1985] 1 SCR 177.

A law that does not comply with the *Bill of Rights* and that does not contain a declaration that it shall operate notwithstanding the *Bill* is inoperative.[58]

2) Section 7 and the Quebec *Charter*

The Quebec *Charter of Human Rights and Freedoms*[59] came into force in 1976 and was significantly amended in 1982. The Quebec *Charter* is most plausibly characterized as a quasi-constitutional statute,[60] and its impact on Quebec law has been much more significant and far-reaching than the impact of the *Canadian Bill of Rights* on federal law. Moreover, the Quebec *Charter* applies to private parties as well as to state action. While it does not (and perhaps could not) give courts or other tribunals the power to declare legislation invalid, it does provide a strong clause concerning derogation:

> 52. No provision of any Act, even subsequent to the *Charter*, may derogate from sections 1 to 38, except so far as provided by those sections, unless such Act expressly states that it applies despite the *Charter*.

This clause has been interpreted to mean that a law that neither complies with nor expressly derogates from the Quebec *Charter*, though not formally declared invalid, is inoperative, thus rendering it invalid in substance.[61]

The combined effect of sections 1 and 9.1 of the Quebec *Charter* is often similar to the effect of sections 7 and 1 of the Canadian *Charter*. Sections 1 and 9.1 of the Quebec *Charter* provide:

> 1. Every human being has a right to life, and to personal security, inviolability and freedom.

> 9.1 In exercising his fundamental freedoms and rights, a person shall maintain a proper regard for democratic values, public order and the general well-being of the citizens of Québec.

---

58   *Drybones*, above note 47 at 294–95.

59   RSQ c C-12.

60   *Béliveau St-Jacques v Fédération des employées et employés de service publics inc*, [1996] 2 SCR 345 at para 116; *Chaoulli v Quebec (AG)*, 2005 SCC 35 at para 25 [*Chaoulli*].

61   See Jacques-Yves André, "La constitutionnalisation progressive de *la Charte de droits et libertés de la personne*" (1987) 21 RJT 25 at 37–42, and compare *Ford*, above note 41 at 788, declaring a Quebec statute "inoperative" ("inopérant").

> In this respect, the scope of the freedoms and rights, and limits to their exercise, may be fixed by law.

The rights guaranteed by section 1 obviously resemble those guaranteed by section 7 of the Canadian *Charter*, but are not qualified with reference to the "principles of fundamental justice." Section 9.1, though worded differently from section 1 of the Canadian *Charter*, has been interpreted as providing essentially equivalent criteria for the justifiable limitation of the rights guaranteed in the Quebec *Charter*.[62] So it is sometimes possible to challenge a Quebec statute under section 1 of the Quebec *Charter* and section 7 of the Canadian *Charter*. If a statute engages section 7 by depriving someone of life, liberty, and security of the person, it will usually affect the rights guaranteed under section 1 of the Quebec *Charter*. Under the Canadian *Charter*, the question of whether the effect on life, liberty, and security of the person is constitutionally permissible is done mainly by considering whether the deprivation is in accord with the principles of fundamental justice; although it is in principle possible to justify a violation of section 7 under section 1, the Supreme Court of Canada has never done so. But under the Quebec *Charter*, the question will be whether the effect on life, liberty, and security of the person is an acceptable limit fixed by law with reference to the values of section 9.1.

Chaoulli v Quebec (AG) (*Chaoulli*) is perhaps the most important example of this overlap between section 7 of the Canadian *Charter* and sections 1 and 9.1 of the Quebec *Charter*. The applicants challenged a Quebec regulation prohibiting individuals from purchasing insurance for health services that were covered by the provincial health insurance plan. Deschamps J held that the prohibition infringed the right to life and to security of the person under section 1 of the Quebec *Charter*[63] and, applying the *Oakes* test[64] for a justification under section 1 of the Canadian *Charter*, held that the infringement was not justified under section 9.1 of the Quebec *Charter*.[65] The other three judges who constituted the majority (McLachlin CJC and Major and Bastarache JJ) agreed with this analysis, but reached the same conclusion under the Canadian *Charter*.[66] While Deschamps J did not have to consider whether the deprivation was in accord with the principles of fundamental justice, many of the considerations she relied on in

---

62 *Ford, ibid* at 768–71.
63 *Chaoulli*, above note 60 at paras 37–45.
64 *Oakes*, above note 10.
65 *Chaoulli*, above note 60 at paras 48–99.
66 *Ibid* at para 159.

rejecting the justification appear in the reasons of McLachlin CJC and Major J as aspects of the constitutional norm against arbitrariness. For example, Deschamps J found that the prohibition was not minimally impairing of the rights to life and security because the government had not established its effectiveness and had not shown the ineffectiveness of other ways of achieving its objectives.[67] McLachlin CJC and Major J found that the prohibition was arbitrary because the evidence did not establish a connection between the prohibition and the objective of maintaining the quality of the public health care system.[68] Following *Chaoulli*, a claim that a statute unjustifiably infringes the rights guaranteed in section 1 of the Quebec *Charter* can often be recast as a claim that a statute infringes section 7 on the ground of arbitrariness, overbreadth, or gross disproportionality (see Chapter 4, Section B).

E. CONCLUSION

Section 7 of the *Charter* has had a profound effect on Canadian law. On its face, it protects an individual's most basic interests (life, liberty, and security of the person) by requiring any state action affecting those interests to comply with the principles of fundamental justice. Because of its constitutional status, it gives courts a central role in deciding whether legislation and other state action meet that requirement. The Supreme Court of Canada has held that the *Charter* is applicable to a wide range of state conduct (see Chapter 2), has interpreted the phrase "life, liberty, and security of the person" broadly (see Chapter 2) and the phrase "principles of fundamental justice" even more broadly (see Chapters 3 through 5). Moreover, the Court has never upheld a violation of section 7 under section 1 (see Chapter 6). And there is reason to believe that federal and provincial ministries and legislatures have taken the demands of the *Charter*, including section 7, seriously

---

67 *Ibid* at para 97.

68 *Ibid* at para 152. Another example of overlap between the two Charters is *Godbout v Longueuil (City)*, [1997] 3 SCR 844, where a majority found that a municipal bylaw violated s 5 of the Quebec *Charter* and was not justified under s 9.1, and declined to consider the applicant's argument under the Canadian *Charter*; the minority agreed, but found that the bylaw also violated s 7 of the Canadian *Charter* and was not justified under s 1. Again, the state's failure to provide a satisfactory rationale for the bylaw played a double role, supporting the finding that the bylaw was not justified under s 9.1 and that it was inconsistent with the principles of fundamental justice.

in drafting legislation.[69] Section 7 is thus a very powerful tool for the protection of rights through litigation rather than through legislative action. The case law concerning section 7 is therefore a useful testing-ground for any argument for or against the legitimacy of judicial review of legislation (see Chapter 7).

FURTHER READINGS

ANDRÉ, JACQUES-YVES. "La constitutionnalisation progressive de *la Charte de droits et libertés de la personne*" (1987) 21 RJT 25.

CAMERON, JAMIE. "The *Charter*'s Legislative Override: Feat or Figment of the Constitutional Imagination?" (2004) 23 Sup Ct L Rev (2d) 135.

HIEBERT, JANET. "Is It Too Late to Rehabilitate Canada's Notwithstanding Clause?" (2004) 23 Sup Ct L Rev (2d) 169.

KAHANA, TSVI. "The Notwithstanding Mechanism and Public Discussion: Lessons from the Ignored Practice of Section 33 of the *Charter*" (2001) 44 Can Pub Admin 255.

————. "Understanding the Notwithstanding Mechanism" (2002) 52 UTLJ 221.

LASKIN, BORA. "An Inquiry Into the Diefenbaker *Bill of Rights*" (1959) 37 Can Bar Rev 77.

MCWHINNEY, EDWARD. *Canada and the Constitution 1979–1982* (Toronto: University of Toronto Press, 1982).

MONAHAN, PATRICK J. *Constitutional Law*, 3d ed (Toronto: Irwin Law, 2006) ch 5.

RUSSELL, PETER H. "Standing Up for Notwithstanding" (1991) 29 Alta L Rev 293.

————. *Constitutional Odyssey*, 3d ed (Toronto: University of Toronto Press, 2004) ch 8.

---

69 See, among others, Kent Roach, "The Dangers of a *Charter*-Proof and Crime-Based Response to Terrorism" in Ronald J Daniels, Patrick Macklem, & Kent Roach, eds, *The Security of Freedom* (Toronto: University of Toronto Press, 2001) 131; Andrew Petter, *The Politics of the Charter* (Toronto: University of Toronto Press, 2010) at 209–18.

ROMANOW, ROY, ET AL. *Canada . . . Notwithstanding* (Toronto: Carswell/ Methuen, 1984).

SHARPE, ROBERT J, & KENT ROACH. *The Canadian Charter of Rights and Freedoms*, 4th ed (Toronto: Irwin Law, 2009) ch 1.

TARNOPOLSKY, WALTER SURMA. *The* Canadian Bill of Rights, 2d rev ed (Toronto: McClelland & Stewart, 1975).

WEINRIB, LORRAINE E. "Learning to Live with the Override" (1990) 35 McGill LJ 541.

CHAPTER 2

ENGAGING SECTION 7

A. INTRODUCTION

By the mid-1980s, the Supreme Court of Canada had decided three issues that are very basic to the application of section 7 of the *Charter*. First, the Court held that while the *Charter* applied to "state action" of several types, it did not apply to disputes between private parties that relied wholly on the common law. Second, the Court held that section 7 rights, though available only to natural persons and not to corporations, are available to all natural persons who are subject to Canadian law. Third, the Court rejected the view that section 7 created one right to life, liberty, and security of the person and a second, distinct right to be treated in accordance with the principles of fundamental justice; instead, it interpreted section 7 as guaranteeing the right not to be deprived of life, liberty, and security of the person except in accordance with the principles of fundamental justice. Thus, to demonstrate a violation of her section 7 rights, a *Charter* applicant must demonstrate the following elements:

(1) there is some state conduct to which the *Charter* applies;
(2) the applicant is a natural person or has standing to invoke a natural person's section 7 rights;
(3) the state conduct affects the applicant's (or natural person's) life, liberty, or security of the person; and

(4) the state conduct is not in accordance with the principles of fundamental justice.

The first three elements engage section 7; that is, if the applicant can demonstrate them, then section 7 applies to the matters in dispute. The first element arises in all *Charter* litigation, while the second and third are particular to section 7. This chapter discusses these three elements. The fourth element—whether the state conduct conforms to the principles of fundamental justice—is considered in Chapters 3 through 5. If all four elements are established, then the applicant's section 7 rights are violated.

B. STATE CONDUCT

The application of the *Charter* is, in the first instance, governed by section 32:

32(1) This *Charter* applies

(a) to the Parliament and government of Canada in respect of all matters within the authority of Parliament including all matters relating to the Yukon Territory and the Northwest Territories; and

(b) to the legislature and government of each province in respect of all matters within the authority of the legislature of each province.

Given this wording, the potential range of the *Charter*'s application is very broad. Since every matter that can be regulated by law is, ultimately, "within the authority of" either the federal Parliament or the provincial legislatures, it might be argued that the *Charter* applies in every legal dispute.[1] But the Supreme Court of Canada has rejected that interpretation, holding instead that there must be some element of state action before the *Charter* applies.[2] In the rest of Section B, I discuss the

---

1   See, for example, Brian Slattery, "*Charter of Rights and Freedoms*: Does It Bind Private Persons?" (1985) 63 Can Bar Rev 148; David Beatty, "Constitutional Conceits: The Coercive Authority of Courts" (1987) 37 UTLJ 183.

2   *Retail, Wholesale and Department Store Union, Local 580 v Dolphin Delivery Ltd*, [1986] 2 SCR 573 [*Dolphin Delivery*]. See also the discussion in Robert J Sharpe & Kent Roach, *The Charter of Rights and Freedoms*, 4th ed (Toronto: Irwin Law, 2009) at 98–100; Peter W Hogg, *Constitutional Law of Canada*, 5th ed supplemented (Scarborough, ON: Thomson Carswell, 2007) ch 37.

application of the *Charter* to various types of laws and disputes, with particular attention to cases where section 7 was invoked.

1) Statutes and Regulations

It is clear that all statutes and regulations have to comply with the *Charter*, and this is so whether the statute or regulation comes into play in a dispute between the state and a private individual or between two private individuals.[3] Therefore, any statute or regulation that deprives a person of one of the three interests protected by section 7 (life, liberty, or security of the person) must comply with the principles of fundamental justice, whether or not the legal relationship governed by the statute or regulation involves the state. The legislative enactment of the statute in question, or the making of a law under a delegated power, usually provides the element of state action that makes the *Charter* applicable.

Many statutes have been scrutinized under section 7. Examples include statutes concerning crime,[4] child protection,[5] immigration,[6] extradition proceedings,[7] public health insurance,[8] and adoption records.[9] Similarly, there are many examples of regulations, municipal bylaws, and other forms of delegated legislation being challenged under the *Charter*. The subordinate legislation challenged includes regulations

---

3   *Dolphin Delivery, ibid* at 601–2.

4   For example, *R v Martineau*, [1990] 2 SCR 633 (s 7 challenge to one of the definitions of murder in the *Criminal Code*); *R v Malmo-Levine*, 2003 SCC 74 [*Malmo-Levine*] (s 7 challenge to the offence of simple possession of marijuana).

5   For example, *Winnipeg Child and Family Services v KLW*, 2000 SCC 48 (s 7 challenge to statutory provisions defining a power of warrantless apprehension of a child).

6   For example, *Charkaoui v Canada (Citizenship and Immigration)*, 2007 SCC 9 [*Charkaoui*] (s 7 challenge to the statutory scheme for determining the reasonableness of ministerial certification that a permanent resident or foreign national is a threat to the security of Canada).

7   For example, *United States v Ferras*, 2006 SCC 33 (s 7 challenge to the procedures for committal for extradition).

8   For example, *Chaoulli v Quebec (AG)*, 2005 SCC 35 [*Chaoulli*] (a s 7 challenge to a statutory prohibition on certain forms of private health insurance).

9   For example, *Cheskes v Ontario (AG)*, [2007] OJ No 3515, 2007 CanLII 38387 (SCJ) [*Cheskes*] (a s 7 challenge to a statute allowing access to certain information concerning adoptions without the consent of the person being identified).

concerning immigration,[10] assisted conception,[11] and health insurance.[12] Moreover, it is generally held that municipalities are part of the government for *Charter* purposes,[13] so that municipal bylaws are, like other forms of delegated legislation, subject to *Charter* challenge.[14]

A statute or regulation can also be challenged under the *Charter* even if it does not authorize any conduct by state officials but instead governs a legal relationship between private parties. In *Retail, Wholesale and Department Store Union, Local 580 v Dolphin Delivery Ltd* (*Dolphin Delivery*), the Supreme Court of Canada held that the *Charter* would apply to a statute whether that statute was relied upon in public or private litigation.[15] Examples from private litigation are less common than examples from public law, but include section 7 challenges to limitation periods,[16] to a notice period for commencing litigation against a municipality,[17] to a statutory provision permitting the Court

---

10   For example, *De Guzman v Canada (Minister of Citizenship and Immigration)*, 2005 FCA 436 [*De Guzman*] (s 7 challenge to a regulation made under the *Immigration and Refugee Protection Act*, SC 2001, c 27).

11   *Susan Doe v Canada (AG)*, 2007 ONCA 11 [*Susan Doe*], aff'g (2006), 79 OR (3d) 586 (SCJ).

12   *Flora v Ontario (Health Insurance Plan, General Director)*, 2008 ONCA 538, aff'g (2007), 278 DLR (4th) 45 (Ont Div Ct).

13   Hogg, above note 2, ch 37.2(c) argues persuasively that the *Charter* applies to municipal bylaws. In *Godbout v Longueuil (City of)*, [1997] 3 SCR 844 [*Godbout*], only three of the nine judges of the Court found it necessary to hold that s 7 of the *Charter* applied to municipalities (see the reasons of La Forest J, L'Heureux-Dubé and McLachlin JJ concurring, at paras 50–55), the other judges preferring to decide the case on other grounds. See in particular para 118, Cory J (Gonthier and Iacobucci JJ concurring), recognizing that the *Charter* can apply to municipal bylaws, but expressing hesitation about the application of s 7. In cases like *Montréal (City of) v 2952-1366 Québec Inc*, 2005 SCC 62, and *Ramsden v Peterborough (City)*, [1993] 2 SCR 1084, the court assumed without discussion that the *Charter* was applicable to the bylaws in question, perhaps because the *Charter* applicants in those cases were charged with offences (compare *McKinney v University of Guelph*, [1990] 3 SCR 229 at 270 [*McKinney*]).

14   *Adult Entertainment Assn of Canada v Ottawa (City)*, 2007 ONCA 389. All of the challenges cited in notes 10 through 14 failed not because there was no state action but for other reasons.

15   *Dolphin Delivery*, above note 2 at 599. Compare Philip H Osborne, *The Law of Torts*, 4th ed (Toronto: Irwin Law, 2011) at 439.

16   *Heuman (Next Friend of) v Andrews*, 2005 ABQB 832; *Wittman (Guardian ad litem of) v Emmott* (1991), 77 DLR (4th) 77 (BCCA).

17   *Filip v Waterloo (City of)* (1992), 98 DLR (4th) 534 (Ont CA).

to override an agreement concerning child support,[18] and to legislation concerning pension plans.[19]

2) Governmental Entities

Bodies established or regulated by governments may or may not be part of the state for *Charter* purposes depending on their functions and on the extent to which they are controlled by the state. An "entity" can be part of the government "either by its very nature or in virtue of the degree of governmental control exercised over it."[20] An entity carrying out a governmental function is subject to the *Charter* regardless of the precise decree of control that the state exercises over it; an entity that is not exercising a governmental function may nonetheless be part of the government if the state exercises a sufficient degree of control over it.

The fact that an institution operates under a statutory grant of power or with heavy reliance on government funding does not make it subject to the *Charter* if it operates with a sufficient degree of independence from the government or is not carrying out specific government policies. If it can be said that the "routine or regular control"[21] of the institution does not lie in the government's hands but in the hands of an independent board, it is likely that the institution will not be considered part of the government for *Charter* purposes. On this basis, universities and hospitals, though usually considered part of the "public sector," are not generally subject to the *Charter*.[22] So the rules, policies, and procedures enacted by the governing bodies of universities and by hospital boards will not generally be subject to challenge under section 7.

If an institution is set up to serve as an instrument of government policy,[23] or if the government exercises a substantial degree of control

---

18 *Jane Doe v Alberta*, 2007 ABCA 50, leave to appeal to SCC refused (2007), 279 DLR (4th) vi (SCC) [*Doe*].

19 *Melanson v New Brunswick (AG)*, 2007 NBCA 12. All of the challenges cited in notes 16 through 19 failed, but not because the element of state action was lacking.

20 *Eldridge v British Columbia (AG)*, [1997] 3 SCR 624 at para 44 [*Eldridge*].

21 *Stoffman v Vancouver General Hospital*, [1990] 3 SCR 483 at 513 [*Stoffman*].

22 *McKinney*, above note 13 (universities); *Stoffman*, ibid (hospitals). For a surprising exception to this principle, see *Eldridge*, above note 20, where the hospital in question was seen as carrying out a particular government policy. See the discussion in Patrick J Monahan, *Constitutional Law*, 3d ed (Toronto: Irwin Law, 2006) at 407–10; Hogg, above note 2, ch 37.2(e).

23 See, for example, *Insurance Corp of British Columbia v Suska*, 2008 BCSC 1204 (an insurance corporation established to forward government policy was subject

over it,[24] then its conduct is likely subject to *Charter* scrutiny. In contrast, a private body not controlled by the government is not subject to the *Charter* even if it receives some government funding and works closely with government to achieve its objectives.[25]

3) Exercises of Statutory Powers and Discretion

A difficult problem of *Charter* application arises where a statute, the constitutional validity of which is not itself in issue, grants an official a discretionary power to do something that affects an applicant's constitutionally protected interest. In such a case, the target of the *Charter* challenge is not the validity of the statute but the legality of the particular decision of the official. Parallel issues arise when an administrative tribunal makes a decision that affects constitutional interests. The caselaw leaves no doubt that courts can review such decisions on *Charter* grounds, but the approach to be taken by the reviewing court is not wholly clear. The Supreme Court of Canada's decisions in this area adopt two different and potentially inconsistent approaches.[26]

On the first approach, which might be called the "administrative" approach, the decision is reviewed on ordinary administrative law grounds. The statute, being assumed to be valid, must be taken to authorize some intrusion on constitutionally-protected interests, but the decision is nonetheless reviewable in the same way as any other decision. So the administrative law question about the standard of review, or degree of deference, applicable to the various aspects of the decision

---

to the *Charter*). It is most unlikely that a private insurer would be subject to the *Charter*—though statutes or regulations that require policies of insurance to contain particular terms are subject to the *Charter*: see, for instance, *Miron v Trudel*, [1995] 2 SCR 418.

24 See, for example, *Greater Vancouver Transportation Authority v Canadian Federation of Students—British Columbia Component*, 2009 SCC 31 (the policies of two transit authorities were subject to the *Charter*).

25 Such was VANOC, the committee responsible for the 2010 Olympic Winter Games in Vancouver: *Sagen v Vancouver Organizing Committee for the 2010 Olympic and Paralympic Winter Games*, 2009 BCCA 522, leave to appeal to SCC refused, [2009] SCCA No 459 (*Charter* not applicable to VANOC). Given the extent to which the governments of Canada, British Columbia, and Vancouver associated themselves with the Winter Games and encouraged the patriotic fervour associated with them, and the amount of public money that supported both the Games themselves and the Canadian athletes who participated in them, the conclusion that the *Charter* applied to VANOC would have been quite defensible.

26 See the discussion in David Mullan, "Section 7 and Administrative Law Deference: No Room at the Inn?" (2006) 34 Sup Ct L Rev (2d) 227.

would arise and would be decided in roughly the same way as in a case where no constitutional interests were at stake—though with particular attention to the constitutionally-protected interests at stake.[27]

On the second approach, which might be called the "constitutional" approach, the decision must be correct because it affects constitutionally-protected interests; thus, the task of the reviewing court is simply to decide whether the decision maker made the constitutionally correct decision, and the decision is entitled to no deference. On the constitutional approach, it might be said that all aspects of the tribunal's decision raise questions going to jurisdiction. As Lamer J put it in *Slaight Communications Inc v Davidson*:

> . . . an adjudicator exercising delegated powers does not have the power to make an order that would result in the infringement of the *Charter*, and he exceeds his jurisdiction when he does so.[28]

The constitutional approach appeared to be decisively endorsed in *Multani v Commission scolaire Marguerite-Bourgeoys* (*Multani*) and in *Canada (AG) v PHS Community Services Society* (*PHS*).[29] In *Multani*, the applicant challenged a decision of a school board on the ground that it unjustifiably interfered with his religious freedom. A majority of the Supreme Court of Canada expressly rejected the minority's proposal that the decision was entitled to some deference, commenting that this proposal "could well reduce the fundamental rights guaranteed by the *Canadian Charter* to mere administrative law principles."[30] Since "the constitutionality of the *decision*"[31] was at issue, the Court, giving no deference to the board's reasoning, decided whether the board had violated the applicant's religious freedom and, if so, whether that violation was justified under section 1.[32]

---

27 Compare *Pinet v St Thomas Psychiatric Hospital*, [2004] 1 SCR 528 at para 78 [*Pinet*].

28 *Slaight Communications Inc v Davidson*, [1989] 1 SCR 1038 at 1078 [*Slaight Communications*], Lamer J dissenting in part on other grounds. Dickson CJC for the majority expressed at 1048 "complete agreement" with this aspect of Lamer J's reasons, but disagreed on the application of the principles to the facts of the case. Compare *Ross v New Brunswick School District No 15*, [1996] 1 SCR 85 at para 31; *Multani v Commission scolaire Marguerite-Bourgeoys*, 2006 SCC 6 at para 17 [*Multani*].

29 *Canada (AG) v PHS Community Services Society*, 2011 SCC 44 [*PHS*].

30 *Multani*, above note 28 at para 16.

31 *Ibid* at para 21 [emphasis in original].

32 *Ibid* at paras 32–79. As Mullan, above note 26 at 241, points out, it is arguable that even if the Court had taken the administrative law approach proposed by the minority, a full analysis of the constitutional claim might have been re-

PHS[33] arguably goes even further down the path of the constitutional approach. In 2003, as a response to a very serious problem of illegal intravenous drug use in a particular area of downtown Vancouver (the Downtown East Side), the Vancouver Coastal Health Authority (VCHA) established "Insite," a safe injection site for drug addicts. The federal Minister of Health granted Insite an exemption from the trafficking and possession provisions of the *Controlled Drugs and Substances Act* (*CDSA*),[34] pursuant to section 56 of that Act. Insite does not provide addicts with drugs and its staff does not perform injections; instead, it provides clean injection equipment, monitoring of the users' administration of drugs, and medical care in the event of an emergency. The section 56 exemption was extended from time to time until 30 June 2008. The Minister of Health then declined to act on VCHA's request for a further exemption. The organization that operated Insite, two drug addicts, and the Attorney General of British Columbia applied for, *inter alia*, an order requiring the Minister of Health to continue the exemption. The evidence at trial showed that Insite had dramatically reduced the number of overdose deaths without increasing the level of crime in the DTES and the surrounding area.[35] The Supreme Court of Canada rejected the applicants' various constitutional challenges to the *CDSA* and its application at Insite. But the Court agreed that the failure to extend the exemption engaged the applicants' interests in life and security of the person and held that the Minister of Health's failure to provide Insite with an exemption was contrary to the principles of fundamental justice because it was arbitrary and grossly disprortionate (see Chapter 4, Section B). And the Court expressed some doubt as to whether a section 1 justification for this violation of section 7 would even be possible.[36] The Court went so far as to grant "an order in the nature of mandamus," requiring the Minister to grant the exemption "forthwith."[37] There was no hint of any deference to the Minister's decision not to grant an exemption. The Court held, in essence, that the Minister was constitutionally required to exercise his discretion under section 56 of the *CDSA* in a particular way: to grant the exemption sought.

---

quired in any event because the board gave "very short shrift to [the applicant's] freedom of religion assertion"; there was, in terms of the values at play, not much reasoning to defer to.

33   Above note 29.

34   SC 1996, c 19.

35   *PHS*, above note 29 at para 28.

36   "If a s. 1 analysis were required, a point not argued, no s. 1 justificaion could succeed." *Ibid* at para 137.

37   *Ibid* at para 150.

Notwithstanding *Multani* and *PHS*, the "administrative" approach dominates the cases considered in this book. In judicial review of extradition and deportation decisions, Canadian courts regularly entertain claims that an exercise of statutory discretion under a valid statute violated the applicant's section 7 rights, but do so using the tools of administrative law. The leading case on point is, arguably, *Suresh v Canada (Minister of Citizenship and Immigration) (Suresh)*.[38] The applicant, a Convention refugee, sought judicial review of a decision of the Minister of Citizenship and Immigration to deport him on grounds of terrorism and danger to the security of Canada. There was good reason to believe that he would face a risk of death or torture if he was returned to his home country. He argued that section 53(1)(*b*) of the *Immigration Act*, which authorized deportation of a refugee, was unconstitutional to the extent that it permitted deportation to torture. The Court held that section 53(1)(*b*) was constitutionally valid because the Minister was required to exercise her discretion in accordance with the *Charter*. The relevant principle of fundamental justice was the proper balancing of interests (compare Chapter 3, Section B(4)). Given that principle, section 53(1)(*b*) did not contravene section 7 because the section does not authorize deportation to torture where the principle would forbid it; that is, where torture would be disproportionate to the interests furthered by deportation. Rather, section 53(1)(*b*) gives the Minister a discretion, the exercise of which affects the interests protected by section 7. In these circumstances, the Court says, "The Minister is obliged to exercise the discretion conferred upon her by the *Immigration Act* in accordance with the Constitution" and she "should generally decline to deport refugees where on the evidence there is a substantial risk of torture."[39] Moreover, the Minister's decision must be procedurally fair in its context. To determine the content of the duty of fairness, the Court applied a constitutionalized version of the administrative law duty of fairness,[40] bearing in mind that the interest at stake was deportation to face torture. Thus, *Suresh* suggests that exercises of a discretionary power that affects the interests protected by section 7 of the *Charter* must be exercised with attention to those interests and is reviewable on ordinary administrative law grounds.

---

38   *Suresh v Canada (Minister of Citizenship and Immigration)*, 2002 SCC 1 [*Suresh*].

39   *Ibid* at para 77. This much-criticized *obiter dictum* leaves open the possibility that refoulement to be tortured might be consistent with s 7: see Chapter 5, Section C(3)(b).

40   For the duty of fairness in administrative law, see *Baker v Canada (Minister of Citizenship and Immigration)*, [1999] 2 SCR 817 [*Baker*].

Similarly, in *Lake v Canada (Minister of Justice)*,[41] the Supreme Court of Canada considered the standard of review applicable on a Court of Appeal's review of the Minister of Justice's decision to surrender a person for extradition. Since there is no doubt that the decision to extradite profoundly implicates the person's section 7 interests,[42] it might be thought that the Minister would have to reach the correct decision (as a number of lower courts had held). But the Supreme Court held that the standard of review applicable to the surrender decision itself was reasonableness. Although the Minister is, of course, required to apply the correct legal test, which is whether the surrender is in accordance with the principles of fundamental justice, and to consider the appropriate factors, the Minister's assessment of the factors relevant to surrender is entitled to deference and is only to be set aside if unreasonable, just as if it were reviewed under ordinary administrative law principles.[43]

Suresh and *Lake* support the administrative approach;[44] *Multani* and especially *PHS* support the constitutional approach. One way to understand the difference is to assume that, when reviewing an exercise of an otherwise constitutionally valid discretion that affects *Charter*-protected interests, the Court sometimes uses a correctness standard and sometimes uses a reasonableness standard. Thus, although a constitutionally valid discretion must be exercised constitutionally, the standard of review applicable to the decision is not necessarily that of correctness; the decision may attract deference and be reviewable on the standard of reasonableness. The requirement that the discretion be exercised constitutionally may mean, depending on the context, that the official exercising the discretion may have to give the person affected certain procedural rights, even if those rights are not required by the statute, or that the official exercising discretion may have to consider substantive factors that are not expressly contemplated by the statute. Courts have long imposed such requirements on ordinary administra-

---

41   *Lake v Canada (Minister of Justice)*, 2008 SCC 23 [*Lake*].

42   See, among many other cases, *Canada v Schmidt*, [1987] 1 SCR 500 at 521, and Chapter 5, Section C. The *Charter* right at issue in *Lake* was the mobility right under s 6, but the Court's reasoning applies generally to the surrender decision "when a fugitive's *Charter* rights are engaged": *Lake*, *ibid* at para 20.

43   The Court remarked that the review of the Minister's decision on the grounds set out in the *Extradition Act* itself and the review of the decision on constitutional grounds involve "similar considerations" and therefore "overlap somewhat": *Lake*, *ibid* at para 24.

44   *Multani* is not cited in *Lake*. *Slaight Communications* is cited in *Suresh*, above note 38 at para 46, but only for some general propositions about identifying the principles of fundamental justice and not on the question of judicial review of a discretionary decision or a tribunal's ruling.

tive law grounds, but in some circumstances they will be constitutionally required and cannot be ousted by ordinary legislation.[45]

But, the question of the standard of review applicable to decisions
that affect a constitutionally protected interest cannot be answered
simply by choosing between correctness and reasonableness. In every
case where section 7 interests are affected by discretionary state action,
the very fact that the interests at stake are so vital points to correctness;
but the fact that the statute validly entrusts the decision to a decision
maker other than a court points to the need for some deference. Rather
than asking whether the decision is correct or reasonable, it is more
useful to ask what, in the particular case, justifies deference to the decision. As Dyzenhaus has suggested, such a decision is entitled to respect
if the reasons for it are supportable in light of the values underlying the
law that grants the decision maker the power to make it.[46] Where an
applicant's constitutionally protected interests are at stake, the underlying values must of course include the relevant constitutional values.
If the decision does take those values seriously, the decision is entitled
to some deference and should stand even if the reviewing court might
not have made precisely the same decision. Thus, in *Multani* itself, deference was not particularly appropriate, not because the appropriate
standard of review was correctness, but because the original decision
maker simply did not take the applicant's religious freedom into account at all. Similarly, in *PHS*, deference was not appropriate because
the evidence, including the evidence available to the Minister, over-
whelmingly pointed in the direction of granting the exemption. In *Lake*
and *Suresh*, on the other hand, some deference might possibly be justified by the executive's traditional role and expertise in foreign relations;
though even in such cases, it is hard to see how deporting someone to
face torture could be a reasonable exercise of a statutory discretion.

---

45 Contrast *Ocean Port Hotel Ltd v British Columbia (General Manager, Liquor
    Control and Licensing Branch)*, 2001 SCC 52, where there was no remedy for the
    legislature's express derogation from a principle of natural justice; the applicant
    made no *Charter* argument, no doubt because no s 7 interests were engaged.

46 David Dyzenhaus, "The Politics of Deference: Judicial Review and Democracy"
    in M. Taggart, ed, *The Province of Administrative Law* (Oxford: Hart, 1997) 279,
    esp. at 302–7; see also David Dyzenhaus, "Constituting the Rule of Law: Fun-
    damental Values in Administrative Law" (2002) 27 Queen's LJ 445. Compare
    Baker, above note 40 at para 65, asking whether the decision maker's reasons
    showed "that his decision was inconsistent with the values underlying the grant
    of discretion."

4) Laws Governing Private Litigation

a) General Considerations

As noted above, the wording of section 32(1) of the *Charter* does not, in itself, exclude the possibility that the *Charter* applies to disputes between private parties. While it would be implausible to argue that private parties were required to respect constitutional norms in their dealings with each other, it would be quite plausible to argue that where one private party invoked the state-authorized and state-funded machinery of litigation to obtain a remedy against another private party, both the substantive and procedural laws on which they relied would have to respect the Constitution. The substantive and procedural legal rules on which the parties rely are either statutory or common law rules, and so subject to the *Charter*; the facilities that the parties use to resolve their disputes are provided by the state; the judges who make court orders are state officials; and the procedures for enforcing court orders are largely matters of public law. But in *Dolphin Delivery*, a strong majority of the Court held that "the *Charter* does not apply to private litigation" because the word "government," as it appears in the phrases "Parliament and government" and "legislature and government" in section 32(1) "must . . . refer to the executive or administrative branch of government."[47] A legislature could infringe the *Charter* by enacting unconstitutional legislation, but only the executive and administrative branch could carry out an action to which the *Charter* applied. Nor was the fact that a private action would ultimately end in a court order sufficient to make the private action subject to the *Charter*, because a court order was not government action for *Charter* purposes.[48]

Thus, any legislation on which private parties rely to advance their positions in private litigation is subject to the *Charter*. But the *Charter* does not apply to a dispute between private parties where the source of the applicable legal rules was in the common law: "Where . . . private party 'A' sues private party 'B' relying on the common law and where no act of government is relied upon to support the action, the *Charter* will not apply."[49]

Dolphin Delivery itself involved a dispute between Dolphin, a company, and the RWDSU, a trade union. Dolphin applied for an injunction

---

47   *Dolphin Delivery*, above note 2 at 597–98, McIntyre J.
48   *Ibid* at 600. But see *BCGEU v British Columbia*, [1988] 2 SCR 214, where the *Charter* applied to a court order made on the court's own motion, and see the discussion in Hogg, above note 2, ch 37.2(f).
49   *Dolphin Delivery*, *ibid* at 603.

to restrain the union's secondary picketing. Since the *Canada Labour Code* was silent on this subject, Dolphin relied on the common law governing the legality of secondary picketing. The union argued that this common law violated the *Charter*. On these facts, the Supreme Court held that the *Charter* did not apply. The dispute in question was between two private parties: the RWDSU and Dolphin. The legal rule upon which Dolphin relied to restrain the union's picketing was not statutory but was a matter of the common law of British Columbia.[50]

While *Dolphin Delivery* has never been overruled, later cases have softened its impact. In *Hill v Church of Scientology* (*Church of Scientology*),[51] the defendants argued that the *Charter* should apply to the common law of defamation,[52] particularly because, on the facts of the case, the plaintiff was an official (a Crown attorney) acting in his professional capacity when he was defamed. The Court, applying *Dolphin Delivery*, found that there was no state action and so rejected this argument. The majority, *per* Cory J, noted that the defendants had "impugned the character, competence and integrity of [the plaintiff], himself, and not that of the government," and that the plaintiff had brought the action in his private capacity.[53] However, the Court went on to hold that "the common law must be interpreted in a manner which is consistent with *Charter* principles"[54] and that "it is appropriate for the courts to make such incremental revisions to the common law as may be necessary to have it comply with the values enunciated in the *Charter*."[55] Lest this holding appear to undermine *Dolphin Delivery*, Cory J continued:

---

50   *Ibid* at 603–4. The decision attracted considerable scholarly criticism, both from those who thought that the *Charter* should apply to all law, regardless of the status of the parties to the litigation, and from those who thought any effort to draw a principled distinction between public and private for the purposes of *Charter* application was doomed to fail. For examples of the former critique, see Beatty, above note 1; for the latter, see Allan C Hutchinson & Andrew Petter, "Private Rights / Public Wrongs: The Liberal Lie of the *Charter*" (1988) 38 UTLJ 278. For an argument linking *Charter* application to the proper scope of judicial review of legislation, see Robin Elliot & Robert Grant, "The *Charter*'s Application in Private Litigation" (1989) 23 UBC L Rev 459; for an argument linking *Charter* application to the nature and purpose of the particular *Charter* right invoked, see Brian Slattery, "The *Charter*'s Relevance to Private Litigation: Does *Dolphin* Deliver?" (1987) 32 McGill LJ 905.

51   *Hill v Church of Scientology of Toronto*, [1995] 2 SCR 1130 [*Church of Scientology*].

52   They did not challenge a statute that had modified the common law of defamation.

53   *Church of Scientology*, above note 51 at para 75.

54   *Ibid* at para 91.

55   *Ibid* at para 92.

Private parties owe each other no constitutional duties and cannot found their cause of action upon a *Charter* right. The party challenging the common law cannot allege that the common law violates a *Charter* <u>right</u> because, quite simply, *Charter* rights do not exist in the absence of state action. The most that the private litigant can do is argue that the common law is inconsistent with *Charter* <u>values</u> . . . .
in the context of litigation involving only private parties, the *Charter* will "apply" to the common law only to the extent that the common law is found to be inconsistent with *Charter* values.[56]

Church of Scientology directs the courts to develop the common law governing private disputes in accordance with *Charter* values, even though the common law governing private disputes is not strictly speaking subject to *Charter* challenge. This direction significantly limits the impact of *Dolphin Delivery*.[57] In *Grant v Torstar Corp*, for example, the defendant in a defamation action persuaded the Supreme Court of Canada to revise the defences to the tort of defamation so that they would give "proper weight . . . to the constitutional value of free expression on matters of public interest."[58] It is difficult to see what more the defendant could have achieved through a formal *Charter* challenge to the common law rule at issue, or what difference the formal challenge would have made to the evolution of the common law.[59] Nonetheless, some procedural *Charter* claims have been rejected in litigation between two private parties on the ground that there is no state action. For example, in some circumstances, there is a section 7 right to state -

---

56   *Ibid* at para 95 [emphasis in original].
57   See also Sharpe & Roach, above note 2 at 99–102; Hogg, above note 2, ch 37.2(g).
58   *Grant v Torstar Corp*, 2009 SCC 61 at para 65.
59   Compare *R v NS*, 2010 ONCA 670. The applicant was a witness in a preliminary inquiry. She challenged the presiding judge's ruling that she had to remove her *niqab* in order to testify, arguing that the ruling violated her religious freedom under s 2(*a*) of the *Charter*. This challenge faced at least two significant obstacles: first, the holding in *Dolphin Delivery* that court orders were not state action to which the *Charter* applied; and second, the holding in *R v Mills*, [1986] 1 SCR 863, that a judge presiding over a preliminary inquiry has no jurisdiction to grant a remedy under s 24(1) of the *Charter*. But Doherty JA reasoned that a preliminary inquiry judge was required to "exercise his or her statutory powers in accordance with the *Charter*" (*R v NS*, *ibid* at para 36). The applicant could have achieved nothing more if her challenge to the preliminary inquiry judge's decision had been formally subject to the *Charter*.

funded counsel in criminal cases and child-protection proceedings; but there is no right to state-funded counsel in private litigation.[60]

b) Tort Law

A long line of cases holds, in brief, that "s. 7 of the *Charter* does not embrace the right to bring an action for the recovery of damages for personal injury. A civil action is economic and proprietary in nature and as such outside the range of interests protected by s. 7."[61] As applied to litigation between private parties, this holding is consistent with *Dolphin Delivery*: if the *Charter* does not apply in private litigation based on the common law, then section 7 of the *Charter* does not protect one private party's right to bring a common law tort action against another private party. Moreover, where the plaintiff's injury is caused by a private party, it might be said that the element of state action required for *Charter* application is lacking.[62]

However, statutes that affect the common law of tort, for example by limiting recovery or by eliminating a cause of action, are in principle susceptible to *Charter* review because the enactment of the statute provides the necessary element of state action (see Section B(1), above in this chapter). The view that the right of recovery is a mere economic interest not protected by section 7 (compare Section D(5)(a), below in this chapter) should not preclude this scrutiny. The primary right protected by the law of personal-injury torts is the plaintiff's interest in bodily integrity, which is an aspect of security of the person; the right to recover is a secondary right.[63] Thus, to the extent that such statutes affect security of the person by affecting the individual's right to recover for violations of his bodily integrity, they should be subject to section 7 scrutiny.[64] This is not, of course, to say that restrictions on tort damages or other statutory interventions in the law of tort would violate

---

60   See, for example, *Holland (Guardian ad litem of) v Marshall*, 2010 BCCA 164 at para 16.

61   *Rogers v Faught* (2002), 212 DLR (4th) 366 at para 34 (Ont CA).

62   Compare *Whitbread v Whalley* (1988), 51 DLR (4th) 509 at 522 (BCCA), aff'd without reference to the s 7 argument, [1990] 3 SCR 1273 [*Whitbread*].

63   On the distinction between primary rights and secondary rights in private law, see *Photo Productions Ltd v Securicor Transport Ltd*, [1980] AC 827 at 848–49, Lord Diplock. The distinction between primary and secondary rights is central to the analysis of tort law offered by Robert Stevens, *Torts and Rights* (Oxford: Oxford University Press, 2007); see also Allan Beever, *Rediscovering the Law of Negligence* (Oxford: Hart, 2007) at 210–14.

64   Compare Jeremy Taylor, "Re-thinking *Whitbread v Whalley*: Liberal Justice and the Judicial Review of Damage Caps under Section 7 of the *Charter of Rights and Freedoms*" (2006) 29 Dal LJ 199.

section 7; it is merely to say that the cases holding that section 7 does not even apply to statutes concerning tort law should be reconsidered.

5) The Common Law in Public Law Litigation

In *Dolphin Delivery*, it was held that the *Charter* applies to the common law, provided that the required element of state action was also present. This holding was based primarily on the language of section 52(1) of the *Constitution Act, 1982*, to the effect that "any law that is inconsistent with the provisions of the Constitution is, to the extent of the inconsistency, of no force or effect." "Any law," in the Court's view, included the common law:

> To adopt a construction of section 52(1) which would exclude from *Charter* application the whole body of the common law which in great part governs the rights and obligations of the individuals in society, would be wholly unrealistic and contrary to the clear language employed in section 52(1) . . . .[65]

Thus, provided there is some state action, such as a criminal prosecution, a common law rule may be challenged under section 7 of the *Charter*. To put the point more strongly, any common law rule that is implicated in public law litigation is subject to section 7 challenge.

A prominent instance of a section 7 challenge to a common law rule arose in *Swain*.[66] A person who had been found not guilty of an offence by reason of insanity challenged several aspects of the legal regime governing the defence of insanity, including the common law rule that the Crown was entitled to lead evidence of insanity even though insanity was, in principle, a defence that benefited the accused. The challenge was allowed to proceed on the basis that "in cases where the *Charter* is generally applicable to the litigation in question (within the meaning of section 32), the *Charter* applies to common law rules as well as to statutes and regulations."[67]

Other common law rules that have been subject to *Charter* challenge include the common law rules governing publication bans,[68] the

---

65   *Dolphin Delivery*, above note 2 at 593, McIntyre J.

66   *R v Swain*, [1991] 1 SCR 933. In the end, the challenge succeeded, and the common law rule was invalidated. *Swain* is discussed further in Chapter 4, Section D(3)(c).

67   *Ibid* at 968.

68   *R v Mentuck*, 2001 SCC 76 (a challenge under s 2(b)).

common law definition of the offence of contempt of court,[69] and an aspect of the common law of civil procedure.[70]

6) Other State Conduct

If conduct by state actors, particularly police officers, is neither expressly or impliedly authorized nor forbidden by a statute or by the common law, the *Charter* in general, and section 7 in particular, nonetheless applies to that conduct. Consider the following two examples.

a) Investigative Conduct

Police officers have both common law and statutory duties to investigate crime. But the existence of the duty does not, in itself, provide a police officer with any particular powers.[71] In carrying out the duty to investigate crime, a police officer may, of course, exercise any powers that she is given by statute or at common law. But the officer may also do many things that are neither specifically forbidden nor specifically authorized by law: interviewing potential witnesses, observing publicly accessible locations, obtaining information in which there is no reasonable expectation of privacy, and talking to suspects (whether they are in custody or not). This conduct is state action, so the *Charter* applies to it. If the conduct impinges on an interest protected by section 7, it must comply with the principles of fundamental justice; if the conduct does not comply with the principles of fundamental justice, it violates the person's section 7 right and cannot be justified under section 1. Although the conduct is not independently unlawful, it is not "prescribed by law" because not specifically authorized by law. And one would expect state conduct that impinges on the basic interests protected by section 7 to be specifically authorized by law.

These points are exemplified in two 1990 decisions of the Supreme Court of Canada, *R v Duarte* and *R v Hebert*, which considered the constitutionality of previously accepted investigative techniques that were

---

69 *United Nurses of Alberta v Alberta (AG)*, [1992] 1 SCR 901; *Alberta v The Edmonton Sun*, 2003 ABCA 3.

70 *Doucette (Litigation Guardian of) v Wee Watch Day Care Systems Inc*, 2006 BCCA 262, rev'd on other grounds (*sub nom Juman v Doucette*) 2008 SCC 8. The British Columbia Court of Appeal considered the constitutional status of the common law implied undertaking rule on the assumption that the *Charter* applied to it. The Supreme Court of Canada did not deal with this aspect of the dispute.

71 This duty is one of the elements of the test for common law police powers set out in *R v Waterfield*, [1963] 3 All ER 659 (CCA) and *R v Mann*, 2004 SCC 52, but the duty does not by itself establish the existence of a common law power.

not independently unlawful. *Duarte*[72] concerned electronic surveillance of a conversation with the consent of one of the parties involved: the police recorded the accused's conversations with an informant, with the informant's consent. The police did not obtain a warrant, but relied on what is now section 184(2)(*a*) of the *Criminal Code*. It is, in general, an offence under section 184(1) for anyone to electronically intercept private communications, but pursuant to section 184(2)(*a*), the prohibition does not apply to "a person who has the consent to intercept, express or implied, of the originator of the private communication or of the person intended by the originator thereof to receive it." So the police conduct did not violate section 184: the officers had the informant's consent to intercept the communication between the accused and the informant. Moreover, police forces had been using this technique since what is now Part VI of the *Criminal Code* had been enacted in the 1970s. Nonetheless, the Court held that the accused had a reasonable expectation of privacy in the conversations and that the police should therefore have obtained a warrant to intercept them.[73] The warrantless recording violated section 8 of the *Charter*. Could it be justified under section 1? The Court's analysis of this point is brief and cryptic. The Court commented that participant surveillance could not be justified under section 1 because "the police could employ the same investigatory tool with or without a warrant."[74] This reasoning looks like a holding that warrantless electronic surveillance with the consent of a participant pursuant to section 184(2)(*a*) is not a minimal impairment of the target's section 8 right;[75] but no declaration of invalidity is issued in respect of any part of section 184 itself. So it might be more satisfactory to read *Duarte* as implicitly holding that the police conduct in question could not be justified under section 1 because it was not "prescribed by law": although neither the police nor the informant violated the *Criminal Code* through the method of consent interception, neither the Code nor any other law authorized the police to use consent interceptions in their investigations.[76]

In *R v Hebert*,[77] the Court revisited, under the *Charter*, an investigative technique that was accepted at common law. The accused was

---

72   *R v Duarte*, [1990] 1 SCR 30.

73   *Ibid* at 42–49.

74   *Ibid* at 57.

75   That is, that the technique fails the proportionality test from *R v Oakes*, [1986] 1 SCR 103, discussed in Chapter 6.

76   The *Criminal Code* was subsequently amended to authorize this method: see s 184.2.

77   *R v Hebert*, [1990] 2 SCR 151 [*Hebert*].

charged with robbery. On arrest, he spoke to counsel and declined to make a statement. The police placed an undercover officer in his cell to engage him in conversation, and thereby obtained a statement.[78] There is no question that the accused's statements would have been admissible at common law,[79] but the court found that the officer's conduct violated the accused's right to silence under section 7 of the *Charter* and excluded the statement under section 24(2).[80] The Supreme Court of Canada ultimately upheld this decision. The important point, for present purposes, is that the Court did not invalidate any statute or common law rule, or find that the officer's conduct was independently unlawful; rather, the holding was simply that the officer's conduct violated the accused's section 7 rights. Any question about whether a statute or common law rule was in issue was removed by McLachlin J's reasoning concerning the application of section 1 of the *Charter*. She held that "the conduct here in question is not a limit 'prescribed by law' within section 1" and added:

> The police conduct here at issue . . . was not done in execution of or by necessary implication from a statutory or regulatory duty, and it was not the result of application of a common law rule.[81]

Thus, a section 7 violation can result from conduct of state actors that, though not independently illegal, is not authorized by a statute, regulation, or common law rule.

b) Tortious State Conduct

A private party may sue the state in tort, either for the government-specific tort of misfeasance in public office or for the general tort of negligence. A statute could, of course, abolish these torts in whole or in part, or could create defences to them that do not exist at common law. However, it is not clear whether tortious state conduct engages section 7 of the *Charter*. The argument in favour of recognizing state torts as engaging, and indeed violating, section 7 is fairly straightforward. If officials conduct themselves in such a way that the government is liable in tort, then the involvement of state agents would seem to supply the element of state action necessary to make the *Charter* applicable to the dispute. If, further, the state's tortious conduct affects the plaintiff's life, liberty, or security of the person, it would seem that the tort engaged section 7. Once these two elements were established, the finding that

---

78   *Ibid* at 159.
79   Compare *Rothman v R*, [1981] 1 SCR 640.
80   These aspects of *Hebert* are discussed in more detail in Chapter 4, Section E(1).
81   *Hebert*, above note 77 at 187.

section 7 was violated would seem to be irresistible, as the commission of a tort would violate the principle of fundamental justice requiring the state to obey the law (see Chapter 4, Section B(6)). In the absence of a statutory defence, no section 1 justification would be possible because committing a tort could not be authorized by law (and note that if the state conduct was authorized by law, it could not be a tort). So, it would seem that a tort that is committed by the state and that affects life, liberty, or security of the person must always amount to a *Charter* breach, entitling the plaintiff to a remedy under section 24(1) as well as a remedy at common law.

As noted above in this chapter (Section B(4)(b)), the weight of authority holds that section 7 does not apply to tort law; this holding has often been maintained even where the tort action is brought against the state.[82] But in these cases, the element of state action is present, and as argued above, it is unsatisfactory to characterize the plaintiff's interest as a purely economic one that is not protected by section 7. So it might be argued that (depending on the tort in question) the interest protected is the right to life, liberty, and security of the person; the state's tortious action provides the necessary element of state action; and the damages award is the remedy for the violation of the plaintiff's right against the state.[83] Some judicial decisions have accepted this line of reasoning; most have not.

i) Misfeasance in Public Office

An action for misfeasance in public office involves a claim by the plaintiff that the defendant, the holder of a public office, has in some way misused his public office to the plaintiff's detriment. In *Odhavji Estate v Woodhouse*,[84] the Supreme Court of Canada summarized the elements of the tort of misfeasance in public office as follows:

---

82 See, for example, *Rogers v Faught*, above note 61 (constitutional action against public bodies regulating dentistry); *Filip v Waterloo (City)*, above note 17 (negligence action against a municipality); *Taylor v Canada (Minister of Health)* (2007), 285 DLR (4th) 296 at paras 51–57 (Ont SCJ) (negligence action against two federal ministers).

83 This kind of reasoning was considered and rejected, albeit in the context of a tort action between two private parties, in *Whitbread v Whalley*, above note 62 at 520–21. See also *Trang v Alberta (Edmonton Remand Centre)*, 2007 ABCA 263 at para 36 [*Trang*], expressing doubt about whether "every public sector tort or potential tort [is] a breach of s 7."

84 *Odhavji Estate v Woodhouse*, 2003 SCC 69 [*Odhavji Estate*]; see also Lewis N. Klar, *Tort Law*, 4th ed (Toronto: Thomson Carswell, 2008) at 318–24.

First, the public officer must have engaged in deliberate and unlawful conduct in his or her capacity as a public officer. Second, the public officer must have been aware both that his or her conduct was unlawful and that it was likely to harm the plaintiff.[85]

If the misfeasance in public office affected life, liberty, or security of the person, and if the public officer is one to whom the *Charter* otherwise applies,[86] then it is arguable that the commission of this tort would also be a violation of section 7. However, there appear to be no cases recognizing this possibility.

ii) *Malicious Prosecution*

The tort of malicious prosecution, if committed by a public officer rather than a private prosecutor, seems inevitably to involve not just engaging but breaching section 7. The elements of this tort are as follows:

(1) The defendant initiated the prosecution;
(2) The prosecution ended in the plaintiff's favour;
(3) The plaintiff had no reasonable and probable grounds for the prosecution; and
(4) The defendant was motivated by malice.[87]

If the defendant is a public prosecutor, the necessary element of state action would be present. Section 7 would apply to his or her conduct because any prosecution where imprisonment is a possibility engages the section 7 liberty interest (see Section D(3)(b), below in this chapter). And a tortious prosecution could not possibly comply with the principles of fundamental justice. Thus, "in many, if not all cases of malicious prosecution by an Attorney General or Crown Attorney, there will have been an infringement of an accused's rights as guaranteed by sections 7 and 11 of the *Canadian Charter of Rights and Freedoms*."[88] However, in

---

85   *Odhavji Estate*, *ibid* at para 23.
86   There is some authority for the proposition that this tort can be committed by a public officer to whom the *Charter* does not apply. In *Freeman-Maloy v Marsden* (2006), 267 DLR (4th) 37 (Ont CA), a university student brought an action for misfeasance in public office against the president of the university. Sharpe JA accepted the point that the *Charter* was not applicable to the defendant, but held at paras 17–28 that it was not plain and obvious that the defendant was not a public officer for the purposes of this tort. Accordingly, the defendant's motion to strike out that part of the plaintiff's claim was dismissed. In such a case, the element of state action would be lacking, so the *Charter* would not even apply to the dispute.
87   *Nelles v Ontario*, [1989] 2 SCR 170 at 193; *Miazga v Kvello Estate*, 2009 SCC 51 at paras 53–57.
88   *Nelles v Ontario*, *ibid* at 194.

its most recent consideration of this tort, the Supreme Court of Canada does not mention section 7.[89]

iii) Negligence

The state and its agents can also be found liable in negligence, though the element of policy in the determination of liability is even stronger in negligence actions against the state than in negligence actions between private parties.

In any negligence action, the plaintiff must establish the following elements:

- the defendant owed a duty of care to the plaintiff;
- the defendant breached his or her duty of care;
- the plaintiff was injured;
- the defendant's breach of duty caused the plaintiff's injury in fact; and
- the defendant's breach of duty caused the plaintiff's injury in law, in that the injury was a reasonably foreseeable consequence of the breach of duty.[90]

The defendant may then seek to establish a partial or complete defence such as contributory negligence.

Where the plaintiff alleges that the state is liable in negligence, the same basic elements must be established, but because of the need for the state to make policy decisions about how best to allocate its resources in the public interest, and because of the necessarily discretionary nature of much public decision making, courts are more hesitant to recognize a duty of care than they might be in a similar action between private parties.[91]

In *Neilsen v Kamloops* and *Cooper v Hobart*,[92] the Supreme Court of Canada has specified the elements that have to be proved before the state can be found liable in negligence, relying heavily on the English case of *Anns v Merton London Borough Council*.[93] First, the plaintiff must establish that the state owed him a private law duty of care, in light of the following questions:

---

89   *Miazga v Kvello Estate*, above note 87.
90   *Mustapha v Culligan of Canada Ltd*, 2008 SCC 27.
91   Compare Osborne, above note 15 at 217–18; Klar, above note 84 at 291–313; and compare *Holland v Saskatchewan*, 2008 SCC 42 at para 10 (refusing to recognize a tort of negligent breach of statutory duty).
92   *Neilsen v Kamloops*, [1984] 2 SCR 2; *Cooper v Hobart*, 2001 SCC 79.
93   *Anns v Merton London Borough Council*, [1978] AC 728 [*Anns*].

> (1) is there a sufficiently close relationship between the parties . . . so
> that, in the reasonable contemplation of the [public] authority, care-
> lessness on its part might cause damage to that person?[94]

This step has itself been subdivided into two parts: in deciding whether to recognize a duty of care, a court should ask whether "the harm
that occurred [was] the reasonably foreseeable consequence of the defendant's act" and whether "there [are] reasons, notwithstanding the
proximity between the parties established in the first part of this test,
that tort liability should not be recognized here." These reasons would
typically relate to "factors arising from the *relationship* between the
plaintiff and the defendant."[95] If a duty suggests itself at the first stage,
a second question arises:

> (2) are there any considerations which ought to negative or limit (a)
> the scope of the duty and (b) the class of persons to whom it is owed
> or (c) the damages to which a breach of it may give rise?[96]

The policy considerations relevant at the second stage are "residual" in
that they "are not concerned with the relationship between the parties,"
but with the systemic effects of recognizing a new duty of care:

> Does the law already provide a remedy? Would recognition of the
> duty of care create the spectre of unlimited liability to an unlimited
> class? Are there other reasons of broad policy that suggest that the
> duty of care should not be recognized?[97]

The kind of decision at issue is an important consideration at the second
stage. Courts have relied heavily on a distinction between "policy" decisions and "operational" decisions. A policy decision is a choice to
engage in a particular activity; an operational decision is one made in
the course of carrying out a policy.[98]

There is no tort liability for policy decisions because "it is inappropriate for courts to second-guess elected legislators on policy matters",
but there may be tort liability for the negligent execution of operational
decisions.[99] The distinction between policy and operational decisions,

---

94 *Neilsen v Kamloops*, above note 92 at 10.
95 *Cooper v Hobart*, above note 92 at para 30.
96 *Neilsen v Kamloops*, above note 92 at 10–11, paraphrasing *Anns*, above note 93 at
    751–52.
97 *Cooper v Hobart*, above note 92 at para 37.
98 *Neilsen v Kamloops*, above note 92 at 8–131; compare *Cooper v Hobart*, *ibid* at
    para 38.
99 *Cooper v Hobart*, *ibid* at para 38.

though "elusive,"[100] continues to play a central role in negligence actions against the state.[101] As the Supreme Court of Canada recently put it:

> Policy decisions about what acts to perform under a statute do not give rise to liability in negligence. On the other hand, once a decision to act has been made, the government may be liable in negligence for the manner in which it *implements* that decision.[102]

The injury suffered by the plaintiff need not affect life, liberty, or security of the person;[103] if it does not, section 7 would not be engaged. But if the plaintiff's injury does involve life, liberty, or security of the person, then it is arguable that the government's negligence would also amount to a section 7 breach. For example, the tort of negligent investigation, which was recognized in *Hill v Hamilton-Wentworth Regional Police* (*Hill*) as a cause of action under the *Anns* test,[104] typically engages the plaintiff's interest in liberty because the tort arises in the criminal process (see Section D(3)(b), below in this chapter); the liberty interest is engaged both by the prospect of imprisonment on conviction and by the likelihood of pre-trial custody. In *Hill* itself, McLachlin CJC commented that imposing a duty of care on police officers investigating crime was "consistent with the values and spirit underlying the *Charter*,"[105] though she did not expressly hold that a failure to live up to this duty would be a violation of the *Charter*.

The well-known tort action in *Jane Doe v Metropolitan Toronto (Municipality) Commissioners of Police* (*Jane Doe*) illustrates how a tort of negligence committed by a public official can also be a violation

100 Osborne, above note 15 at 219; compare the discussion in Klar, above note 84 at 300–11.
101 See especially the cases concerning the maintenance of highways, a public function that inevitably involves a complicated and highly discretionary mixture of policy and operational decisions (as anyone who has endured a Canadian winter knows): *Just v British Columbia*, [1989] 2 SCR 1228 (highway department's system of inspection and repair of rocky slopes a policy decision); *Brown v British Columbia (Minister of Transportation and Highways)*, [1994] 1 SCR 420 (continuing summer schedule for snow and ice removal until November a policy decision).
102 *Holland v Saskatchewan*, above note 91 at para 14 [emphasis in original].
103 In *Anns*, above note 93, the plaintiffs alleged property damage. In *Cooper v Hobart*, above note 92, and *Edwards v Law Society of Upper Canada*, 2001 SCC 80, the damage alleged by the plaintiffs was purely financial. Neither type of injury would, by itself, engage s 7.
104 *Hill v Hamilton-Wentworth Regional Police*, 2007 SCC 41.
105 *Ibid* at para 38.

of section 7.[106] The plaintiff was raped by a serial rapist. She was his fifth known victim. She sued the police for a negligent failure to warn her, as a member of the class of women likely to be targeted, of the danger posed by the rapist. The trial judge found that the plaintiff had established the elements of the tort of negligence. She also found that the conduct of the police amounted to a violation of the plaintiff's section 7 rights. Her security of the person was engaged by the police's "subjecting her to the very real risk of attack by a serial rapist."[107] The "discriminatory and negligent" conduct of the investigation was inconsistent with the principles of fundamental justice.[108] And section 1 of the *Charter* was inapplicable because the conduct was not prescribed by law: "the plaintiff's *Charter* rights have been infringed by police conduct—not a legislative enactment or a common law rule."[109]

However, *Jane Doe* is difficult to reconcile with the long line of cases holding that whether or not a plaintiff can maintain an action in negligence against the state, the state's tortious conduct is not a breach of section 7 because "the right to security of the person under section 7 does not embrace the civil right to bring an action for the recovery of damages for personal injury."[110] Most recently, in *Trang v Alberta (Edmonton Remand Centre)* (*Trang*), it is suggested in *obiter dicta* that government torts are not violations of section 7 because section 7 "relate[s] primarily to the procedures and methods by which the legal rights of the citizens are engaged [but] does not engage any general obligation to design government programs only after adverting to the interests of all those potentially affected."[111] The reasoning in *Trang* seems to give insufficient weight to the distinction between policy and operational decisions. The extent to which the state adverts to the interests of all would be a policy decision for which the state is not liable in tort;[112] to the extent that the state negligently carries out its own policies and thereby affects a person's life, liberty, and security of the person, all the elements of a section 7 claim would appear to be present. Moreover,

---

106 *Jane Doe v Metropolitan Toronto (Municipality) Commissioners of Police* (1998), 160 DLR (4th) 697 (Ont Ct Gen Div).

107 *Ibid* at 734.

108 *Ibid* at 735.

109 *Ibid*.

110 *Filip v Waterloo (City)*, above note 17 at 537–38; see also the other cases cited in note 82.

111 *Trang*, above note 83 at para 38.

112 Compare *Abarquez v Ontario*, 2009 ONCA 374 at para 49, holding that the Ontario government's policy-driven response to a public health emergency was not arbitrary in the s 7 sense because the province had legitimately weighed a number of interests in formulating its response.

even if section 7 relates primarily to the determination of legal rights, it is clear from *Chaoulli v Quebec (Attorney General)* (*Chaoulli*),[113] among many other cases, that section 7 does not relate *solely* to proceedings involving the determination of legal rights and may be engaged by state action that deprives individuals of life, liberty, and security of the person in other ways.

7) Conduct outside Canada

Section 32 does not in itself limit the geographical reach of the *Charter*; instead, it speaks of "all matters within the authority" of Canadian legislative bodies. Thus, the *Charter* does not apply to the conduct of foreign state officials, even where they gather evidence that is later used in a Canadian proceeding,[114] or where they are acting in response to a request from Canadian officials.[115] But it might be argued that the *Charter* applies to the conduct of Canadian state officials while they are operating abroad. While a *Charter* remedy could not be obtained from a foreign court,[116] it could be obtained from a Canadian court. On the other hand, it might be argued that to apply the *Charter* in these circumstances would be inappropriate, as it would amount to saying that individuals can have *Charter* rights anywhere in the world, which would impinge on the sovereignty of other states.

The Supreme Court of Canada has wrestled with this issue on a number of occasions. The leading cases are *R v Cook* (*Cook*) and *R v Hape* (*Hape*),[117] which take very different approaches to determining how the *Charter* applies to the conduct of Canadian state agents abroad.

In *Cook*, the Court adopted a two-step approach to extraterritorial application of the *Charter*. The first step was to decide whether the conduct could properly be characterized as state action under section 32(1) of the *Charter*; the second step was to decide whether applying the *Charter* would, in the circumstances, be consistent with the sovereignty of the foreign state. The accused was charged with murder. The

---

113 *Chaoulli*, above note 8.

114 *R v Harrer*, [1995] 3 SCR 562 [*Harrer*].

115 *R v Terry*, [1996] 2 SCR 207 [*Terry*]. *Harrer* and *Terry* are discussed in more detail in Chapter 5, Section B(3)(b).

116 It is difficult to envisage circumstances under which a foreign court would recognize itself as a "court of competent jurisdiction" for the purposes of making an order under s 24(1) of the *Charter* or as having the jurisdiction to make a declaration of invalidity under s 52, or under which circumstances such an order or declaration would be enforced in Canada by a Canadian court.

117 *R v Cook*, [1998] 2 SCR 597 [*Cook*]; *R v Hape*, 2007 SCC 26 [*Hape*].

victim was killed in Vancouver. The accused was arrested in the state
of Louisiana and was informed of his rights under American law. He
did not make a statement. Two days later, while in custody in New
Orleans, he was interviewed by officers from the Vancouver Police Department. The officers gave him an explanation of his right to counsel that did not comply with section 10(b) of the *Charter*. The accused
made a statement denying that he killed the victim. This statement was
not introduced during the Crown's case in chief, but it turned out to be
inconsistent with his trial testimony, and the Crown was permitted to
cross-examine him on it to undermine his credibility. The accused was
convicted. The British Columbia Court of Appeal dismissed his appeal
from conviction on the ground that the statement was properly admitted under section 24(2) of the *Charter* for the purpose of undermining
the accused's credibility. The accused's further appeal to the Supreme
Court of Canada was allowed and a new trial was ordered. On the question of whether the *Charter* applied to the conduct of the Vancouver officers when they interviewed the accused in New Orleans, the majority,
per Cory and Iacobucci JJ, adopted the following approach. In general,
the *Charter* would not apply abroad because that would inconsistent
with the general principle of territorial sovereignty; however, because
of the wording of section 32 and because of the possibility of jurisdiction based on nationality, the *Charter* could apply to the conduct of
Canadian state agents acting abroad. In particular, "the *Charter* applies
to the actions of *Canadian law enforcement authorities* on foreign territory (which satisfies section 32(1)), provided that the application of
Charter standards would not interfere with the sovereign authority of
the foreign state."[118] On the facts of the case, both elements of this test
were satisfied: the officers' interview of the accused "was conducted by
Canadian detectives, as opposed to foreign officials, in accordance with
their powers of investigation as derived from Canadian law";[119] and
in the circumstances, there was no interference with the sovereignty
of the United States.[120] So the conclusion in the courts below that the
statement was obtained via a *Charter* breach was affirmed; but unlike
the lower courts, the majority went on to exclude the statement under
section 24(2).[121]

---

118 *Cook, ibid* at para 46 [emphasis in original].
119 *Ibid* at para 49.
120 *Ibid* at para 50.
121 *Ibid* at paras 64–78. Bastarache J, Gonthier J concurring, concurred in the result,
     but took a different approach to the question of *Charter* application. He held
     that the *Charter* always applied to Canadian officials abroad (*ibid* at para 122),
     but that its application to a particular investigation would depend on a number

In *Hape*, the Court took a fundamentally different approach. The accused was charged with money laundering. The Crown led evidence that had been gathered in the Turks and Caicos Islands. On 7 and 8 February 1998, officers of the Turks and Caicos Police Force, accompanied by RCMP officers, surreptitiously and without a warrant, entered the accused's business premises at might and conducted a search. On 14 March, RCMP officers, again acting surreptitiously and without a warrant, entered and searched the premises again. In February 1999, RCMP officers, accompanied by Turks and Caicos police officers and acting without a warrant, seized more than 100 boxes of documents from the premises. These searches, had they occurred in Canada, would clearly have violated section 8 of the *Charter*. Based on the test from *Cook*, the trial judge found that the *Charter* did not apply because the legality of the entry into the premises was governed entirely by Turks and Caicos law; accordingly, the application of *Charter* standards to the search would be an objectionable extra-territorial effect, and the argument for *Charter* application failed at the second step. The evidence was admitted and the accused was convicted of money laundering. His appeal to the Ontario Court of Appeal was dismissed, and he appealed to the Supreme Court of Canada.

Given the trial judge's factual findings, the case could have been decided in the Crown's favour on the basis of the *Cook* approach, and Binnie J would have dismissed the appeal for that reason.[122] Bastarache J would have dismissed the appeal on the ground that, although the *Charter* did apply to them, the RCMP officers did not violate the accused's section 8 rights because there was no evidence that the search was unreasonable under the law of the Turks and Caicos. [123]

But the majority in *Hape*, *per* LeBel J, overruled the approach in *Cook*. LeBel J interpreted section 32(1) of the *Charter* in light of two principles of international law: the principle of respect for sovereignty and the principle of comity. These two principles implied that, in

---

of factors concerning "who was in control of the specific feature of the investigation which is alleged to constitute the *Charter* breach": *ibid* at para 126. If the Canadian officers were in control of a particular part of the investigation, then the *Charter* would apply to that part. L'Heureux-Dubé J, McLachlin J concurring, dissented on the grounds that the *Charter* did not apply to the conduct of the Vancouver officers and that the evidence obtained should not be excluded under *Harrer*, above note 114, and *Terry*, above note 115.

122 *Hape*, above note 117 at para 189.

123 *Ibid* at paras 176–79; this holding is consistent with his approach in *Cook*, above note 117 at para 122. It might also be said that the accused had no reasonable expectation of privacy against a search that was lawful in the jurisdiction where it occurred.

general the *Charter* could not apply to the conduct of Canadian state officials outside Canada because "Canadian law, whether statutory or constitutional, cannot be enforced in another state's territory without the other state's consent."[124] The point is put even more strongly in the course of LeBel J's critique of the reasoning in *Cook*:

> . . . Canadian law cannot be enforced in another state's territory without that state's consent. Since extraterritorial enforcement is not possible, and enforcement is necessary for the *Charter* to apply, extraterritorial application of the *Charter* is impossible.[125]

Illustrating the point with respect to the facts of the case, LeBel J pointed out that the kind of warrant required to make the searches lawful in Canada was apparently unavailable in the Turks and Caicos, and commented that it would interfere with that state's sovereignty "to require that country's legal system to develop a procedure for issuing a warrant in the circumstances simply to comply with the dictates of the *Charter*."[126]

After *Hape*, there appear to be two ways that the *Charter* can apply to the conduct of Canadian officials operating abroad, or two "*Hape* exceptions." First, the foreign state might consent to the application of the *Charter*.[127] The Court in *Hape* did not discuss the issues that would arise in establishing this fact in a Canadian court: for example, whether such consent would have to be given expressly or could arise by implication,[128] or who has the burden of proof on the issue of the foreign state's consent.

Second, LeBel J affirmed that Canadian officials abroad must conduct themselves in accordance with Canada's "international obligations in respect of human rights," even if the law of the foreign state did not require compliance with those norms, and that the *Charter* will apply where the applicant's *Charter* rights in Canada are affected:

> I would leave open the possibility that, in a future case, participation by Canadian officers in activities in another country that would violate Canada's international human rights obligations might justify

---

124 *Hape*, above note 117 at para 69.
125 *Ibid* at para 85.
126 *Ibid* at para 86.
127 *Ibid* at para 106.
128 Both explicit and implicit consent of a foreign state were considered, and rejected on the facts, in *Amnesty International Canada v Canada (Canadian Forces)*, 2008 FC 336 at paras 152–84, aff'd 2008 FCA 401, leave to appeal to SCC refused, [2009] 1 SCR v [*Amnesty*].

a remedy under section 24(1) of the *Charter* because of the impact of those activities on *Charter* rights in Canada.[129]

This reasoning must mean that, notwithstanding the general rule that the *Charter* cannot apply outside Canada, Canadian participation in violating Canada's international human rights obligations abroad is indeed a *Charter* violation, at least where the effect of that violation is felt in Canada—otherwise a section 24(1) remedy would not be available.

The Supreme Court's first opportunity to consider the application of *Hape* involved the second *Hape* exception. In *Canada (Justice) v Khadr (Khadr)*[130] the applicant was a Canadian citizen who was (and, as of February 2011, still is) held at the United States' notorious prison camp in Guantanamo Bay, Cuba, for suspected terrorists who are not US citizens. He was captured in battle in Afghanistan in 2002. In 2003, and at other times, he was interviewed at Guantanamo Bay by agents of the Canadian Security and Intelligence Service (CSIS) and other Canadian officials. Information from those interviews was provided to US officials. In 2005, Khadr was charged with the murder of an American soldier. He sought disclosure from various Canadian government sources[131] of information relevant to the charges against him. The government argued, on the basis of *Hape*, that the *Charter* did not apply to the Canadian officials who conducted the interviews with Khadr. The Supreme Court framed this issue as follows:

> If the Guantanamo Bay process under which Mr. Khadr was being held was in conformity with Canada's international obligations, the *Charter* has no application and Mr. Khadr's application for disclosure cannot succeed . . . . However, if Canada was participating in a process that was violative of Canada's binding obligations under international law, the *Charter* applies to the extent of that participation.[132]

The Court noted that the United States Supreme Court had found that the "Guantanamo Bay process" violated the Geneva Conventions;[133] indeed, that "the regime providing for detention and trial of Mr. Khadr at the time of the CSIS interviews constituted a clear violation of funda-

---

129 *Hape*, above note 117 at para 101.
130 *Canada (Justice) v Khadr*, 2008 SCC 28 [*Khadr*].
131 Specifically, the Minister of Justice and Attorney General of Canada, the Minister of Foreign Affairs, the Director of CSIS, and the Commissioner of the Royal Canadian Mounted Police.
132 *Khadr*, above note 130 at para 19.
133 The court cites *Rasul v Bush*, 542 US 466 (2004) and *Hamdan v Rumsfeld*, 126 S Ct 2749 (2006).

mental human rights protected by international law."[134] Moreover, the Geneva conventions are part of Canadian law.[135] Consequently, "the *Hape* comity concerns that would ordinarily justify deference to foreign law have no application here" and the *Charter* applied to Canada's participation "in a process that violated Canada's international obligations."[136] Since Khadr's liberty was at stake, section 7 of the *Charter* applied, and the government had to conduct itself in accordance with the principles of fundamental justice.[137]

The result in *Khadr* indicates that the second *Hape* exception is considerably broader than was contemplated in *Hape* itself. On the most natural reading of *Hape*, the applicant's *Charter* rights are engaged only where (1) Canadian officials participate "in activities in another country that would violate Canada's international human rights obligations" *and* (2) the applicant's *Charter* rights in Canada are affected.[138] Yet in *Khadr*, the applicant's liberty interest in Canada was not affected. He was detained at Guantanamo by US officials, but had never been detained in Canada, and faced no proceeding in Canada. His ability to receive disclosure was certainly affected in Canada, but the right to receive disclosure is not a free-standing *Charter* right; rather, it is a principle of fundamental justice that applies if the applicant's section 7 interests are engaged.[139] In *Khadr*, although the applicant did not face a deprivation of liberty in Canada, the Court compelled the government

---

134 *Khadr*, above note 130 at para 24.

135 *Geneva Convention for the Amelioration of the Condition of the Wounded and Sick in Armed Forces in the Field*, 75 UNTS 31, Can TS 1965 No 20; *Geneva Convention for the Amelioration of the Condition of Wounded, Sick and Shipwrecked Members of Armed Forces at Sea*, 75 UNTS 85, Can TS 1965 No 20; *Geneva Convention Relative to the Protection of Civilian Persons in Time of War*, 75 UNTS 287, Can TS 1965 No 20; *Geneva Convention Relative to the Treatment of Prisoners of War*, 75 UNTS 135, Can TS 1965 No 20; *Geneva Conventions Act*, RSC 1985, c G-3.

136 *Khadr*, above note 130 at para 26.

137 *Ibid* at para 29. This holding was reaffirmed in *Canada (Prime Minister) v Khadr*, 2010 SCC 3 at paras 14–18 (*Khadr SCC*), where the court found that the government of Canada had violated Khadr's *Charter* rights because Canadian officials had participated in interviews with Khadr under conditions that were illegal and contrary to Canada's international obligations (para 24). But the remedy for this violation was limited to a declaration that Khadr's rights had been violated (paras 46–47), in essence leaving it to the federal government to choose an appropriate remedy. The government's response was to ask the US not to use the evidence unlawfully obtained from Khadr: Sarah Boeswald, "Ottawa Asks U.S. to Omit Evidence in *Khadr* Case" *Globe & Mail* (17 February 2010) A7.

138 *Hape*, above note 117 at para 101.

139 Compare *R v Stinchcombe*, [1991] 3 SCR 326, discussed in Chapter 5, Section B(4).

of Canada to provide him with a *Charter* remedy because Canadian officials had, while in another country, participated in a process that violated Canada's international obligations, and because the government of Canada was in a position to provide him with a procedural right (disclosure) that he would have received if he had faced a deprivation of liberty in Canada. None of these factors by itself would have generated a *Charter* remedy. So *Khadr* implies that the second *Hape* exception should be reformulated as follows: the applicant's *Charter* rights are engaged where (1) Canadian officials participate "in activities in another country that would violate Canada's international human rights obligations," (2) the applicant's *Charter*-protected interests are affected anywhere in the world, or at least in the other country. The government of Canada would then be required to provide a remedy, linked to its participation in the unlawful activity abroad, that responded in some way to the threat to the applicant's *Charter* rights.

This reading of the second *Hape* exception casts doubt on the correctness of the decision in *Amnesty International Canada v Canada (Canadian Forces)*, another case arising from Canada's participation in the so-called "global war on terror." The applicants[140] sought judicial review of "the conduct of Canadian Forces personnel in relation to individuals detained by the Canadian Forces in Afghanistan, and the transfer of those individuals to the custody of Afghan authorities."[141] Specifically, they sought to prevent the Canadian Forces (CF) from transferring detainees without adequate assurances that the detainees would not be tortured. The applications rested on the detainees' section 7 right to security of the person. Mactavish J, deciding the matter before the decision in *Khadr* was relesed, applied *Hape* and dismissed the application on the ground that the *Charter* was not applicable to CF personnel operating in Afghanistan. After reviewing the legal basis for the CF's presence in Afghanistan, she concluded that Afghanistan had not consented to the application of Canadian law.[142] She considered the argument that the *Charter* applied when the CF had "effective military control" of detainees, and rejected it on several grounds, including its inconsistency with *Hape*.[143] Finally, she considered whether the *Charter* would apply if the applicants could establish that the detainees faced a substantial risk of torture on being transferred to Afghan authorities, and held that this fact would not engage the *Charter* because it would

---

140 Amnesty International Canada and the British Columbia Civil Liberties Association.
141 *Amnesty*, above note 128 at para 1 (FC).
142 *Ibid* at paras 152–84.
143 *Ibid* at paras 187–298.

have no impact on *Charter* rights in Canada.[144] In other words, she held that "*Hape* did not create a 'fundamental human rights exception' justifying the extraterritorial assertion of *Charter* jurisdiction where such jurisdiction would not otherwise exist"; some impact on *Charter* rights in Canada was required.[145]

The Federal Court of Appeal agreed with these findings and holdings,[146] but since *Khadr* had been decided, had also to decide whether the *Hape* exceptions were broader than Mactavish J thought. On the interpretation of the second *Hape* exception proposed above, the fundamental human rights exception applies when section 7 interests are "engaged by Canada's participation in a foreign process that is contrary to Canada's international human rights obligations,"[147] no matter where in the world the engagement occurs. Thus, if the conduct of the CF meant that Afghan detainees faced a substantial risk of torture, section 7 of the *Charter* would be engaged. But the Federal Court of Appeal rejected this interpretation of the *Hape* exception and so dismissed the applicants' appeal. The court held that while "deference and comity end where clear violations of international law and fundamental human rights begin," the end of deference and comity "does not mean that the *Charter* then applies as a consequence of these violations."[148] All the circumstances had to be considered; the circumstances here included the commitment of the CF and the government of Afghanistan to the application of "international law, including international humanitarian law" to "the treatment of detainees in Canadian custody,"[149] and the limited extent to which the government of Afghanistan had consented to the application of Canadian law.[150] The court distinguished *Khadr* on the ground that Khadr was a Canadian citizen, unlike the Afghan detainees, who have "no attachment whatsoever to Canada or its laws."[151] But there is no reason why all of these circumstances, in particular the question of citizenship, should defeat the claim. Khadr's Canadian citizenship plays no role in the Supreme Court of Canada's reasoning; the second *Hape* exception, as interpreted and applied in the *Khadr* decisions, applies "in the case of Canadian participation in activities of a foreign state or its agents that are contrary to Canada's international

---

144 *Ibid* at para 326.
145 *Ibid* at paras 324–25.
146 *Amnesty*, above note 128 (CA).
147 *Khadr*, above note 130 at para 27.
148 *Amnesty*, above note 128 at para 20 (CA).
149 *Ibid* at para 29.
150 *Ibid* at paras 31–32.
151 *Ibid* at para 14.

obligations or fundamental human rights norms," regardless of the citizenship of the person affected.[152]

Finally, although after *Hape* the *Charter* will not always apply to Canadian officials operating abroad, Canadian trial courts retain the power to exclude evidence obtained abroad if its admission would make the trial unfair, pursuant to sections 7 and 11(*d*) of the *Charter*.[153]

8) State Inaction

The failure of the state to act will rarely amount to state action for *Charter* purposes in general and for section 7 purposes in particular. Suppose, for example, that someone thinks it would be a good idea for a provincial legislature to enact a statute establishing a new private cause of action or providing a new social program that would improve the legal protection of security of the person, but the legislature does not do so. If an individual were to bring a *Charter* action or application to compel the government to provide a particular social program or to compel the legislature to create one, the action or application would undoubtedly be dismissed on the grounds that the state's failure to act does not amount to state action for *Charter* purposes or that the relief sought would itself be an unconstitutional interference with the proper division of functions between the government, the legislature, and the judiciary—even though the legislation, if enacted, would undoubtedly be subject to *Charter* scrutiny.[154] However, the possibility that inaction might count as state action for *Charter* purposes, and for section 7 purposes in particular, has always been left open.[155] Moreover, it is argu-

---

152   *Khadr* (SCC), above note 137 at para 14.

153   *Hape*, above note 117 at paras 108–11. This power is discussed in more detail in Chapter 5, Section B.

154   See, for example, *Beauchamp v Canada (AG)*, 2009 FC 350. The federal Cabinet failed to proclaim in force legislation that would arguably have enhanced the applicant's security of the person; the applicant argued that this failure violated s 7. Justice Barnes, though ultimately dismissing the applicant's claim on other grounds, was very doubtful that this failure amounted to state action and even more doubtful that ordering Cabinet to proclaim legislation in force would be an appropriate remedy (*ibid* at para 22).

155   For example in *Daigle v Tremblay*, [1989] 2 SCR 530, a man sought to enjoin his pregnant girlfriend from having an abortion. The Supreme Court found it unnecessary to decide whether a foetus was a person entitled to s 7 protection because the *Charter* did not apply to the dispute between the parties: at 571. The court commented that "[t]he issue as to whether s 7 could be used to ground an affirmative claim to protection by the state was not raised": at 571. This question was also raised in *Borowski v Canada (AG)*, [1989] 1 SCR 342, but not dealt with as the appeal was dismissed for mootness. A motion to amend the

able that on at least one occasion the Supreme Court has accepted the proposition that a failure to enact basic protections for physical integrity would engage section 7 (see Section D(4)(a), below in this chapter).

Although it is unlikely that failure to create a particular statutory scheme or to provide a particular benefit for everyone will be construed as state action for *Charter* purposes, there is no doubt that an underinclusive scheme can be challenged as contrary to section 15 of the *Charter*. The leading case is *Vriend v Alberta*.[156] The applicant challenged the omission of sexual orientation as a prohibited ground of discrimination from a province's human rights statute. The Supreme Court of Canada specifically rejected the proposition that the omission did not amount to state action. Cory J commented that "the language of section 32 does not limit the application of the *Charter* merely to positive actions encroaching on rights or the excessive exercise of authority"[157] and that "[t]he application of the *Charter* is not restricted to situations where the government actively encroaches on rights."[158] The Court did not have to decide, and specifically refrained from commenting on, whether a province was constitutionally required to enact particular pieces of legislation;[159] but the code that the province had chosen to enact was subject to *Charter* scrutiny for underinclusiveness. Similarly, the Court has on one occasion held that a statute withdrawing a protection that would otherwise be available engages section 7 of the *Charter*.[160]

The most important case on state inaction for section 7 purposes is *Gosselin v Quebec (AG)* (*Gosselin*),[161] but even though the section 7 claim

---

draft *Charter* to preserve Parliament's power to legislate concerning abortion was defeated in the House of Commons on 23 April 1981; a motion to define the unborn child as a person for s 7 purposes and to add a section preserving Parliament's power to legislate concerning "the rights of unborn children" was defeated in the Senate on 8 December 1981. See *House of Commons Debates*, 23 April 1981 at 9471–73; *Senate Debates*, 8 December 1981 at 3395–99. For the view that the foetus is not a person for s 7 purposes, see Martha Shaffer, "Foetal Rights and the Regulation of Abortion" (1994) 39 McGill LJ 58.

Similarly, in *Eldridge* above note 20, La Forest J declined to decide whether the *Charter* "oblige[s] the state to take positive actions, such as provide services to ameliorate the symptoms of systemic or general inequality": at para 73; compare *McKinney*, above note 13 at 412, Wilson J.

156 *Vriend v Alberta*, [1998] 1 SCR 493.
157 *Ibid* at para 55.
158 *Ibid* at para 60.
159 *Ibid* at paras 63–64.
160 *Canadian Foundation for Children, Youth and the Law v Canada (AG)*, 2004 SCC 4 [*Canadian Foundation*]; see also Section D(4)(a), below in this chapter.
161 *Gosselin v Quebec (AG)*, 2002 SCC 84 [*Gosselin*].

in that case failed, the question of whether state inaction could engage the section 7 interests was left open. The plaintiff, representative of a class, challenged a Quebec legislative scheme in place between 1985 and 1989 under which social welfare recipients under the age of thirty received substantially fewer benefits than recipients over thirty. The section 7 claim failed on the ground that the plaintiff had not shown that her section 7 rights were engaged. The majority, *per* McLachlin CJC,[162] expressed considerable doubt about whether the state's failure to protect life, liberty, and security of the person could engage section 7:

> Section 7 speaks of the right *not to be deprived of* life, liberty and security of the person, except in accordance with the principles of fundamental justice. Nothing in the jurisprudence thus far suggests that section 7 places a positive obligation on the state to ensure that each person enjoys life, liberty or security of the person. Rather, section 7 has been interpreted as restricting the state's ability to *deprive* people of these. Such a deprivation does not exist in the case at bar.[163]

However, this holding appears to have been based on the absence of "sufficient evidence in this case to support the proposed interpretation of section 7";[164] thus, *Gosselin* should not be read as rejecting outright the idea that state inaction could engage the section 7 interest. Indeed, McLachlin CJC commented that "[o]ne day section 7 may be interpreted to include positive obligations,"[165] thus leaving open "the possibility that an affirmative right to basic subsistence might one day be protected by section 7."[166]

---

162 Gonthier, Iacobucci, Major, and Binnie JJ concurred with McLachlin CJC.

163 *Gosselin*, above note 161 at para 81 [emphasis in original].

164 *Ibid* at para 83.

165 *Ibid*. Bastarache J, dissenting in the result, would not have left this opening; in his view, "a s 7 claim has to arise as a result of some determinative state action that in and of itself deprives the claimant of the right to life, liberty and security of the person": *ibid* at para 213. LeBel J generally agreed with this aspect of Bastarache J's reasons: *ibid* at para 414. Arbour J, dissenting, wrote at some length in support of the view that the *Charter* in general, and s 7 in particular, could impose positive obligations on the state: *Gosselin*, *ibid* at paras 310–58. Moreover, she found that the evidence showed that "the legislated exclusion of young adults from the full benefits of the social assistance regime substantially interfered with their s 7 rights, in particular their right to security of the person," so that s 7 was engaged: *ibid* at para 371, and see also paras 372–77. L'Heureux-Dubé J, dissenting, generally agreed with these aspects of Arbour J's analysis: *ibid* at para 99.

166 Sharpe & Roach, above note 2 at 231.

There may be no state action for section 7 purposes where the law grants a benefit that would not otherwise be available but does not otherwise affect life, liberty, and security of the person. For example, in *Flora v Ontario (Health Insurance Plan, General Manager)*,[167] the applicant challenged a regulation that required Ontario's provincial health plan to compensate a person for medical services rendered outside Canada if "the treatment is generally accepted in Ontario as appropriate for a person in the same medical circumstances as the insured person" and was either unavailable in Ontario or available only with a delay "that would result in death or medically significant irreversible tissue damage."[168] The court found that the regulation provided a benefit that was not otherwise available and did "not prohibit or impede anyone from seeking medical treatment"; accordingly, it did not deprive anyone of the right to life, liberty, and security of the person.[169] Similarly, in *Wynberg v Ontario*,[170] a provincial program that provided a particular type of therapy to autistic children between the ages of two and five, but not to children over five, did not deprive the children of anything they were entitled to under section 7 and so did not engage section 7.[171] Such distinctions may, of course, raise issues about whether the equality guarantee in section 15(1) of the *Charter* has been violated, but a violation of section 15 is not necessarily a violation of section 7 (see Chapter 1, Section C(3)(c)).

C. EVERYONE

Section 7 of the *Charter* grants rights to "[e]veryone." The main issues in interpreting this word were whether section 7 rights were restricted to Canadian citizens or included anyone subject to Canadian state actions, and whether section 7 rights were restricted to natural persons or could also be asserted by corporations and other artificial persons. These controversies have now been settled. Both citizens and non-citizens have section 7 rights, but section 7 rights are available only to living natural persons.

---

167 *Flora v Ontario (Health Insurance Plan, General Manager)*, 2008 ONCA 538 [*Flora*], aff'g (2007), 278 DLR (4th) 45 (Ont Div Ct).

168 RRO 1990, Reg 552, s 28.4(2).

169 *Flora*, above note 167 at para 101.

170 *Wynberg v Ontario* (2006), 269 DLR (4th) 435 (Ont CA).

171 *Ibid* at para 220 (concerning the interest in security of the person) and at para 231 (concerning the liberty interest).

1) Citizens and Others

Singh v Canada (Minister of Employment and Immigration) (Singh),[172] a very early *Charter* case, established that all natural persons physically present in Canada have the rights granted by section 7. The applicants challenged procedural aspects of the system then in place for determining refugee claims. Before reaching this question, the court had to determine whether section 7 of the *Charter* applied to the system in the first place. The federal government argued that refugee claimants were not entitled to section 7 protection because they were not Canadian citizens. Three members of the Supreme Court of Canada rejected this argument,[173] holding that the word "everyone" in section 7 "includes every human being who is physically present in Canada and by virtue of such presence amenable to Canadian law."[174] This holding is undoubtedly the most natural grammatical reading of section 7, particularly when that section is contrasted with other sections of the *Charter* that grant rights to specified persons or persons in specific situations: for example, "[e]very citizen" in sections 3 and 6, "[e]veryone on arrest or detention" in section 10, or "[a]ny person charged with an offence" in section 11. But the holding is also consistent with Canada's commitment to international human rights norms. Whether or not there is any specific treaty commitment to grant any particular section 7 right to citizens and non-citizens alike, the idea that state protection for a person's most fundamental interests (life, liberty, and security of the person) could vary depending on their citizenship is repugnant to the idea that every individual has basic and inalienable human rights.[175] If the decision in *Singh* had gone the other way—if the Court had restricted section 7 protections to Canadian citizens—the implications would have gone well beyond the fairness of the scheme for determining refu-

---

172 *Singh v Canada (Minister of Employment and Immigration)*, [1985] 1 SCR 177 [*Singh*].

173 A panel of seven heard the appeal. One member of the court did not participate in the judgment. Wilson J, Dickson CJC and Lamer J concurring, held that the impugned immigration provisions violated the *Charter*; Beetz J, Estey and McIntyre JJ concurring, held that the impugned provisions violated s 2(*e*) of the *Canadian Bill of Rights*, SC 1960, c 44, and expressed no opinion on the *Charter* issues. There was thus no clear majority on the *Charter* issues; however, Wilson J's reasons for judgment are generally taken to represent the court's position in *Singh*, and there is nothing in the subsequent cases to cast doubt on her resolution of the meaning of the word "Everyone" in s 7.

174 *Ibid* at 202, Wilson J.

175 Compare the discussion of *Amnesty*, above note 128, in Section B(7), above in this chapter.

gee claims. Non-citizens could, for instance, be deprived of their liberty in defiance of the principles of fundamental justice.

Moreover, if the reading of *Khadr* presented in Section B(7), above in this chapter, is correct, then section 7 rights are also available to non-citizens abroad when the second *Hape* exception applies. Nothing in the Court's reasoning in the *Khadr* decisions depended on the fact that the applicant was a Canadian citizen; rather, it was the nature of the participation of Canadian officials and the effect on Khadr's rights in Canada that were essential to the outcome.

2) Natural and Artificial Persons

The section 7 interests in life, liberty, and security of the person are available only to natural persons and not to corporations or other artificial persons. In *Irwin Toy Ltd v Quebec (AG)*, the Supreme Court of Canada, though deeply divided on other issues, was unanimously of the view that the word "everyone" in section 7 should mean "only human beings," not "corporations and other artificial entities incapable of enjoying life, liberty or security of the person."[176] Since a corporation has no section 7 interests, the state is not constitutionally required to respect the principles of fundamental justice in its dealings with a corporation. On this ground, the Court refused to entertain a corporation's vagueness challenge to a statute.[177] Similarly, a corporation has no right against self-incrimination[178] and no section 7 rights in civil proceedings.[179]

However, anyone charged with an offence, including a corporation, can argue that the statute is invalid because it offends any part of the *Charter*, including section 7, even if the statute would be constitutionally valid if applied in that accused's case.[180] Thus, a corporation charged with an offence can argue that a statute is invalid because it would of-

---

176 *Irwin Toy Ltd v Quebec (AG)*, [1989] 1 SCR 927 at 1004 [*Irwin Toy*], Dickson CJC and Wilson and Lamer JJ; compare *ibid* at 1009, McIntyre J (Beetz J concurring) dissenting on other grounds.

177 *Irwin Toy*, *ibid* at 1002–4. The corporation was not charged with an offence; if it had been, it would have had standing to challenge the constitutionality of the offence under the cases cited in note 181 below.

178 *R v Amway Corp*, [1989] 1 SCR 21.

179 *Dywidag Systems International, Canada Ltd v Zutphen Brothers Construction Ltd*, [1990] 1 SCR 705 at 709.

180 See *R v Heywood*, [1994] 3 SCR 761, where the court invalidated a provision of the *Criminal Code* for overbreadth even though on the facts of the case, the accused would likely have been found guilty under a properly crafted version of the provision.

fend section 7 if applied to a natural person, even though the statute would be immune from section 7 review if it applied to corporations only.[181] This rule of standing reflects a very basic principle of legality: everyone, whether a natural or an artificial person, has a right not to be convicted of an offence under an unconstitutional statute. Moreover, by analogy with penal proceedings, a corporation may raise a *Charter* argument by way of defence to a civil action brought against it by the state.[182] And even if none of these routes is available, a court has a "residuary discretion" to permit a corporation to raise a *Charter* argument if the question is one of public importance.[183]

Although *Charter* rights are available to all natural persons, it appears that a right of action arising under the *Charter* does not normally survive the death of the natural person; or, put another way, that a person's estate cannot usually commence or continue a *Charter* claim. In *Hislop v Canada (AG) (Hislop)*,[184] the Supreme Court of Canada held that a section 15 claim could not be commenced by an estate because, in the section 15 context,

> an estate is just a collection of assets and liabilities of a person who has died. It is not an individual and has no dignity that may be infringed . . . . In this sense, it may be said that section 15 rights die with the individual.[185]

The Court recognized exceptions for an individual who died after the completion of argument, or who had obtained judgment while still alive and died pending appeal.[186]

The decision in *Hislop* is, strictly speaking, limited to section 15 of the *Charter*. However, to the extent that the reasoning is based on the individual interest in human dignity, it likely applies to other *Charter* rights that have a dignitary aspect, and perhaps to all *Charter* rights

---

181   See, for example, *R v Wholesale Travel Group Inc*, [1991] 3 SCR 154. Both a natural person and a corporation were charged with offences, but the natural person was not a party to the appeal. See also *R v 1260448 Ontario Ltd; R v Transport Robert Ltée* (2003), 180 CCC (3d) 254 (Ont CA) [*Transport Robert*]. Similarly, in *R v Big M Drug Mart*, [1985] 1 SCR 295 [*Big M*], a corporation was permitted to invoke freedom of religion to challenge the constitutionality of a statute under which it was charged with an offence, even though only natural persons have religious freedom. The Court commented at 313 that "no one can be convicted of an offence under an unconstitutional law."

182   *Canadian Egg Marketing Agency v Richardson*, [1998] 3 SCR 157 at paras 37–47.

183   *Ibid* at para 33.

184   *Hislop v Canada (AG)*, 2007 SCC 10.

185   *Ibid* at para 73, LeBel and Rothstein JJ.

186   *Ibid* at paras 74–75.

that can be characterized as personal. On the latter basis, in *Giacomelli Estate v Canada (AG)*,[187] the Ontario Court of Appeal applied the rule in *Hislop* to dismiss claims made under sections 7 and 15 where the applicant had died after commencing the action but before any evidence was heard at trial.[188]

Similarly, it appears that a person's claim for a remedy for a *Charter* violation, including a violation of section 7, cannot be assigned to another person;[189] in particular, a claim by a natural person cannot be assigned to another natural person or to a corporation.

D. LIFE, LIBERTY, AND SECURITY OF THE PERSON

1) The Structure of the Section 7 Rights

The English version of section 7 uses the word "right" twice: it says that "Everyone has the *right* to life, liberty, and security of the person and the *right* not to be deprived thereof except in accordance with the principles of fundamental justice" (emphasis added). So does the French version, but after guaranteeing the right to life, liberty, and security of the person, it goes on to state that: « il ne peut être porté atteinte *à ce droit* qu'en conformité avec les principes de justice fondamentale » (emphasis added). Thus, on its face, the English version might suggest that there are two separate rights—first, a right to life, liberty, and security, and second, a right to be treated in accordance with the principles of fundamental justice—while the French version might suggest that only one right is in play. The "two-right" interpretation of section 7 would be broader, in that section 7 would be infringed by state action that *either* effects a deprivation of life, liberty, and security of the person *or* departs from the principles of fundamental justice, while on the "one-right" interpretation, section 7 is infringed only when state action does both.

In *Re BC Motor Vehicle Act* (*Motor Vehicle Reference*), Wilson J proposed a version of the "two-right" interpretation. She held that if state action impaired life, liberty, or security of the person without complying with the principles of fundamental justice, then section 7 would

---

187 *Giacomelli Estate v Canada (AG)*, 2008 ONCA 346.

188 *Ibid* at paras 15–20.

189 *PSC Industrial Canada Inc v Ontario (Ministry of the Environment)* (2005), 258 DLR (4th) 320 at paras 24–26 (Ont CA).

be infringed and, moreover, no section 1 justification for the infringement would be possible. But even if the state action complied with the principles of fundamental justice, the impairment of the right to life, liberty, and security of the person would have to be justified under section 1.[190] This interpretation recognized, in effect, two section 7 rights: a right not to deprived of life, liberty, and security of the person except in accordance with the principles of fundamental justice, and a right not to be deprived of life, liberty, and security of the person even in accordance with the principles of fundamental justice. A violation of the former right could not be justified under section 1, but the latter might. However, Wilson J agreed with the majority that section 7 did not guarantee "a right to the principles of fundamental justice *per se*."[191]

However, the Supreme Court of Canada has adopted a "one-right" interpretation. It is clear from the subsequent cases, if not from the *Motor Vehicle Reference* itself,[192] that section 7 is infringed only where state conduct deprives one of life, liberty, and security of the person *and* where the deprivation is not in accordance with the principles of fundamental justice. Thus, section 7 is not infringed where life, liberty, and security of the person is not affected, or where life, liberty, and security of the person is affected but the principles of fundamental justice are respected.

Once a *Charter* claimant has established that the *Charter* applies to the dispute in question and that she is a natural person, the next step is to show how a particular *Charter* right is engaged. In light of the dominant "one-right" interpretation, under section 7 the claimant must show that the state action at issue deprived her of her "right to life, liberty [or] security of the person." There is considerable caselaw on the meaning of these terms.[193]

---

190 *Re BC Motor Vehicle Act*, [1985] 2 SCR 486 at 523 [*Motor Vehicle Reference*].

191 *Ibid*.

192 "On the facts of this case it is not necessary to decide whether [s. 7] gives any greater protection, such as deciding whether, absent a breach of the principles of fundamental justice, there still can be . . . a violation of one's rights to life, liberty and security of the person": *ibid* at 500, Lamer J.

193 The phrase "life, liberty, security of the person and enjoyment of property" appears in s 1(*a*) of the *Canadian Bill of Rights*, above note 173. However, the case law interpreting that section focused principally on the meaning of the phrase "the right not to be deprived thereof except by due process of law"; see, for instance, *Curr v R*, [1972] SCR 889. Consequently, these cases had no impact on the interpretation of "life, liberty and security of the person" under s 7 of the *Charter*.

2) "Life"

The section 7 interest in life would be engaged where state conduct deprived a person of his life. The imposition of the death penalty would be the clearest instance. However, the death penalty was abolished under the *Criminal Code* in 1976, before the *Charter* came into force in 1982.[194] The death penalty was an available punishment under the *National Defence Act* until 1998,[195] but there are no instances of a court martial imposing the death penalty between 1982 and 1998. Thus, there is no caselaw dealing with the death penalty and the *Charter* under domestic law in Canada.[196] In the extremely unlikely event that the prosecution sought the death penalty for an offence that was committed before the abolition of the death penalty, the accused would be entitled to "the benefit of the lesser punishment" under section 11(*i*) of the *Charter*, and would therefore be liable only for life imprisonment under the provisions of the current *Criminal Code*.[197] It would not be necessary to consider the accused's rights under sections 7 or 12.

The death penalty may, however, be inflicted by foreign states with which Canada has extradition treaties, notably the United States. The constitutionality of extraditing a suspect or fugitive to face the death penalty has twice been considered by the Supreme Court of Canada.[198] The Court has treated extradition to face the death penalty as state action that engages liberty and security interests, rather than the interest in life, because the lives of the persons sought were, though at risk, not certain to be taken away.[199] It would be equally plausible to hold that the interest in life was at stake because the requesting state actively seeks to impose the death penalty. These cases are discussed in more detail in Chapter 5, Section C.

---

194 See SC 1974-75-76 (23-24-25 Eliz. II), c 105, in force 26 July 1976.

195 The death penalty was formerly available for many offences under the *National Defence Act*, RSC 1985, c N-5—including misconduct in the face of the enemy (ss. 73, 74) and being drunk while on guard duty (s. 75(*h*)), if the offence was committed "traitorously"—as well as offences such as spying and mutiny (ss. 78, 79, 80). The death penalty under this Act was removed by SC 1998, c 35, in force 1 September 1999.

196 In *Miller and Cockriell v R*, [1977] 2 SCR 680, the Supreme Court of Canada held that capital punishment for the murder of a peace officer was not "cruel and unusual" within the meaning of s 2(*b*) of the *Bill of Rights*.

197 See also *Criminal Law Amendment Act (No 2), 1976*, SC 1974-75-76, c 105, s 25(2).

198 *Kindler v Canada (Minister of Justice)*, [1991] 2 SCR 779 [*Kindler*]; *Reference re Ng Extradition (Can)*, [1991] 2 SCR 858; *United States v Burns*, 2001 SCC 7 [*Burns*].

199 *Kindler, ibid* at 831, La Forest J and at 790, Sopinka J dissenting; *Burns, ibid* at para 59.

Interestingly, the Supreme Court has recognized the section 7 interest in life in a civil context. In *Chaoulli*,[200] the applicant physician argued, *inter alia*, that a prohibition on private health insurance, combined with the existence of significant delays in providing his patients with necessary medical care in the public health care system, violated section 7 of the *Charter*. The six members of the Court who dealt with the section 7 claim agreed that this combination of prohibition and state-created delay engaged the s. 7 interest in life. As McLachlin CJC and Bastarache J (Major J concurring) put it:

> . . . there is unchallenged evidence that in some serious cases, patients die as a result of waiting lists for public health care. Where lack of timely health care can result in death, s 7 protection of life itself is engaged.[201]

Binnie and LeBel JJ (Fish J concurring), dissenting on other grounds, seemed to agree on this point.[202] Similarly, in *PHS*, the Court held that the proposed closure of a safe injection site for intravenous drug users, which had been shown to save lives, engaged the users' right to life.[203] In light of these holdings, it would be more straightforward to treat extradition to face the death penalty as engaging the right to life as well as the right to security of the person. These cases are discussed in more detail in Chapter 4, Section B(3).

Along similar lines, British Columbia courts have held that government decisions that might threaten a person's survival engage the section 7 right to life: a municipal prohibition on panhandling,[204] and a municipal prohibition on the erection of temporary overhead shelters in public places.[205]

---

200   Above note 8.
201   *Ibid* at para 123.
202   *Ibid* at para 191. Justice Deschamps held that the interest in life under the Quebec *Charter* was engaged: *ibid* at para 45.
203   *PHS*, above note 29 at paras 91 and 126.
204   *Federated Anti-Poverty Groups of BC v Vancouver (City of)*, 2002 BCSC 105 at paras 201–2; contrast *R v Banks*, 2007 ONCA 19 at para 81 [*Banks*], where the individual's interest in panhandling is treated as an economic interest that is not protected under s 7: see Section D(5), below in this chapter.
205   *Victoria (City of) v Adams*, 2009 BCCA 563, var'g 2008 BCSC 1363 at para 145 [*Victoria (City)*].

3) "Liberty"

a) The Scope of the Liberty Interest

The word "liberty" means many different things in legal and political discourse.[206] Under section 7 of the *Charter*, the liberty interest is engaged by deprivations of liberty by state action. Yet even in this context, the word "liberty" might mean many things. In its narrowest sense, "liberty" under section 7 would mean freedom from state-imposed or state-authorized imprisonment or detention; in its widest sense, "liberty" under section 7 would mean freedom from *any* state-imposed or state-authorized constraint on action. On the narrow reading, the liberty interest would be engaged only by state action that might result in imprisonment or another form of detention. On the widest reading, the liberty interest would always be engaged because the law always limits someone's freedom of action.[207] Although many laws do not on their face prohibit actions but enable persons to take actions they would not otherwise be able to take,[208] once the legal relationship created by the enabling law is in place, someone's freedom of action is constrained. For example, the law of contract permits two people to enter into arrangements that they would otherwise be unable to achieve; the law of wills enables people to dispose of their property after their death. But once the contract is signed or the will is made, someone's freedom of action is limited. The parties to the contract have to perform; the executor of the estate has to act in accordance with the will. If these enabling laws take the form of statutes or regulations, they will, according to the approach in *Dolphin Delivery*, satisfy the state action requirement and are therefore subject to the *Charter*; and even if they are common

---

206 For an influential discussion of the possible meanings of the word "liberty," see Isaiah Berlin, "Two Concepts of Liberty" in *Four Essays on Liberty* (Oxford: Oxford University Press, 1969) 118. Berlin distinguished between "negative freedom" and "positive freedom"; the former was concerned with absence of interference within a defined area in which one is permitted and able to act, while the latter was concerned with being one's own master. He was quite skeptical about the value of positive freedom as a political goal because taking it seriously permitted an easy slide into the authoritarian or totalitarian view that there were certain ends or goals that everyone must adopt: *ibid* at 141–54. However, his conception of negative freedom does not correspond to freedom from state action; in his view, state action that increased a person's ability to act, for example the provision of basic necessities of life, would increase that person's negative freedom. Even the widest meaning of the word "liberty" under s 7 of the *Charter* remains narrower than Berlin's conception of negative freedom.

207 Sharpe & Roach, above note 2 at 201.

208 See, for example, HLA Hart, *The Concept of Law* (Oxford: Clarendon Press, 1961) at 26–48.

law rules, they will, according to the approach in *Church of Scientology*, have to be construed in accordance with *Charter* values.[209] So if "liberty" under section 7 was given its widest meaning, section 7 would be engaged by a very wide range of laws indeed: not only by prohibitions but by enabling laws that resulted in restrictions on action. Moreover, some very basic civil liberties are guaranteed in other sections of the *Charter*. For example, the liberty to believe in and follow the teachings of a particular religion is protected under section 2(*a*); the liberty to associate with like-minded individuals is protected under section 2(*d*); and fundamental political liberties are protected under sections 2 and 3. So to construe liberty in the widest sense might make the rest of the *Charter* redundant.

For these reasons, the Supreme Court of Canada was quick to reject the widest possible reading of "liberty." In *R v Edwards Books and Art Ltd*,[210] various businesses challenged a Sunday closing law on *Charter* grounds. One of the *Charter* applicants argued that the law infringed his liberty simply because it prevented him from doing something. The majority, *per* Dickson CJC, rejected this claim, because "'liberty' in section 7 of the *Charter* is not synonymous with unconstrained freedom." Dickson CJC then quoted approvingly from Wilson J's concurring judgment in the *Motor Vehicle Reference*:

> . . . all regulatory offences impose some restriction on liberty broadly construed. But I think it would trivialize the *Charter* to sweep all those offences into s. 7 as violations of the right to life, liberty and security of the person even if they can be sustained under section 1.[211]

Many such claims can in any event be made under another section of the *Charter* (compare Chapter 1, Section C(3)). For example, in *R v Big M Drug Mart*,[212] another case about Sunday closing, the applicant was able to rely on the right to freedom of religion under section 2(*a*) of the *Charter*.

But rejecting the widest possible reading of "liberty" did not resolve the debate about the scope of the section 7 liberty interest. Lamer CJC was a champion of the narrow view that the liberty interest under section 7 was engaged only in penal proceedings, or in other pro-

---

209 *Dolphin Delivery*, above note 2; *Church of Scientology*, above note 51.

210 *R v Edwards Books & Art Ltd*, [1986] 2 SCR 713 [*Edwards Books*].

211 *Motor Vehicle Reference*, above note 190 at 524, as quoted in *Edwards Books, ibid* at 786.

212 *Big M*, above note 181.

ceedings where imprisonment or detention was a possibility,[213] while Wilson J and La Forest J took the broad view that the liberty interest might also be engaged by state interference with certain fundamental decisions that an individual might take. Wilson J, for instance, held in *R v Morgentaler* (*Morgentaler*)[214] that "the right to make fundamental personal decisions without interference from the state" was "a critical component of the right to liberty."[215] In *R v Jones*,[216] where the majority preferred to assume without deciding that the liberty interest was engaged,[217] she held that the liberty interest extended to a parent's right "to raise his children in accordance with his conscientious beliefs."[218]

The two views confronted each other directly in *B(R) v Children's Aid Society of Metropolitan Toronto* (*B(R)*).[219] The applicants were Jehovah's Witnesses. Their child was born prematurely and was in hospital for the first several weeks of her life. When the child was a month old, the Children's Aid Society (CAS) successfully applied for an order making her a ward of the state for a period of seventy-two hours (later extended to twenty-one days) so that she could receive blood transfusions — a procedure that the applicants would not have consented to. The applicants appealed these orders, and challenged the constitutionality of the statutory provisions under which the CAS had acted. The Supreme Court of Canada was deeply divided as to whether these facts engaged the applicants' section 7 liberty interest. La Forest J, Gonthier and McLachlin JJ concurring, adopted Wilson J's view from *Morgentaler* that the section 7 liberty interest extended beyond freedom from imprisonment or detention:

> On the one hand, liberty does not mean unconstrained freedom . . . .
> On the other hand, liberty does not mean mere freedom from physical restraint. In a free and democratic society, the individual must be left room for personal autonomy to live his or her own life and to make decisions that are of fundamental personal importance.[220]

---

213 See also Eric Colvin, "Section 7 of the *Charter of Rights and Freedoms*" (1989) 68 Can Bar Rev 560; Philip Bryden, "Section 7 of the *Charter* outside the Criminal Context" (2005) 38 UBC L Rev 507.

214 *R v Morgentaler*, [1988] 1 SCR 30 [*Morgentaler*].

215 *Ibid* at 166.

216 *R v Jones*, [1986] 2 SCR 284 [*Jones*].

217 *Ibid* at 302.

218 *Ibid* at 319.

219 *B(R) v Children's Aid Society of Metropolitan Toronto*, [1995] 1 SCR 315 [*B(R)*].

220 *Ibid* at para 80. See also La Forest J's reasons in *Godbout*, above note 13 at para 66.

This conception of liberty included some forms of "parental liberty," including "the right to nurture a child, to care for its development, and to make decisions for it in fundamental matters such as medical care."[221] Since the statute affected this form of liberty, it had to comply with the principles of fundamental justice. Iacobucci and Major JJ, writing jointly, agreed with La Forest J that the section 7 liberty interest included parental liberty, but held that parental liberty did not extend to making the decision to deny a child necessary medical treatment.[222] Since the statute did not affect liberty in this sense, it was not necessary to consider whether it conformed with the principles of fundamental justice. In stark contrast with these approaches, Lamer CJC held that because fundamental justice "essentially involves the judicial system and the decision-making bodies whose decisions are enforceable through the state's coercive power . . . the subject matter of s. 7 must be the conduct of the state when the state calls on law enforcement officials to enforce and secure obedience to the law, or invokes the law to deprive a person of liberty . . ."[223] Accordingly, the section 7 liberty interest would typically be engaged by the loss of physical liberty "through the operation of the legal system."[224] The "parental liberty" identified by La Forest J would not be included.[225]

The Court ultimately adopted a version of La Forest J's broader view of the liberty interest. In *Blencoe v British Columbia (Human Rights Commission)* (*Blencoe*),[226] the applicant applied for judicial review of a human rights commission's delay in dealing with a complaint against him. He argued, *inter alia*, that the delay infringed his rights under section 7; specifically, that his rights to liberty and security of the person had been infringed. Bastarache J, for the majority, quoted approvingly from La Forest J's reasons in *B(R)* and from Wilson J's reasons in *Morgentaler*, and characterized the liberty interest as follows:

> The liberty interest protected by s. 7 of the *Charter* is no longer restricted to mere freedom from physical restraint . . . . "liberty" is engaged where state compulsions or prohibitions affect important and fundamental life choices . . . . In our free and democratic society, in-

---

221 *B(R)*, above note 219 at para 83. Gonthier and McLachlin JJ concurred with La Forest J; L'Heureux-Dubé J concurred with this part of La Forest J's reasons.
222 *Ibid* at paras 212–21.
223 *Ibid* at para 21.
224 *Ibid* at para 22; compare para 33.
225 *Ibid* at para 1.
226 *Blencoe v British Columbia (Human Rights Commission)*, 2000 SCC 44 [*Blencoe*].

dividuals are entitled to make decisions of fundamental importance free from state interference.[227]

However, there has yet to be a case where a majority of the Supreme Court has held that the government has affected the section 7 liberty interest by interfering with fundamental personal choices (see Section D(3)(e), below in this chapter).

b) Penal Proceedings

The early section 7 cases established that the section 7 liberty interest is engaged in any proceedings where there is a possibility of imprisonment. In the *Motor Vehicle Reference*, the Court considered a section 7 challenge to a statute that imposed a mandatory sentence of seven days' imprisonment for the offence of driving while prohibited.[228] Since the sentence was mandatory, it was obvious that the liberty interest was engaged; but the majority made it clear that the *possibility* of imprisonment also engaged the liberty interest:

> Obviously, imprisonment (including probation orders) deprives people of their liberty. An offence has that potential as of the moment it is open to the judge to impose imprisonment. There is no need that imprisonment . . . be made mandatory.[229]

This approach makes sense. In proceedings where imprisonment was not mandatory on conviction, it would be odd if the principles of fundamental justice came into play only at the point where the accused had been convicted and the judge had decided to imprison him, or if the content of the applicable principles was different depending on whether the Crown announced its intention to seek a term of imprisonment before the trial began. The approach taken in the *Motor Vehicle Reference* ensures that the principles of fundamental justice will always apply in penal proceedings, whether or not imprisonment, another form of detention, or probation will ultimately be imposed.

---

227 *Ibid* at para 49, Bastarache J (McLachlin CJC and L'Heureux-Dubé, Gonthier, and Major JJ concurring). The minority, LeBel J (Iacobucci, Binnie, and Arbour JJ concurring) decided the case on administrative law grounds and did not find it necessary to determine the *Charter* issues: *ibid* at para 187.

228 See the *Motor Vehicle Act*, RSBC 1979, c 288, s 94, as amended by the *Motor Vehicle Amendment Act, 1982*, SBC 1982, c 36, s 19.

229 *Motor Vehicle Reference*, above note 190 at 515, Lamer J. McIntyre J and Wilson J, concurring in the result, appear to have deliberately limited their reasoning to the case of mandatory imprisonment: see *ibid* at 522, McIntyre J; and at 534, Wilson J.

The basic point that section 7 is engaged whenever there is a possibility of imprisonment in penal proceedings has often been reiterated. The only serious difficulty has arisen where the prospect of imprisonment is truly remote, not in the sense that imprisonment is rarely imposed for the offence in question (minor theft, for example), but in the sense that although imprisonment is not available for the offence in question, conviction for that offence may ultimately expose the accused to imprisonment in some other way. The most common scenario is the following. The accused is convicted of an offence for which imprisonment is not a possible penalty, and is sentenced to pay a fine.[230] Under the relevant statutory scheme for enforcing the payment of the fine, imprisonment is a possibility. Is the section 7 liberty interest engaged in the prosecution for the offence? The answer depends on exactly how the consequence of imprisonment is connected to the non-payment of the fine. If the defaulting offender can be imprisoned through a process or proceeding that does not address her fault or ability to pay the fine, then the liberty interest is engaged in the original proceedings.[231] But if imprisonment can result only from a separate proceeding in which there is a fault element for not paying the fine, then "the risk of imprisonment in default [is] sufficiently remote as not to engage a liberty interest under s. 7."[232]

Where imprisonment is not a possible sanction and payment of a fine is the only consequence of a conviction, the section 7 liberty interest is not engaged.[233]

c) Extradition Proceedings

i) Extradition from Canada
There is no doubt that the section 7 liberty interest is engaged when the Canadian state invokes the procedures in the *Extradition Act* to extradite an individual from Canada to face prosecution in another state.[234] As Arbour J put it, "Section 7 permeates the entire extradition process

---

230 If the sentence consists of a fine with imprisonment for default of payment, as is possible under s 734 of the *Criminal Code* or under provincial penal statutes, then the s 7 liberty interest is directly engaged throughout the proceedings. The problem arises where imprisonment is imposed as a penalty for the distinct offence of not paying the fine.

231 *R v Nickel City of Transport (Sudbury) Ltd* (1993), 104 DLR (4th) 340 at 372–73 (Ont CA), Arbour JA.

232 *London (City of) v Polewsky* (2005), 202 CCC (3d) 257 at para 4 (Ont CA).

233 *Transport Robert*, above note 181.

234 *Canada v Schmidt*, [1987] 1 SCR 500 at 520–22.

. . ."[235] The person sought may be detained while the extradition request is dealt with, and will certainly be detained if that request is granted. The impact of section 7 on the extradition process is discussed in more detail in Chapter 5, Section C(1).

ii) Extradition to Canada

It is likely that the section 7 liberty interest is engaged when Canadian officials decide to seek the extradition of an individual from another country to face prosecution in Canada. While the *Charter* does not apply to the conduct of the foreign officials who respond to the request, the Canadian extradition request may be "so closely and directly linked to the deprivation of the [individual's] liberty" that it engages the individual's section 7 rights.[236] However, this point has not been finally decided.[237]

d) Other Proceedings Where Liberty Is at Stake

The section 7 liberty interest is always engaged when the individual's physical liberty is at stake, whether or not the proceedings are penal in nature. This conclusion flows from both the wording and the purpose of section 7. The section does not refer directly to penal proceedings, but speaks in general of "life, liberty and security of the person"; moreover, it would be at odds with the purposive interpretation of *Charter* rights to hold that imprisonment or detention did not engage the *Charter* because the proceedings that led to the loss of liberty were not penal. Section 7 is meant to ensure that any state-imposed deprivation of liberty complies with the principles of fundamental justice. For example, the liberty interest is engaged in civil contempt proceedings if incarceration is a possible consequence on a finding of contempt,

---

235 *United States v Cobb*, 2001 SCC 19 at para 34.

236 *R v McIntosh*, 2008 NSCA 124 at para 40 [*McIntosh*]. Cromwell JA, writing for the court, commented that *Schreiber v Canada (AG)*, [1998] 1 SCR 841, might be read as supporting the position that s 7 was not engaged. However, he noted that the core of the reasoning in *Schreiber* was that the applicant's s 8 rights were not engaged by a request from Canadian officials to Swiss officials, whose actions affecting the applicant's privacy interests were not subject to the *Charter*; in contrast, an extradition request has direct consequences for the applicant's s 7 liberty interest, both in the foreign jurisdiction and, eventually, in Canada: *McIntosh*, ibid at para 40.

237 In *McIntosh*, ibid, Cromwell JA held that the procedures challenged by the applicant complied with the principles of fundamental justice (paras 42–75); it was therefore not necessary to decide whether s 7 was engaged (para 41).

even though the proceedings as a whole might not be characterized as penal.[238]

Any doubt about this point was put to rest in *Charkaoui v Canada (Citizenship and Immigration) (Charkaoui)*.[239] The applicants were subjected to security certificates issued under the *Immigration and Refugee Protection Act*,[240] and were detained for lengthy periods of time pursuant to that statute. They brought several constitutional challenges to the security certificate scheme. The government submitted that the applicants had no section 7 rights because the proceedings concerned immigration rather than criminal or penal law.[241] The Supreme Court of Canada decisively rejected this submission and confirmed that it was the fact of detention, not the legal heading under which the detention occurred, that engaged the liberty interest:

> While the deportation of a non-citizen may not *in itself* engage s. 7 of the *Charter*, some features associated with deportation, such as detention in the course of the certificate process or the prospect of deportation to torture, may do so.
>
> In determining whether s. 7 applies, we must look at the interests at stake rather than the legal label attached to the impugned legislation . . . :
>
>> Many of the principles of fundamental justice were developed in criminal cases, but their application is not restricted to criminal cases: they apply whenever one of the three protected interests is engaged. Put another way, the principles of fundamental justice apply in criminal proceedings, not because they are criminal proceedings, but because the liberty interest is always engaged in criminal proceedings . . . .[242]

Thus, whenever a person faces a risk of deprivation of liberty by the state for any reason, the section 7 liberty interest is engaged.

---

238 *McClure v Backstein* (1987), 17 CPC (2d) 242 at 248 (Ont H Ct J); *Burgoyne Holdings v Magda* (2005), 74 OR (3d) 417 at para 22 (SCJ).

239 *Charkaoui*, above note 6.

240 SC 2001, c 27.

241 "The government argues . . . that s 7 does not apply because this is an immigration matter:" *Charkaoui*, above note 6 at para 16.

242 *Ibid* at paras 17–18 [emphasis in original], quoting from Hamish Stewart, "Is Indefinite Detention of Terrorist Suspects Really Constitutional?" (2005) 54 UNBLJ 235 at 242 [emphasis removed].

i)   Prison Conditions

A convicted offender in custody has already lost his liberty; however, decisions by corrections officials that further restrict the offender's liberty engage the section 7 liberty interest.[243] So where the offender's liberty is restricted as a form of prison discipline or where the offender is transferred from a lower to a higher security institution, section 7 applies to the decision and the process must comply with the principles of fundamental justice. This doctrine is a constitutionalized version of the common law position that "[t]he continuation of an initially valid deprivation of liberty can be challenged by way of *habeas corpus* . . . if it becomes unlawful."[244]

ii)   Parole Eligibility

An offender who is on parole is still serving her sentence and may be subject to various conditions restricting her liberty. Nonetheless, a paroled offender has more liberty than an imprisoned offender. Consequently, decisions concerning parole engage the section 7 liberty interest.[245] Indeed, the Supreme Court of Canada has recognized the liberty interest in a situation where the offender was ineligible for parole because she had been sentenced under the wrong provision of the *Criminal Code.*[246]

iii)   Psychiatric Detention

The section 7 liberty interest is engaged by involuntary detention for psychiatric purposes, whether the detention occurs as a result of a verdict of not criminally responsible on account of mental disorder (NCR) under the *Criminal Code*[247] or as a result of civil commitment procedures.[248] Once detained for psychiatric reasons, the detainee retains a

---

243 *May v Ferndale Institution*, 2005 SCC 82 at para 76; compare *R v Miller*, [1985] 2 SCR 613.

244 *Dumas v Leclerc Institute*, [1986] 2 SCR 459 at 464.

245 *Cunningham v Canada*, [1993] 2 SCR 143 at 150–51 [*Cunningham*].

246 *R v Gamble*, [1988] 2 SCR 595 at 645.

247 See, for example, *Ontario (Crown Attorney) v Hussein* (2004), 191 CCC (3d) 113 at para 19 (Ont SCJ) (detention while awaiting assessment pursuant to s 672.11 of the *Criminal Code* engages the s 7 liberty interest); *Phaneuf v Ontario* (2007), 285 DLR (4th) 727 (Ont SCJ).

248 See, for example, *McCorkell v Riverview Hospital Review Panel* (1993), 104 DLR (4th) 391 at 412 (BCSC) (the point was conceded by the hospital); *Mullins v Levy*, 2005 BCSC 1217 at para 213, var'd on other grounds 2009 BCCA 6.

residual liberty interest, which is engaged by decisions to change the conditions of detention or the conditions of a conditional discharge.[249]

iv) Detention Incidental to Deportation Proceedings
The Supreme Court of Canada has held both that deportation in and of itself does not engage section 7[250] and that detention incidental to deportation proceedings does engage section 7.[251] The tension between these two holdings is briefly discussed in Section D(3)(g)(i), below in this chapter.

e) Fundamental Personal Choices
As noted above, the Supreme Court of Canada has held that the liberty interest may be engaged by state interference with fundamental personal choices. Some members of the Court have recognized this interest in specific cases. Wilson J, speaking for herself in *Morgentaler*,[252] held that a woman's decision to continue or to terminate a pregnancy was one of fundamental personal importance, such that state interference with it would engage the section 7 liberty interest. In *Godbout v Longueil (City of)*,[253] La Forest J, speaking for himself and two other judges, held that "choosing where to establish one's home is . . . a quintessentially private decision going to the very heart of personal or individual autonomy."[254]

The Ontario Court of Appeal has recognized this type of liberty interest in the context of access to marijuana for medical purposes. In *R v Parker*,[255] the accused used marijuana in combination with other medications to control epileptic seizures, as lawful methods had been found to be ineffective in his case.[256] The court held that by limiting "a person's choice of treatment through threat of criminal prosecution" the state had interfered with "the right to make decisions of fundamental personal importance."[257]

---

249 See for example *Penetanguishene Mental Health Centre v Ontario (AG)*, 2004 SCC 20 at para 24; *Pinet*, above note 27.
250 *Medovarski v Canada (Minister of Citizenship and Immigration)*, 2005 SCC 51 [*Medovarski*].
251 Above notes 247–49.
252 *Morgentaler*, above note 214 at 166.
253 *Godbout*, above note 13.
254 *Ibid* at para 66. L'Heureux-Dubé and McLachlin JJ concurred with La Forest J. The remaining six members of the court decided the case on other grounds and found it unnecessary to consider the plaintiff's s 7 claim.
255 *R v Parker* (2000), 146 CCC (3d) 193 (Ont CA) [*Parker*].
256 *Ibid* at paras 55–56.
257 *Ibid* at para 92; compare *Hitzig v Canada* (2003), 177 CCC (3d) 449 at para 93 (Ont CA) [*Hitzig*].

The British Columbia Court of Appeal has also recognized an instance of the liberty interest in decisions of fundamental personal importance. The court considered a municipal bylaw prohibiting the erection of temporary overhead shelters in public parks, in a context where the municipality had not provided sufficient shelters for homeless persons and where the absence of shelter posed significant health risks to that population. The trial judge reasoned that homeless people "have no choice but to sleep on public property," that the prohibition "interferes with the individuals' choice to protect themselves," and that "creating shelter to protect oneself from the elements is a matter critical to an individual's dignity and independence."[258] The Court of Appeal agreed, commenting that the prohibition engaged homeless persons' liberty interest because it amounted to "a significant interference with their dignity and independence."[259]

Nonetheless, a majority of the Supreme Court of Canada has yet clearly to recognize a set of facts where fundamental personal choices were affected so as to interfere with the section 7 liberty interest (though the Court has been willing to recognize this effect as an aspect of security of the person if it causes sufficient psychological stress: see Section D(4)(b), below in this chapter). In *Blencoe*, where this kind of interest was accepted in principle as engaging section 7, it was not recognized on the facts. The applicant argued that his section 7 rights were violated by a human rights commission's delay in dealing with a complaint against him. Bastarache J held that this delay did not engage the liberty interest as "the state has not prevented the [applicant] from making any 'fundamental personal choices.'"[260] In *R v Malmo-Levine*, a challenge to the offence of simple possession of marijuana, the Court characterized the decision to smoke marijuana as a "lifestyle choice" and held that such choices were not protected by the liberty interest: "the Constitution cannot be stretched to afford protection to whatever activity an individual chooses to define as central to his or her lifestyle."[261]

---

258 *Victoria (City)*, above note 205 at para 148 (BCSC).

259 *Ibid* at para 109.

260 *Blencoe*, above note 226 at para 54; compare *Lavallee v Alberta (Securities Commission)*, 2010 ABCA 48 at para 28 [*Lavallee*].

261 *Malmo-Levine*, above note 4 at para 86. See also *B(K) (Litigation Guardian of) v Toronto District School Board* (2008), 290 DLR (4th) 66 at paras 65–67 (Ont Div Ct) (decision to transfer two students from one high school to another did not engage the liberty interest because their choice of school was not a fundamental life choice).

Other courts have also been quite reluctant to recognize state action as affecting the liberty interest in fundamental personal choices under section 7.

In *Susan Doe v Canada (AG) (Susan Doe)*,[262] a lesbian couple wished to conceive a child with their friend D and, to this end, wanted to take advantage of the federal government's assisted conception plan. D was not an eligible sperm donor under the plan because he was over forty years old and gay; in order for him to donate his semen, a physician would have to apply to the program for a "special access authorization," which would issue after the semen had tested negative for various infectious agents, had been quarantined, and had again tested negative. However, D was unwilling to have his semen stored as required for the special access authorization. So Doe applied for a declaration that the relevant regulation was invalid to the extent that it prevented D's participation in the plan. The court held that although the liberty interest "includes the right to conceive a child with the person of the woman's choice," it did not include the right "to attempt to conceive . . . through assisted conception without that semen being screened or tested for infections or disease."[263] A preferable view might be that decisions about conception are indeed fundamental personal choices, and that the interest in screening the semen is a public interest that would better be considered as an aspect of the applicable principles of fundamental justice or under section 1 of the *Charter*.

In *Jane Doe v Alberta*,[264] a woman gave birth to a child using the sperm of an anonymous donor. She and the man with whom she lived intended to execute an agreement relieving the man of all parental obligations in relation to the child; however, because of the statutory provisions applicable to such agreements,[265] they could not be certain that the agreement would in fact determine their obligations. They applied for a declaration that the legislation in question was invalid. The Alberta courts refused to grant the declaration, holding that the man could avoid his parental obligations by not living with the woman; put another way, the impact on his liberty flowed from his choice and not from the actions of the state.[266] As in *Susan Doe*, it might be preferable to accept that statutes governing the arrangements that parents make

---

262 *Susan Doe*, above note 11.

263 *Ibid* at para 141 (SCJ).

264 *Doe*, above note 18.

265 *Family Law Act*, SA 2003, c F-4.5, particularly ss. 53 and 85, which clearly indicate that an agreement between parents concerning support is not binding on a court.

266 *Doe*, above note 18 at para 28.

for their children do engage the liberty interest, and consider the societal interests that might justify interfering with those arrangements as an aspect of the applicable principles of fundamental justice or under section 1.

In *De Guzman v Canada (Minister of Citizenship and Immigration)*,[267] the applicant applied for and obtained permanent resident status, having falsely stated on her original immigration application that she had no children. She subsequently tried to sponsor her children to come to Canada; however, because she had not disclosed them on her original application, they were not defined as members of the family class under the relevant immigration regulation, so she was unable to sponsor them. She challenged the regulation under section 7. The court recognized that her decision to come to Canada was a fundamental life choice, but noted that the decision was subject to Canadian law and held that any impact on liberty and security of the person was generated by the applicant's decision to misrepresent her family status rather than by the regulation itself.[268] Given the court's recognition that the decision to emigrate is fundamental, it might be preferable to assume that section 7 is engaged and resolve the case on the basis that the regulation is not procedurally unfair. It would be very plausible to conclude that the requirement that a potential immigrant be truthful, combined with a regulation that does not punish her for making an untrue statement but merely holds her to it, would not violate the principles of fundamental justice.

In *Marchand v Ontario*,[269] the applicant, a woman who had been adopted as an infant, sought identifying information about the man whom she believed to be her father. The Adoption Disclosure Registrar refused to provide the information because the man in question had not consented to its disclosure. The applicant challenged the statutory provisions that enabled the man to prevent disclosure, arguing that she needed this information to make fundamental life choices. The applications judge held that the liberty interest did not include the right to obtain this information;[270] while the Court of Appeal found it unnecessary to decide whether this holding was correct,[271] it does appear consistent with the Supreme Court of Canada's approach to the liberty interest.

---

267 *De Guzman*, above note 10.
268 *Ibid* at paras 63–64.
269 *Marchand v Ontario* (2006), 81 OR (3d) 172 (SCJ), aff'd 2007 ONCA 787, leave to appeal to SCC refused, [2008] SCCA No 37 [*Marchand*].
270 *Ibid* at paras 110–16 (SCJ).
271 *Ibid* at para 12 (CA).

In *Tadros v Peel Regional Police Service*,[272] the applicant had been charged in Peel Region with sexual offences, but the charges were withdrawn after he agreed to enter into a peace bond without admitting the offences. After the peace bond expired, in connection with applications for employment, the applicant signed forms authorizing the Toronto Police Service to conduct a number of Vulnerable Persons Searches. During these searches, the Toronto police contacted the Peel police, who sent the Toronto police the information they had concerning the withdrawn charges. The applicant applied for an order requiring the Peel police to remove all information concerning the withdrawn charges and argued, *inter alia*, that the conduct of the Peel police infringed his rights under section 7. The Ontario Court of Appeal held that the applicant's liberty interest was not engaged: "the disclosure by one police service to another of information obtained through the public prosecution of an individual" did not engage liberty understood as the right to make fundamental personal choices.

f) Privacy Interests as Liberty Interests

In *R v O'Connor*,[273] L'Heureux-Dubé J held that section 7 of the *Charter* would protect a person's reasonable expectation of privacy in therapeutic records,[274] and that an infringement of that expectation would engage the liberty interest in section 7.[275] Although it is far from clear that her views on this issue were shared by a majority of the Court,[276] it is now generally accepted that individual interests in privacy can engage section 7, either via the interest in security of the person (see Section D(4), below in this chapter) or via the liberty interest. In *Cheskes v Ontario (Attorney General)*,[277] for example, the applicants challenged

---

272 *Tadros v Peel Regional Police Service*, 2009 ONCA 442 [*Tadros*].
273 *R v O'Connor*, [1995] 4 SCR 411 [*O'Connor*].
274 *Ibid* at para 118.
275 *Ibid* at para 113.
276 La Forest and Gonthier JJ concurred with L'Heureux-Dubé J. Justice McLachlin also concurred in separate reasons. The other five judges did not explicitly address this point (Lamer CJC and Sopinka J, dissenting in the result, agreed that "important privacy interests" (para 8) attached to the records at issue in the case, but did not indicate the precise constitutional status of these interests; Cory J, Iacobucci J concurring, concurred in the result with L'Heureux-Dubé, and Major J, dissenting in the result, did not discuss this point). In *R v Mills*, [1999] 3 SCR 668 at paras 77–89, the privacy interest at stake in *O'Connor* was considered primarily under s 8 rather than s 7.
277 *Cheskes*, above note 9.

amendments to the *Vital Statistics Act*[278] that allowed access to information identifying birth parents and adopted children without the consent of the person being identified. The applicants were adoptees and birth parents who did not want their identities to be disclosed. Belobaba J held that the applicants had a reasonable expectation of privacy in the information in question, and that this privacy interest gave rise to a liberty interest.[279]

The section 7 privacy interest may explain a puzzling aspect of the Supreme Court of Canada's decision in *R v B(D)*.[280] The accused young offender challenged the provisions of the *Youth Criminal Justice Act*[281] (*YCJA*) that, for certain "presumptive" offences, required him to establish that he should be sentenced as a youth rather than as an adult and that he was entitled to a publication ban.[282] The majority, *per* Abella J, held that the reversal of onus on the publication ban issue engaged the section 7 liberty interest, apparently because it makes the sentence "more severe."[283] But as the minority, *per* Rothstein J, pointed out, it is not obvious that publication of the young person's identity affects liberty because it does not amount to an additional period of imprisonment or probation, or otherwise restrict the offender's liberty in a physical sense, or interfere with his fundamental life choices.[284] Since Abella J notes the *YCJA*'s emphasis on the young offender's privacy interests,[285] her holding is perhaps best understood as follows. The *YCJA* itself grants young persons accused of crime a reasonable expectation of privacy in their identity, and because reasonable expectations of privacy are an aspect of the section 7 liberty interest, the publication ban provisions of the *YCJA* engage that interest.

---

278 RSO 1990, c V-4, as amended by the *Adoption Information Disclosure Act*, SO 2005, c 25.

279 *Cheskes*, above note 9 at para 182. On the other side of the coin, in *C(PS) v British Columbia (AG)*, 2007 BCSC 895 at paras 148–52, the federal registration requirements for convicted sexual offenders were held not to engage an offender's reasonable expectation of privacy.

280 *R v B(D)* [*B(D)*], 2008 SCC 25.

281 *Youth Criminal Justice Act*, SC 2002, c 1 [*YCJA*].

282 *YCJA, ibid*, ss 62, 63, 64(1) & (5), 70, 72(1) & (2), 73(1) (sentence), ss 75, 110(2) (publication ban). The "presumptive offences" are defined in s 2(1).

283 *B(D)*, above note 280 at para 87, Abella J.

284 *Ibid* at para 171, Rothstein J dissenting.

285 *Ibid* at para 84, Abella J.

g) State Action That Does Not Engage the Liberty Interest

i) Deportation

Do deportation proceedings, as such, engage the section 7 liberty interest? The point was left open in *Chiarelli v Canada (Minister of Employment and Immigration)*,[286] but was subsequently settled in *Medovarski v Canada (Minister of Citizenship and Immigration) (Medovarski)*.[287] Both cases involved constitutional challenges to the procedures applicable to deportation for serious criminality. In *Medovarski*, the Court held that deportation as such did not engage section 7 because "non-citizens do not have an unqualified right to enter or remain in Canada."[288] The reasoning that connects this limit on a non-citizen's mobility rights with the absence of a section 7 liberty interest is elusive, and the Court does not spell it out. The Court may have meant to say something like the following: since non-citizens can be excluded under section 6, excluding them cannot be contrary to another section of the *Charter*. But the fact that non-citizens do not have mobility rights under section 6 of the *Charter* does not mean that they do not have rights under section 7 of the *Charter*. Indeed, the contrary proposition is well established. One of the earliest section 7 cases held that the word "everyone" in section 7 includes non-citizens physically present in Canada,[289] and this holding has never seriously been questioned. To establish that deportation as such does not engage the section 7 interest, a more careful analysis of the nature and effect of deportation on a person present in Canada would have to be carried out. A more satisfactory solution would be to hold that deportation does indeed engage the liberty interest because a deportation order includes the possibility of detaining the deportee in order to carry it out, just as penal proceedings engage the liberty interest because a finding of guilt includes possibility of imprisonment as punishment. This solution would by no means give non-citizens "an unqualified right to enter or remain in Canada"; it would, however, require the legal rules governing deportation from Canada to comply with the principles of fundamental justice. Given the importance to a permanent resident or Convention refugee of remaining in Canada, such a requirement would be quite appropriate.

Shortly after *Medovarski* was decided, the Court held in *Charkaoui* that detention incidental to deportation proceedings does engage the

---

286 *Chiarelli v Canada (Minister of Employment and Immigration)*, [1992] 1 SCR 711 at 731.

287 *Medovarski*, above note 250.

288 *Ibid* at para 46.

289 *Singh*, above note 172.

liberty interest (see Section D(3)(d), above in this chapter). There is a tension between *Medovarski* and *Charkaoui* on this point. Criminal proceedings, and most other penal proceedings as well, have to comply with section 7 from the outset because of the potential for imprisonment that they create (see Section D(3)(b), above in this chapter). Because of the holding in *Medovarski*, this logic apparently does not apply to deportation proceedings; thus, in *Poshteh v Canada (Minister of Citizenship and Immigration)*, the Federal Court of Appeal held that the initial steps in proceedings that may lead to deportation, such as a finding that a person is inadmissible to Canada, do not engage section 7 because those initial steps do not necessarily mean that individual will ever be detained. [290] But because of the holding in *Charkaoui*, there must be some point in the proceedings where the likelihood of detention incidental to deportation is sufficiently high that the liberty interest is engaged and section 7 applies.

ii) Driving Prohibitions

Driving a motor vehicle is a licensed activity: no-one is legally permitted to drive without obtaining a driver's licence, and there are also typically licensing and insurance requirements applicable to the vehicle driven. But it is not especially difficult to obtain a driver's licence, and most adult Canadians have one. Moreover, for some adult Canadians, the legal ability to drive is a practical necessity for their livelihood. [291] Thus, the freedom to drive might seem to qualify as a kind of "liberty" protected by section 7. Nonetheless, Canadian courts have consistently held that holding a driver's licence is not protected by the section 7 liberty interest. In *Buhlers v British Columbia (Superintendent of Motor Vehicles)*, [292] the leading case, the British Columbia Court of Appeal conducted an extensive review of authority concerning both driving under the *Charter* and the meaning of "liberty" in section 7, and concluded that notwithstanding the expansion of the liberty interest to include matters of fundamental personal importance, the liberty interest "does not extend to the driving of a motor vehicle on a public highway. It is not a matter that is fundamental or inherently personal to the individual. It is not a matter that goes to the root of a person's dignity and independence." [293] Accordingly, a provincial statute providing for an im-

---

290 *Poshteh v Canada (Minister of Citizenship and Immigration)*, 2005 FCA 85.

291 Compare *Alberta v Hutterian Brethren of Wilson Colony*, 2009 SCC 37 at para 201, LeBel J dissenting (though s 7 was not in issue in that case).

292 *Buhlers v British Columbia (Superintendent of Motor Vehicles)*, 1999 BCCA 114, leave to appeal to SCC refused (1999), 181 DLR (4th) vii (SCC).

293 *Ibid* at para 109.

mediate driving prohibition where a police officer believed on reasonable grounds that a driver had committed impaired driving offences under the *Criminal Code* did not engage section 7 of the *Charter* (and so did not have to comply with the principles of fundamental justice). The same reasoning has been applied to similar statutory schemes for administrative licence suspension in other provinces.[294] Thus, the administrative procedures for granting, suspending, or revoking a driver's licence do not, as a matter of constitutional law, have to comply with the principles of fundamental justice.

iii) Offences without Imprisonment

As noted above, where the available penalties for an offence do not include imprisonment or other restrictions on personal liberty, the section 7 liberty interest is not engaged.[295]

4) "Security of the Person"

Security of the person refers to both the bodily integrity and the psychological integrity of the individual. The Supreme Court of Canada's first extensive consideration of the interest in security of the person came in *Morgentaler*.[296] The accused were charged with procuring abortions, contrary to what was then section 251 of the *Criminal Code*.[297] Section 251 prohibited abortion in general, but created an exception for an abortion approved by the therapeutic abortion committee of an accredited and approved hospital. The accused physicians had performed abortions in a private clinic and thus did not come within the statutory exception. The accused challenged section 251 on the ground that it violated the section 7 rights of women. In a complex split decision, a 5:2 majority of the Supreme Court of Canada ultimately agreed with the accused, declared that the section was invalid, and acquitted the accused. However, there was no clear majority on the questions of how section 251 engaged or violated section 7. Dickson CJC, Lamer J concurring, held that security of the person would be engaged by "state

---

294 *Horsefield v Ontario (Registrar of Motor Vehicles)* (1999), 134 CCC (3d) 161 (Ont CA); *Thomson v Alberta (Transportation and Safety Board)*, 2003 ABCA 256; *White v Nova Scotia (Registrar of Motor Vehicles)* (1996), 147 NSR (2d) 259 (SC); *R v Leclair* (1990), 25 MVR (2d) 47 (QB); *R v MacCormack* (1999), 134 CCC (3d) 351 (PESCAD).

295 *Transport Robert*, above note 181.

296 Above note 214.

297 *Criminal Code*, RSC 1970, c C-34, s 251; see now *Criminal Code*, RSC 1985, c C-46, s 287.

interference with bodily integrity and serious state-imposed psychological stress, at least in the criminal law context."[298] Beetz J, Estey J concurring, held that security of the person included "some protection from state interference when a person's life or health is in danger."[299] Both judges held that the prohibition on abortion in section 251 engaged the interest in security of the person, though for different reasons. Dickson CJC held that "[f]orcing a woman, by threat of criminal sanction, to carry a foetus to term unless she meets certain criteria unrelated to her own priorities and aspirations, is a profound interference with a woman's body" and that the delay inherent in the procedure for obtaining an exemption from the prohibition "can have profound consequences on the woman's physical and emotional well-being"; for both reasons, security of the person was engaged.[300] Beetz J took a narrower view, holding that the prohibition engaged security of the person where it precluded the woman from obtaining "appropriate medical treatment when . . . her life is in danger."[301] Wilson J, speaking for herself, held that section 251 engaged the interest in security of the person because it effectively put the woman seeking an abortion under the control of the state.[302] Thus, the majority decisions in *Morgentaler* recognized two branches of the interest in security of the person: physical integrity and psychological integrity.

a) Physical Integrity

In general, it can be said that state conduct that involves a non-consensual application of force to a person's body engages security of the person. There are many examples in the caselaw that illustrate this point: the non-consensual taking of bodily samples for forensic DNA analysis or other investigative purposes,[303] the non-consensual taking of fingerprints,[304] the use of force by the police to effect an arrest or to control a suspect,[305] the removal of a child for adoption,[306] and the

---

298 *Morgentaler*, above note 214 at 56.

299 *Ibid* at 90.

300 *Ibid* at 56–57.

301 *Ibid* at 90.

302 *Ibid* at 173.

303 *R v Stillman*, [1997] 1 SCR 607 at para 51; compare *R v B(SA)*, 2003 SCC 60 at paras 44–47.

304 *R v Beare; R v Higgins*, [1988] 2 SCR 387 at 402, expressing agreement with the reasons of Cameron JA in the court below, [1987] 4 WWR 309 at 362 (Sask CA).

305 *R v Nasogaluak*, 2010 SCC 6 at para 38; *R v C(M)*, 2007 ONCJ 164 at para 56.

306 *T(R) (Re)*, 2004 SKQB 503 at paras 67–68.

forcible provision of beneficial but unwanted medical treatment[307] all engage the interest in security of the person.

Unlawful state conduct that affects physical integrity — that is, an assault by a state agent — not only engages security of the person but necessarily violates section 7 of the *Charter*[308] and cannot be justified under section 1. An illegal act cannot comply with the principles of fundamental justice and is not "prescribed by law" for section 1 purposes.

Interestingly, in *Canadian Foundation for Children, Youth and the Law v Canada (AG)*,[309] the Court held unanimously that a statute withdrawing a criminal law protection that would otherwise be available engaged the potential victims' security of the person. The Canadian Foundation for Children, Youth, and the Law was granted public interest standing to challenge the constitutionality of section 43 of the *Criminal Code*, which permits parents, teachers, and persons *in loco parentis* to use "force by way of correction toward a pupil or child"; the section thus partially withdraws from children the protection of the law of assault. Although the Court was sharply divided on the interpretation and the constitutionality of section 43, and although the difference between children and adults might well have been considered under section 15 alone,[310] the Crown conceded that the children's security of the person was engaged. The Court had no hesitation in accepting this concession. As Arbour J, dissenting on other grounds, said,

> The absence of this protective force [of the criminal law], and the correlative sanction by the state of what would otherwise be an assault, suffices, in my view, to amount to a deprivation of children's security of the person interest.[311]

Moreover, it is hard to believe that the majority, *per* McLachlin CJC, would have gone to such lengths to reject the claim that section 43 violated the principles of fundamental justice if the Court had not thought the Crown's concession well-founded. It might have been argued that Parliament's refusal to extend the protection of the criminal law to these potential victims was an instance of state inaction rather than

---

307 *AC v Manitoba (Director of Child and Family Services)*, 2009 SCC 30 at para 100, Abella J for the majority, and compare *ibid* at para 136, McLachlin CJC, Rothstein J, concurring, and at para 220, Binnie J dissenting.

308 *Hawley v Bapoo* (2005), 76 OR (3d) 649 at para 149 (SCJ).

309 *Canadian Foundation*, above note 160.

310 See the reasons of Binnie J, dissenting in part.

311 *Ibid* at para 176. Deschamps J, dissenting, agreed with Arbour J's reasons on the s 7 issue. See also para 3, McLachlin CJC.

state action to which the *Charter* applied. The Court's implicit rejection of this argument suggests that section 7 may require the state to provide positive protection for security of the person, at least by providing a basic set of criminal law protections for bodily integrity.

On the basis of the majority holdings in *Morgentaler*, security of the person will also be engaged by "deprivation by means of a criminal sanction of access to medication reasonably required for the treatment of a medical condition that threatens life or health . . . ."[312] Other obstacles to obtaining necessary medical care may also engage security of the person; in *Chaoulli*, the combination of a prohibition on private insurance and lengthy delays in the public sector engaged patients' physical security of the person.[313]

In a different medical context, when a person is in custody, the right to security of the person very likely includes the right to be provided with necessary health care. This view seems implicit in *R v Monney*.[314] The accused had ingested a significant amount of heroin for the purpose of smuggling it into Canada. He was detained at the border and customs officials maintained a "bedpan vigil" until the heroin passed through his system. He argued that his section 7 rights had been violated because the "bedpan vigil" had not been conducted under medical supervision; rather than having a physician present, customs officials were prepared "to provide prompt medical attention if requested by the suspect, or should the need arise."[315] The Court commented that it would have been preferable to have a physician present, as contemplated in the relevant customs policy manual; however, "[c]onstitutional protection of life and security of the person pursuant to s. 7 of the *Charter* does not extend to providing access to medical supervision during a passive 'bedpan vigil' over and above the rejection of medical attention by the suspect being detained."[316] There is little doubt that if the accused had requested or had required necessary medical care, and had been denied it, his section 7 rights would have been engaged and indeed infringed.

A more difficult class of cases consists of those where state action creates a risk, but not a certainty, of an intrusion on physical integrity. It might seem obvious that the creation of such risks engages security

---

312 *Parker*, above note 255 at para 97. See also *Hitzig*, above note 257 at paras 93–94; *PHS*, above note 29 at paras 91–93 (interest in security of the person engaged by the closing of a safe injection site for heroin addicts).

313 *Chaoulli*, above note 8 at paras 111–16.

314 *R v Monney*, [1999] 1 SCR 652.

315 *Ibid* at para 54.

316 *Ibid* at para 56.

of the person, but because of the wide range of tasks undertaken by government, virtually any statute, policy, or program might be said to impose a physical risk on some persons, even if it ameliorates risks for others. Thus, all government action would engage security of the person. This tension was exposed quite early in the *Charter* era. Although the Court quickly recognized that some state-imposed risks to physical integrity engaged security of the person, it also recognized that some state-imposed risks are so infused with policy that it is difficult to bring them under the kind of judicial review contemplated in section 7.

In *Singh*, as noted above, the applicants sought to challenge certain aspects of the system for determining refugee claims. Three members of the Court held that the denial of rights to a person who qualified as a refugee under the Refugee Convention "must amount to a deprivation of security of the person"[317] because of the risk that the person faced on being deported. Similarly, as noted in Section D(3)(c), above in this chapter, in the cases involving extradition to face the death penalty, the Supreme Court of Canada has treated the risk of being executed as engaging security of the person, rather than as engaging the interest in life.[318]

In *Operation Dismantle v R* (*Operation Dismantle*),[319] the applicants challenged a decision of the federal cabinet to permit the United States to test cruise missiles in Canada. They alleged that the decision affected the security of every person in Canada by increasing the risk of nuclear war. The Court, somewhat surprisingly, held that the decision was subject to judicial review;[320] but the majority avoided deciding whether security of the person could be engaged by holding that the link between the cabinet's decision and the alleged effect on security of the person was too speculative to require further consideration.[321] Section 7 would be engaged only "where it can be said that a deprivation of life and security of the person could be proven to result from the impugned government act."[322] By handing the issue this way, the Court left open the possibility that an executive decision to go to war, or one that could be shown to increase the danger of war, highly political and discretionary as that decision might be, would engage section 7 of the *Charter* by affecting everyone's security of the person. Justice Wilson,

---

317 *Singh*, above note 172 at 207. See note 173 above for a description of the various judges' dispositions of the case.

318 *Kindler*, above note 198 at 831, La Forest J and at 790, Sopinka J dissenting; *Burns*, above note 198 at para 59.

319 *Operation Dismantle v R*, [1985] 1 SCR 441.

320 *Ibid* at 455.

321 *Ibid* at 452–57.

322 *Ibid* at 456.

concurring in the result, agreed with the majority that the cabinet's decision was in principle reviewable under the *Charter* but held that the drafters of the *Charter* could not have intended the courts to review all government decisions that "incidentally increase the risk to the lives or personal security of some or all of the state's citizens."[323] Therefore, this kind of decision did not in itself engage security of the person.[324]

In *Trang*,[325] the difficulty of deciding what decisions are apt for judicial review was arguably central to the reasoning. Several inmates at the Edmonton Remand Centre brought an application for relief under section 7 of the *Charter*, alleging that the conditions in the vans used to transport them to and from the jail were unsafe. The trial judge granted a declaration to this effect. The Alberta Court of Appeal set the declaration aside on the ground that declaratory relief was not appropriate;[326] however, in extensive *obiter dicta*, the court also expressed serious doubts about the merits of the inmates' claim. After referring to Wilson J's minority reasons in *Operation Dismantle*, the court commented that "Merely because the risks of riding in the prison vans may be greater than the risk of riding in some other vehicle does not engage the *Charter*" and rejected the proposition that "every state action that imposes a greater risk of personal injury on a citizen is a breach of s. 7."[327] The court must be correct to reject this general proposition, and to give the state some margin of appreciation in how it handles security arrangements for inmates; but the proposition that "mere risk" can never engage section 7 of the *Charter*[328] cannot be correct. The cases involving deportation of refugees and the extradition of fugitives to face a risk of death or torture clearly show that a risk can engage section 7. Moreover, the court's reasons show little sensitivity to the particular situation of the applicants. As persons in custody, they have no choice about whether to ride in prison vans; if they could demonstrate with evidence that the conditions under which they were transported failed to meet some threshold of safety, then surely their security of the person would be engaged.

In contrast to *Trang*, the British Columbia Court of Appeal held in *Victoria (City of) v Adams (Adams)* that a municipal prohibition on temporary erection of overhead shelter engaged a homeless person's

---

323 *Ibid* at 489.
324 *Ibid* at 488–91.
325 *Trang*, above note 83.
326 *Ibid* at paras 13–25.
327 *Ibid* at paras 29–30.
328 The court does not expressly state this proposition, but see *ibid* at para 28.

security of the person because it exposed him to health risks.[329] It is not entirely clear what factors might be involved to distinguish *Trang* from *Adams*;[330] while the facts of the two cases are of course entirely different, one might have thought that the corrections context of *Trang* would be more, not less, amenable to judicial scrutiny than the difficult problem of homelessness that formed the context in *Adams*.

b) Psychological Integrity

In *Blencoe*, briefly described in Section D(3)(a), above in this chapter, the Supreme Court of Canada held that the individual's interest in security of the person could be engaged by "serious psychological incursions resulting from state interference with an individual interest of fundamental importance."[331] The threshold for finding such an interference is both objective and high. In *New Brunswick (Minister of Health and Community Services) v G(J) (G(J))*,[332] Lamer CJC described it as flows:

> For a restriction of security of the person to be made out . . . , the impugned state action must have a serious and profound effect on a person's psychological integrity. The effects of the state interference must be assessed objectively, with a view to their impact on the psychological integrity of a person of reasonable sensibility. This need not rise to the level of nervous shock or psychiatric illness, but must be greater than ordinary stress or anxiety.[333]

In that case, the Minister of Health and Community Services applied for an order extending the removal of the applicant's children from her care and custody. This state action engaged the interest in security of the person:

> . . . state removal of a child from parental custody pursuant to the state's *parens patriae* jurisdiction constitutes a serious interference with the psychological integrity of the parent . . . . Besides the obvious distress arising from the loss of companionship of the child, direct state interference with the parent-child relationship, through a procedure in which the relationship is subject to state inspection and review, is a gross intrusion into a private and intimate sphere. Further, the parent is often stigmatized as "unfit" when relieved of

---

329 *Victoria (City)*, above note 205 at paras 102–10.
330 *Trang* is not cited in *Adams*.
331 *Blencoe*, above note 226 at para 82.
332 *New Brunswick (Minister of Health and Community Services) v G(J)*, [1999] 3 SCR 46 [*G(J)*].
333 *Ibid* at para 60.

custody. As an individual's status as a parent is often fundamental to personal identity, the stigma and distress resulting from a loss of parental status is a particularly serious consequence of the state's conduct.[334]

However, Lamer CJC held that not all state action that severed the parent-child relationship would engage security of the person: "a parent's security of the person is not restricted when, without more, his or her child is sentenced to jail or conscripted into the army . . . [or] is negligently shot and killed by a police officer."[335]

Despite the high threshold, courts have on occasion recognized that a particular state interference with a fundamentally important individual interest creates sufficient psychological stress to engage section 7. In *Rodriguez v British Columbia (AG)*,[336] the applicant sought a declaration that section 241(*b*) of the *Criminal Code*, prohibiting assisted suicide, was invalid. She suffered from a degenerative disease and wished to choose for herself the time and manner of her death; section 241(*b*) interfered with this choice because it would prevent her from obtaining assistance in killing herself once the disease reached the point where she was unable to kill herself on her own. The majority recognized that this effect of section 241(*b*) engaged her security of the person:

> . . . personal autonomy, at least with respect to the right to make choices concerning one's own body, control over one's physical and psychological integrity, and basic human dignity are encompassed within security of the person, at least to the extent of freedom from criminal prohibitions which interfere with these.

---

334 *Ibid* at para 61. Section 7 is not engaged where another relative seeks custody of a child in protection proceedings: *New Brunswick (Minister of Social Development) v S(T)*, 2009 NBCA 67; *R(J) v New Brunswick (Minister of Social Development)*, 2010 NBCA 81.

335 *G(J)*, above note 332 at para 63. In support of the last example, Lamer CJC cites *Augustus v Gosset*, [1996] 3 SCR 268 [*Augustus*], a case decided under Quebec's *Charter of Human Rights and Freedoms*. In *Augustus*, L'Heureux-Dubé J commented at para 53 that "neither the Canadian *Charter* nor the Quebec *Charter* protects the right to maintain and continue a parent-child relationship," a comment that must at least be qualified to the extent that *G(J)* holds that state interference with the parent-child relationship can constitute a deprivation of security of the person.

336 *Rodriguez v British Columbia (AG)*, [1993] 3 SCR 519.

. . . the prohibition in s. 241(*b*) deprives the [applicant] of autonomy over her person and caused her physical pain and psychological stress in a manner which impinged upon the security of her person.[337]

In *Chaoulli*—untypical in this respect as in so many others—the Court found that the psychological stress created by delays in obtaining necessary medical treatment amounted to the kind of state-imposed psychological stress that would engage section 7.[338]

Courts have frequently found that the requisite level of state-imposed stress is not established on the facts. Many of these cases involve the stress inherent in participation in legal proceedings. In *Blencoe*, the applicant complained of the delay in processing a human rights complaint against him, and the evidence amply documented the stress and psychological harm that the delay had caused him. Nonetheless, the Court held that his interest in security of the person had not been engaged: "The state has not interfered with the [applicant's] right to make decisions that affect his fundamental being."[339] The kind of stress that the applicant faced was an inevitable by-product of his involvement in the proceedings. Similarly, in *Bouzari v Iran (Islamic Republic)* it was held that failure to provide a civil cause of action in Canada for acts of torture committed abroad by a foreign state did not cause the degree of psychological harm necessary to engage security of the person.[340] In *R v 1260448 Ontario Ltd; R v Transport Robert Ltée*, it was held that prosecution for a traffic safety offence does not engage "the kind of exceptional state-induced psychological stress . . . that would trigger the security of the person guarantee," even where the fine upon conviction was quite large.[341] There are many other examples where various forms of involvement in legal proceedings, though undoubtedly stressful, have been held not to engage security of the person.[342]

---

337 *Ibid* at 588–89. Compare *ibid* at 618–19, McLachlin J (L'Heureux-Dubé J concurring) dissenting. Cory J dissenting saw the prohibition as engaging the interest in life: "the right to die with dignity should be as well protected as is any other aspect of the right to life": *ibid* at 630. Lamer CJC, dissenting, decided the case under s 15 of the *Charter* and did not consider the s 7 challenge.

338 *Chaoulli*, above note 8 at paras 122–23.

339 *Blencoe*, above note 226 at para 86.

340 *Bouzari v Iran (Islamic Republic)* (2004), 243 DLR (4th) 406 at paras 96–103 (Ont CA), rejecting a constitutional challenge to s 3 of the *State Immunity Act*, RSC 1985, c S-18.

341 *Transport Robert*, above note 181 at para 27.

342 See *Kostuch (Informant) v Alberta (AG)* (1995), 101 CCC (3d) 321 (Alta CA) (Attorney General's power to intervene in private prosecution does not engage informant's security of the person); *I(A) v Ontario (Director, Child and Family Services Act)* (2005), 75 OR (3d) 663 at paras 70–74 (Div Ct) (applicants were

5) Interests That Are Not Protected

a) Economic Interests

Section 7 of the *Charter* does not expressly protect economic interests such as property rights. In this respect, it is unlike section 1(*a*) of the *Bill of Rights*[343] or the 5th and 14th Amendments to the *Constitution* of the United States, all of which provide a right not to be deprived of "property" except in accordance with due process of law. The omission of property interests was deliberate,[344] and, although the interpretation of section 7 is not determined by the actual intentions of its drafters,[345] Canadian courts have been very reluctant to interpret the right to life, liberty, and security of the person as including property interests or other purely economic interests.

Interests that have been identified as purely economic, and so not entitled to recognition under section 7, include the "unconstrained right to transact business whenever one wishes,"[346] the right to sue in tort,[347] the right to sue for breach of the duty of fair representation in

---

the foster parents of a child who was the ward of the Children's Aid Society; the child's removal from their custody for an adoption placement did not engage their security of the person); *Medovarski*, above note 250 at para 46 (deportation as such does not engage security of the person); *Malmo-Levine*, above note 4 at para 88 (prohibition of non-addictive marijuana did not engage security of the person); *R v N(D)*, 2004 NLCA 44 at paras 35–43 (security of the person not engaged where proceedings stayed by Crown counsel rather than by trial judge); *Tadros*, above note 272 (security of the person not engaged by retention and lawful dissemination of information concerning a sexual assault charge that had been withdrawn); *Polewsky v Home Hardware Stores Ltd* (2003), 229 DLR (4th) 308 (Ont Div Ct) (stress caused by the plaintiff's inability to pay the fees required to commence a small claims action not sufficiently serious to engage s 7); *Beals v Saldanha*, 2003 SCC 72 at para 78 (s 7 does not protect "a Canadian defendant from the enforcement of a foreign judgment"; appears that security of the person not engaged); *Marchand*, above note 269 at para 121 (SCJ) ("a curiosity amongst adopted persons as to their birth family . . . does not meet the test of serious psychological stress").

343 *Canadian Bill of Rights*, above note 173.

344 See Sujit Choudhry, "The *Lochner* Era and Comparative Constitutionalism" (2004) 2 International Journal of Constitutional Law 1 at 15–27. A motion to amend the draft *Charter* to add property interests to s 7 was defeated in the House of Commons on 23 April 1981: see *House of Commons Debates*, 23 April 1981, 9471–73.

345 See Chapter 3, Section B.

346 *Edwards Books*, above note 210 at 786.

347 See *Whitbread*, above note 62, rejecting a s 7 challenge to a statute limiting tort liability.

collective bargaining,[348] pension rights,[349] the right to recover the costs of pursuing a human rights claim,[350] the interest in cash held while crossing an international boundary,[351] and the right to inherit upon the intestacy of a parent.[352]

It has often been held that section 7 does not protect "the right to unrestrained business activity or to practise a particular profession."[353] This holding has been applied to many ways of earning a living: prostitution,[354] operating video lottery terminals,[355] being a landlord,[356] begging,[357] dentistry,[358] and architecture.[359] Certain earlier cases that recognized "the right to choose one's occupation and where to pursue it" as a protected interest under section 7 must be considered wrongly decided.[360] In *Gosselin*, the majority appears to have considered the applicant's interest in receiving social welfare benefits to be a purely economic interest, given that she did not show that section 7 should be reinterpreted to guarantee a more basic interest in subsistence.[361]

Despite these authorities, a statute or official decision that deprived a person of the possibility of making a living in any way — for example, by prohibiting her from seeking any employment or participating in any business venture — might be characterized as going beyond purely economic interests and as affecting security of the person. This pos-

---

348 *Rowell v Manitoba*, 2006 MBCA 14.

349 *Melanson v New Brunswick (AG)* (2007), 280 DLR (4th) 69 at para 21 (NBCA); *Clitheroe v Hydro One Inc* (2009), 96 OR (3d) 203 (SCJ).

350 *Quereshi v Ontario (Human Rights Commission)* (2006), 268 DLR (4th) 281 (Ont Div Ct).

351 *Tourki v Canada (Minister of Public Safety and Emergency Preparedness)*, 2007 FCA 186 at para 46, aff'g 2006 FC 50. The applicant challenged the constitutionality of a statute providing for seizure and forfeiture of currency for failure to report the importation or exportation of currency valued at more than $10,000.

352 *Marshall Estate (Re)*, 2008 NSSC 93 at paras 26–30.

353 *Lister v Ontario (AG)* (1990), 72 OR (2d) 354 at 365 (Ont HCJ) [*Lister*]; compare *Lavallee*, above note 260 at para 27.

354 *Reference re ss 193 and 195.1(1)(c) of the Criminal Code*, [1990] 1 SCR 1123 at 1169–71, Lamer J concurring in the result; the other members of the majority did not decide the point: *ibid* at 1140–41.

355 *Siemens v Manitoba (AG)*, 2003 SCC 3 at paras 45–46.

356 *A&L Investments Ltd v Ontario* (1997), 36 OR (3d) 127 (CA).

357 *Banks*, above note 204 at paras 73–81.

358 *Lister*, above note 353.

359 *Guthrie v Ontario Association of Architects* (1988), 29 OAC 146 at para 5 (Div Ct).

360 *Wilson v Medical Services Commission of British Columbia* (1988), 30 BCLR (2d) 1 at 18 (CA).

361 *Gosselin*, above note 161 at para 81.

sibility has been left open in a number of cases.[362] Similarly, a law or official action that deprived a person of all or substantially all of his property interests would certainly affect security of the person because the person would then be unable to provide for his most basic bodily needs. Thus, the question should not be whether the interest in question is economic, but whether it is *merely* economic (in which case it is not protected under section 7) or whether, though having an economic dimension, it nonetheless affects the interests that are protected by section 7.

b) Interests Arising in Private Disputes

As noted in Section B(4)(a), above in this chapter, in *Dolphin Delivery*, the Supreme Court of Canada held that the *Charter* does not apply to private disputes that depend solely on the common law, although the parties can challenge any statutes that apply to the dispute. In accordance with these holdings, courts have been unwilling to permit section 7 challenges to proceed in private disputes, even where life, liberty, and security of the person are arguably at stake, because the element of state action is lacking.[363] Consider a custody dispute between a mother and a father. From the parent's perspective, the interest in security of the person at stake here is arguably the same as in *G(J)*,[364] but the element of state action is lacking because it is not the state that seeks to deprive the parent of the child. For this reason, in *W(R) v W(E)*,[365] it was held that there was no right to state-funded counsel in a private custody dispute, even though *G(J)* recognized a right to state-funded counsel in some cases where the state seeks to take custody of the child from the parents.

---

362 *A&L Investments*, above note 356 at 136; *Banks*, above note 204 at para 81.

363 Consider *Hobbs v Robinson*, 2004 BCSC 1508, rev'd 2006 BCCA 65. A hospital patient who was a Jehovah's Witness refused a blood transfusion and was required to sign a release. After she died, her family brought an action against the hospital and the treating physicians. They argued that the hospital's requirement that she sign a release violated s 7. The trial judge held that there was no state action, so s 7 was not engaged. The Court of Appeal ordered a new trial for procedural reasons and did not consider the merits of this claim.

364 Above note 332.

365 *W(R) v W(E)*, 2004 NBCA 13. Similarly, in *Green v Millar*, 2004 BCCA 590, there was no violation of s 7 where a judge granted interim orders concerning custody and the matrimonial home in the absence of one of the parties, where the absent party had had actual notice of the hearing but believed it to be defective. It is not entirely clear whether the court's view was that s 7 was not engaged or that s 7, though engaged, was not violated because the motions judge's decision to proceed in the circumstances was not unfair; see paras 20*ff*.

c) Trivial Infringements of Life, Liberty, and Security of the Person

Section 7, like other sections of the *Charter*, does not protect individuals against insignificant or trivial effects of state action on their constitutionally protected interests.[366] As McLachlin J put it in *Cunningham v Canada* (*Cunningham*), in the context of decisions concerning the liberty of offenders in custody:

> The *Charter* does not protect against insignificant or "trivial" limitations of rights . . . . It follows that qualification of a prisoner's expectation of liberty does not necessarily bring the matter within the purview of section 7 of the *Charter*. The qualification must be significant enough to warrant constitutional protection. To require that all changes to the manner in which a sentence is served be in accordance with the principles of fundamental justice would trivialize the protections under the *Charter*.[367]

However, in *Cunningham* itself, the section 7 interest was engaged. The case involved a challenge to the statutory framework for granting parole, a decision that has a substantial effect on an offender's liberty.

6) Life, Liberty, and Security Revisited

The challenge in interpreting the phrase "life, liberty and security of the person" is to give it a sufficiently generous meaning to capture the constitutional significance of these interests without making section 7 so expansive that it makes the rest of the *Charter* redundant. The Supreme Court of Canada's jurisprudence on the requirements for engaging section 7 by and large meets this challenge. The possibility of detention or imprisonment engages the liberty interest, as it should; in keeping with the common law presumption in favour of liberty, any use of state power that deprives individuals of the most basic interest in freedom should be fundamentally just. State action that interferes with decisions of "fundamental personal importance" should also be fundamentally just; although the scope of this phrase is not entirely clear, it represents a plausible extension of the notion of liberty to interests that, though not captured by other sections of the *Charter* such as the fundamental freedoms of section 2, are sufficiently basic to a legal order committed to individual freedom and dignity that they should be con-

---

366 Compare *Edwards Books*, above note 210 at 759 (trivial burden on exercise of religion would not offend s 2(*a*)); *Lavigne v Ontario Public Service Employees Union*, [1991] 2 SCR 211 at 259 (fact that infringement of s 2(*d*) right was trivial relevant to s 1 justification).

367 *Cunningham*, above note 245 at 151.

stitutionally recognized. Security of the person, similarly, is engaged by state action that intrudes on both physical and psychological integrity, interests of a similar nature to the liberty interests. While the standard of "state-imposed psychological stress" required to engage psychological integrity is a high one, it also rests on the idea that the state should respect individual freedom and dignity. If state action did have a sufficiently severe impact on an individual to meet the high threshold, it would be appropriate to determine whether the state had acted in a fundamentally just manner in doing so. The tests for engaging section 7 of the *Charter*, though sometimes uncertain of application, are appropriate to section 7's role in ensuring that state action that affects the most basic individual interests is fundamentally just.

FURTHER READINGS

BEATTY, DAVID. "Constitutional Conceits: The Coercive Authority of Courts" (1987) 37 UTLJ 183.

BRYDEN, PHILIP. " Section 7 of the *Charter* outside the Criminal Context" (2005) 38 UBC L Rev 507.

CHOUDHRY, SUJIT. "The *Lochner* Era and Comparative Constitutionalism" (2004) 2 International Journal of Constitutional Law 1.

COLVIN, ERIC. "Section 7 of the *Charter of Rights and Freedoms*" (1989) 68 Can Bar Rev 560.

DYZENHAUS, DAVID. "The Politics of Deference: Judicial Review and Democracy" in M TAGGART, ed, *The Province of Administrative Law* (Oxford: Hart, 1997) 279.

————. "Constituting the Rule of Law: Fundamental Values in Administrative Law" (2001–2002) 27 Queen's LJ 445.

ELLIOT, ROBIN, & ROBERT GRANT, "The *Charter*'s Application in Private Litigation" (1988–1989) 23 UBC L Rev 459.

HUTCHINSON, ALLAN C, & ANDREW PETTER, "Private Rights/Public Wrongs: The Liberal Lie of the *Charter*" (1988) 38 UTLJ 278.

MULLAN, DAVID."Section 7 and Administrative Law Deference: No Room at the Inn?" (2006) 34 Sup Ct L Rev (2d) 227.

SHAFFER, MARTHA. "Foetal Rights and the Regulation of Abortion" (1994) 39 McGill LJ 58.

SHARPE, ROBERT J. "Antonio Lamer and Section 7 of the *Charter*: A Law Reformer's Ambition, A Judge's Restraint" in Adam M Dodek & Daniel Jutras, eds, *The Sacred Fire: The Legacy of Antonio Lamer* (Markham, ON: LexisNexis Canada, 2009) 423.

SHARPE, ROBERT J, & KENT ROACH, *The Canadian Charter of Rights and Freedoms*, 4th ed (Toronto: Irwin Law, 2009) ch 6.

SLATTERY, BRIAN. "*Charter of Rights and Freedoms*: Does It Bind Private Persons?" (1985) 63 Can Bar Rev 148.

————. "The *Charter*'s Relevance to Private Litigation: Does *Dolphin* Deliver?" (1986–1987) 32 McGill LJ 905.

CHAPTER 3

DEFINING THE PRINCIPLES OF FUNDAMENTAL JUSTICE

A. INTRODUCTION

In Chapter 2, I considered the question of when section 7 is engaged; that is, when state action affects an individual's life, liberty, and security of the person to such an extent that section 7 applies. If section 7 is engaged, the state action must comply with the principles of fundamental justice; if the *Charter* applicant can show that the state action does not comply with the principles of fundamental justice, then she has established a violation of section 7.

But what are "the principles of fundamental justice"? On its face, the phrase is extraordinarily open-ended and admits of many possible interpretations. In this chapter, I consider the Court's approach to determining whether a proposed principle qualifies as a principle of fundamental justice. In the two following chapters, I provide a comprehensive list of legal principles that have been recognized as principles of fundamental justice. The major, generally applicable substantive principles are considered in Chapter 4. Procedural fairness as a principle of fundamental justice is the subject matter of Chapter 5.

B. THE PRINCIPLES OF FUNDAMENTAL JUSTICE: METHODS AND SOURCES

1) Procedure and Substance

In *Re BC Motor Vehicle Act* (*Motor Vehicle Reference*), the Supreme Court of Canada held that the principles of fundamental justice were not limited to principles of procedural fairness or natural justice but also included substantive legal norms.[1] To fully appreciate the significance of this holding, it is helpful to consider its legal background.

The phrase "principles of fundamental justice" was little known to Canadian law before the *Charter* came into force. It did, however, appear in section 2(*e*) of the *Bill of Rights*, which provided that "no law of Canada shall be construed or applied so as to . . . deprive a person of the right to a fair hearing in accordance with the principles of fundamental justice for the determination of his rights and obligations."[2] Given that section 2(*e*) was expressly directed at the conduct of hearings, it was unsurprising that in this context the phrase was interpreted to refer to procedural fairness—the administrative law concept of natural justice. The leading case, though not attempting "a final definition," held that the phrase should be interpreted to mean that "the tribunal which adjudicates upon [a person's] rights must act fairly, in good faith, without bias and in a judicial temper, and must give to him the opportunity adequately to state his case."[3] Moreover, there is little doubt that the drafters of the *Charter* thought that the phrase "principles of fundamental justice" was equivalent to the administrative law concept of "natural justice." Some early drafts of the *Charter* used the phrase "due process of law,"[4] and the substitution of the phrase "principles of fundamental justice" was in part an attempt to avoid the importation of American due process doctrine, particularly its substantive aspects,

---

1   *Re BC Motor Vehicle Act*, [1985] 2 SCR 486 [*Motor Vehicle Reference*], aff'g (1983), 4 CCC (3d) 243 (BCCA); this view was anticipated in *R v Young* (1984), 13 CCC (3d) 1 at 23 (Ont CA).

2   *Canadian Bill of Rights*, SC 1960, c 44, s 2(*e*).

3   *R v Duke*, [1972] SCR 917 at 923, and compare *R v Lowry* (1972), [1974] SCR 195 (holding that the *Bill of Rights* required a court of appeal, which allowed the Crown's appeal from an acquittal, to give the accused an opportunity to be heard before being sentenced). See also the discussion in Walter Surma Tarnopolsky, *The Canadian Bill of Rights*, 2d ed (Toronto: McClelland & Stewart, 1975) at 259–64.

4   See, for instance, the drafts of October and November 1979, in Anne Bayefsky, ed, *Canada's Constitution Act 1982 & Amendments: A Documentary History* (Toronto: McGraw-Hill Ryerson, 1989) vol 2 at 575 and 588–89.

into Canadian constitutional law.[5] Thus, in the early 1980s, it appeared likely that the "principles of fundamental justice" guaranteed by section 7 were principles of procedural fairness or natural justice.[6] Under this interpretation, section 7 would guarantee that the rules of procedural fairness would be observed where a person's life, liberty, and security of the person were at stake: the person would have the right to be heard, the right to lead evidence, the right to challenge evidence put against her, the right to have her case heard by an impartial tribunal, and so forth.[7] But the principles of fundamental justice would not have included any guarantees relating to the substantive fairness of the law to which the individual was subject, and probably would not have applied at all outside formal judicial or administrative proceedings.

In the *Motor Vehicle Reference*, the Supreme Court of Canada rejected this procedural understanding of "fundamental justice." The Court was faced with a British Columbia statute that imposed a mandatory period of imprisonment for the offence of driving while prohibited.[8] The statute expressly stated that the offence was "an absolute liability offence in which guilt is established by proof of driving, whether or not the defendant knew of the prohibition or suspension."[9] Thus, the prosecution was not required to demonstrate that the defendant was at fault in any way, nor was there any way that the defendant could avoid liability by showing absence of fault. The prosecution did not have to prove that the defendant was aware of the prohibition or even that he had been notified of it; and the defendant's due diligence in determining whether or not he was subject to a prohibition was no defence. The only defences would be those negating the *actus reus* of the offence (for example, the defendant was not prohibited or was not driving), or

---

5   See Sujit Choudhry, "The *Lochner* Era and Comparative Constitutionalism" (2004) 2 International Journal of Constitutional Law 1 at 15–27.

6   Compare Peter W Hogg, *Canada Act 1982 Annotated* (Toronto: Carswell, 1982) at 26–29.

7   In *Singh v Canada (Minister of Employment and Immigration)*, [1985] 1 SCR 177, one of the earliest cases, the parties agreed that the principles of fundamental justice included "the notion of procedural fairness" (at 212), and those judges who decided the case on *Charter* grounds readily accepted this agreement. The Court did not explain in any detail why procedural fairness was a principle of fundamental justice, though there is considerable discussion of the content of procedural fairness.

8   See the *Motor Vehicle Act*, RSBC 1979, c 288, s 94, as amended by the *Motor Vehicle Amendment Act, 1982*, SBC 1982, c 36, s 19. The legislative history of this provision is briefly described in Andrew Petter, *The Politics of the Charter* (Toronto: University of Toronto Press, 2010) at 68–71.

9   *Motor Vehicle Act, ibid*, s 94(2).

arising after the elements of the offence were established (for example, the defence of necessity). The government of British Columbia referred the question of the constitutionality of this offence to the British Columbia Court of Appeal, and that court struck down section 94(2). The government appealed to the Supreme Court of Canada. If the principles of fundamental justice were equivalent to the rules of natural justice, the appeal would have been allowed: section 94(2), though imposing a harsh form of penal liability, did not interfere with a defendant's procedural rights. He was entitled to a hearing before an independent tribunal, to cross-examine the witnesses against him, and so forth. But because the offence was one of absolute liability, these rights would not be of much help to the defendant who did not know that his licence was suspended.

The Court rejected the province's argument that the principles of fundamental justice were exhausted by the rules of natural justice. In a holding of great significance for Canadian constitutional interpretation generally and for section 7 in particular, the Court held that the meaning of section 7 was not determined by the intentions of its drafters. Evidence relating to those intentions, though admissible, was of "minimal weight," for at least two reasons. First, the relevant "intentions" were not those of the civil servants who wrote the words of the *Charter*, but of the "multiplicity of individuals who played major roles in the negotiating, drafting and adoption of the *Charter*"; and there was no prospect of determining those intentions through evidence.[10] Second, and perhaps more important, to equate the meaning of the words in the Charter with the intentions of the drafters would mean that "the rights, freedoms and values embodied in the *Charter* in effect become frozen in time to the moment of adoption with little or no possibility of growth, development and adjustment to changing societal needs."[11] Unshackled by the intentions of the drafters, and in light of the important interests protected by section 7, the Court held that the principles of fundamental justice, though including procedural fairness, might on a case-by-case basis be extended to substantive principles as well.[12] Whether characterized as procedural or substantive, the principles of fundamental justice were "essential elements of a system for the administration of justice which is founded upon the belief in the dignity and worth of the human person and the rule of law."[13]

---

10   *Motor Vehicle Reference*, above note 1 at 508.
11   *Ibid* at 509. In the same paragraph, Lamer J echoes the metaphor of the constitution as a "living tree": *Edwards v Canada (AG)*, [1930] AC 124 at 136.
12   *Motor Vehicle Reference*, *ibid* at 500–4.
13   *Ibid* at 512; see also Chapter 4, Section C(2).

The Court went on to recognize its first substantive principle of fundamental justice: penal liability requires proof of fault, or to put it another way, "absolute liability in penal law offends the principles of fundamental justice."[14] Since the statute at issue affected liberty (through mandatory imprisonment) and offended the principles of fundamental justice, it infringed section 7: "Absolute liability and imprisonment cannot be combined."[15]

In holding that the principles of fundamental justice included both procedural and substantive principles, the Court not only broadened the grounds of judicial review of legislation in penal law, but also made it inevitable that a wide range of laws would be scrutinized under section 7. If the principles of fundamental justice were limited to procedural rules, it would be difficult indeed to apply them outside the context of proceedings in which the state sought to deprive an individual of life, liberty, and security of the person. But since the principles of fundamental justice include substantive principles, it would be highly artificial to limit them to proceedings.[16] Consider, for example, the principle that the laws should not be arbitrary (see Chapter 4, Section B(3)). If an arbitrary law affects life, liberty, and security of the person, there is no compelling reason to distinguish between laws involving proceedings between the state and the individual and other sorts of laws. In both cases, the interest affected and the substantive principle at stake are the same.

2) Approaching the Principles: 1982–1993

Having decided that the principles of fundamental justice could be either procedural or substantive, and having decided that section 7 applied to a very wide range of laws,[17] the Court still had to decide which principles proposed by *Charter* applicants were so basic or important that they qualified as "principles of fundamental justice" under section 7. The Court's methods for determining this question are extremely important because of the consequences of identifying a principle of fundamental justice. Once the Supreme Court of Canada recognizes a particular legal rule or normative idea as a principle of fundamental justice (and

---

14   *Ibid* at 514.
15   *Ibid* at 492; see also 515.
16   Though Lamer J himself, the author of the majority reasons in the *Motor Vehicle Reference*, maintained this view throughout his judicial career: see Chapter 2, Section D(3)(a).
17   See Chapter 2.

it is likely that only a court can do so),[18] a person has the right that the principle be respected when his or her life, liberty, and security of the person is at stake; that is, the principle of fundamental justice has the same status as rights that are more explicitly described in the *Charter*, such as the right to freedom of expression or the right to counsel on arrest or detention.[19] Moreover, the Court has never withdrawn its recognition of a principle of fundamental justice. And, finally, violations of section 7 are extremely difficult to justify under section 1 of the *Charter*.[20] When the Court transforms a normative idea into a principle of fundamental justice under section 7, it entrenches that idea in the Canadian Constitution in a particularly powerful way.

The early section 7 cases show that the Court was well aware of the significance of identifying a principle of fundamental justice. In the *Motor Vehicle Reference*, Lamer J tried to identify the sense in which these principles were basic or fundamental:

> . . . the principles of fundamental justice are to be found in the basic tenets of our legal system. They do not lie in the realm of general public policy but in the inherent domain of the judiciary as guardian of the justice system.[21]

The principles of fundamental justice were exemplified by the guarantees in sections 8 through 14 of the *Charter*; they might also be expressed in "presumptions of the common law [or] . . . . international conventions on human rights."[22] But the common thread among these principles was not their historical association with a particular legal system or international order but their connection with a normative idea about the function of the law:

> All [of these constitutional, common law, and international principles] have been recognized as elements of a system for the administration of justice which is founded upon a belief in "the dignity and

---

18   Any federal or provincial statute declaring that a particular rule or principle was a principle of fundamental justice for s 7 purposes would likely have little effect. It would not prevent the legislature from enacting another statute that operated notwithstanding the first, or that repealed the first; and it would not be binding on courts.

19   In this sense, the identification of a principle of fundamental justice is similar to the identification of an analogous ground of discrimination under s 15(1) of the *Charter*: compare *Vriend v Alberta*, [1998] 1 SCR 493.

20   See Chapter 6.

21   *Motor Vehicle Reference*, above note 1 at 503; compare 512.

22   *Ibid* at 503.

worth of the human person" (preamble to the *Canadian Bill of Rights*
. . .) and on "the rule of law" (preamble to the *Canadian Charter of
Rights and Freedoms*).[23]

In the *Motor Vehicle Reference* itself, the principle identified was that
penal liability should not be imposed without proof of fault. This principle was an aspect of a larger one: "that the innocent not be punished,"
a principle "founded upon a belief in the dignity and worth of the human person and on the rule of law."[24] Absolute liability offended the
principle that the innocent not be punished because it permitted the
conviction of those who, though they had committed a prohibited act,
were in no way at fault in doing so. The requirement of fault was supported with reference to the ancient maxim *actus non facit reum nisi
mens sit rea*, to academic authority, and to the presumption that penal
statutes should be interpreted to require fault.[25]

It would, no doubt, have been possible to use similar sources to
argue that the principle of no liability without fault was not fundamental, not a basic tenet of our legal system; this argument would have
been based on the existence of absolute liability offences in penal statutes, including the *Criminal Code* itself, and on the historical fact that
mens rea principles were not always securely recognized at common
law but developed gradually over time. But this interpretive possibility
does not show that the Court was wrong to conclude that the principle of no liability without fault was a principle of fundamental justice
under section 7; it shows, rather, that the identification of a principle
of fundamental justice is not a purely historical exercise. Instead, it is
an exercise in identifying and giving legal recognition to those values
that are appropriate to a constitutional order founded upon principles
that include respect for human dignity, the recognition of basic human
rights, and the rule of law.[26] It is the Court's reading of its sources in
the light of those values that makes the principle of no liability without
fault into a basic tenet of the legal system. The process of determining the principles of fundamental justice is informed by the history of
our legal system and by the intentions of the drafters of the constitution, but it is not reducible to those sources; it is rather a process of
determining the values that are sufficiently fundamental to restrain

---

23   *Ibid.*
24   *Ibid.*
25   *Ibid* at 513–15. The English and Canadian (pre-*Charter*) authorities cited in fa-
     vour of this presumption are *Harding v Price*, [1948] 1 KB 695; *R v Beaver*, [1957]
     SCR 531; *R v Sault Ste Marie (City)*, [1978] 2 SCR 1299 [*Sault Ste Marie*].
26   Compare *Reference re Secession of Quebec*, [1998] 2 SCR 217 at paras 49–82.

the exercise of state power when the subject's most vital interests—life, liberty, and security of the person—are at stake.

In light of the approach in the *Motor Vehicle Reference*, the principles of fundamental justice recognized in subsequent cases were usually linked not only to important legal ideas that pre-existed the *Charter* but also to the values appropriate to a constitutional order that respected human dignity. In *R v Nova Scotia Pharmaceutical Society*,[27] for example, the Court held that it was a principle of fundamental justice that the law should not be vague. The recognition of this principle was supported by early *Charter* cases,[28] American constitutional decisions,[29] and the jurisprudence of the European Court of Human Rights; but its content was crucially informed by two rationales that run through these sources: "fair notice to the citizen and limitation of [law] enforcement discretion."[30] These rationales themselves derive from the requirement that the state treat its subjects with respect: without that overarching requirement, there would be no particular reason to provide fair notice or to limit the discretion of law enforcement officials.

The Court's decision in *R v Hebert* (*Hebert*),[31] recognizing a pre-trial right to silence as a principle of fundamental justice, proceeds similarly. The right to silence is connected with pre-*Charter* doctrines such as the confessions rule and the statutory privilege against self-incrimination[32] and to other *Charter* rights such as the right to counsel on arrest (section 10(*b*)) and the right against self-incrimination at trial (section 11(*c*)).[33] But the Court could just as easily have used these sources to support the conclusion that the right to silence was not a fundamental tenet of our justice system. There was an abundance of pre-*Charter* material suggesting that there was no right to silence as such, merely an absence of statutory obligation to co-operate with the police;[34] the

---

27 *R v Nova Scotia Pharmaceutical Society* (1992), 15 C.R. (4th) 1 (SCC) [*Nova Scotia Pharmaceutical Society*].

28 Particularly *Reference re ss 193 and 195.1(1)(c) of the Criminal Code*, [1990] 1 SCR 1123 [*Prostitution Reference*]; and *Committee for the Commonwealth of Canada v Canada*, [1991] 1 SCR 139.

29 Particularly *Village of Hoffman Estates v Flipside, Hoffman Estates, Inc*, 455 US 489 (1982).

30 *Nova Scotia Pharmaceutical Society*, above note 27 at 2. The content of the doctrine of vagueness is discussed in more detail in Chapter 4, Section B(1).

31 *R v Hebert*, [1990] 2 SCR 151 [*Hebert*].

32 *Ibid* at 165–75.

33 *Ibid* at 176–79.

34 See for example Ed Ratushny, *Self-Incrimination* (Toronto: Carswell, 1979) at 185–87, and the doubts about *Hebert* expressed by Stanley Schiff, *Evidence in the Litigation Process*, 4th Master ed (Scarborough, ON: Carswell, 1993) at 1441–43.

precise police trick used in *Hebert* had been held to be unobjectionable at common law;[35] and sections 8 through 14 of the *Charter*, though recognizing a right to silence at trial,[36] are silent about the pre-trial right to silence. Thus, the crucial move in *Hebert* is the recognition that the pre-trial right to silence is required on normative grounds to protect the detainees' right to choose whether or not to speak to persons in authority, a right flowing from the requirement that the state make its case against the accused without her forced testimony;[37] but this limit on state power is in turn required because the state is required to respect the human dignity of the individual accused in the investigative process.

The process of identifying a principle of fundamental justice by considering not just the principles actually embodied in the Canadian legal system but also its implicit normative values was extended to a limit perhaps never to be exceeded in *R v Vaillancourt* (*Vaillancourt*) and *R v Martineau* (*Martineau*).[38] These cases involved constitutional challenges to so-called "constructive murder." The core definition of murder, embodied in section 229(*a*) (formerly section 212(*a*)) of the *Criminal Code*, defines murder as a culpable homicide committed with one of three mental states, all of which require proof of some form of subjective intention to cause the death of the victim; but section 230 (formerly section 213) of the Code also defines murder as causing death "while committing or attempting to commit" one of several stated offences in defined circumstances, whether or not the Crown can prove the mental states mentioned in section 229. These forms of murder are called "constructive" because proof of the circumstances defined by section 230 is a substitute for the usual requirement that the Crown prove intent; in the absence of section 230, such a culpable homicide would be manslaughter. In *Vaillancourt*, the Supreme Court of Canada held that one type of constructive murder[39] was unconstitutional because it offended a principle of fundamental justice: "that, absent proof beyond a reasonable doubt of at least objective foreseeability, there . . .

---

35 See *R v Rothman*, [1981] 1 SCR 640.

36 *Canadian Charter of Rights and Freedoms*, Part I of the *Constitution Act, 1982*, being Schedule B to the *Canada Act 1982* (UK), 1982, c 11, s 111(*c*) [*Charter*].

37 See Hamish Stewart, "The Confessions Rule and the *Charter*" (2009) 54 McGill LJ 517.

38 *R v Vaillancourt*, [1987] 2 SCR 636 [*Vaillancourt*]; *R v Martineau*, [1990] 2 SCR 633 [*Martineau*]. These cases are discussed in more detail in Chapter 4, Section C(4).

39 The section at issue was the subsequently repealed s 213(*d*) of the *Criminal Code*, RSC 1970, c C-34.

cannot be a murder conviction."[40] In *Martineau*, the Court replaced this principle with a stronger one, holding that "the stigma and punishment attached to a murder conviction must be reserved to those who either intend to cause death or who intend to cause bodily harm that they know will likely cause death."[41] But where did these principles come from? There is no doubt that the core definition of murder is deeply rooted in the common law tradition; but so is the doctrine of felony murder that lies behind section 230 and that remains in force in many American jurisdictions.[42] It would be very difficult to show via a purely historical analysis that the core definition of murder was any more fundamental than felony murder. So Lamer J, writing for the majority in both cases, relied on an explicitly normative argument in support of the proposition that the fault-based distinction between murder and manslaughter was a principle of fundamental justice: murder was a crime carrying a "special stigma," the stigma of one who intentionally causes death, and the most severe penalty in the *Criminal Code*; accordingly, it was unjust to label and penalize those who did not intend to cause death as if they had. Lamer J held that murder was constitutionally different from manslaughter not just because the offence of culpable homicide developed historically to distinguish between intentional and unintentional killing, but also because justice requires there to be a difference.

3) A Three-Part Test: 1993 and After

It was perhaps inevitable that the broad and generous but somewhat vague approach to identifying principles of fundamental justice would, in due course, give way to a more structured method. In *Rodriguez v British Columbia (AG)* (*Rodriguez*), decided in 1993, Sopinka J summarized the approach to determining the principles of fundamental justice, as laid out in the *Motor Vehicle Reference* and subsequent cases, as follows:

> . . . the principles of fundamental justice . . . [are], as the term implies, principles upon which there is some consensus that they are vital or fundamental to our societal notion of justice . . . . Principles of

---

40   *Vaillancourt*, above note 38 at 654.

41   *Martineau*, above note 38 at 646.

42   For an attempt to explain and rationalize some of the doctrinal features of the American felony murder doctrine, see Claire Finkelstein, "Merger and Felony Murder" in RA Duff & Stuart Green, eds, *Defining Crimes: Essays on the Special Part of the Criminal Law* (Oxford: Oxford University Press, 2005) 218.

fundamental justice must not, however, be so broad as to be no more than vague generalizations about what our society considers to be ethical or moral. They must be capable of being identified with some precision and applied to situations in a manner which yields and understandable result. They must also . . . be legal principles.[43]

In subsequent cases, this summary has been read as establishing a three-part test for determining whether a proposed norm qualifies as a principle of fundamental justice under section 7. In 2004, McLachlin CJC summarized this approach as follows:

> . . . a "principle of fundamental justice" must fulfill three criteria . . . . First, it must be a legal principle. . . . Second, there must be sufficient consensus that the alleged principle is "vital or fundamental to our societal notions of justice" . . . . The principles of fundamental justice are the shared assumptions upon which our system of justice is grounded. They find their meaning in the cases and traditions that have long detailed the basic norms for how the state deals with its citizens. Society views them as essential to the administration of justice. Third, the alleged principle must be capable of being identified with precision and applied to situations in a manner that yields predictable results.[44]

A few words on each element of this test are in order.

The first and third elements of the test, taken together, require that a principle of fundamental justice be a legal principle capable of being identified with some precision. These requirements are unsurprising and unexceptional. The Constitution, with all of its components including the *Charter*, is the "supreme law" of Canada[45]—the requirement that a principle of fundamental justice be a legal principle simply restates the legal quality of the *Charter*. But this requirement need not be especially restrictive; it does not exclude legal principles that have moral content or that have parallels in morality. For example: it is a principle of fundamental justice that a law not be vague,[46] but a norm against vagueness could also apply to moral rules and principles; the principle of no blame without fault might apply to judgments of moral culpability as well as to judgments of legal culpability. The requirement

---

43   *Rodriguez v British Columbia (AG)*, [1993] 3 SCR 519 at 590–91 [*Rodriguez*].

44   *Canadian Foundation for Children, Youth and the Law v Canada (AG)*, 2004 SCC 4 at para 8; see also *R v Malmo-Levine; R v Caine*, 2003 SCC 74 at paras 112–13, Gonthier and Binnie JJ [*Malmo-Levine*], aff'g 2000 BCCA 335 [*Malmo-Levine (CA)*].

45   *Charter*, above note 36, s 152(1).

46   See Chapter 4, Section B(1).

that a principle of fundamental justice be capable of being identified with some precision reflects, at the constitutional level, the same requirement of certainty that is itself a principle of fundamental justice (in the form that a law should not be vague). Where a court measures the content of legislation against a constitutionalized legal principle, and has the power to invalidate the legislation if it does not comply with that principle, it is essential that the principle be sufficiently precise that the public, the legislature, and other courts and tribunals understand exactly what is the defect in the legislation that leads to its invalidation and how that defect might be cured. A generalized assessment of the injustice of the legislation, or "vague generalizations about what our society considers to be ethical or moral,"[47] would not be adequate for these purposes.

The second element—the requirement of "sufficient consensus"—is more difficult to understand and to apply. These difficulties flow in part from the Court's unfortunate suggestion that whether a legal principle is a principle of fundamental justice is a matter of societal consensus. The exercise of interpreting the Constitution according to the intentions or opinions of a specific group of actual persons (the drafters of the *Charter*) was rejected on both practical and principled grounds in the *Motor Vehicle Reference*—the existence of a social consensus that the principle of "no liability without fault" is fundamental to the justice system would be significantly harder to prove or define. Moreover, while the early cases indicate that the principles of fundamental justice are "fundamental" in the sense that they are basic to the operation of the justice system, they also make it clear that these principles are not matters of "general public policy," to which societal consensus in the empirical sense might indeed be relevant, but lie "in the inherent domain of the judiciary as guardians of the justice system."[48] In light of this understanding, it is very difficult to imagine that a court could accept, for example, opinion surveys or poll results as evidence relevant to the recognition of a proposed legal principle as a principle of fundamental justice.

Fortunately, the second requirement can be understood in a way that is more consistent with the early section 7 cases and with the constitutional status of the principles of fundamental justice. The principles of fundamental justice are norms that control the content of the law and the process of the administration of justice in a legal order committed to respecting human dignity and the rule of law: these val-

---

47 *Rodriguez*, above note 43 at 591.
48 *Motor Vehicle Reference*, above note 1 at 503.

ues themselves provide the societal consensus necessary to the recognition of a principle of fundamental justice. Sopinka J's reasoning in *Rodriguez* itself provides an example. In that case, the Court addressed the difficult legal question of whether a legislative prohibition on assisted suicide was consistent with the principles of fundamental justice. While recognizing that the legal history of this prohibition was "helpful" in resolving the question, Sopinka J also pointed to the limits of history as a determinant of the principles of fundamental justice:

> It is not sufficient . . . to conduct a historical review and conclude that because neither Parliament nor the various medical associations had ever expressed a view that assisted suicide should be decriminalized, that to prohibit it could not be contrary to the principles of fundamental justice. Such an approach would be problematic for two reasons. First, a strictly historical analysis will always lead to the conclusion in a case such as this that the deprivation is in accordance with fundamental justice . . . . Second, such reasoning is somewhat circular, in that it relies on the continuing existence of the prohibition to find the prohibition to be fundamentally just.[49]

The way out of this circularity was to consider "not just at the existence of the practice itself . . . , but at the rationale behind that practice and the principles that underlie it,"[50] which is to say, its normative justification in the context of the Canadian legal order, including the *Charter* itself.

Like a purely historical analysis, a strictly empirical investigation into societal views cannot be decisive in determining whether a particular principle is or is not a principle of fundamental justice; the decisive question is what role the principle plays in a legal order that is committed to the values expressed in the *Charter*. The fact that those values are reflected in existing legal rules or are supported by a significant social consensus shows that the principle has been recognized as fundamental in other contexts but does not by itself make it a principle of fundamental justice; similarly, a refusal to recognize the principle in other contexts does not mean that it is not a principle of fundamental justice if it can be shown by a normatively infused legal argument to be fundamental to the system of justice. And, as will be seen in more detail in Chapters 4 and 5, courts applying the three-part test for determining a principle of fundamental justice have never conducted the kind of empirical investigation suggested by the phrase "societal

---

49 *Rodriguez*, above note 43 at 591–92.
50 *Ibid* at 592.

consensus" but have engaged in the type of normative analysis that is appropriate to section 7 of the *Charter*.

4) The Balancing of Interests

a) Balancing and the Principles of Fundamental Justice

Although the principles of fundamental justice constrain the state's pursuit of its objectives by protecting the most basic individual interests, it has frequently been held that the principles of fundamental justice do not only reflect the interests of the individual *Charter* applicant. For example, the right to a fair trial, though it is the right of the individual accused person, is not the right to the most favourable procedure imaginable.[51] Nor could it be: taken to its illogical extreme, the right to a trial most favourable to the accused would be the right to be acquitted regardless of the prosecution's evidence, which would not be a right to a "trial" in any meaningful sense of the word. So the *Charter* right to a fair trial is constructed not with reference to the accused's interest in being acquitted, but with reference to the societal interest in a just resolution of the prosecution's allegations against her; this interest includes both the accused's interest in being tried fairly and the public interest in getting at the truth of the allegations against her. So, for example, one aspect of the constitutional right to a fair trial is the accused's right to cross-examine Crown witnesses and to lead other evidence, but the accused may be prevented from leading evidence where the prejudicial effect of that evidence substantially outweighs its probative value.[52] Admitting this kind of evidence, though it might increase the accused's chances of being acquitted, would interfere with the societal interest in a just resolution of the case by increasing the chance that an acquittal would be based on improper reasoning by the trier of fact. Excluding it does not make the trial unfair.

In light of this kind of rationale, it is sometimes said that the principles of fundamental justice represent a balance between individual and societal interests. Indeed, at one time it appeared that the requirement to strike a proper balance between these interests might itself be a principle of fundamental justice. In *Cunningham v Canada* (*Cunningham*),[53] an inmate serving a sentence for manslaughter challenged certain changes to the *Parole Act*[54] that made it more difficult for him to be

---

51   See, for example, *R v Lyons*, [1987] 2 SCR 309 at 361–62 [*Lyons*]; *R v Rose*, [1998] 3 SCR 262 at para 99.

52   *R v Seaboyer*, [1991] 2 SCR 577.

53   *Cunningham v Canada*, [1993] 2 SCR 143 [*Cunningham*].

54   RSC 1985, c P-2.

paroled. Specifically, before the change, he was entitled to release after serving two-thirds of his sentence with good behaviour; but after the change, the Commissioner of Corrections could (and did) refer him to the National Parole Board within six months of his anticipated release date for continued detention on the ground that he was likely to commit an offence causing death or serious bodily harm before the expiration of his sentence. The Court, speaking unanimously *per* McLachlin J, rejected his challenge. Although the changes to the *Parole Act* engaged the applicant's liberty interest, they were not contrary to the principles of fundamental justice:

> The principles of fundamental justice are concerned not only with the interest of the person who claims his liberty has been limited, but with the protection of society. Fundamental justice requires that a fair balance be struck between these interests, both substantively and procedurally. . . . In my view the balance struck in this case conforms to this requirement.[55]

This comment naturally led some readers to conclude that "striking a fair balance" was itself a principle of fundamental justice. But McLachlin J went on to hold that the changes to the *Parole Act* did not offend any substantive or procedural principles of fundamental justice. On the substantive side, she noted that parole, though affecting the liberty interest, is in effect a "change in the form in which a sentence is served" and that such a change "is not, in itself, contrary to any principle of fundamental justice."[56] This reasoning would be easier to follow if she had specified the particular substantive principles against which the changes to the *Parole Act* were being measured, but one can speculate that she would have held, for example, that the changes did not offend the principle against arbitrariness because they were justified by the need to protect the public.[57] On the procedural side, she noted that the inmate had notice of the commissioner's referral of his case to the board and was entitled to a hearing before the board and to further review of the detention: "These requirements provide safeguards against arbitrary, capricious orders and ensure that curtailment of release on mandatory supervision occurs only when it is required to protect the public and then only after the interests of the prisoner in obtaining the release have been fully and fairly canvassed."[58] In other

---

55   *Cunningham*, above note 53 at 151–52.
56   *Ibid* at 152.
57   *Ibid* at 153.
58   *Ibid* at 153–54.

words, *Cunningham* can be read as holding that the changes to the *Parole Act* were not arbitrary and that the new procedure they created was procedurally fair; thus, no recognized principle of fundamental justice was violated, and it was not necessary to recognize a new principle of "fair balancing."[59]

Moreover, a broad principle of "fair balancing" would suffer from precisely the imprecision and vague generalization that the three-part test for a principle of fundamental justice strives to avoid. The idea of fair balancing, though undoubtedly an aspect of various principles of fundamental justice, does not in itself point to any particular virtue or defect that a law or an administrative decision might have; more specific principles do. For example, the principle that a law should not be arbitrary (see Chapter 4, Section B) requires that there should be a good reason for affecting a section 7 interest; the principle that a law should not be overbroad (see Chapter 4, Section B(3)) requires that a law should not affect the interest protected by section 7 in situations where doing so would not advance the purposes of the law. Such principles cover much of the ground that a principle of fair balancing would cover, but do so in a more focused way.

In *R v Malmo-Levine*[60] (*Malmo-Levine*), the Supreme Court confirmed the view that "striking a fair balance" was not a principle of fundamental justice as such. The *Charter* applicants argued that the prohibition on marijuana possession under the *Controlled Drugs and Substances Act* was contrary to the *Charter* in various ways. The British Columbia Court of Appeal treated balancing— "whether the impugned provision strikes the right balance between the rights of the individual and the interests of the State"[61]—as a distinct step in the section 7 analysis, in addition to the question of whether the legislation violated a recognized principle of fundamental justice. Having recognized the harm principle as a principle of fundamental justice and having con-

---

59 See, in the same vein, *Godbout v Longueil (City)*, [1997] 3 SCR 844. A municipal employee challenged a rule of the municipality requiring new employees to live within its boundaries. The majority resolved the case under the Quebec *Charter*. A minority of three judges characterized the s 7 issue as follows (at para 76): "whether the right to life, liberty or security of the person asserted by the individual can, in the circumstances, justifiably be violated given the interests or purposes sought to be advanced in doing so." The minority found that the municipal rule did not satisfy this requirement. This approach to the s 7 issue resembles the principle of "fair balancing" apparently advanced in *Cunningham* but can be rationalized in the same way: a law that failed this test would be arbitrary in the s 7 sense.

60 *Malmo-Levine*, above note 44.

61 *Malmo-Levine* (CA), above note 44 at para 59.

cluded that the prohibition on marijuana possession did not violate it, the Court of Appeal went on to ask whether the prohibition struck the right balance.[62] The Supreme Court rejected this approach, holding that the correct balancing of interests is neither a "free-standing" step in the section 7 analysis nor "an overarching principle of fundamental justice" in its own right.[63] Instead, the balancing of interests may play a role in the identification of the principles of fundamental justice: "The balancing of individual and societal interests within s. 7 is only relevant when elucidating a particular principle of fundamental justice."[64] So a particular principle of fundamental justice, like the right to a fair trial mentioned above, may contain a balancing of interests within it. But the balancing of interests "is not in and of itself a freestanding principle of fundamental justice."[65]

b) Case-by-Case Balancing

Despite this rejection of balancing as a free-standing principle of fundamental justice, there is one context in which the idea of striking a fair balance does function, for all intents and purposes, as a principle of fundamental justice. As noted in Chapter 2, Section B(3), a discretionary decision by a state official can be challenged under the *Charter* even though the statute under which the decision was made is not itself challenged. Where the *Charter* challenge is based on section 7, it is rarely argued that the decision infringed any particular principle of fundamental justice; rather, it is usually argued simply that the decision violated the applicant's section 7 rights because it did not correctly balance the interests at stake — the applicant's interest in life, liberty, and security of the person on the one hand, and the public purposes forwarded by the decision on the other.

Thus, in making a specific decision, pursuant to an otherwise valid discretionary power, that engages the section 7 interests, a decision maker is required to balance interests; and in reviewing that decision, the court is revisiting the balance, with the degree of deference appropriate to the decision. Although the proper balancing of interests is not a principle of fundamental justice applicable in reviewing legislation, it appears to be a principle of fundamental justice applicable in the review of particular discretionary decisions. Section 7 challenges

---

62   *Ibid* at paras 144–57.
63   *Malmo-Levine*, above note 44 at para 96.
64   *Ibid* at para 98.
65   *R v Demers*, 2004 SCC 46 at para 45.

of this kind are particularly common in deportation and extradition proceedings.

i)   Balancing in Deportation Proceedings

Suresh v Canada (Minister of Citizenship and Immigration) (*Suresh*)[66] provides a dramatic example of this sort of reasoning. The applicant, a Sri Lankan national, had been granted refugee status in Canada, but the Minister of Citizenship and Immigration sought to deport him to Sri Lanka on security grounds.[67] The applicant resisted deportation on the ground that he faced a substantial risk of torture on his return, and that to return him in these circumstances would be contrary to the principles of fundamental justice. In considering the constitutionality of otherwise valid statutory provisions that, on their face, permitted the government to return the applicant to be tortured, the Court did not invoke any particular principles of fundamental justice,[68] and in particular did not hold that deportation to torture was itself contrary to the principles of fundamental justice. Instead, the Court held that, in effect, the statutory provisions were constitutionally valid because the Minister had to conduct a constitutionally adequate balancing of interests before deporting to torture. While the fact that the applicant faced torture weighed very heavily against deportation, the issue was ultimately one of balancing:

> The Minister is obliged to exercise the discretion conferred upon her by the *Immigration Act* in accordance with the Constitution. This requires the Minister to balance the relevant factors in the case before her. . . . the balance struck by the Minister must conform to the

---

66   *Suresh v Canada (Minister of Citizenship and Immigration)*, 2002 SCC 1 [*Suresh*]. *Suresh* was decided less than two years before *Malmo-Levine* but is not cited in the Court's discussion of the balancing of interests.

67   More specifically, the Solicitor General and the Minister of Citizenship and Immigration issued a security certificate under a predecessor to current s 77 of the *Immigration and Refugee Protection Act*, SC 2001, c 27 [*IRPA*], and a judge of the Federal Court found the certificate to be reasonable; accordingly, it became a deportation order, which was issued by an adjudicator. The Minister issued a danger opinion under s 115(2) of *IRPA*, which enabled him to return the applicant to Sri Lanka notwithstanding his refugee status. The applicant applied for judicial review of the Minister's decision.

68   The Court did consider some specific s 7 claims: it rejected the applicant's contention that some phrases in the statute were unconstitutionally vague (*Suresh*, above note 66 at paras 80–99) and held that s 7 required the Minister to treat the applicant fairly (*ibid* at paras 113–28). But its decision on these points did not determine the question of whether it was constitutional to deport the applicant to torture.

principles of fundamental justice under s. 7 of the *Charter*. It follows that insofar as the *Immigration Act* leaves open the possibility of deportation to torture, the Minister should generally decline to deport refugees where on the evidence there is a substantial risk of torture.

We do not exclude the possibility that in exceptional circumstances, deportation to face torture might be justified, either as a consequence of the balancing process mandated by s. 7 of the *Charter* or under s. 1. . . . [T]he fundamental justice balance. . . . generally precludes deportation to torture when applied on a case-by-case basis.[69]

The Court's accepting the possibility that deportation to torture might be consistent with the principles of fundamental justice is extremely troubling. Torture is such a profound assault on the victim's physical and psychological integrity, indeed on the victim's very sense of himself or herself as a person,[70] that neither its infliction by an agent of the Canadian state nor the Canadian state's involvement in sending a person to be tortured by another state can comply with the principles of fundamental justice. Moreover, deporting a refugee to face torture is contrary to Canada's international obligations, which are themselves a source of the principles of fundamental justice. Torture is so abhorrent, and the norm against refoulement to torture is so well established in international law, that deportation to torture surely cannot be consistent with section 7, regardless of the degree of procedural fairness afforded to the *Charter* applicant during the decision-making process.[71] And any compelling interest that Canada might have in the deportation of a refugee could be satisfied, consistently with the principles of fundamental justice, by seeking and obtaining assurances that the refugee would not be tortured; if such assurances could not be obtained or were not satisfactory, the danger that the refugee might pose in Canada could be controlled under domestic Canadian law, including if necessary the peace bond procedure in section 810.01 of the *Criminal Code*. The right

---

69 *Ibid* at paras 77–78.

70 See Elaine Scarry, *The Body in Pain* (New York: Oxford University Press, 1985) ch 2.

71 Many commentators have made these points: see, among others, Jutta Brunnée & Stephen J Toope, *Legitimacy and Legality in International Law* (Cambridge: Cambridge University Press, 2010) at 220–70; D Jenkins, "Rethinking *Suresh*: Refoulement to Torture under Canada's *Canadian Charter of Rights and Freedoms*" (2009) 47 Alta L Rev 125; Kent Roach, "Must We Trade Rights for Security? The Choice Between Smart, Harsh, or Proportionate Security Strategies in Canada and Britain" (2006) 27 Cardozo L Rev 2151.

solution in *Suresh* would have been to recognize a right against deportation to torture under section 7 of the *Charter,* either as a principle of
fundamental justice in its own right, or through the doctrine of *per se*
gross disproportionality (see Chapter 4, Section B(4)). Put another way,
torture has such a severe impact on the interests protected by section 7
that no state interest could be proportionate to it.

Indeed, the suggestion in *Suresh* that the principles of fundamental
justice might permit a person to be deported to torture is so implausible that it casts additional doubt on the very idea of case-by-case balancing under section 7. Where the fundamental individual interests
protected by section 7 are at stake, the individual has a right not just to
have those interests taken into account or weighed against other interests, but to have those interests protected unless their deprivation is in
accord with an identifiable principle of fundamental justice. Nonetheless, case-by-case balancing often occurs in judicial review of certain
kinds of executive decisions.

ii)   Balancing in Extradition Proceedings

Where the Minister of Justice orders a person's surrender to face criminal trial in another state, the decision is subject to review on section 7
grounds even though the power under which the Minister acts is constitutionally valid.[72] The Minister's exercise of discretion to surrender
the person sought will violate the principles of fundamental justice
"where the nature of the criminal procedures or penalties in a foreign
country sufficiently shocks the conscience"[73] or where the situation the
person surrendered would face is "simply unacceptable."[74] The Court's
application of this standard to the Minister's surrender decision does
not involve a reassessment of the Minister's balancing of the factors
in favour of and against surrender, but an assessment of whether "the
Minister's decision falls within a range of reasonable outcomes."[75]

---

72   *Kindler v Canada (Minister of Justice),* [1991] 2 SCR 779 at 850–57 [*Kindler*]
     (Minister's power to surrender fugitive constitutionally valid, but Minister's
     conduct in surrendering fugitive subject to s 7 scrutiny); *United States v Burns,*
     2001 SCC 7 at paras 32–35 [*Burns*]. See also *Argentina (Republic) v Mellino,*
     [1987] 1 SCR 536 at 555–56; *United States v Allard,* [1987] 1 SCR 564 at 572
     (surrendering a person for trial in accordance with foreign procedures does not
     itself offend the principles of fundamental justice).

73   *Canada v Schmidt,* [1987] 1 SCR 500 at 522. This standard has been restated
     many times: see, for example, *Burns, ibid* at para 60; *Lake v Canada (Minister of
     Justice),* 2008 SCC 23 at para 32 [*Lake*].

74   *Kindler,* above note 72 at 791.

75   *Lake,* above note 73 at para 41.

It is rare for a surrender decision to be set aside on these grounds. The requesting state is in the great majority of cases the United States of America, which has a criminal justice system that is in many respects significantly harsher than the Canadian one. The principle of double criminality enshrined in the relevant extradition treaty[76] ensures that no-one will be extradited to the United States for conduct that is not an offence in Canada. But the sentencing regime in the United States, under both state and federal criminal law, is often much more severe than in Canada. Generally speaking, even extreme disparities in sentencing will not amount to conditions that shock the conscience so as to require the Minister to refuse, on constitutional grounds, to surrender the person sought.[77]

The Supreme Court of Canada has, however, recognized that there are situations in which the surrender of the person sought would violate that person's section 7 rights. Where the death penalty is an available punishment for the offence in the requesting state (usually the United States), the Minister of Justice must normally seek and obtain assurances that the death penalty will not be imposed; failure to do so would usually violate the person's section 7 rights.[78] In reaching this conclusion, the Supreme Court considered, or balanced, factors favouring extradition without assurances: these included the need to bring charged individuals to trial in the jurisdiction where the offence was allegedly committed[79] and the need to maintain the "international network of mutual assistance that enables states to deal both with crimes in their own jurisdiction and transnational crimes with elements that occur in more than one jurisdiction."[80] The factors favouring extradition dependent on assurances included the abolition of the death penalty around the world and in Canada itself,[81] state practice supporting extradition with assurances,[82] and perhaps most importantly, a substantial body of evidence indicating the real possibility of wrongful convictions, particularly in murder cases.[83] None of the factors weighing for or against extradition with assurances had anything

---

76   *Treaty on Extradition Between the Government of Canada and the Government of the United States*, 3 December 1971, Can TS 1976 No 3, Art 2(1).
77   See, for example, *United States v K(JH)* (2002), 165 CCC (3d) 449 (Ont CA), leave to appeal to SCC refused, [2002] SCCA No 501; *United States v Magnifico*, 2007 ONCA 535.
78   *Burns*, above note 72 at paras 124–32.
79   *Ibid* at para 72.
80   *Ibid* at para 73.
81   *Ibid* at paras 76–81 and paras 90–92.
82   *Ibid* at paras 82–84.
83   *Ibid* at paras 95–117.

to do with the nationality or other circumstances of the two persons sought, the crime they allegedly committed, or the particular concerns of the requesting state. The Court found that the balance between these factors usually requires the Minister to seek and obtain assurances whenever the requesting state seeks to impose the death penalty.[84]

In *Karas v Canada (Minister of Justice)*,[85] Thailand sought the fugitive's extradition on a charge of murder for which the death penalty was available. The relevant extradition treaty did not provide for assurances; however, on the basis of material provided by Thai authorities, the Minister concluded that "it could not reasonably be anticipated that the [fugitive] would face the jeopardy of execution in Thailand if convicted."[86] The British Columbia Court of Appeal found that in these circumstances the Minister's decision to surrender the fugitive without seeking assurances was not unreasonable.[87]

The Supreme Court of Canada has, however, left open the possibility that in an exceptional case, the Minister might be able to justify the surrender decision under section 1 of the *Charter*;[88] in such a case, the balancing of interests that the Court contemplates under section 7 in *Suresh*[89] would occur under section 1 instead, and would be open to the same objections.

Cases where the extradition proceeding itself is impugned as an abuse of process are considered in Chapter 5, Section C.

5) Some Rejected Principles

The Supreme Court of Canada has considered and rejected a number of proposed principles of fundamental justice. Its reasons for doing so help to illustrate its methodology for defining a principle of fundamental justice.

---

84 *Burns* must therefore also be read as reversing *Kindler*, above note 72, where a majority found that the s 7 balance did not generally require the Minister to seek or obtain assurances.

85 *Karas v Canada (Minister of Justice)*, 2009 BCCA 1 [*Karas*].

86 *Ibid* at para 15.

87 *Ibid* at para 32.

88 *Burns*, above note 72 at para 133. The Minister took the view that *Karas* was such an exceptional case, and the British Columbia Court of Appeal found it unnecessary to decide the point: *Karas*, above note 85 at para 33.

89 *Suresh*, above note 66.

a) Principles Related to the Criminal Law Power

In *Reference re ss 193 and 195.1(1)(c) of the Criminal Code* (the *Prostitution Reference*),[90] the Court held that the principles of fundamental justice did not require what might be called "direct" criminalization of an undesirable activity; "indirect" criminalization is constitutionally permissible. The issue arose as follows. In Canadian criminal law, in contrast to the criminal law of many American states, an act of prostitution is not an offence. It is not a crime for an adult to engage in sexual activity in exchange for money or other favours.[91] But most activities ancillary to prostitution are offences: keeping a common bawdy-house,[92] procuring a person to engage in "illicit sexual intercourse,"[93] living "wholly or in part on the avails of prostitution,"[94] communicating in a public place for the purpose of prostitution.[95] In short, while adult prostitution is not an offence, it is very difficult to carry on prostitution as a business without committing an offence. In the *Prostitution Reference*, it was argued that "by creating a legal environment indirectly making it, in effect, impossible for a prostitute to sell sex, Parliament has offended the principles of fundamental justice."[96] Dickson CJC rejected this argument, commenting that while Parliament had "chosen a circuitous path" to achieve its objective, there was no constitutional impediment to its doing so.[97] Although Dickson CJC does not put the point this way, it might be said that there is nothing in either our legal traditions or the normative idea of a rights-protecting state that requires the state to criminalize undesirable activity directly rather than indirectly.

In *United Nurses of Alberta v Alberta (AG)*, the Court held that the principles of fundamental justice did not require the codification of all criminal offences.[98] In rejecting the proposed principle, McLachlin J referred mainly to legal history and to some realities of statutory interpretation:

---

90 *Prostitution Reference*, above note 28.
91 It is an offence if the person providing the sexual services is under 18: *Criminal Code*, RSC 1985, c C-46, s 212(4).
92 *Criminal Code, ibid*, s 210.
93 *Ibid*, s 212(1)(a).
94 *Ibid*, ss 212(1)(j), (2), & (2.1).
95 *Ibid*, s 213.
96 *Prostitution Reference*, above note 28 at 1142, Dickson CJC, characterizing a constitutional challenge.
97 *Ibid*. Lamer J rejected this argument for a different reason: he saw it as amounting to a claim that s 7 protected the right to carry on a particular profession, and held that it did not; thus, the claim did not engage the liberty interest. Compare Chapter 2, Section D(3)(a).
98 *United Nurses of Alberta v Alberta (AG)*, [1992] 1 SCR 901 at 930.

For many centuries, most of our crimes were uncodified and were not viewed as violating this fundamental rule. Nor, conversely, is codification a guarantee that all is made manifest in the *Code*. Definition of elements of codified crimes not infrequently requires recourse to common law concepts . . . .[99]

In light of the three-part test for identifying a principle of fundamental justice, it might be said that, no matter how precise the statutory definition of an offence appears to be, given our legal traditions and practices and in particular the strong presumption in favour of *mens rea*,[100] there is no consensus that all crimes must be codified.

In *Canadian Foundation for Children, Youth and the Law v Canada (AG)* (*Canadian Foundation*), the Ontario Court of Appeal commented that while "it is an essential purpose of the criminal law to protect members of society from invasion of their physical security," no principle of fundamental justice requires Parliament to do so.[101] While the Supreme Court of Canada did not expressly disagree with this holding, there is reason to believe that the Court implicitly accepted the proposition that Parliament's failure to enact any protections for physical security would at least engage section 7 of the *Charter* (see Chapter 2, Section D).

b) Substantive Principles

In *Malmo-Levine*, the Court held that the "harm principle" was not a principle of fundamental justice. The accused persons challenged the offence of simple possession of marijuana. They submitted, among other points, that conduct could not be criminalized unless it caused harm to someone other than the user. The Court understood this submission as an effort to constitutionalize John Stuart Mill's version of the harm principle, according to which "the only purpose for which power can be rightfully exercised over any member of a civilised community, against his will, is to prevent harm to others."[102] The majority held that Mill's harm principle was not a principle of fundamental justice

---

99 *Ibid.*

100 See particularly *Sault Ste Marie*, above note 25; *Sweet v Parsley*, [1970] 1 AC 132 (HL).

101 *Canadian Foundation for Children, Youth and the Law v Canada (AG)* (2002), 57 OR (3d) 511 at para 32 (CA), aff'd 2004 SCC 4 [*Canadian Foundation*].

102 John Stuart Mill, "On Liberty" in *Collected Works, vol 18: Essays on Politics and Society* ed by JM Robson (Toronto: University of Toronto Press, 1977) at 223; quoted from a different source and emphasized in *Malmo-Levine*, above note 44 at para 106. There are many other versions of the harm principle in the secondary literature on criminalization; see, for example, Joel Feinberg, *Harm*

because there was no consensus that the causation of harm was a necessary condition for criminalization, or that conduct that harms only oneself cannot be criminalized.[103] This lack of consensus was demonstrated largely with reference to the existing offences in the *Criminal Code*, not with reference to sociological data such as public opinion polls; the Court's conclusion would, however, be stronger if it had also considered normative arguments against insisting on harm as a necessary condition for criminalization, in particular the ways in which insisting on the harm principle is in tension with rights protection.[104] The majority also held that the harm principle was not a "manageable standard" because it was possible to make a harm-based argument for or against any given legal prohibition.[105] Thus even assuming that the harm principle was a legal principle it failed the other two steps in the three-part test for identifying a principle of fundamental justice.[106]

In *Canadian Foundation*, the Court rejected the proposition that "the best interests of the child" is a principle of fundamental justice. The applicants argued that section 43 of the *Criminal Code*, permitting parents, teachers, and others in the place of parents to use reasonable force "by way of correction toward a pupil or child," was unconstitutional because, among other things, it was not in the best interests of children for them to be subjected to corporal punishment. The majority held that the requirement that laws affecting children be in the best interests of children was a legal principle, but that there was an insufficient consensus that it was vital or fundamental to justice: there were many legal contexts in which the best interests of a child had to yield to other interests.[107] Moreover, it was not a manageable standard because "[i]ts application is inevitably highly contextual and subject

---

to Others (New York: Oxford University Press, 1984); Joseph Raz, *The Morality of Freedom* (Oxford: Clarendon Press, 1986) at 412–14.

103 *Malmo-Levine*, above note 44 at paras 115–26.

104 See, for instance, Arthur Ripstein, "Beyond the Harm Principle" (2006) 34 Phil & Pub Aff 216; Hamish Stewart, "The Limits of the Harm Principle" (2010) 4 Crim Law and Phil 17.

105 *Malmo-Levine*, above note 44 at paras 127–29. For this point, the majority relies in part on Bernard Harcourt, "The Collapse of the Harm Principle" (1999) 90 J Crim L & Criminology 109, who argues that harm has so often and so successfully been invoked as a justification for penalizing conduct that the harm principle has no constraining effect on American penal law.

106 Arbour J, dissenting in part, accepted a Millian version of the harm principle as a principle of fundamental justice: *Malmo-Levine*, above note 44 at paras 235–51.

107 *Canadian Foundation*, above note 44 at para 10.

to dispute; reasonable people may well disagree about the result of its application."[108]

The majority may well have been correct to reject the principle on the ground of insufficient consensus, though once again the holding would be stronger if it showed some constitutionally acceptable normative reasons for overriding the best interests of the child in some contexts. But it is difficult to accept the holding that the best interests of the child is not a manageable standard, given its widespread use in family law; moreover, the fact that reasonable people disagree about the application of a principle cannot be a bar to recognizing it as a principle of fundamental justice, as that will be the case for many possible principles, including those the Court has already recognized.

A number of cases have held that "respect for human dignity," though it is one of the most important values promoted by section 7, is not itself a principle of fundamental justice.[109] In *Rodriguez*, Sopinka J was concerned that recognizing human dignity as a principle of fundamental justice would collapse the two distinct stages of section 7 analysis: "To state that 'respect for human dignity and autonomy' is a principle of fundamental justice . . . is essentially to state that the deprivation of the [applicant's] security of the person is contrary to the principles of fundamental justice because it deprives her of security of the person."[110] This concern does not seem sufficient in itself to reject respect for human dignity as a principle of fundamental justice; it is not difficult to imagine effects on security of the person (for example, the taking of bodily samples for forensic DNA analysis[111]) that comply with a principle of respect for human dignity because they are conducted lawfully and are minimally intrusive. However, it is likely that the Court would continue to reject "respect for human dignity" as a principle of fundamental justice on the ground that it is insufficiently precise to define acceptable intrusions on life, liberty, and security of the person. Human dignity may be better protected by defining more precise principles of fundamental justice.

---

108 *Ibid* at para 11. The majority does not cite, but must be taken to have overruled, Lamer CJC's recognition of the best interests of the child as a principle of fundamental justice in *New Brunswick (Minister of Health and Community Services) v G(J)*, [1999] 3 SCR 46, 177 DLR (4th) 124 at para 70.

109 *Rodriguez*, above note 43 at 592; *Eutenier v Lee* (2005), 260 DLR (4th) 123 at para 63 (Ont CA).

110 *Rodriguez*, ibid.

111 Compare *R v B(SA)*, 2003 SCC 60.

c) Procedural Principles

i) Prosecutorial Discretion

The existence of prosecutorial discretion does not offend the principles of fundamental justice;[112] put another way, it is not a principle of fundamental justice that the prosecution should have no discretion about how to proceed. "A system that attempted to eliminate discretion would be unworkably complex and rigid."[113] Indeed, it would be more plausible to argue that the prosecutorial discretion is itself a principle of fundamental justice, since it is so basic to the operation of the justice system.

The Supreme Court of Canada has identified the core aspect of prosecutorial discretion as decision making regarding "the nature and extent of the prosecution."[114] This core of decision making includes at least five kinds of decisions:

> (a) the discretion whether to bring the prosecution of a charge laid by police; (b) the discretion to enter a stay of proceedings in either a private or a public prosecution . . . ; (c) the discretion to accept a guilty plea to a lesser charge; (d) the discretion to withdraw from criminal proceedings altogether . . . ; and (e) the discretion to take control of a private prosecution . . . .[115]

The Crown's decision making in these areas is immune from judicial review. The existence and the exercise of prosecutorial discretion in these areas cannot offend the principles of fundamental justice but are rather consistent with them.

Outside these core areas, prosecutorial decision making is not immune from review, but the standard of review is highly deferential. Only in the "rare" cases where "there is conspicuous evidence of improper motives or bad faith or of an act so wrong that it violates the conscience of the community, such that it would genuinely be unfair and indecent to proceed," will the court "intervene to prevent an abuse of process that could bring the administration of justice into disrepute."[116] In such a case, it would not be the existence of prosecutorial discretion but the abuse of that discretion that would violate the principles of fundamental justice.

---

112 *Lyons*, above note 51 at 348; *R v Beare*, [1988] 2 SCR 387 at 410–12 [*Beare*]; *R v VT*, [1992] 1 SCR 749 at 759–64; *R v Cook*, [1997] 1 SCR 1113 at 1122–24.

113 *Beare*, ibid at 410.

114 *Krieger v Law Society of Alberta*, 2002 SCC 65 at para 47.

115 *Ibid* at para 46.

116 *R v Power*, [1994] 1 SCR 601 at 616.

An exercise of prosecutorial discretion was, however, reviewed in *R v C(G)*.[117] The accused, a young person, was charged with manslaughter arising out of a highly publicized homicide. He elected trial by judge alone, but pursuant to section 67(6) of the *Youth Criminal Justice Act*,[118] the Crown sought a direction from the Attorney General that he be tried by judge and jury. Defence counsel made submissions to the Attorney General as to why the accused's election should be respected and asked what the Crown's reasons were for seeking the direction, so that he could respond to them. The Attorney General did not respond to these requests and directed that the accused be tried by judge and jury. The accused applied to the trial judge for an order setting aside the direction. The trial judge found that the Crown's failure to disclose the basis for its request and the Attorney General's failure to give any reasons for his decision amounted to procedural unfairness.[119] The record indicated not only that the accused preferred a trial by judge alone but that there were several reasons to believe it would be easier to conduct a fair trial without a jury.[120] In the absence of any explanation for the Crown's request for a jury trial, the trial judge concluded "that an informed person viewing the matter realistically and practically would conclude that the Crown was seeking a favourable jury, not an impartial one."[121] Accordingly, the conduct of the Crown and the Attorney General were abusive. The remedy was to set aside the direction and restore the accused's election.

ii) Other Procedural Rights

The principles of fundamental justice do not always guarantee the full array of procedural protections such as notice[122] and rights of appeal.[123] However, it would be unwise to commit oneself to the contrary proposition that the principles of fundamental justice never require notice or rights of appeal. Procedural fairness is undoubtedly a principle of fundamental justice; the question whether a specific procedural right is required for procedural fairness has to be considered in the particu-

---

117 *R v C(G)*, 2010 ONSC 115 [*C(G)*].

118 *Youth Criminal Justice Act*, SC 2002, c 1.

119 *C(G)*, above note 117 at paras 31–42.

120 *Ibid* at paras 58–60.

121 *Ibid* at para 64.

122 *R v Dyck*, 2008 ONCA 309 at para 131; *Taylor v Canada (Minister of Citizenship and Immigration)*, 2007 FCA 349 at paras 85–98 (FCA); *R v Rodgers*, 2006 SCC 15.

123 *R v Meltzer*, [1989] 1 SCR 1764 at 1773–74; *Chiarelli v Canada (Minister of Citizenship and Immigration)*, [1992] 1 SCR 711 at 739; *Charkaoui v Canada (Minister of Citizenship and Immigration)*, 2007 SCC 9 at para 136.

lar context in which it arises. Some of these contexts are discussed in Chapter 5.

FURTHER READINGS

CAMERON, JAMIE. "From the *MVR* to *Chaoulli v Quebec*: The Road Not Taken and the Future of Section 7" (2006) 34 Sup Ct L Rev (2d) 105.

CARTER, MARK. "Fundamental Justice in Section 7 of the *Charter*: A Human Rights Interpretation" (2003) 52 UNBLJ 243.

COLVIN, ERIC. "Section 7 of the *Charter of Rights and Freedoms*" (1989) 68 Can Bar Rev 560.

HUSCROFT, GRANT. "A Constitutional 'Work in Progress'? The *Charter* and the Limits of Progressive Interpretation" (2004) 23 Sup Ct L Rev (2d) 413.

ROACH, KENT. "Must We Trade Rights for Security? The Choice Between Smart, Harsh, or Proportionate Security Strategies in Canada and Britain" (2006) 27 Cardozo L Rev 2151.

SHARPE, ROBERT J, & KENT ROACH. *The Canadian Charter of Rights and Freedoms*, 4th ed (Toronto: Irwin Law, 2009) ch 13.

SINGLETON, THOMAS J. "The Principles of Fundamental Justice, Societal Interests and Section 1 of the *Charter*" (1995) 74 Can Bar Rev 446.

STUART, DON. *Charter Justice in Canadian Criminal Law*, 4th ed (Toronto: Thomson Carswell, 2005) ch 2.4.

CHAPTER 4

SUBSTANTIVE PRINCIPLES OF FUNDAMENTAL JUSTICE

A. INTRODUCTION

Because the principles of fundamental justice include both the principles of natural justice (or procedural fairness) and principles of substantive justice,[1] the classification of a norm as "substantive" or "procedural" has no special importance under section 7. Nonetheless, for the sake of expository convenience, I have divided my discussion of the principles of fundamental justice as follows. In this chapter, I consider the principles of fundamental justice that have been recognized by Canadian courts and are usually characterized as substantive; in Chapter 5, I consider the extent to which natural justice or the principles of procedural fairness have been recognized as principles of fundamental justice. If some of the principles discussed in Chapter 4 seem more naturally characterized as procedural than substantive, or vice versa, the reader is asked to remember that the distinction does not affect the characterization of a principle as fundamental.

Section B deals with certain principles of fundamental justice that apply generally to any law affecting the interests protected by section 7, while the remaining Sections consider the principles of fundamental justice that apply particularly in criminal law.

---

1   *Re BC Motor Vehicle Act*, [1985] 2 SCR 486 [*Motor Vehicle Reference*].

B. GENERALLY APPLICABLE SUBSTANTIVE PRINCIPLES

Substantive principles of fundamental justice are most often seen in constitutional challenges to statutes, regulations, and common law rules; they apply not only to the procedures for determining legal disputes but also to the general norms that govern those disputes.

1) A Law Must Not Be Overly Vague

It is a principle of fundamental justice that a law must not be overly vague. Stated positively, it is a principle of fundamental justice that a law must be precise enough "to give sufficient guidance for legal debate."[2]

The requirement of sufficient precision flows from the idea of the rule of law. If the law is to guide human behaviour, it must be sufficiently precise that individuals can determine in advance the legal implications of their conduct with a reasonable degree of certainty. If the law does not have this quality of sufficient precision, it cannot guide conduct and to that extent is incompatible with the rule of law: "obscure and incoherent legislation can make legality unattainable by anyone."[3] This degree of certainty, though particularly important in the criminal law,[4] is a desirable feature of laws of all kinds,[5] and is constitutionally required whenever section 7 is engaged.

In *R v Nova Scotia Pharmaceutical Society* (*Nova Scotia Pharmaceutical Society*), Gonthier J linked these rule of law requirements to two related ideas. First, the law should provide the citizen with fair notice of the legal implications of her conduct.[6] A vague law does not give fair notice; it might, or might not, prohibit or permit any conduct. In *Reference re ss 193 and 195.1(1)(c) of the Criminal Code* (the *Prostitution Reference*), Lamer J provided a historical example. A section of the penal code of Nazi-era Danzig provided that "Any person who commits an act . . .

---

2   *R v Nova Scotia Pharmaceutical Society,* [1992] 2 SCR 606 at 639 [*Nova Scotia Pharmaceutical Society*].

3   Lon Fuller, *The Morality of Law* (New Haven: Yale University Press, 1964) at 63.

4   *Reference re ss 193 and 195.1(1)(c) of the Criminal Code,* [1990] 1 SCR 1123 at 1152 [*Prostitution Reference*].

5   The vagueness standard "applies to all enactments, irrespective of whether they are civil, criminal, administrative or other:" *Nova Scotia Pharmaceutical Society,* above note 2 at 642.

6   *Nova Scotia Pharmaceutical Society, ibid* at 633–35; see also *Prostitution Reference,* above note 4 at 1155.

which is deserving of punishment according to the fundamental conceptions of a penal law and sound popular feeling, shall be punished."[7] No-one could tell in advance what this law prohibited or permitted, or whether his conduct might be punishable under it. Second, the law should limit the discretionary power of officials.[8] A vague law does not limit the actions that officials can take under it and therefore makes the interests protected by section 7 vulnerable to their discretion. The Danzig penal law might again serve as an example: since any conduct might be found to infringe it, there would be no criteria for making the decision to arrest or to prosecute someone for violating it. In contrast, under a system of reasonably precise penal law, there are meaningful thresholds before a police officer can exercise the power of arrest.

The requirement of sufficient precision "does not require that a law can be absolutely certain: no law can meet that standard."[9] There will always be uncertainty about how even the most carefully and precisely drafted law applies to a given situation. This uncertainly flows from both the irreducible imprecision of language and from the inevitably value-laden nature of legal interpretation. So a law will not be unconstitutionally vague simply because it leaves room for debate about its application; indeed, the fact that there can be an intelligible debate about the boundaries of the law's application itself indicates that the law is sufficiently precise. A law will meet the constitutional standard if it can "enunciate some boundaries, which create a zone of risk"; but a law will be unconstitutionally vague if it "does not provide an adequate basis for legal debate, that is for reaching a conclusion as to its meaning by reasoned analysis applying legal criteria."[10] In other words, "a law will not be struck down as vague simply because reasonable people disagree as to its application to particular facts";[11] but rather if it provides no intelligible standard at all.[12]

The test of sufficient precision is relatively easy to satisfy. Very few Canadian laws are so devoid of intelligible content that they are unconstitutionally vague. Even where statutes incorporate relatively im-

---

7   *Prostitution Reference, ibid* at 1151. See also *Consistency of Certain Danzig Legislative Decrees with Constitution of Free City, Advisory Opinion,* 1935 PCIJ (ser A/B) No 65, giving the opinion that the law was inconsistent with the city's constitution.

8   *Nova Scotia Pharmaceutical Society,* above note 2 at 635–36.

9   *Prostitution Reference,* above note 4 at 1156.

10 *Nova Scotia Pharmaceutical Society,* above note 2 at 639.

11 *Cochrane v Ontario (AG),* 2008 ONCA 718 at para 44 [*Cochrane*].

12 An "unintelligible provision gives insufficient guidance for legal debate and is therefore unconstitutionally vague": *Nova Scotia Pharmaceutical Society,* above note 2 at 638.

precise concepts such as "reasonableness" or "undueness," Canadian courts provide those concepts with more determinate content through the process of statutory interpretation and application to specific fact situations; therefore, courts have generally been unwilling to find them unconstitutionally vague.[13] In *Nova Scotia Pharmaceutical Society* itself, the leading case on the standard for vagueness, the Court upheld a provision penalizing conspiracy "to prevent, or lessen, *unduly*, competition . . . ."[14] The Court agreed with the applicants that the undueness standard "cannot readily be applied to a factual situation to yield an answer."[15] But to show that the standard was intelligible, the Court considered interpretations of the word "undue" in other legal contexts and, perhaps more importantly, reviewed the cases that gave the standard its content:[16] proof of the offence required proof that the accused had some market power and had engaged in some behaviour that was likely to injure competition in that market.[17] Without this judicially developed content, the standard of "undue lessening of competition" might have been more vulnerable to a vagueness challenge.

In light of this reasoning, it is not surprising that most vagueness challenges have failed. The offence of contempt of court, though not codified, has been rendered sufficiently precise at common law that "[a] person can predict in advance whether his or her conduct will constitute a crime";[18] the common law definition of the offence is therefore not vague. An environmental offence requiring proof that the accused emitted or permitted the emission of a "contaminant" that "causes or is likely to cause impairment to the quality of the natural environment,"[19] though "broad and general,"[20] was not unconstitutionally vague. The terms "contaminant" and "natural environment" were defined in the statute, in such a way that there was a "basis for legal debate" about their application in a particular situation.[21] The terms "impairment"

---

13 Compare Fuller, above note 3 at 64: "Sometimes the best way to achieve clarity is to take advantage of, and incorporate into the law, common sense standards that have grown up in the ordinary life lived outside legislative halls . . . . Nor can we ever . . . be more exact than the nature of the subject matter with which we are dealing admits. A specious clarity can be more damaging than an honest open-ended vagueness."

14 *Combines Investigation Act*, RSC 1970, c C-23, s 32(1)(c) [emphasis added].

15 *Nova Scotia Pharmaceutical Society*, above note 2 at 650.

16 *Ibid* at 648–58.

17 *Ibid* at 650.

18 *United Nurses of Alberta v Alberta (AG)*, [1992] 1 SCR 901 at 933.

19 *Environmental Protection Act*, RSO 1980, c 141, s 13(1)(a).

20 *Ontario v Canadian Pacific Ltd*, [1995] 2 SCR 1031 at para 43.

21 *Ibid* at para 61.

and "use," though not defined in the statute, could easily be interpreted in accordance with the usual principles of statutory interpretation to permit a reasoned application of the statute to particular fact situations.[22] The "best interests of the child" standard, widely used in family and child protection law, is "a fairly broad legislative concept" but has given rise to a very extensive body of case law giving it sufficient content to make it "capable of application to the circumstance of each case";[23] accordingly, it is not unconstitutionally vague. The criminal offence of defamatory libel[24] is sufficiently well defined to guide prosecutorial discretion and so is not vague.[25]

Indeed, the Supreme Court of Canada has only once found a law unconstitutionally vague, and that decision was made under another section of the *Charter*. In *R v Morales* (*Morales*),[26] the Court considered the constitutionality of the provisions governing bail (judicial interim release) in proceedings by way of indictment. At the time, there were two possible grounds for denying bail. The primary ground was the need to ensure the accused's attendance at trial. If the primary ground was not established, bail might be refused "on the secondary ground . . . that his detention is necessary in the public interest or for the protection of safety of the public, having regard to all the circumstances . . . ."[27] The accused argued that the denial of bail on the ground of "the public interest" denied him the right "not to be denied reasonable bail without just cause" under section 11(*e*) of the *Charter*. The Court, adapting the section 7 vagueness analysis to the context of section 11(*e*),[28] held that the considerable body of case law interpreting the "public interest" had provided "no guidance for legal debate" about the application of the standard to particular cases.[29] The standard was "completely discre-

---

22   *Ibid* at paras 62–70.
23   *P(D) v S(C)*, [1993] 4 SCR 141 at 180.
24   *Criminal Code*, RSC 1985, c C-46, ss 298–300.
25   *R v Lucas*, [1998] 1 SCR 439, 132 CCC (3d) 97 at paras 29–30.
26   *R v Morales*, [1992] 3 SCR 711 [*Morales*].
27   *Criminal Code*, above note 24, s 515(1)(*b*), as it then read.
28   In the companion case of *R v Pearson*, [1992] 3 SCR 665 at 688–89 [*Pearson*], the court held that the accused's claim should be decided under s 11(*e*) rather than under s 7 because the s 7 claim added nothing to the accused's complaint under s 11(*e*); however, if the section violated s 11(*e*), it would also violate s 7. The content of the vagueness standard applied to s 11(*e*) was the same as that articulated under s 7 in *Nova Scotia Pharmaceutical Society*, above note 2. The Court held that "there cannot be just cause for the denial of bail where the statutory criteria for denial are vague and imprecise": *Morales*, above note 26 at 727.
29   *Morales*, *ibid* at 732.

tionary" and authorized a "standardless sweep, as the court can order imprisonment whenever it sees fit."[30]

Parliament responded to the decision in *Morales* by re-drafting the bail provisions to provide three grounds for refusal of bail: the need to ensure attendance at court, the protection of the public, and the following tertiary ground:

> . . . the detention of an accused in custody is justified . . . on any other just cause being shown and, without liming the generality of the foregoing, where the detention is necessary in order to maintain confidence in the administration of justice, having regard to all the circumstances, including the apparent strength of the prosecution's case, the gravity and nature of the offence, the circumstances surrounding its commission and the potential for a lengthy term of imprisonment.[31]

This ground was partially invalidated in *R v Hall*.[32] The majority held that the phrase "on any other just cause being shown" was unconstitutionally vague and contrary to section 11(*e*) for the reasons given in *Morales*: it conferred a "broad discretion" and did "not specify any particular basis upon which bail could be denied."[33] But the majority held that the rest of the ground was constitutionally valid: maintaining "confidence in the administration of justice" was a constitutionally permissible ground for denying bail and the circumstances in which this ground would be established were sufficiently precise to satisfy the norm against vagueness.[34]

---

30   *Ibid* at 731–32.
31   *Criminal Code*, above note 24, s 515(10)(*c*).
32   *R v Hall*, 2002 SCC 64.
33   *Ibid* at para 22.
34   *Ibid* at paras 24–41. The minority would have struck down s 515(10)(*c*) altogether.

Most vagueness challenges made under section 7 have been re-jected.[35] *O'Neill v Canada (AG)*[36] provides a rare instance of a success-ful challenge. The RCMP obtained and executed warrants to search a reporter's home and office, based on the allegation that the reporter had committed offences under the *Security of Information Act (SOIA)*.[37] The reporter and the newspaper applied to quash the warrants and to have the seized material returned, arguing among other things that the allegedly violated sections of the *SOIA* were unconstitutionally vague. Ratushny J noted that the key terms in the *SOIA* definition of the of-fence — "secret official" and "official" information — were not defined in the statute; more significantly, she held that these terms could not be interpreted so as to define a zone of risk that could guide the conduct of individuals and structure law enforcement discretion.[38] Therefore, the

---

35   See *Cochrane*, above note 11 (statutory definition of "pit bull" not vague); *R v Shand*, 2011 ONCA 5 at para 187 [*Shand*] (definition of murder in s 229(*c*) of the *Criminal Code* not unconstitutionally vague); *D'Almeida v Baron*, 2010 ONCA 564 (test for capacity to consent in s 4 of *Health Care Consent Act, 1996*, SO 1996, c 2, Sched A, not unconstitutionally vague); *Adult Entertainment Assn of Canada v Ottawa (City)*, 2007 ONCA 389 (bylaw regulating "adult entertain-ment parlours" not vague); *R v Banks*, 2007 ONCA 19 (provincial offences of aggressive soliciting and soliciting person in stopped vehicle not vague); *R v Khawaja* (2006), 214 CCC (3d) 399 at paras 14–21 (Ont SCJ), leave to appeal to SCC refused (2007), [2006] SCCA No 505 [*Khawaja*] (definition of "terror-ist activity" in s 83.01(1)(*b*) not vague); *R v Lindsay*, 2009 ONCA 532 [*Lindsay*] (definition of "criminal organization" in *Criminal Code*, above note 24, s 467.1(1) not vague); *I(A) v Ontario (Director, Child and Family Services Act)* (2005), 75 OR (3d) 663 (Div Ct) (criteria for director's review of child placement decision not vague); *Mussani v College of Physicians and Surgeons of Ontario* (2004), 248 DLR (4th) 632 at paras 62–67 (Ont CA) [*Mussani*] (rule requiring automatic licence revocation for physician found to have committed professional misconduct by engaging in sexual relationship with patient not vague); *R v Tse*, 2008 BCSC 211 at paras 135–86 (*Criminal Code*, above note 24, s 184.4, permitting warrantless interception of electronic communications under certain circumstances, not void for vagueness if properly interpreted); *Tourki v Canada (Minister of Public Safety and Emergency Preparedness)*, 2006 FC 50, aff'd on other grounds 2007 FCA 186 (statute providing for seizure and forfeiture of currency valued at more than $10,000 and not reported on import or export not vague); *Johnson v British Columbia (Securities Commission)*, 2001 BCCA 597 (offence of acting contrary to the "public interest" in securities transactions not unconstitution-ally vague).

36   *O'Neill v Canada (AG)* (2006), 213 CCC (3d) 389 (Ont SCJ) [*O'Neill*].

37   RSC 1985, c O-5.

38   *O'Neill*, above note 36 at para 71.

offences in question were "unconstitutionally vague for not sufficiently delineating the risk zone for criminal sanction."[39]

2) A Law Must Not Be Overbroad

It is a principle of fundamental justice that a law must not be overbroad in relation to its own purposes. Put positively, it is a principle of fundamental justice that a law must be drafted with a degree of precision appropriate to its purposes.

The Supreme Court recognized the norm against overbreadth as a principle of fundamental justice in *R v Heywood* (*Heywood*).[40] The accused was charged with an offence under section 179(1)(*b*) of the *Criminal Code*, which reads as follows:

> 179 (1) Every one commits vagrancy
>
>   . . .
>
> (*b*) having at any time been convicted of [sexual assault and other sexual offences] is found loitering in or near a school ground, playground, public park or bathing area.

The charge arose as follows. In 1987, the accused had been convicted of two counts of sexual assault. On 16 June 1989, he was found in a public park with a camera. A police officer informed him about the prohibition created by section 179(1)(*b*). But on 5 July 1989, the accused was again found in a public park with a camera. This time, he was arrested and charged. A search revealed that he was in possession of photographs of the clothed genital areas of young girls. The accused was convicted as charged. His argument that section 179(1)(*b*) was unconstitutionally overbroad succeeded on appeal to the British Columbia Court of Appeal and again in the Supreme Court of Canada.

Cory J recognized a constitutional norm against overbreadth in the following terms:

> Overbreadth analysis looks at the means chosen by the state in relation to its purpose. In considering whether a legislative provision is overbroad, a court must ask the question: are those means necessary to achieve the State's objective? If the State, in pursuing a legitimate objective, uses means which are broader than is necessary to accomplish that objective, the principles of fundamental justice will be

---

39   *Ibid* at para 72. The Crown did not appeal the decision, but the relevant sections of the *SOIA* have yet to be amended or repealed.

40   *R v Heywood*, [1994] 3 SCR 761 [*Heywood*].

violated because the individual's rights will have been limited for no reason.[41]

He interpreted the word "loiters" in section 179(1)(b) in a broad and ordinary sense, "namely to stand idly around, hang around, linger, tarry, saunter, delay, dawdle, etc."[42] Under this interpretation, a person convicted of one of the offences listed in section 179(1)(b) was, for the rest of his life, criminally prohibited from spending any time in any of the listed locations (school grounds, playgrounds, public parks, public bathing areas). The purpose of section 179(1)(b) was "to protect children from becoming victims of sexual offences."[43] In light of this purpose, the prohibition was overbroad in three respects. First, it was geographically overbroad, applying not only to schoolyards and playgrounds where children were likely to be present but to all public parks, including "vast and remote wilderness parks."[44] Second, it was temporally overbroad, in that it applied to persons convicted of the predicate offences even where they no longer posed a danger to children.[45] Third, it applied to all persons convicted of the predicate offences even if they never posed a danger to children (because, for example, their offences involved adult complainants).[46] Finally, Cory J noted that there was no mechanism by which a person convicted of a predicate offence would be notified of the prohibition created by section 179(1)(b),[47] though this defect in the law does not depend on its being overbroad. Section 179(1)(b) therefore offended section 7. Moreover, precisely because it was overbroad, it failed the minimal impairment branch of the *Oakes* test[48] and so could not be justified under section 1.[49]

---

41   *Ibid* at 792–93.

42   *Ibid* at 789.

43   *Ibid* at 794.

44   *Ibid* at 795.

45   *Ibid* at 796–97.

46   *Ibid* at 798–800.

47   *Ibid* at 800–2.

48   *R v Oakes*, [1986] 1 SCR 103 at 138–40 [*Oakes*].

49   *Heywood*, above note 40 at 802–3. Justice Cory noted that s 161 of the *Criminal Code*, above note 24, then recently enacted, was "much more carefully and narrowly fashioned to achieve the same objective as s 179(1)(b)," thus demonstrating a less impairing alternative (indeed, it appears that s 161 does not offend s 7 at all and so does not need to be justified under s 1). The dissenting minority, *per* Gonthier J, interpreted the word "loiter" in s 179(1)(b) narrowly to include a mental element related to the predicate offences, and held that the section so interpreted did not offend the *Charter*. It is not entirely clear whether the minority accepted the majority's view that there was a distinct norm against overbreadth under s 7.

The norm against overbreadth recognized as a principle of fundamental justice in *Heywood* has rarely been invoked in subsequent Supreme Court of Canada cases[50] and has rarely succeeded in lower-level decisions.[51] Nonetheless, as late as 2004, the Court in *R v Demers* (*Demers*) described it as "well-established."[52] The accused was charged with sexual assault and was found unfit to stand trial. The Court held that the provisions of the *Criminal Code* that applied to a person found *permanently* unfit to stand trial were overbroad in that they did not permit the review board to discharge the person absolutely where there was no evidence that he was a threat to public safety. Permanent restriction of a person's liberty "where there is clear evidence that capacity [to stand trial] will never be recovered and there is no evidence of a significant threat to public safety . . . [is] not necessary to achieve the State's objective" and is therefore unconstitutionally overbroad.[53]

The standard to be met for a finding that a law is overbroad is not entirely clear. To assess a claim of overbreadth, a court must identify the purposes of the impugned law and then must consider whether the law is a necessary means for achieving those purposes. But it is not clear whether a law is overbroad merely because it goes farther than required to achieve its objective, or whether a law is overbroad only when it goes so far as to be grossly disproportionate to its objective. I will call the first standard "mere overbreadth" and the second standard "grossly disproportionate overbreadth." *Heywood* and *Demers* suggest that mere overbreadth is all that has to be shown: if the purposes can be achieved with a more narrowly drafted restriction on behaviour, then the impugned law is overbroad. But in *R v Clay* (*Clay*), the Supreme Court of Canada commented that a law is overbroad only "where the adverse effect of a legislative measure on the individuals subject to its strictures is *grossly* disproportionate to the state interest the legislation seeks to protect."[54] If the standard for a violation of section 7 is mere over-

---

50 In *R v Clay*, 2003 SCC 75 at paras 34–40 [*Clay*], the majority held that a criminal prohibition on the simple possession of marijuana was not overbroad.

51 See, for instance, *Mussani*, above note 35 at paras 68–74 (rule requiring automatic licence revocation for physician found to have committed professional misconduct by engaging in sexual relationship with patient not overbroad); *R v Gibbons*, 2010 ONCJ 470 (s 127 of *Criminal Code*, above note 24, creating offence of breaching court order, not overbroad); *Shand*, above note 35 at para 186 (definition of murder in s 229(*c*) of the *Criminal Code* not overbroad).

52 *R v Demers*, 2004 SCC 46 at para 37 [*Demers*].

53 *Ibid* at para 43. For Parliament's response, see Section B(3)(d), below in this chapter.

54 *Clay*, above note 50 at para 38 [emphasis in original]; see also the discussion in Section B(5)(c), below in this chapter.

breadth, then legislation must be drafted with greater precision than if the standard is grossly disproportionate overbreadth. The relationship between the norm against overbreadth and the other substantive norms is discussed in more detail in Section B(5), below in this chapter.

3) A Law Must Not Be Arbitrary

It is a principle of fundamental justice that a law must not be arbitrary. Similarly, a government decision, taken pursuant to an otherwise valid law, that affects the interests protected by section 7 can be set aside if it is arbitrary.

The test for arbitrariness is not entirely clear. It has been said that a law is arbitrary if it is not necessary to achieve the objective of the legislation in question,[55] if "it bears no relation to, or is inconsistent with, the objective that lies behind the legislation,"[56] if there is no "real connection on the facts to the purpose the interference is said to serve,"[57] or if it is not "rationally connected to a reasonable apprehension of harm."[58] At a minimum, to avoid being arbitrary, a law or decision must have some positive effect on the purpose it is supposed to serve; otherwise, the section 7 interests will have been affected for no good reason. Like the norm against overbreadth, the norm against arbitrariness requires a court to identify the purposes of the law and to assess the connection between those purposes and the limits on life, liberty, or security created by the law.

a) Unsuccessful Arbitrariness Challenges
To hold that a law is arbitrary is to hold that the legislature which enacted it was, in a very basic sense, irrational: the legislature had an acceptable objective in mind, but chose a completely unsuitable means for achieving it. A court will understandably be quite reluctant to attribute this level of irrationality to the legislature, and so claims of arbitrariness have frequently been rejected.[59]

---

55 *Canada (AG) v PHS Community Services Society*, 2011 SCC 44 at para 132 [*PHS*].

56 *Rodriguez v British Columbia (AG)*, [1993] 3 SCR 519 at 620–21, McLachlin J [*Rodriguez*].

57 *Chaoulli v Quebec (AG)*, 2005 SCC 35 at para 134, McLachlin CJC and Major J [*Chaoulli*].

58 *R v Malmo-Levine; R v Caine*, 2003 SCC 74 at para 136 [*Malmo-Levine*].

59 See, for example, *R v Beare; R v Higgins*, [1988] 2 SCR 387 at 408–12 (fingerprinting of arrestees under *Identification of Criminals Act*, RSC 1985, c I-1, not arbitrary); *R v Arkell*, [1990] 2 SCR 695 at 702–4 (statutory criteria for classifying certain murders as "first degree" not arbitrary); *Chiarelli v Canada (Minister of Employment and Immigration)*, [1992] 1 SCR 711 (provisions for deportation

In *Rodriguez v British Columbia (AG)*[60] (*Rodriguez*), the Court considered the constitutionality of the prohibition on assisted suicide in section 241(*b*) of the *Criminal Code*. The applicant suffered from amyotrophic lateral sclerosis (ALS, or "Lou Gehrig's disease"), a wasting illness that would eventually deprive her of all muscular control while leaving her mental processes intact. She applied for a declaration that section 241(*b*) was invalid because she wanted to choose the time and manner of her own death; "by the time she no longer is able to enjoy life, she will be physically unable to terminate her life without assistance."[61] She argued, among other points, that the prohibition was arbitrary in the section 7 sense. The majority found that the purpose of the prohibition was "the protection of the vulnerable who might be induced in moments of weakness to commit suicide" and linked this purpose with a broader state interest in "protecting life" and a societal commitment to recognizing "the sanctity of human life."[62] In light of these purposes and of the broad consensus against assisted suicide in Western democracies, the prohibition was not arbitrary. Three dissenting judges held that the prohibition was indeed arbitrary, for the following reasons. There was no general prohibition on suicide in Canadian criminal law; however, a person in the applicant's situation would be unable to commit suicide without assistance. Given the purpose identified by the majority, that of protecting the vulnerable, this restriction was arbitrary: the applicant was not among the vulnerable that the prohibition sought to protect.[63]

---

of permanent resident for serious criminality not arbitrary); *R v Skalbania*, [1997] 3 SCR 995 (Court of Appeal's power under *Criminal Code*, above note 24, s 686(4)(*b*)(ii) to substitute verdict of guilt on appeal from acquittal by judge alone not arbitrary); *R v Jones*, [1986] 2 SCR 284 at 303–4 (statutory process for ensuring that all children receive education of a certain quality not "manifestly unfair"); *Flora v Ontario (Health Insurance Plan, General Manager)* (2007), 278 DLR (4th) 45 (Ont Div Ct), aff'd 2008 ONCA 538 [*Flora*] (health insurance regulation defining insured service so as to prevent reimbursement for treatment received abroad in certain circumstances not arbitrary); *Melanson v New Brunswick (AG)*, 2007 NBCA 12 (legislation concerning rights of participation in underfunded pension plan of bankrupt employer not arbitrary); *Toussaint v Canada (AG)*, 2010 FC 810 (denial of medical coverage to person remaining illegally in Canada not arbitrary).

60 *Rodriguez*, above note 56.
61 *Ibid* at 531, Lamer CJC dissenting.
62 *Ibid* at 595, Sopinka J.
63 *Ibid* at 619–22, McLachlin J dissenting, L'Heureux-Dubé J concurring in the dissent. Justice Cory, dissenting, expressed at 629 substantial agreement with this reasoning.

In *AC v Manitoba (Director of Child and Family Services)*,[64] there was a similar difference of opinion in another difficult case of life and death. The applicant, a fourteen-year-old Jehovah's Witness, refused a life-saving blood transfusion. The Manitoba Director of Child and Family Services apprehended her as a child in need of protection and applied for a court order authorizing the transfusion. The applicable statute provided that such an order was not to be made where a child was under sixteen without the child's consent unless the child was unable "to understand the information that is relevant to making a decision to consent, or . . . to appreciate the reasonably foreseeable consequences" of consenting or not consenting.[65] The applicant argued that the statute was arbitrary in that it drew the line at sixteen years of age for no reason. The majority of the Supreme Court held that it would indeed be arbitrary "to assume that no one under the age of sixteen has the capacity to make medical treatment decisions,"[66] but held that the statute, properly interpreted, was not arbitrary because it required an assessment of the capacity of a child under sixteen to make a decision about treatment; the more mature the child, the more weight his views would be entitled to.[67] Justice Binnie, dissenting, held that the statute was arbitrary precisely because it did not enable a child to rebut the presumption that he was incapable of deciding for himself; accordingly, it bore no relation to "the legislative goal of protecting children who *lack* such capacity."[68]

In *May v Ferndale Institution*,[69] the Court considered a new procedure for classifying the security risk posed by inmates in federal penitentiaries. The Court held, unanimously on this point, that the application of a new procedure was not arbitrary because it struck "the proper balance"[70] between "the interest of inmates deprived of their residual liberty and the interest of the state in the protection of the public";[71] moreover, no inmate was reclassified without an individualized assessment.[72]

---

64   *AC v Manitoba (Director of Child and Family Services)*, 2009 SCC 30 [*AC*].

65   *Child and Family Services Act*, CCSM c C80, s 25(8).

66   *AC*, above note 64 at para 107, Abella J.

67   *Ibid* at paras 80–98 and 103–8.

68   *Ibid* at para 223, Binnie J dissenting [emphasis in original].

69   *May v Ferndale Institution*, 2005 SCC 82.

70   *Ibid* at para 84.

71   *Ibid* at para 83.

72   *Ibid* at para 85, LeBel and Fish JJ; McLachlin CJC and Binnie, Deschamps, and Abella JJ concurring; Charron J dissenting; Major and Bastarache JJ concurring in the dissent; agreed with this aspect of the majority reasons: *ibid* at para 124.

b) *Morgentaler, Chaoulli,* and *PHS*

There is no case in which a majority of the Court has clearly invoked the section 7 norm against arbitrariness to invalidate a law. But in two cases, *R v Morgentaler (Morgentaler)* and *Chaoulli v Quebec (AG) (Chaoulli)*, the reasons of the various judges who constitute the majority may fairly be read as striking down statutes for arbitrariness. Moreover, in *Canada (AG) v PHS Community Services Society (PHS)*,[73] the Supreme Court of Canada set aside a decision of the federal Minister of Health on the ground of arbitrariness.

In *Morgentaler*,[74] the Supreme Court of Canada considered section 251 (now section 287) of the *Criminal Code*, prohibiting abortion except in accordance with a procedure laid out in section 251(4). Section 251(4) provided in effect that an abortion was lawful if performed by "a qualified medical practitioner" in "an accredited or approved hospital" after the hospital's "therapeutic abortion committee" had "by certificate in writing stated that in its opinion the continuation of the pregnancy of [the] female person would or would be likely to endanger her life or health" (the physician performing the abortion could not himself or herself be a member of the committee). Morgentaler and his co-accused were qualified medical practitioners, but performed abortions in a clinic that was not part of an approved hospital and, *a fortiori*, were not approved by a committee. By a 5:2 majority, the Court held that section 251 violated section 7 of the *Charter* and could not be justified under section 1. But there was no clear majority on the applicable principle of fundamental justice, as the five judges in the majority divided 2:2:1 on the defects in section 251. Justice Beetz, Estey J concurring, held that a prohibition on abortion as such was not contrary to the principles of fundamental justice.[75] But the procedure for obtaining an abortion, considered in light of the facts surrounding its operation in practice, created delays which were "unnecessary, given Parliament's objectives in establishing the administrative structure."[76] For example, the requirement that all abortions take place in hospitals was unnecessary to Parliament's objectives and had been shown to contribute to these delays; it was therefore "manifestly unfair" and "serve[d] no real purpose."[77] Though Beetz J does not say that section 251 is "arbitrary," his reasons track the concept of arbitrariness as developed in the subsequent cases. Chief Justice Dickson, Lamer J concurring, held that

---

73   Above note 55.
74   *R v Morgentaler*, [1988] 1 SCR 30 [*Morgentaler*].
75   *Ibid* at 109–10.
76   *Ibid* at 114.
77   *Ibid* at 119 & 120.

section 251 offended the principles of fundamental justice because it purported to provide a defence but in fact made the defence nearly impossible to invoke (see Section G(1), below in this chapter). Justice Wilson went much farther than the other members of the majority, holding that the section 7 rights to liberty and security of the person included a woman's "right to decide for herself whether or not to terminate her pregnancy"[78] and that section 251 deprived a woman of the ability to exercise that right conscientiously, a violation of section 2(a) which was itself contrary to the principles of fundamental justice.[79] To the extent that Dickson CJC's reasoning, like Beetz J's, can be read as implicitly invoking the concept of arbitrariness, and to the extent that Wilson J agreed with that analysis (while holding that it did not go far enough),[80] it may fairly be said that the majority in *Morgentaler* struck down section 251 because it was an arbitrary law.[81]

In *Chaoulli*,[82] the applicant physician challenged Quebec statutes that prohibited "private insurance for health care services that are available in the public system."[83] A 4:3 majority of the Court held that the prohibition violated the Quebec *Charter*; in addition, three members of the majority[84] held that the prohibition was arbitrary. The purpose of the prohibition was to protect public health care by preventing the diversion of resources from the public to the private system.[85] But Quebec had not established this threat to the public system, and while an apprehension of harm might suffice, the evidence at trial concerning experience in other countries suggested that public health care and private insurance could co-exist. Consequently, there was "no real connection in fact between prohibition of health insurance and the goal of a quality public health system,"[86] so the prohibition was arbitrary. The three dissenting judges found, to the contrary, that the government of Quebec had established at trial the required connection between

---

78   *Ibid* at 172; compare 174.
79   *Ibid* at 174–80.
80   *Ibid* at 173.
81   The Supreme Court has sometimes but not always read *Morgentaler* this way: see *Rodriguez*, above note 56 at 619–20, McLachlin J (reading *Morgentaler* as a case applying the norm against arbitrariness); and contrast *Chaoulli*, above note 57 at paras 132–33, McLachlin CJC and Major J (distinguishing between Dickson CJC's and Beetz J's reasoning).
82   *Ibid*.
83   *Ibid* at para 2.
84   Chief Justice McLachlin and Major J, Bastarache J concurring.
85   *Chaoulli*, above note 57 at para 135.
86   *Ibid* at para 139.

the legislature's objectives and the prohibition.[87] But, to the extent that Deschamps J's reasoning under the Quebec *Charter* is similar to McLachclin CJC and Major J's analysis under section 7, *Chaoulli* may fairly be read as the second case in which the Supreme Court has invalidated a law on the ground of arbitrariness.

The majority decision in *Chaoulli* was quite surprising because one would have expected the Court to show more deference to legislative policy choices on matters of health care policy.[88] Many commentators regarded the decision as at best an unwise assertion of judicial power in an area particularly unsuited to regulation by constitutional means and at worst as catastrophic for Canada's public health care system. One commentator asked whether it was "worse than *Lochner*,"[89] another described it as "a moment of judicial folly"[90] comparable to *Dred Scott*.[91] However, other commentators predicted that the decision would have little impact.[92] This prediction was correct. Quebec responded to the decision as narrowly as possible, allowing private health insurance only for certain specified procedures and taking measures to reduce wait times; and litigation inspired by *Chaoulli* in other provinces was generally unsuccessful.[93] Moreover, most critics of the decision in *Chaoulli* understand the facts differently than the Court did. The majority was somehow persuaded, contrary to the trial judge's findings of legislative fact, that the government's "monopoly" on health care, combined with its failure to provide the system with enough resources, threatened people's lives, and that the introduction of private health

---

87 *Ibid* at paras 231–58, Binnie and LeBel JJ dissenting, Fish J concurring in the dissent.

88 There is a substantial secondary literature on *Chaoulli*; see, in particular, Colleen M Flood, Kent Roach, & Lorne Sossin, eds, *Access to Care, Access to Justice* (Toronto: University of Toronto Press, 2005); "Symposium on *Chaoulli*" (2006) 44 Osgoode Hall LJ 249.

89 Sujit Choudhry, "Worse than *Lochner*?" in *Access to Care, Access to Justice, ibid* at 86; compare *Lochner v New York*, 198 US 45 (1905), a 5:4 decision invalidating on due process grounds a law regulating hours of work.

90 Lawrie MacFarlane, "Supreme Court Slaps For-sale Sign on Medicare" (2005) 173 Can Med Assoc J 269.

91 *Scott v Sandford*, 60 US 393 (1856) [*Dred Scott*], holding that an African-American could not be a citizen of any of the United States.

92 Colleen Flood & Terence Sullivan, "Supreme Disagreement: The Highest Court Affirms an Empty Right" (2005) 173 Can Med Assoc J 142.

93 See Colleen Flood & Sujith Xavier, "Health Care Rights in Canada: The *Chaoulli* Legacy" (2008) 27 Med L 617; Daniel Cohn, "*Chaoulli* Five Years On: All Bark and No Bite?" (Paper delivered at the 2010 Annual Meeting of the Canadian Political Science Association, Concordia University, Montreal, 2010) [unpublished]; *Flora*, above note 59.

insurance would not damage the system of public insurance.[94] But it seems unlikely that if the Court were to revisit the issues in *Chaoulli*, it would again take such an eccentric view of the facts. The importance of *Chaoulli* is that it appears to authorize courts to scrutinize the rationality of legislation quite closely in determining whether it is arbitrary.[95]

PHS was a challenge to a decision of the Federal Minister of Heath, declining to renew an exemption under section 56 of the *Controlled Drugs and Substances Act*. In 2003, in an act of "cooperative federalism," the federal Minister of Health and the Vancouver Coastal Health Authority (VCHA) established a safe injection site called "Insite" for intravenous drug users, and the federal Minister of Health granted Insite an exemption from the trafficking and possession provisions of the *Controlled Drugs and Substances Act* (*CDSA*),[96] pursuant to section 56 of that Act. The function of Insite is not to provide users with drugs or to administer drugs, but to provide clean injection equipment, to monitor of the users' self-administration of drugs, and to provide medical care in the event of an emergency. In 2008, a different Minister of Health declined to act on VCHA's request for a further exemption. The organization that operated Insite, two drug addicts, and the Attorney General of British Columbia applied for, *inter alia*, an order requiring the Minister of Health to continue the exemption. The evidence at trial showed that Insite had reduced the number of overdose deaths without increasing the level of crime in the area.[97] The trial judge granted the applicants a constitutional exemption from the operation of the *CDSA*. The Supreme Court of Canada provided a somewhat different remedy for a similar reason. The Court accepted the trial judge's factual findings and the trial judge's holding that the Minister's decision engaged the applicants' section 7 interests.[98] The deprivation of the section 7 interests was arbitrary because the refusal to continue the exemption was not consistent with the purposes of the *CDSA*, namely, "the protec-

---

94   *Chaoulli*, above note 57 at para 106. On the factual issues in the case, see Flood & Xavier, *ibid* at 620–26; Theodore R Marmor, "Canada's Supreme Court and its National Health Insurance Program: Evaluating the Landmark *Chaoulli* Decision from a Comparative Perspective" (2006) 44 Osgoode Hall LJ 311; Charles J Wright, "Different Interpretations of 'Evidence' and Implications for the Canadian Healthcare System" in *Access to Care, Access to Justice* above note 88 at 220; Hamish Stewart, "Implications of *Chaoulli* for Fact-Finding in Constitutional Cases," *ibid* at 207.

95   See Section B(3)(a), above in this chapter, and Section B(3)(d), below in this chapter, for further discussion of this point.

96   SC 1996, c 19 [*CDSA*].

97   *PHS*, above note 55 at para 28.

98   See Chapter 2, Section D.

tion of health and public safety";[99] indeed, the decision was contrary to those purposes because providing Insite with an exemption "does not undermine the objectives of public health and safety, but furthers them."[100] The Court granted a remedy in the nature of the administrative law remedy of mandamus, ordering the Minister "to grant an exemption to Insite under section 56 of the *CDSA* forthwith."[101]

In all three cases, it is the inconsistency of the law or the decision with the objectives of the law that makes the law or decision arbitrary. Thus, applying the norm against arbitrariness requires not only a determination of the purposes of the law but an empirical assessment of the effectiveness of the law or decision in serving those purposes. Often, social science evidence may be required. But claims of arbitrariness do not depend on social science evidence alone; they also depend on the extent to which the court is willing to defer to the government's assertion that it is reasonable to believe that the law in question will have a beneficial effect on its objectives. The more deferential the court, the less the social-science evidence will affect the court's empirical assessment.[102]

c) Marijuana: Recreational and Medical

In *R v Malmo-Levine; R v Caine* (*Malmo-Levine*),[103] the accused challenged the offence of simple possession of marijuana[104] on several grounds, including the assertion that it was arbitrary because a criminal prohibition was not a rational way to deal with the harms (if any) caused by possession of marijuana. The majority rejected the accused's claim, holding that Parliament had a reasonable apprehension that marijuana use caused a number of harms[105] and that the prohibition was "rationally connected" to this apprehension of harm.[106] Two dissenting judges found the prohibition to be arbitrary.[107]

Despite the outcome in *Malmo-Levine*, the norm against arbitrariness has played a central role in the development of a medical exception to the criminal prohibition on the possession and production of

---

99   *PHS*, above note 55 at para 129.
100 *Ibid* at para 131.
101 *Ibid* at para 150.
102 See Section B(3)(d), below in this chapter.
103 Above note 58.
104 *CDSA*, above note 96, s 4(1) and Sched II.
105 *Malmo-Levine*, above note 58 at paras 40–61 and 135.
106 *Ibid* at para 136.
107 *Ibid* at para 280, LeBel J dissenting and at paras 289–99, Deschamps J dissenting. Justice Arbour dissented on other grounds.

marijuana. Although the cases do not always expressly invoke the norm, they are best understood as instance of it.

Under the *Controlled Drugs and Substances Act* (*CDSA*) it is an offence to possess, to traffic, or to produce marijuana without an authorization.[108] Section 56 gives the federal Minister of Health a discretion "to exempt any person or class of persons" from the provisions of the *CDSA* "if, in the opinion of the Minister, the exemption is necessary for a medical or scientific purpose or is otherwise in the public interest." There is some evidence indicating that smoking or otherwise ingesting marijuana can effectively control certain symptoms of disease, such as pain and nausea, and can provide other therapeutic benefits, such as reducing the convulsions associated with epilepsy.[109] The prohibition on marijuana possession therefore engages the section 7 interest in security of the person of those who would derive some therapeutic benefit from it (see Chapter 2, Section D(4)). Thus, to comply with section 7, the prohibition must not be arbitrary. A number of courts have found that the prohibition, even with the possibility of an exemption under section 56, is arbitrary, and that some aspects of the federal government's efforts to remedy this arbitrariness are themselves arbitrary.

In *R v Parker* (*Parker*), the accused, an epileptic, cultivated and smoked marijuana for the purpose of reducing the incidence of the seizures to which he was subject. The evidence indicated that, in his case, smoking marijuana was more effective than conventional (and legal) medications. The trial judge held, and the Ontario Court of Appeal agreed, that in cases such as the accused's, the prohibition did "little or nothing to enhance the state's interest."[110] The Crown argued that because the accused could seek an exemption under section 56, his section 7 rights were not violated; however, the court held that leaving "an unfettered discretion in the hands of the Minister" was inadequate to protect the right.[111]

The Crown chose not to seek leave to appeal the decision in *Parker*; instead, the government enacted the *Marihuana Medical Access Regulations* (*MMAR*)[112] to structure the Minister's exercise of discretion under section 56. The basic structure of the *MMAR*, as they originally read,

---

108 *CDSA*, above note 96, ss 4(1), 5(1), 6(1), and 7(1); and see Sched II.

109 See *R v Parker* (2000), 146 CCC (3d) 193 at paras 42–53 (Ont CA) [*Parker*]; *R v Beren*, 2009 BCSC 429 at paras 36–37, leave to appeal refused, [2009] SCCA No 272 [*Beren*].

110 *Parker*, *ibid* at para 113, quoting from *Rodriguez*, above note 56 at 594; see also para 153.

111 *Parker*, *ibid* at para 187.

112 *Marihuana Medical Access Regulations*, SOR/2001-227.

was as follows. An individual would seek an authority to possess (ATP) from the Minister of Health on the basis of a declaration from a medical practitioner and a specialist. The ATP, if granted, permitted the holder to produce marijuana, to obtain marijuana from another designated person (the holder of a "designated-person licence" or DPL), or to obtain marijuana from a licensed dealer. Holders of DPLs were prohibited from being compensated, from operating in groups of larger than three persons, and from providing marijuana for more than one holder of an ATP. However, as of 2003, no dealers had been licensed.

In *Hitzig v Canada* (*Hitzig*),[113] the Ontario Court of Appeal held in effect that the *MMAR* responded inadequately to the problem identified in *Parker*. While the *MMAR* did provide very significant structure for the Minister's decision to grant an exemption under section 56, it provided no lawful means for the holder of an ATP or a DPL to obtain plants, cuttings, or seeds. Because no dealers had been licensed and because the government itself did not supply marijuana, the *MMAR* "create[d] an alliance between the Government and the black market whereby the Government authorizes possession of marihuana for medical purposes and the black market supplies the necessary product."[114] This situation was contrary to the principle of fundamental justice that requires the state to obey the law.[115] To remedy this defect, the court invalidated the provisions of the *MMAR* that prevented the holder of a DPL from being compensated, from growing in common with more than two other holders of DPLs, and from growing for more than one holder of an ATP.[116] The court also invalidated the "second specialist" requirement that applied to some applicants, finding that it did nothing to advance the state's interest that had not already been done by requirement for a declaration by one specialist.

The government responded to *Hitzig* by repealing the "second specialist" requirement, and by allowing holders of ATPs to purchase marijuana from Prairie Plant System (PPS), a firm that has the monopoly on supplying cannabis to the federal government for research purposes.[117] However, most of the restrictions on holders of DPLs were re-enacted: they could now be compensated, but were again prohibited from growing in common with more than two other holders of DPLs

---

113 *Hitzig v Canada* (2003), 177 CCC (3d) 449 (Ont CA), leave to appeal to SCC refused, [2004] SCCA No 5 [*Hitzig*].

114 *Ibid* at para 116.

115 *Ibid* at para 115, and see Section B(6), below in this chapter.

116 *Ibid* at para 165.

117 See *Beren*, above note 109 at para 19.

(section 54.1), and from growing for more than one holder of an ATP (section 41(b.1)).

This response set the sage for a second round of challenges. In *Sfetkopoulos v Canada (AG) (Sfetkopoulos)*,[118] several holders of ATPs challenged section 41(b.1) in the context of an application in Federal Court for judicial review of a decision of the Minister of Health refusing to grant a corporation a DPL for more than one holder of an ATP. Strayer DJ held that section 41(b.1) was arbitrary because it caused considerable difficulty to holders of ATPs in obtaining marijuana without advancing the state's interests. He found as a fact that only 20 percent of holders of ATPs were able to obtain marijuana from PPS, so that the rule-of-law problem identified in *Hitzig* had not really been solved.[119] The matter was remitted to the Minister for reconsideration in light of the invalidity of section 41(b.1). Section 54.1, which was not in issue in *Sfetkopoulos*, was invalidated by the British Columbia Supreme Court in *R v Beren*, again on the ground of arbitrariness.[120]

The government has responded to these decisions by repealing sections 41(1.b) and 54.1 of the *MMAR*, and by revising its policies on access to marijuana from PPS.[121] Whether these responses are adequate to the problems identified in the cases will no doubt require another round of litigation.

d) Demonstrating Arbitrariness

It is not easy to reconcile those cases where arbitrariness has been successfully argued with those where it has not. In cases like *Rodriguez* and *Malmo-Levine*, the allegation of arbitrariness failed because the government had demonstrated a rational connection between the legislation and a reasonable apprehension of the harm the legislation was intended to address. Uncertainty about the effectiveness of the prohibition in practice did not affect this conclusion. In *Chaoulli*, on the other hand, the three judges who found the prohibition in question to be arbitrary considered the effectiveness of the prohibition in much greater detail and, contrary to the trial judge's express factual findings, found that the required connection was not established; accordingly,

---

118 *Sfetkopoulos v Canada (AG)*, 2008 FC 33, aff'd 2008 FCA 328, leave to appeal to SCC refused, [2008] SCCA No 531.

119 *Ibid* at para 19; see also *Beren*, above note 109.

120 *Beren*, *ibid* at paras 127–28.

121 See Health Canada, Controlled Substances and Tobacco Directorate, *Policy on Health Canada's Supply of Marihuana Seeds and Dried Marihuana for Medical Purposes*, in force 30 November 2009.

the prohibition was arbitrary.[122] In defence of their rejection of the trial judge's factual findings, McLachlin CJC and Major J commented that "The task of the courts . . . is to evaluate the issue in the light, not just of common sense or theory, but of the evidence."[123] If the Court had taken this approach in *Malmo-Levine*—if the Court had considered whether the evidence supported the proposition that prohibiting marijuana was an effective way to assist vulnerable users — the analysis would certainly have been different, and so might the result.

However, recent decisions suggest that the more demanding *Chaoulli* approach may prevail. In *PHS*,[124] the applicants challenged the constitutionality of the criminal prohibition on the possession of drugs in section 4(1) of the *CDSA*,[125] in the context of a challenge to a decision of the federal Minister of Justice to withdraw an exemption that had been granted to Insite, a "safe injection site", under a statutory discretion. Insite provided clean needles and a safe environment for users of unlawful intravenous drugs,[126] with a view to preventing the spread of blood borne diseases through re-use of needles and to providing health care for drug users, particularly in cases of overdose.[127] The trial judge found that Insite had reduced the injection of drugs in public, without increasing the rate of crime in the neigbourhood, and he appears to have found that Insite reduced the number of overdose deaths of addicts.[128] In light of these factual findings, the Supreme Court of Canada held that the decision of the Minister of Health to refuse to continue Insite's exemption was arbitrary because the exemption did not undermine but furthered the health and safety objectives of the *CDSA*.[129]

In *Bedford v Canada* (*Bedford*),[130] Himel J of the Ontario Superior Court of Justice held that three of the prostitution-related provisions of the *Criminal Code* were invalid. The decision is lengthy and complex, but in essence it holds that these provisions are ineffective in achiev-

---

122 On the assessment of the evidence in *Chaoulli* and its connection with the arbitrariness standard, see note 94, above in this chapter.

123 *Chaoulli*, above note 57 at para 150.

124 *PHS*, above note 55, aff'g 2010 BCCA 15, aff'g (*sub nom PHS Community Services Society v Canada (AG)*), 2008 BCSC 661 [*PHS 2008*]. In *Victoria (City) v Adams*, 2009 BCCA 563, var'g 2008 BCSC 1363, the Court of Appeal overturned the trial judge's holding that a municipal by-law prohibiting the erection of temporary shelters in public parks was arbitrary.

125 Above note 96, s 56.

126 *PHS 2008*, above note 124 at paras 71–77.

127 *Ibid* at paras 31–40.

128 *PHS*, above note 55 at paras 19 and 26–28.

129 *Ibid* at para 132.

130 *Bedford v Canada (AG)*, 2010 ONSC 4264 [*Bedford*].

ing their objectives of controlling the harms and nuisances associated with prostitution and therefore are inconsistent with the principles of fundamental justice. Specifically, the offence of living on the avails of the prostitution of another[131] is arbitrary because it is intended to protect prostitutes from exploitation by pimps, but frustrates that objective by making it unlawful for prostitutes to employ staff who might make their work safer.[132] This conclusion depends not on abstract or common-sense reasoning about the likely effects of the provision, but on close scrutiny of the voluminous empirical evidence filed by the parties concerning the effects of the provision on the working lives of prostitutes.[133]

The approach in *PHS* and *Bedford* resembles the approach taken in *Chaoulli* in that it involves a detailed and careful consideration of the rationality of the state's claim that the instrument it has chosen to pursue its objective does in fact contribute to that objective, in contrast to the approach in *Malmo-Levine*, where a reasoned apprehension that the instrument might contribute to the objective was enough. These cases, if they survive appellate review, evidently have very significant implications for public policy towards potentially harmful behaviour such as narcotics use and prostitution. On the basis of *Malmo-Levine*, one might have thought that the government could refute the allegation that criminalizing the possession of a substance is arbitrary simply by showing that the substance is harmful in some way to some persons; all questions about the effectiveness of the prohibition would be left to the legislative and executive branches.[134] But if *Chaoulli*, *PHS*, and *Bedford* are correct, then the allegation that a particular prohibition is arbitrary can only be established, or indeed refuted, by a careful empirical analysis of its effectiveness in controlling the harm at which it is directed.

---

131 *Criminal Code*, above note 24, s 212(1)(*j*).

132 *Bedford*, above note 130 at para 379.

133 See the summary of Himel J's findings, *ibid* at para 421.

134 Compare *Malmo-Levine*, above note 58 at paras 136–40. Justice Pitfield distinguished *Malmo-Levine* on the ground that it was "concerned with the use of marijuana for purely recreational purposes": *PHS* 2008, above note 124 at para 137. But this ground of distinction has little to do with the appropriate methodology for applying the arbitrariness standard under s 7.

4) The Impact of a Law Must Not Be Grossly Disproportionate

It is a principle of fundamental justice that the impact of a law on the interests protected by section 7 must be proportionate to the effect of the law on its objectives. But the measure of proportionality is not strict: a law will violate this principle of fundamental justice only if its impact on the protected interests is grossly disproportionate to its beneficial effects.

The test for gross disproportionality is whether the law (or other state action) is "so extreme" that it is "*per se* disproportionate to any legitimate government interest."[135] The standard is not one of mere disproportionality or even of overbreadth, but of *gross* disproportionality; accordingly, it allows a "broad latitude" for legislation.[136] It is difficult for a *Charter* applicant to demonstrate that a law fails to comply with this standard, so it is unsurprising that the Supreme Court has never invalidated a law[137] or expressly set aside a decision[138] on this ground. In *Malmo-Levine*, the accused argued that the effects of criminally prohibiting the possession of marijuana were grossly disproportionate to the benefits of the prohibition. The Court stated the issue as follows:

> . . . if the use of the criminal law were shown . . . to be grossly disproportionate in its effects on accused persons, when considered in light of the objective of protecting them from the harm caused by marihuana use, the prohibition would be contrary to fundamental justice and to s. 7 of the *Charter*.[139]

---

135 *Suresh v Canada (Minister of Citizenship and Immigration)*, 2002 SCC 1 at para 47 [*Suresh*]; see also *Malmo-Levine*, above note 58 at paras 142–43; *United States v Burns*, 2001 SCC 7 at para 78 [*Burns*]; *PHS*, above note 55 at para 133.

136 *Malmo-Levine*, ibid at para 175.

137 *Suresh*, above note 135 at paras 76–78 (power of Minister of Citizenship and Immigration to deport, on security grounds, refugee who would face torture constitutionally valid). Gross disproportionality is also the test for a violation of the s 12 right to be free from cruel and unusual treatment or punishment, and the Court has once recognized an infringement of s 12: *R v Smith*, [1987] 1 SCR 1045 [*Smith*].

138 In *Suresh*, ibid, the Minister's decision to deport the applicant to face possible torture was set aside on other grounds. *Burns*, above note 135, is probably best understood as setting aside as disproportionate the Minister of Justice's decision to extradite the *Charter* applicants without obtaining assurances that the death penalty would not be imposed; however, the Court does not expressly invoke the language of proportionality.

139 *Malmo-Levine*, above note 58 at para 169.

The accused relied on three facts about the prohibition on possession: first, a criminal record had adverse consequences apart from conviction; second, the prohibition was ineffective in any event; and third, its deleterious effects outweighed its salutary effects. The majority rejected all of these arguments, not on the facts, but in principle. The adverse effects of a conviction were part of its deterrent value and therefore could not count against it;[140] it would be "inconsistent with the rule of law" to count the ineffectiveness of a criminal prohibition in the disproportionality analysis;[141] and it was not appropriate to import the balance between salutary and deleterious effects from section 7 into section 1.[142]

In light of this reasoning, one wonders how the ill effects of a penal law could ever demonstrate its disproportionality. In *Bedford*, Himel J showed how this might be done. The applicants were three former sex workers who sought a declaration that certain prostitution-related provisions of the *Criminal Code* were unconstitutional. Himel J found that the provisions had a substantial impact not just on the liberty interest but on a prostitute's security of the person, in that they prevented prostitutes, particularly street prostitutes, from taking certain measures to protect their personal safety in their work.[143] She found that these effects on security of the person were grossly disproportionate to the minimal beneficial effects of the legislation,[144] and that they were therefore contrary to the principles of fundamental justice. The ineffectiveness of a criminal prohibition in deterring the prohibited conduct may not be enough to establish gross disproportionality; but if its very effectiveness in deterring the prohibited conduct undermines its effectiveness in achieving its own objectives, it may well cause deleterious effects out of all proportion to its salutary effects.

5) The Relationship between the Substantive Principles

a) Vagueness and Overbreadth
The Court's recognition in *Heywood* of a norm against overbreadth as an independent principle of fundamental justice was something of a surprise, as only two years before, a unanimous panel of the Court had held in *Nova Scotia Pharmaceutical Society* that although vagueness and overbreadth were distinct concepts, there was no distinct norm against overbreadth under the *Charter*. Gonthier J for the Court, had held that

---

140 *Ibid* at para 172.
141 *Ibid* at para 178.
142 *Ibid* at paras 179–82.
143 *Bedford*, above note 130 at para 421.
144 *Ibid* at paras 422–33.

"overbreadth is always related to some limitation under the *Charter*,"[145] whether under section 1 or under another limiting idea such as reasonable search (an overbroad search power might violate section 8) or cruel and unusual punishment (an overbroad power to punish might violate section 12). Nonetheless, the defect of a vague law is substantively different from the defect of an overbroad law. It is arguable that a vague law is necessarily overbroad, but an overbroad law need not be vague: "The intended effect of a statute may be perfectly clear and thus not vague, and yet its application may be overly broad."[146] Moreover, *Heywood* and *Demers* show the value of recognizing an independent norm against overbreadth. The unnecessarily broad and indeed oppressive prohibition created by section 179(1)(*b*) did not infringe any other section of the *Charter* or any other principle of fundamental justice. In particular, it was not vague; on the contrary, it was, if anything, clearer than many other criminal prohibitions. Similarly, there was no unconstitutional vagueness in the provisions at issue in *Demers*. If the Court had not recognized the norm against overbreadth as a principle of fundamental justice, there would have been no way to recognize the particular substantive defect of these laws under the *Charter*.

b) Overbreadth, Arbitrariness, and Disproportionality: How Many Principles?

The norms against overbreadth, arbitrariness, and gross disproportionality all involve failures of instrumental rationality, in the following sense. Whenever a law fails to satisfy one of these norms, there is a mismatch between the legislature's objective and the means chosen to achieve it: the law is inadequately connected to its objective or in some sense goes too far in seeking to attain it. It might be thought that these norms are really three separate ways of identifying the same kind of defect in the law: perhaps these three norms are different facets or aspects of a larger overarching norm requiring a minimal degree of instrumental rationality in legislation. On the other hand, it might be thought that each of them names a distinct failure of instrumental rationality: maybe, for example, a law can be overbroad without being arbitrary or grossly disproportionate. Or it might be thought that while the three norms are not identical, there is enough overlap between them that perhaps the law could manage with fewer than three.

---

145 *Nova Scotia Pharmaceutical Society*, above note 2 at 630.
146 *R v Zundel* (1987), 31 CCC (3d) 97 at 125 (Ont CA), quoted with approval in *Nova Scotia Pharmaceutical Society*, *ibid* at 630; see also *Heywood*, above note 40 at 792.

Thus, there are (at least) three possible ways to understand the relationships among the norms against overbreadth, arbitrariness, and gross disproportionality. The first is to hold that all overbroad laws offend section 7 and that the norms against arbitrariness and gross disproportionality are superfluous; this interpretation requires us to understand overbreadth as grossly arbitrary overbreadth rather than as mere overbreadth (see Section B(2), above in this chapter). The second is to hold that an overbroad law offends section 7 only if it reaches the threshold of being arbitrary or grossly disproportionate. In the first solution, the three norms collapse into one norm against overbreadth; in the second solution, there is no norm against overbreadth—mere overbreadth as such is constitutionally permissible—but there are separate norms against arbitrariness and gross disproportionality. The third approach is to maintain that the norms are independent of each other, that it is possible for a law to respect any two of them while nonetheless infringing the third. On this approach, the norm against gross disproportionality is best understood as a norm against disproportionality "*per se*"; that is, a law offends this norm where it is neither arbitrary (because it has some effectiveness in achieving its objective) nor overbroad (because it affects the protected interests no more than necessary to achieve its objective), but where its impact on the protected interests is too severe to justify whatever beneficial effects it might have. On this understanding, an overbroad law is disproportionate to its objective, but it is possible to imagine a more carefully tailored law would be proportionate, while a grossly disproportionate law could not be more carefully tailored: any version of the law that had a less severe impact on the section 7 interest would also be less effective in achieving its objectives.

There is some support for the first solution in *Heywood*, where Cory J commented that "[t]he effect of overbreadth is that in some applications the law is arbitrary or disproportionate."[147] On this view, a finding of overbreadth entails a finding of arbitrariness or a finding of disproportionality, so the norms against arbitrariness or disproportionality would serve as ways of demonstrating overbreadth. But given the margin of appreciation that the Court is prepared to grant the legislature in finding legal solutions to social problems, it is unlikely that the Court will accept the proposition that any degree of overbreadth renders a law inconsistent with the principles of fundamental justice. Some degree of overbreadth is probably inevitable, and in this regard it is worth noting

---

147 *Heywood, ibid* at 793.

that Cory J did not use the term *gross* disproportionality in explaining the implications of a finding of overbreadth.

There is some support for the second solution in *Clay* and in *Cochrane v Ontario (AG)* (*Cochrane*). In *Clay*, the majority appeared to hold that a law is not overbroad in the section 7 sense unless "the adverse effect of a legislative measure on the individuals subject to its strictures is *grossly* disproportionate to the state interest the legislation seeks to protect," and commented that overbreadth in this sense is "related to arbitrariness."[148] In *Cochrane*, Sharpe JA of the Ontario Court of Appeal proceeded along these lines, treating the norms against arbitrariness and disproportionality as aspects of an overarching norm against overbreadth:

> Overbreadth is a term used to describe legislation that, as drafted, covers more than is necessary to attain the legislature's objective and thereby impinges unduly upon a protected right or freedom. A law is unconstitutionally overbroad if it deprives an individual of "life, liberty and security of the person" in a manner that is "grossly disproportionate" to the state interest that the legislation seeks to protect. Such a law is said to be "arbitrary" . . . . A law . . . is also "arbitrary" unless it is grounded in a "reasoned apprehension of harm."[149]
>
> . . . the test for a breach of s. 7 on grounds of overbreadth is [1] whether the law is "arbitrary" because there is no "reasoned apprehension of harm" or [2] whether the law is "grossly disproportionate" to the legislative objective.[150]

On this approach, the norm against overbreadth is not an independent norm under section 7; rather, to say that a law is "overbroad" is merely a way of saying that it is arbitrary or grossly disproportionate in some respect.

Sharpe JA's approach is consistent with much of what the Supreme Court has done. *Heywood*, which explicitly recognized the norm against overbreadth, can be read as a case where the impact of the prohibition on the persons to whom it applied (convicted sex offenders) was grossly disproportionate to the legislature's objectives (the protection of children) because it restrained the offender's liberty far more than necessary (he would also be prohibited from "loitering" in a remote area of a national park where no children were present). The law held to be

---

148 *Clay*, above note 50 at para 38 [emphasis in original].
149 *Cochrane*, above note 11 at para 18.
150 *Ibid* at para 25 [numbering added]; see also *Lindsay*, above note 35 at para 21.

overbroad in *Demers* can be read as arbitrary because, in the name of public safety, it restricted the liberty of a detainee who posed no risk to public safety, but applied even where there was no risk to public safety and so was, to that extent, inconsistent with its own purpose.

Nonetheless, the approach in *Cochrane* does not reflect the Supreme Court of Canada's explicit practice. In *Malmo-Levine*, the Court considered the claims of arbitrariness and gross disproportionality separately and not as aspects of a larger concept of overbreadth. In *Demers*, the Court held that a law was overbroad without explicitly considering whether it was arbitrary or grossly disproportional. And in *PHS*, the Court treated each of the three principles as distinct, finding that the ministerial decision in question was both arbitrary and grossly disproportionate and declining to consider whether it was overbroad.[151] Similarly, the British Columbia Court of Appeal has continued to recognize the three norms as distinct from each other; in *Victoria (City) v Adams*, for example, that court found a municipal bylaw to be overbroad but not arbitrary.[152]

In the end, the question of which solution to adopt depends not just on precedent but also on the relationship between the content of the three norms, and specifically on whether the content of one (ore more) of them exhausts the content of any of the others. The most plausible view is the third: each norm is distinct from the others because it is possible for a law to offend one of these norms without offending the other two. An overbroad law is broader than reasonably necessary to achieve its objectives; but it is not arbitrary if it does achieve its objectives, and it is not necessarily grossly disproportionate. "Overbreadth" in this sense is not grossly disproportionate overbreadth, but it might be something more than mere overbreadth, to allow the legislature a margin of appreciation in its choice of policy instruments. An arbitrary law is fundamentally ineffective because it is inconsistent with its own objectives; it might be said that such a law is necessarily overbroad because it unnecessarily restricts the section 7 interests, but its real defect is not its overbreadth but its basic irrationality. If overbreadth and arbitrariness are understood this way, then a grossly disproportionate law should be understood as one that has such an extreme impact on the section 7 interests that its benefits are not worth its costs. A grossly disproportionate law is not necessarily overbroad, in that the draconian nature of the law may be the only way for it to achieve its objectives; nor is it necessarily arbitrary, since it may indeed achieve its objectives; but

---

151 *PHS*, above note 55 at paras 127–35.
152 Above note 124.

the costs, in terms of the interests protected by section 7, are simply out of proportion to the objectives achieved.

c) The Substantive Principles and Section 1 of the *Charter*

A limitation of a *Charter* right will be constitutional where the limit is, in the words of section 1 of the *Charter*, "prescribed by law [and] . . . demonstrably justified in a free and democratic society." The *Oakes* test requires the state to demonstrate that the limit is proportional to its objective in that:

(1) the limit is rationally connected to the objective;

(2) the limit is the minimally rights-impairing means of achieving the objective, and

(3) the deleterious impact of the limit on the right is not dispropor-tionate to the beneficial impact of the limit on the objective.[153]

The substantive concepts discussed in Section B of this chapter may well appear in other guises as aspects of the proportionality analysis under section 1 of the *Charter*. A vague law is not "prescribed by law" and therefore cannot be a justified limit under section 1; however, the claim that a law is too vague to amount to a limit prescribed by law has never succeeded in the Supreme Court of Canada[154] (except in cases where the law already violates a *Charter* right on the ground of vague-ness). A vague law may also fail the "minimal impairment" branch of the *Oakes* test because a more precise law would impair the right less.[155] An arbitrary law will not be rationally connected to its objective.[156] An overbroad law cannot be a minimal impairment of the applicant's *Char-ter* right.[157] And a grossly disproportionate law will likely fail at step (iii) of the *Oakes* test.

---

153 *Oakes*, above note 48 at 138–40.

154 The court indicated its reluctance to reject a potential s. 1 justification on this ground in *Osborne v Canada (Treasury Board)*, [1991] 2 SCR 69 at 94–96. In the following cases, the impugned law was not too vague to be justified under s 1: *R v Butler*, [1992] 1 SCR 452 (definition of "obscene" in *Criminal Code*, above note 24, s 163(8) violates s 2(*b*) but justified under s 1); *R v Keegstra*, [1990] 3 SCR 697 (definition of wilful promotion of hatred violates s 2(*b*) but justified under s 1); *Committee for the Commonwealth of Canada v Canada*, [1991] 1 SCR 139 (limit on freedom of expression on government-owned property violates s 2(*b*) and not justified under s 1); *Irwin Toy Ltd v Quebec (AG)*, [1989] 1 SCR 927 (provin-cial law regulating advertising violates s 2(*b*) but justified under s 1).

155 *Nova Scotia Pharmaceutical Society*, above note 2 at 626.

156 *Chaoulli*, above note 57 at para 155; *PHS*, above note 55 at para 137.

157 Compare *R v Sharpe*, 2001 SCC 2. The accused challenged the statutory defini-tion of child pornography on several grounds. The majority found that the

But it would be an error to infer from the dual role of these concepts that they need only be considered either under section 7 or under section 1. The role of vagueness, overbreadth, arbitrariness, and gross disproportionality under section 7 is to establish a violation of the section 7 *Charter* right; the role of these ideas under section 1 is to rebut the state's claim that a limit on a *Charter* right is justified, regardless of which section of the *Charter* has been infringed. There are many cases where these ideas play no role in establishing a limit on a *Charter* right: for example, a limit on freedom of expression is easily established without demonstrating any of the substantive defects discussed here; a limit on the section 8 right to be free from unreasonable search or seizure may, similarly, be established without showing that the law creating the search power is vague or overbroad.

The relationship between section 7 and section 1 of the *Charter* is discussed in more detail in Chapter 6.

6) The State Must Obey the Law

In *Hitzig*, the Ontario Court of Appeal held that "the state's obligation to obey the law is a principle of fundamental justice."[158] The context in which this principle emerged is described more fully in Section B(3)(c), above in this chapter: the federal government had enacted regulations permitting individuals to possess and to cultivate marijuana for medical purposes, but had not provided any lawful means for them to obtain marijuana. The principle was based on the general constitutional value of the rule of law and its manifestations in other *Charter* rights, but perhaps more importantly, on the observation that "Without this obligation [to obey the law], there would be no enforceable limit on the state's power over individuals."[159] The practical importance of this principle is likely to be limited, as the vast majority of section 7 claims involve either challenges to statutes or challenges to particular decisions which are themselves authorized by valid law. Where unlawful state conduct affects the interest protected by section 7 of the *Charter*, courts generally have no difficulty in recognizing that it also violates section 7.[160] The principle might, however, be deployed in a constitu-

---

definition violated s 2(*b*) of the *Charter* but found the violation justified under s 1. The accused's s 7 overbreadth challenge was not considered in any detail because it "wholly replicate[d] the overbreadth concerns that are the central obstacle to the justification of the s 2(*b*) breach" (para 18).

158 *Hitzig*, above note 113 at para 115.

159 *Ibid* at para 113.

160 Compare *R v Nasogaluak*, 2010 SCC 6 at para 38.

tional challenge to section 25.1 of the *Criminal Code*, which creates a scheme under which certain senior police officers can authorize other persons to commit certain criminal offences as an investigative tool. The difficulty would be in deciding whether the very fact that section 25.1 was enacted immunizes this power from scrutiny under the principle, or whether a process authorizing the commission of what would otherwise be a crime itself engages the principle.

C. PRINCIPLES OF PENAL RESPONSIBILITY: ELEMENTS OF OFFENCES

The principles discussed in Section B, above in this chapter, apply to any law that engages the interests protected by section 7. But the Supreme Court of Canada has recognized a number of substantive principles that apply particularly to the definition of criminal and other penal offences and defences; that is, to the question of whether a person is criminally or penally liable for her conduct. These principles, or analogous principles, might be applicable in other legal contexts where the interests protected by section 7 are engaged; but unlike principles of procedural fairness, which apply whenever liberty is at stake for whatever reason (see Chapter 5), the principles to be discussed here seem to relate particularly to the criminal or penal context.

To demonstrate a person's liability for criminal or other penal offence, the prosecution typically has to demonstrate not only that the person committed the prohibited act (often called the *actus reus*) but also that the person was in some way at fault (often called the *mens rea*) in committing the act. This principle was well established in Canadian law before the *Charter*, in the form of a presumption that in the absence of a clear legislative intention to the contrary, penal statutes should be interpreted as requiring proof of some form of fault.[161] But it is also worth remembering that most offences in the *Criminal Code* have always been defined or interpreted to require proof of subjective fault (that is, knowledge or intention with respect to the elements of the prohibited act). Moreover, many of the major twentieth century commentators on criminal law strongly supported the requirement of

---

161 *R v Sault Ste Marie (City)*, [1978] 2 SCR 1299 [*Sault Ste Marie*]; see also *Beaver v R*, [1957] SCR 531; *Harding v Price*, [1948] 1 KB 695 at 700–1; *Sweet v Parsley*, [1970] 1 AC 132.

subjective fault in criminal law.[162] Nonetheless, before the *Charter*, if Parliament or a provincial legislature chose, within its sphere of legislative authority, to explicitly define an offence without a fault element, no formal constitutional challenge to the offence definition was possible. By recognizing a number of legal principles concerning fault as principles of fundamental justice under section 7 of the *Charter*, the Supreme Court of Canada has significantly restricted the legislature's constitutional power to define offences as it sees fit.

1) Penal Liability Requires Proof of Physically Voluntary Behaviour

It is a principle of fundamental justice that a person's conduct must be physically voluntary in order to attract criminal liability. "Conduct that is not voluntary cannot be criminal."[163]

The voluntariness requirement, though infrequently in issue in criminal proceedings, is deeply rooted in our system of criminal justice, in which responsibility for one's actions, and *a fortiori* criminal liability, is attributed on the basis of acting or, in appropriate cases, failing to act. Where a person's conduct is not the product of any decision to act (or not to act), then the conduct is not properly attributed to the person but to the factor, whatever it is, that caused the conduct. In criminal law terms, voluntariness is a threshold requirement without which there is no *actus reus*,[164] let alone any fault.

In Canadian criminal law, one factor that may lead to involuntary conduct is "automatism." Automatism may be succinctly defined as "a mental state in which the conscious mind is disassociated from the part of the mind that controls action."[165] Canadian law currently recognizes two forms of automatism: mental disorder (or insane) automatism, which results in a verdict of not criminally responsible on account of mental disorder (NCRMD), and non-mental-disorder (or non-insane) automatism, which results in an acquittal. Where the accused establishes a proper foundation for the claim of automatism, the trial judge

---

162 Glanville Williams, *Criminal Law: The General Part*, 2d ed (London: Stevens, 1961) at §14; Jerome Hall, *Principles of Criminal Law* (Indianapolis: Bobbs-Merrill, 1947) at 157–68; Don Stuart, *Canadian Criminal Law: A Treatise*, 5th ed (Scarborough: Thomson/Carswell, 2007) at 161–70.

163 *R v Luedecke*, 2008 ONCA 716 at para 53 [*Luedecke*]; see also *R v Daviault*, [1994] 3 SCR 63 at 103 [*Daviault*]; *R v Stone*, [1999] 2 SCR 290 at para 169 [*Stone*].

164 *Luedecke, ibid* at para 56.

165 *Ibid* at para 54.

must decide, as a matter of law, whether the condition pleaded is best characterized as a mental disorder (disease of the mind) or not.[166] This determination is a heavily policy-laden exercise which takes into account both the nature of the factor alleged to have produced the state of automatism (internal to the accused, or an external circumstance) and the continuing danger, if any, posed by the accused's condition.[167] If the condition is properly characterized as mental disorder automatism, the trier of fact will decide whether the accused has established the defence of NCRMD on the facts; if not, the trier of fact will decide whether the accused should be acquitted on the ground of non-mental-disorder automatism. In either case, the burden of proof is on the accused to establish the condition on a balance of probabilities.[168]

The voluntariness principle, though clearly recognized as a principle of fundamental justice, has not yet been invoked to invalidate any statute. In the Supreme Court of Canada's not entirely satisfactory decision in *R v Daviault* (*Daviault*),[169] the principle was invoked to rework a common law rule. The accused, according to the trial judge's factual findings, had sexually assaulted the complainant while in a state of extreme self-induced intoxication akin to automatism. The trial judge acquitted the accused on the ground that the Crown had not proved the voluntariness of his conduct beyond a reasonable doubt. But, according to the "*Leary* rule," self-induced intoxication was not a defence to the offence of sexual assault;[170] thus, the Court of Appeal allowed the Crown's appeal and found the accused guilty. On the accused's appeal to the Supreme Court of Canada, a majority held that the *Leary* rule

---

166 *Stone*, above note 163 at paras 193–95.
167 *Stone*, *ibid* at paras 203–22. In *Luedecke*, above note 163, the accused committed a sexual assault while in a state of parasomnia (sleepwalking). Notwithstanding authority suggesting that sleepwalking would be characterized as non-insane automatism (notably *R v Parks*, [1992] 2 SCR 871 [*Parks*]), the Ontario Court of Appeal held, in light of the evidence led at trial and the approach in *Stone*, that his condition should be characterized as mental disorder automatism.
168 *Stone*, *ibid* at paras 173–92.
169 Above note 163.
170 *R v Leary*, [1978] 1 SCR 29. According to *Leary*, rape is a crime of "general intent" to which the defence of intoxication does not apply; or, more precisely, the trier of fact may not consider the accused's self-induced intoxication in deciding whether the Crown has proved fault. In *R v Bernard*, [1988] 2 SCR 833 [*Bernard*], the Court held that the *Leary* rule continued to apply to the offence of sexual assault. For further discussion of the distinction between crimes of "general intent" and of "specific intent," see Stuart, above note 162 at 432–40; for further discussion of intoxication and sexual assault, see Hamish Stewart, *Sexual Offences in Canadian Law*, loose-leaf (Aurora, ON: Canada Law Book, 2004) at 3:200.20.20 and 3:600.50 [Stewart, *Sexual Offences*].

offended section 7 of the *Charter*. Justice Cory, speaking for himself and three other judges,[171] held that the *Leary* rule impermissibly substituted proof that the accused intended to get drunk for proof of the fault element of the offence;[172] however, he also agreed with two separately concurring colleagues that it would be contrary to section 7 to convict a person who was acting involuntarily because he was in a state of extreme intoxication akin to automatism.[173] So *Daviault* may be read as holding that the *Leary* rule violated section 7 because it permitted the conviction of a person who committed a criminal act while in a state of automatism, contrary to the voluntariness principle. Certainly, the remedy adopted by Cory J is more responsive to this reading than to his holding concerning fault. As has often been pointed out, if the *Leary* rule offended the *Charter* because of the constitutionally impermissible substitution of the intent to get drunk for the intent required by the definition of the offence, the logical remedy would be to eliminate the common law category of "general intent" offences altogether and always permit the trier of fact to consider evidence of intoxication in deciding whether the Crown has proved fault beyond a reasonable doubt.[174] Instead, Cory J created an exception to the *Leary* rule for the accused who is so intoxicated that he is in a state akin to automatism (though, foreshadowing *R v Stone*, he also shifted the burden of proof to the accused to establish this state on a balance of probabilities).[175]

Parliament responded to *Daviault* by enacting section 33.1 of the *Criminal Code*, a complicated and confusing section which is nonetheless clearly intended to overturn *Daviault*. The Supreme Court has not had an opportunity to consider the constitutional validity of section 33.1, but the claim that it is contrary to section 7 would appear to be very strong.[176]

Automatism is not the only way in which a person's conduct can be involuntary for criminal law purposes. Suppose, for example, that person A were to seize control of person B's body and use it as a weapon

---

171   L'Heureux-Dubé, McLachlin, and Iacobucci JJ.

172   *Daviault*, above note 163 at 87–92.

173   *Ibid* at 87–93; compare Lamer CJC at 71 and La Forest J at 72.

174   *Ibid* at 71, Lamer CJC; Stuart, above note 162 at 446–47.

175   *Daviault*, *ibid* at 103–4.

176   The main lower-court cases all hold that s 33.1 violates s 7 but divide on whether the violation is justified under s 1: *R v Brenton* (1999), 180 DLR (4th) 314 (NWTSC), rev'd on other grounds 2001 NWTCA 1; *R v Vickberg* (1998), 16 CR (5th) 164 (BCSC); *R v Dunn*, [1999] OJ No 5452 (SCJ); *R v Jensen*, [2000] OJ No 4870 (SCJ); *R v Dow*, 2010 QCCS 4276. In *Brenton*, *Dunn*, and *Jensen*, the s 1 justification was rejected; in *Vickberg* and *Dow*, it was accepted. See also Stewart, *Sexual Offences*, above note 170 at 3:200.20.20.

or as a projectile. In such a fanciful case, B would not be in a state of automatism because his consciousness would not be "disassociated from the part of the mind that controls action";[177] but his body movements would nonetheless not be under his control and, according to the voluntariness principle, could not be the basis of criminal liability. The voluntariness principle might also be the basis for Canadian recognition of the common law defence of impossibility, according to which an accused person cannot be criminally liable where it was impossible for her to comply with the law that applied to her.[178]

2) Penal Liability Requires Proof of a Minimum Level of Fault

It is a principle of fundamental justice that penal liability requires proof, at a minimum, that the accused or defendant failed to exercise due diligence.

This principle of fundamental justice was established in two stages. First, in *Re BC Motor Vehicle Act* (the *Motor Vehicle Reference*), the Supreme Court held that absolute liability—that is, penal liability without proof of fault—offended the principles of fundamental justice.[179] As discussed in Chapter 3, Section B(1), the Court struck down a British Columbia statute that created an offence of driving while prohibited with no requirement that the prosecution prove that the accused knew, ought to have known, or even had been given notice of the prohibition. But the *Motor Vehicle Reference* did not directly state the minimum level of fault necessary to satisfy section 7. That issue was addressed in *R v Hess; R v Nguyen*.[180] The two accused, in unrelated cases, challenged the constitutionality of the criminal offence of having sexual intercourse with a female under the age of fourteen. The offence definition expressly stated that an accused was guilty "whether or not he believes that [the complainant] is fourteen years of age or more"[181] and was thus an offence of absolute liability in relation to the essence of the *actus reus*: the complainant's age. In light of the *Motor Vehicle Reference*,

---

177 *Luedecke*, above note 163 at para 54.
178 This defence is recognized in *Tifaga v Department of Labour*, [1980] 2 NZLR 235, and was applied to acquit a person in *Finau v Department of Labour*, [1984] 2 NZLR 396.
179 *Motor Vehicle Reference*, above note 1 at 513–15.
180 *R v Hess; R v Nguyen*, [1990] 2 SCR 906, 59 CCC (3d) 161 [*Hess; Nguyen*].
181 *Criminal Code*, RSC 1970, c C-34, s 146(1) [*Criminal Code*, RSC 1970]. This offence and related offences are discussed in some detail in Stewart, *Sexual Offences*, above note 170 at 2:400.

the offence obviously offended section 7; but the Court went on to say that any penal law that "makes it unnecessary for the Crown to prove *mens rea* and that does not provide an accused, at a minimum, with a due diligence defence" was contrary to the principles of fundamental justice.[182] Having found that this infringement of section 7 was not justified under section 1,[183] the Court did not strike down the offence altogether but held that the words removing the defence of mistake of fact were of no force or effect.[184]

The proposition that due diligence is the minimum constitutionally permissible degree of fault was unanimously confirmed in *R v Wholesale Travel Group Inc* (*Wholesale Travel Group*).[185] The Court held both that the defence of due diligence was constitutionally adequate for the offence at issue and that the legislature's attempt to restrict the defence further was unconstitutional. The accused corporation was charged with five counts of false or misleading advertising.[186] The allegation was that the accused advertised vacation packages at "wholesale prices" but charged more than the cost they incurred in supplying them. The offence was punishable by imprisonment, so the section 7 liberty interest was engaged. Section 37.3(2) of the *Competition Act* created a statutory defence to this charge, consisting of four elements to be established by the accused: (*a*) the act or omission was an error; (*b*) the accused "took reasonable precautions and exercised due diligence to prevent . . . the error"; (*c*) the accused or another "took reasonable measures to bring the error to the attention of the class of persons likely to have been reached" by the erroneous advertisement; and (*d*) these measures were taken "forthwith." Chief Justice Lamer and Cory J, writing separately but speaking for the entire Court on this point,[187] held that the defence

---

182 *Hess; Nguyen*, above note 180 at 918, Wilson J.

183 *Ibid* at 919–27, Wilson J for the majority. Chief Justice McLachlin dissenting, Gonthier J concurring in the dissent, would have upheld the infringement under s 1.

184 *Ibid* at 934. I have argued elsewhere that this remedy, combined with the presumption of statutory interpretation in favour of subjective fault for criminal offences, means that for offences alleged to have occurred between 17 April 1982 (when the *Charter* came into force) and 1 January 1988 (when the offence was repealed), the Crown must prove the accused's knowledge, recklessness, or wilful blindness as to the complainant's age: Stewart, *Sexual Offences*, above note 170 at §2:400.20.10.

185 *R v Wholesale Travel Group Inc*, [1991] 3 SCR 154 [*Wholesale Travel Group*].

186 *Competition Act*, RSC 1970, c C-23, s 36(1).

187 *Wholesale Travel Group*, above note 185 at 238–41, Cory J, L'Heureux-Dubé J concurring. Chief Justice Lamer dissenting at 187–89 analyzed the statutory defence and reached the same conclusion (Sopinka and McLachlin JJ concurred in Lamer CJC's dissent; La Forest J dissenting expressed at 209 "substantial

was constitutionally inadequate. Paragraphs (*a*) and (*b*), taken together, created a defence of due diligence, and an offence subject to a defence of due diligence did not offend section 7.[188] But the elements added by paragraphs (*c*) and (*d*) meant that a person could be convicted of the offence despite having exercised due diligence.[189] These paragraphs therefore offended section 7 and could not be justified under section 1.[190] By invalidating a defence that demanded more than due diligence, the Court made it clear that failure of due diligence is indeed the minimum level of fault acceptable under section 7 of the *Charter*.

Several constitutional challenges to offences have failed because the court has interpreted the offence as having a fault element of negligence (or, in other words, the defence of due diligence was available to the accused), by statute or by operation of the *Sault Ste Marie* approach to the interpretation of penal statutes.[191] As noted in Chapter 2, Section D(3), offences of absolute liability do not offend section 7 where they do not affect the interests protected by section 7—typically, where imprisonment is not an available penalty.

A difficult application of the principle of minimum fault arose in *R v Pontes*.[192] The defendant was charged with driving while prohibited. The prohibition arose automatically and with no notice to him because he had been convicted of a driving offence.[193] The relevant highway traffic legislation did not expressly state the fault element for the of-

---

188 *Ibid* at 241, Cory J.

189 *Ibid* at 187–88, Lamer CJC; compare *ibid* at 252–53 (holding that these paragraphs made the offence "tantamount to absolute liability").

190 The Court was unanimous on these points, but divided quite badly on another issue: whether the reverse onus—the requirement that the accused prove due diligence on a balance of probabilities, in contrast to the Crown's proving negligence beyond a reasonable doubt—violated s 11(*d*) of the *Charter* and, if it did, whether the violation could be justified under s 1. In the end, the reverse onus was upheld by a majority comprising two judges who held that it did not violate s 11(*d*) (Cory and L'Heureux-Dubé JJ) and three judges who held that it did violate s 11(*d*) but was justified under s 1 (Iacobucci, Gonthier, and Stevenson JJ).

191 *R v Finlay*, [1993] 4 SCR 103 at 115–18 (former offence of careless storage of a firearm an offence of negligence and so not contrary to s 7); *R v Felderhof*, 2007 ONCJ 345 (offences under provincial securities legislation provide for defence of due diligence and so do not offend s 7). According to *Sault Ste Marie*, above note 161 at 1325–326 regulatory statutes should be interpreted as permitting the accused to raise a defence of due diligence, unless it is clear that the legislature intended to make the offence one of absolute liability.

192 *R v Pontes*, [1995] 3 SCR 44 [*Pontes*].

193 *Motor Vehicle Act*, RSBC 1979, c 288, s 92.

fence and was punishable by a minimum term of imprisonment.[194] The applicable *Offences Act* specified that notwithstanding any other statutory provision, "no person is liable to imprisonment with respect to an absolute liability offence."[195] So the question the Court faced was, strictly speaking, one of statutory interpretation rather than constitutional analysis: if the offence was found to be one of absolute liability, it would not be necessary to provide any constitutional remedy because the *Offences Act* would mean that the offender would not be imprisoned. Justice Cory, for the majority, held that the offence was indeed one of absolute liability, but on a somewhat debatable ground: he held that no fault-based defence to the charge was available and, in particular, it was no defence that the defendant had not been notified of the driving prohibition resulting from the prior conviction.[196] Justice Gonthier dissenting held that the offence was indeed one of strict liability. A defendant's ignorance of the statutory prohibition on driving was a mistake of law that was irrelevant to liability and in particular had no bearing on the question of due diligence.[197] An accused person might nonetheless defend himself on the grounds "that he made a reasonable mistake of fact as to the existence of his conviction, or that he exercised due diligence to ascertain whether he had been convicted of one of the underlying offences."[198] Neither set of reasons for judgment is entirely satisfactory. Cory J's emphasis on the absence of notice is hard to reconcile with the usual rule that mistake of law is, subject to very few exceptions, irrelevant to liability;[199] while Gonthier J's reading of the statutes offers, as he himself recognizes, an extraordinarily narrow range of defences to conduct that can result in imprisonment.[200] Had Gonthier J's reading prevailed, the statute might have been considered to offend the principle of fundamental justice requiring that defences not be illusory (see Section G(1), below in this chapter).

---

194 *Motor Vehicle Act, ibid*, s 94(1). This is the same offence that was at issue in the *Motor Vehicle Reference*, above note 1, but now without the express statement in s 94(2) that it was an offence of absolute liability, which had been struck down and, in 1986, repealed.

195 *Offences Act*, RSBC 1979, c 305, s 4.1. The legislature added this provision after the decision in the *Motor Vehicle Reference*, above note 1.

196 *Pontes*, above note 192 at paras 43–47.

197 *Ibid* at paras 71–80, Gonthier J dissenting.

198 *Ibid* at para 82.

199 Unless we read Cory J as implicitly recognizing a broader defence of mistake of law: on this possibility, see Hamish Stewart, "Mistake of Law under the *Charter*" (1998) 40 Crim LQ 476.

200 *Pontes*, above note 192 at para 83.

3) The Fault Element of an Offence Must Be Proportionate to Its Seriousness

It is a principle of fundamental justice that the fault element of an offence must be proportionate to the seriousness of the offence. As McLachlin J put it in *R v Creighton* (*Creighton*), "the seriousness of the offence must not be disproportionate to the degree of moral fault;"[201] that is, the "element of mental fault or moral culpability" of an offence must be "proportionate to the seriousness and consequences of the offence charged."[202] Similarly, in *R v Hydro-Québec*, the Court commented that the principles of fundamental justice would normally require a higher degree of fault for "true crimes" than for regulatory offences.[203] In *Creighton* itself, the majority held that the fault element of unlawful manslaughter—proof that the accused ought to have foreseen that his dangerous unlawful act would create a risk of serious bodily harm—satisfied this principle of proportionality.

The principle of proportionate fault has rarely been invoked and has never been used to invalidate an offence definition. It is unusual, particularly in the *Charter* era, for the legislature to create a serious offence without proof of a significant degree of fault, this result being accomplished either by expressly defining a fault element such as intention or knowledge, or by leaving room for the offence to be interpreted as demanding proof of such an element. So it is difficult to envisage realistic circumstances in which this principle would be violated. The creation of an offence that had serious consequences and exposed an offender to significant penalties, but had a fault element that was easy to establish and not closely connected to the consequences, might violate it. Consider, for example, the offence of arson. As currently defined, the core offences of arson require proof of, among other elements, that the accused "intentionally or recklessly cause[d] damage by fire or explosion to property . . . ."[204] This offence undoubtedly satisfies the principle of proportionality, as the Crown must prove a significant subjective fault element—intention or recklessness—with respect to the conduct and consequences that are at the core of the offence: dam-

---

201 *R v Creighton*, [1993] 3 SCR 3 at 53, McLachlin J [*Creighton*].

202 *Ibid* at 53–54. *Creighton* is discussed more fully in Section C(3), below in this chapter.

203 *R v Hydro-Québec*, [1997] 3 SCR 213 at para 120.

204 This wording appears in the *Criminal Code*, above note 24, ss 433, 434, 434.1, and 435. There is also an offence of negligent arson under s 436.

aging property by fire or explosion.[205] But suppose Parliament were to redefine the offence of arson as conduct causing damage to property by fire or explosion, plus proof that the accused knew she was handling a flammable substance.[206] This fault element, though subjective, would be so remotely related to the essence of the offence that it would offend the principle of proportionality between offence and fault.

4) Certain Offences Require Proof of a Specific Fault Element

It is a principle of fundamental justice that certain offences, because of the stigma associated with them or the severity of the available penalties, require proof of a specific subjective fault element relating to the nature of the crime. This small group of offences includes murder, attempted murder, theft, war crimes, and crimes against humanity.

a) Murder

The best way to understand this principle of fundamental justice is to consider how it developed in the law of homicide.

Section 222 of the *Criminal Code* defines "homicide" as "directly or indirectly, by any means, . . . caus[ing] the death of a human being."[207] It then goes on to distinguish between culpable and non-culpable homicide,[208] and to state that non-culpable homicide is not an offence.[209] Section 222(5) defines four ways in which a culpable homicide can be committed; but given the extreme rarity of two of them, in the rest of this discussion I will assume that culpable homicide can be committed by means of an unlawful act[210] or by criminal negligence.[211]

---

205 Compare *R v D(SD)*, 2002 NFCA 18 at para 25 [*D(SD)*]. The accused set fire to a bag of chips in a convenience store and unsuccessfully attempted to put out the flames; the fire spread and damaged the store. She was acquitted of offences under ss 433 and 434; though the accused had obviously intended to set fire to the bag of chips, the Crown had proved neither that she intended to damage the store, nor that she was reckless as to that damage.

206 Under this definition, the accused in *D(SD)*, *ibid*, would have been guilty of arson.

207 *Criminal Code*, above note 24, s 222(1).

208 *Ibid*, s 222(2).

209 *Ibid*, s 222(3).

210 *Ibid*, s 222(5)(*a*).

211 *Ibid*, s 222(5)(*b*).

There are three types of culpable homicide: murder, manslaughter, and infanticide.[212] Murder[213] and infanticide[214] are further defined by the Code, but manslaughter is not. Manslaughter, is, therefore, any culpable homicide[215] that does *not* meet the definition of murder or infanticide. It is a residual category of culpable homicide. Given the rarity of prosecutions for infanticide,[216] in the rest of this discussion I will assume that culpable homicide is either murder or manslaughter.

In 1982, when the *Charter* came into force, sections 212 and 213 (now sections 229 and 230) of the *Criminal Code* read as follows:

212. Culpable homicide is murder

(*a*) where the person who causes the death of a human being
   (i) means to cause his death, or
   (ii) means to cause him bodily harm that he knows is likely to cause his death, and is reckless whether death ensues or not;
(*b*) where a person, meaning to cause death to a human being or meaning to him harm that he knows is likely to cause his death, and being reckless whether death ensues or not, by accident or mistake causes death to another human being, notwithstanding that he does not mean to cause death or bodily harm to that human being; or
(*c*) where a person, for an unlawful object, does anything that he knows or ought to know is likely to cause death, and thereby causes death to a human being, notwithstanding that he desires to effect his object without causing death or bodily harm to any human being.

213. Culpable homicide is murder where a person causes the death of a human being while committing or attempting to commit high treason or treason or an offence mentioned in section 62 (sabotage), 76 (piratical acts) 76.1 (hijacking an aircraft), 132 or subsection 133(1) or sections 134 to 136 (escape or rescue from prison or lawful custody), 143 or 146 (rape or attempt to commit rape), 149 or 166 (indecent assault), subsection 246(2) (resisting lawful arrest), 247 (kidnapping and forcible confinement), 302 (robbery), 306 (breaking and entering) or 389 or 390 (arson), whether or not the person means

---

212 *Ibid*, s 222(4).
213 *Ibid*, ss 229 & 230.
214 *Ibid*, s 233.
215 As defined by ss 222(1) and (5), *ibid*.
216 Indeed, there is recent authority for the odd-sounding proposition that infanticide is sometimes not an offence at all, but a defence to a charge of murder: *R v B(L)*, 2011 ONCA 153; *R v Effert*, 2009 ABQB 368.

to cause death to any human being and whether or not he knows that
death is likely to be caused to any human being, if

(a) he means to cause bodily harm for the purpose of
    (i) facilitating the commission of the offence, or
    (ii) facilitating his flight after committing or attempting to com-
        mit the offence,
and the death ensues from the bodily harm;
(b) he administers a stupefying or overpowering thing for a purpose
    mentioned in paragraph (a), and the death ensues therefrom;
(c) he wilfully stops, by any means, the breath of a human being for a
    purpose mentioned in paragraph (a), and the death ensues there-
    from; or
(d) he uses a weapon or has it upon his person
    (i) during or at the time he commits or attempts to commit the
        offence, or
    (ii) during or at the time of his flight after committing or at-
        tempting to commit the offence,
and the death ensues as a consequence.[217]

Section 212 (apart from the phrase "ought to have known" in para. (c))
required a subjective fault element for murder: the prosecution had to
prove that the accused meant to cause death, or meant to cause grievous bodily harm with a high degree of subjective foresight as to the
consequences of that harm. So, if section 212 had been the only section defining murder, the distinction between murder and manslaughter would, roughly, have been a matter of intent: murder would have
been culpable homicide with intent to cause death, and manslaughter
would have been culpable homicide without such intent. But the effect of section 213 was to classify some culpable homicides as murders
even though the accused had no intent in relation to the victim's death:
where the conditions established by section 213 were met, a culpable
homicide was murder whether or not the prosecution was able to prove
intent to cause death. For this reason, murder defined by section 213
was often called "constructive murder," as if intentional unlawful killing was "real" murder, but the offence defined by section 213 was murder only because Parliament said so.[218]

---

217 *Criminal Code*, RSC 1970, above note 181, ss 212 & 213. Section 229 is now
    worded identically to former s 212. The current s 230 differs in certain respects
    from the former s 213, but as s 230 is of no force or effect, these differences are
    of no practical importance.
218 Compare Alan W Mewett & Morris Manning, *Criminal Law*, 2d ed (Toronto:
    Butterworths, 1985) at 536–48; Stuart, above note 162 at 207–8.

In *R v Vaillancourt* (*Vaillancourt*),[219] the accused was charged with murder. He and an accomplice robbed a pool hall. The accomplice shot and killed a patron. There was evidence to suggest that the accused thought that his accomplice's shotgun was not loaded. The Crown's theory of the case was that the accomplice had committed a murder as defined by section 213(*d*), in that he used a weapon while committing the offence of robbery and the victim had died as a result. The accused was a party to the murder by virtue of section 21(2) of the *Criminal Code*, as it was an offence that he knew or ought to have known would be a probable consequence of the unlawful purpose (the robbery). The accused was convicted of second degree murder, and his appeal to the Quebec Court of Appeal was dismissed. The Supreme Court of Canada held that section 213(*d*) was unconstitutional, and ordered a new trial. The majority, *per* Lamer J, reasoned as follows:

> . . . whatever the minimum *mens rea* for the act or the result may be, there are, though very few in number, certain crimes where, because of the special nature of the stigma attached to a conviction therefor or the available penalties, the principles of fundamental justice require a *mens rea* reflecting the particular nature of that crime. Such is theft, where, in my view, a conviction requires proof of some dishonesty. Murder is another such offence. The punishment for murder is the most severe in our society and the stigma that attaches to a conviction for murder is similarly extreme. In addition, murder is distinguished from manslaughter only by the mental element with respect to the death. It is thus clear that there must be some special mental element with respect to the death before a culpable homicide can be treated as a murder. That special mental element gives rise to the moral blameworthiness which justifies the stigma and sentence attached to a murder conviction.[220]

Lamer J's view was that the required "special mental element" was "subjective foresight" of death; however, he was prepared to go "no further than say that it is a principle of fundamental justice that, absent proof beyond a reasonable doubt of at least objective foreseeability, there surely cannot be a murder conviction."[221] Since, in his view, section 213(*d*) did not require proof of objective foresight, it offended section 7, and the infringement of section 7 was not saved by section 1.[222]

---

219 *R v Vaillancourt*, [1987] 2 SCR 636 [*Vaillancourt*].
220 *Ibid* at 653–54.
221 *Ibid* at 654.
222 *Ibid* at 659–60. Justice McIntyre dissented, commenting that "while it may be illogical to characterize an unintentional killing as murder, no principle of fun-

In *R v Martineau* (*Martineau*),[223] the accused was charged with murder, this time on the basis of sections 213(*a*) or (*d*) and 21(2). The accused and his accomplice Tremblay broke into a trailer and robbed the two occupants, whom Tremblay then killed. The accused was convicted of two counts of second degree murder. The Alberta Court of Appeal ordered a new trial, applying *Vaillancourt* to declare section 213(*a*) unconstitutional. The Crown's appeal to the Supreme Court was dismissed. The majority, *per* Lamer CJC, was now prepared to hold that the principles of fundamental justice required proof of subjective foresight of death for a murder conviction:

> . . . in a free and democratic society that values the autonomy and free will of the individual, the stigma and punishment attaching to the most serious of crimes, murder, should be reserved for those who choose to intentionally cause death or who choose to inflict bodily harm that they know is likely to cause death. The essential role of requiring subjective foresight of death in the context of murder is to maintain a proportionality between the stigma and punishment attached to a murder conviction and the moral blameworthiness of the offender. Murder has long been recognized as the "worst" and most heinous of peace time crimes. It is, therefore, essential that to satisfy the principles of fundamental justice, the stigma and punishment attaching to a murder conviction must be reserved for those who either intend to cause death or who intend to cause bodily harm that they know will likely cause death.[224]

Since section 213(*a*) permitted a murder conviction without proof of subjective foresight of death, it offended section 7, and it could not be justified under section 1.[225]

The decision in *Martineau* had clear implications for the rest of section 213, as the section expressly permits a conviction for murder "whether or not the [accused] means to cause death." A year later, the

---

damental justice is offended only because serious criminal conduct, involving the commission of a crime of violence resulting in the killing of a human being, is classified as murder and not in some other manner": *ibid* at 663.

223 *R v Martineau*, [1990] 2 SCR 633 [*Martineau*].

224 *Ibid* at 645–46.

225 *Ibid* at 647. Justice Sopinka concurred on the narrower ground that s 213(*a*) offended the principle of fundamental justice identified in *Vaillancourt*. Justice L'Heureux-Dubé dissented on the ground that s 213(*a*) did *not* offend the principle identified in *Vaillancourt*, above note 219 at 672; in her view, if the Crown could prove all the elements required by that paragraph, the trier of fact would inevitably conclude that a reasonable person in the accused's position would have foreseen the victim's death.

Court struck down section 213(*c*);[226] while the Court has never express-ly addressed section 213(*b*), it must also be unconstitutional for the reasons given in *Martineau*. Similarly, the objective branch of section 212(*c*) (now section 229(*c*)), permitting conviction where the accused "ought to know" that his act will cause death, is unconstitutional.[227]

The precise meaning of the phrase "subjective foresight of death" has been somewhat elusive. While it clearly includes those who in-tend to cause death (compare section 229(*a*)(i)), does it also include those who are subjectively aware that their unlawful act creates a like-lihood or a risk of death? Proof of murder under section 229(*a*)(ii) re-quires proof that the accused intentionally caused serious bodily harm and was aware that death was likely to result, and the Supreme Court of Canada has never appeared to doubt the constitutional validity of this form of murder. Thus, the accused's subjective awareness that his unlawful act is likely to cause death appears to be a constitutional-ly sufficient fault element for murder. This conclusion was explicitly reached by the Ontario Court of Appeal in *R v Shand*[228] in rejecting a constitutional challenge to the subjective branch of section 229(*c*). The court interpreted the section as requiring proof that the accused was intentionally pursuing an unlawful purpose and that he knew that his unlawful act in furtherance of that purpose was likely to cause death. Under this interpretation, the section satisfied the constitutional re-quirement of proof of "subjective foresight of death." Whether "sub-jective foresight of death" can be stretched to include awareness of a mere risk of death, as opposed to awareness of a likelihood of death, is uncertain because under the murder provisions as they now stand, the Crown must prove at least subjective awareness of a likelihood of death.[229] There is no statutory route to a murder conviction on the basis of awareness of a mere risk of death.

b) Attempted Murder

Since before the *Charter* came into force, a conviction for attempted murder has required proof of the specific intention to kill; that is, of the subjective mental state defined by section 229(*a*)(i). The lesser degrees of fault defined elsewhere in sections 229 and 230 were not adequate.

---

226 *R v Sit*, [1991] 3 SCR 124.

227 *Martineau*, above note 223 at 648. The subjective branch of s 229(*c*) was rarely invoked in the decade after *Martineau*, but has enjoyed something of a revival: see Kent Roach, "The Problematic Revival of Murder under Section 229(*c*) of the *Criminal Code*" (2010) 47 Alta L Rev 675.

228 *R v Shand*, above note 35.

229 Under s 229(*a*)(ii) or (*c*) of the *Criminal Code*, above note 24.

This conclusion was reached as a matter of statutory interpretation in the pre-*Charter* case of *R v Ancio*.[230] In *R v Logan* (*Logan*),[231] a companion case to *Martineau*, a similar conclusion was held to be a constitutional imperative. Chief Justice Lamer reasoned that the "stigma associated with a conviction for attempted murder is the same as it is for murder" and, accordingly, that a conviction for attempted murder required proof of subjective foresight of death.[232] Since, in a case of attempted murder, the victim does not die, this element should presumably be understood not as subjective foresight but as subjective belief that the victim will die.[233]

c)   Theft

The Supreme Court of Canada has, in *obiter dicta*, recognized the following principle of fundamental justice: a conviction for theft requires proof of dishonesty.[234] This principle has no practical effect on the law of theft because the statutory definition of theft already requires proof of dishonesty; that is, a fraudulent taking, without colour of right, and with intent to deprive the owner of his property rights (*Criminal Code*, section 322). If the accused negligently takes another's property, she has not committed theft as defined in the *Criminal Code*; according to the Court's *obiter* in *Vaillancourt*, if Parliament were to redefine theft to include negligent takings, that definition would offend section 7 of the *Charter*. The same reasoning would, presumably, apply to the offences resembling theft[235] and to the offence of fraud.[236] All of these offences mark the offender with the stigma of dishonesty.

In *Wholesale Travel Group*, the accused corporation was charged with false advertising offences under the *Competition Act*. It argued that

---

230 *R v Ancio*, [1984] 1 SCR 225. The facts of the case illustrate the point very well. The accused, carrying a sawed-off shotgun, broke into the home of his estranged wife's new companion. The shotgun discharged, but no one was injured. This conduct would have been murder under former s 213(*d*) if someone had died, but since no one died, the offence was not murder, and since Ancio did not intend to kill anyone, the offence was not attempted murder.

231 *R v Logan*, [1990] 2 SCR 731, 58 CCC (3d) 391 [*Logan*].

232 *Ibid* at 743.

233 Compare *United States v Dynar*, [1997] 2 SCR 462 at para 69 [*Dynar*], explaining the *mens rea* of an attempt as a subjective belief that the elements of the offence are present.

234 *Vaillancourt*, above note 219 at 654.

235 For example: *Criminal Code*, above note 24, s 335 (taking motor vehicle without consent); s 336 (criminal breach of trust); s 338 (fraudulently taking cattle); s 342 (theft of credit card).

236 *Ibid*, s 380.

these offences were like theft and fraud, in that they stigmatized the offender as dishonest, and therefore required proof of subjective fault (not just negligence). The Court rejected this argument, on the ground that the offence did not carry a stigma of dishonesty because a conviction could be based "on a variety of facts, many of which will not reveal any dishonesty but, rather, carelessness."[237] Although the conclusion is not necessarily wrong, the reasoning is seriously incomplete. The stigma analysis is driven by the possibility that the stigma associated with conviction for a certain named offence may imply a degree of fault greater than the law requires for conviction. If the legal definition of the offence determined its stigma, it would never be possible to strike down an offence on the basis that its stigma is not appropriate to its legal definition. Murder carries the stigma of intentional killing, so a person cannot be convicted of murder under a statutory definition that does not require proof of subjective foresight of death. So the questions in *Wholesale Travel Group* should have been what kind of stigma was associated with a conviction for false advertising; what fault element was appropriate to that stigma; and whether the legal definition required proof of that fault element. The fact that the offence could be committed carelessly was relevant to, but not determinative of, the stigma associated with a conviction.[238]

d) Genocide, War Crimes, and Crimes against Humanity

Genocide, war crimes, and crimes against humanity, as legal concepts, were originally developed in international criminal law as a response to the crimes of the Nazi regime, and have been developed in the jurisprudence of the *ad hoc* international tribunals set up in response to the Yugoslav civil war of the early 1990s and the Rwandan genocide of 1994.[239] In 1985, Parliament gave Canadian criminal courts jurisdiction over war crimes and crimes against humanity by enacting section 7(3.71) of the *Criminal Code;*[240] more recently, Parliament enacted a separate statute dealing with these offences, as well as the offence of genocide.[241] One would think that a conviction for any these offences would give rise to a stigma at least as great as that of the crime of mur-

---

237 *Wholesale Travel Group Inc*, above note 185 at 185, Lamer CJC dissenting on other grounds.

238 Compare Hamish Stewart, "*R v Darrach*: A Step Forward in the Constitutionalization of Fault?" (1999) 4 Can Crim L Rev 9 at 18 [Stewart, "Step Forward"].

239 See Robert Cryer *et al*, *An Introduction to International Criminal Law and Procedure* (Cambridge: Cambridge University Press, 2007) chs 10, 11, & 12.

240 RSC 1985, c 27 (1st Supp) s 5, in force 4 December 1985.

241 *Crimes Against Humanity and War Crimes Act*, SC 2000, c 24.

der and would therefore require proof of an appropriate subjective fault element. In *R v Finta* (*Finta*),[242] the Supreme Court of Canada decided, at least by implication, that section 7 did require proof of such a fault element.

The accused Finta was charged with 8,617 counts of unlawful confinement, robbery, kidnapping, and manslaughter, arising out of the accused's alleged participation in the deportation of Jews from Budapest in May and June 1944.[243] The Crown alleged that these offences were war crimes and crimes against humanity, so that a Canadian court would have jurisdiction pursuant to section 7(3.71) of the *Criminal Code* (as it read at the time the charges were laid). A majority of the Supreme Court, *per* Cory J, held that the Crown was required at trial to prove not only the elements of the offences themselves but also a mental element with respect to the allegation that these offences amounted to war crimes and crimes against humanity: "The degree of moral turpitude that attaches to crimes against humanity and war crimes must exceed that of the domestic offences of manslaughter or robbery."[244] The difference was that, to amount to war crimes or crimes against humanity, the offences had to be committed in circumstances of cruelty and barbarism. So the Crown would have to prove "an element of subjective knowledge on the part of the accused of the factual conditions which render the actions a crime against humanity," though it was "not necessary to establish that the accused knew that his or her actions were inhumane."[245]

The reasoning in *Finta* was framed as a matter of statutory interpretation rather than *Charter* analysis.[246] Nonetheless, Cory J's reasons strongly suggest that the additional mental element is required not just by statute but also as a matter of constitutional law. He refers repeatedly to *Martineau* and other cases constitutionalizing fault requirements; moreover, he expressly connects the additional mental element with section 7 of the *Charter*:

> To convict someone of an offence when it has not been established beyond a reasonable doubt that he or she was aware of conditions that would bring to his or her actions that requisite added dimen-

242 *R v Finta*, [1994] 1 SCR 701 [*Finta*].
243 The charges were therefore laid under the *Criminal Code*, RSC 1927, c 36.
244 *Finta*, above note 242 at 818.
245 *Ibid* at 819.
246 The *Charter* did not, strictly speaking, apply as Finta's alleged offences were committed before it came into force. Compare *R v Stevens*, [1988] 1 SCR 1153.

sion of cruelty and barbarism violates the principles of fundamental justice.[247]

Thus, *Finta* is most plausibly read as holding that crimes against humanity and war crimes are, like murder and theft, special stigma offences under section 7.

The Supreme Court revisited these offences, in a different factual context, in *Mugesera v Canada (Minister of Citizenship and Immigration)* (*Mugesera*).[248] The federal government sought to deport the applicant on the ground that he had committed acts outside Canada which, if committed within Canada, would have amounted to war crimes or crimes against humanity. The Court now had the benefit of a substantial jurisprudence on the meaning of these offences from the International Criminal Tribunal for the Former Yugoslavia and the International Criminal Tribunal for Rwanda; in light of this jurisprudence, it held that the elements of a "crime against humanity" were the following:

(1) An enumerated proscribed act was committed (this involves showing that the accused committed the criminal act and had the requisite guilty state of mind for the underlying act);

(2) The act was committed as part of a widespread or systematic attack;

(3) The attack was directed against any civilian population or any identifiable group of persons; and

(4) The person committing the proscribed act knew of the attack and knew or took the risk that his or her act comprised a part of that attack.[249]

With respect to the fourth element, the Court added that "the accused must have knowledge of the attack and must know that his or her acts comprise part of it <u>or</u> take the risk that his or her acts will comprise part of it,"[250] and emphasized that his knowledge was sufficient: the accused's motive for participation in the attack was irrelevant.[251] The Court referred to Cory J's reasons in *Finta*, but did not comment on his view that an additional mental element was constitutionally required.

The fault element articulated in *Mugesera* is arguably different from that articulated in *Finta*, but it is constitutionally adequate. To convict

---

247 *Finta*, above note 242 at 818.
248 *Mugesera v Canada (Minister of Citizenship and Immigration)*, 2005 SCC 40 [*Mugesera*].
249 *Ibid* at para 119
250 *Ibid* at para 173 [emphasis in original].
251 *Ibid* at para 174.

the accused of a war crime, the Crown must prove not only the underlying criminal act, already a serious act in itself, but also the accused's awareness of or recklessness to the fact that his crime was part of a widespread and systematic attack against a civilian population or identifiable group. This fault element is entirely appropriate to the stigma associated with a conviction for a crime against humanity.

When the facts underlying the decisions in *Finta* and *Mugesera* arose, war crimes and crimes against humanity were not themselves distinct offences in Canadian law. The offences alleged were ordinary offences under the *Criminal Code*; if they were properly characterized as war crimes or as crimes against humanity, section 7(3.71) of the *Criminal Code* gave a Canadian criminal court jurisdiction over them regardless of where they were committed, and if they were not so characterized, the court lacked jurisdiction to try them at all. For this reason, the dissenting judges in *Finta* reasoned that the stigma doctrine had no application. In their view, whether the offences were war crimes or crimes against humanity was to be decided by the trial judge in determining whether the court had jurisdiction over the offences, but the Crown did not have to prove any mental element to satisfy the trial judge on this issue. If the trial judge found that the offences alleged were properly characterized as war crimes or crimes against humanity, the Crown would then have to prove before the jury the elements of the offences themselves (in this case, unlawful confinement, robbery, kidnapping, and manslaughter), but would not have to prove any fault element associated with the court's previous finding that it had jurisdiction.[252] Thus, on the dissenters' view, the Crown was not required to prove a mental element for war crimes or crimes against humanity at any point in the trial.

The dissenters' reasoning, however plausible it might have been at the time *Finta* was decided, would no longer apply. Section 4 of the *Crimes Against Humanity and War Crimes Act*[253] now creates and defines (in part with reference to international criminal law) the indictable offences of genocide, war crimes, and crimes against humanity. This statute was already in force when *Mugesera* was decided, and there is every reason to think that the Court's articulation of the elements of the offences of war crimes and crimes against humanity applies as much to the new offences as to the former section 7(3.71).[254] The offence of genocide, not expressly discussed in *Mugesera*, is no doubt also a stigma offence.

---

252 *Finta*, above note 242 at 738–51.

253 Above note 241.

254 The Court in *Mugesera*, above note 248 at para 118, noted that the definition of crimes against humanity in the *Crimes Against Humanity and War Crimes Act*

e) Stigma Analysis and Party Liability

It is a curious coincidence that in *Vaillancourt*, *Martineau*, and *Logan*, the leading cases on stigma offences, the accused was not alleged to have committed the offence in question, but was alleged to have been a party to the offence by virtue of section 21(2) of the *Criminal Code*. The various forms of party liability in Canadian criminal law have their own fault elements, raising an issue of constitutional sufficiency for stigma offences. There are at least eight forms of party liability in Canadian criminal law. A person is a party to an offence where she:

(1) "actually commits it" (section 21(1)(*a*));

(2) is a "co-perpetrator" of the offence;[255]

(3) "does or omits to do anything for the purpose of aiding any person to commit it" (section 21(1)(*b*));

(4) "abets any person in committing it" (section 21(1)(*c*));

(5) has an intention in common to carry out an unlawful purpose with others and "knew or ought to have known that the commission of the offence was a probable consequence of carrying out the common purpose" (section 21(2));

(6) "counsels another person to be a party to [the] offence" (section 22(1));

(7) has counselled another to commit an offence, and the other committed an offence "in consequence of the counselling that the person who counselled knew or ought to have known was likely to be committed in consequence of the counselling" (section 22(2));

(8) uses another person as an innocent agent to commit it.[256]

To prove that the accused is a party to an offence by any means other than actually committing it or co-perpetration, the Crown has to prove the offence[257] and the elements of the relevant form of participation. Thus, on the plain wording of the Code, a person can be convicted of

---

"differs slightly from the definition in [former s 7(3.76)]" but commented that "the differences are not material to the discussion that follows"; namely, to the re-articulation of the offence elements.

255 *R v Biniaris*, [2000] 1 SCR 381, 2000 SCC 15; see also *R v McMaster*, [1996] 1 SCR 740 at para 33.

256 For an example of innocent agency, see *R v Devgan* (2007), 226 CCC (3d) 312 (Ont SCJ).

257 Section 23.1 of the *Criminal Code*, above note 24, provides that the accused can be convicted as a party "notwithstanding the fact that the person whom the accused aids or abets [etc] . . . cannot be convicted of the offence." So the accused can be convicted of murder as an aider, even if the person who actually committed the murder is, for example, acquitted or dead. But there must be an offence

murder because he "ought to have known" that a murder would be a probable consequence of carrying out an unlawful purpose, or of theft because he "ought to have known" that a theft would be a probable consequence of his counselling the commission of a different offence. It is clear from the reasoning in *Martineau* that imposing liability on this basis would offend the principles of fundamental justice because the accused would be stigmatized without proof of the special mental element required for the offence of theft. The solution is to read down the statutory provisions where necessary. So where the accused is charged with murder and the Crown argues that he is liable as a party under section 21(2), the words "or ought to have known" are ignored and the Crown is required to prove that the accused was subjectively aware that murder was a probable consequence of the unlawful purpose.[258] Where the Crown's theory is that the accused is a party to an attempted murder under section 21(2), the Crown must prove that the accused knew "that it [was] probable that his accomplice would do something with the intent to kill in carrying out the common purpose."[259] Similarly, where the accused is charged with murder on the theory that she counselled someone to commit an offence and the murder was a probable consequence, the words "or ought to have known" in section 22(2) are ignored and the Crown must prove the accused's subjective awareness that the victim's death was a probable consequence of that counselling.[260]

It is important to note that this constitutional "reading-up" of the party liability provisions arises not merely because the offence is one of subjective fault, but because the element of subjective fault is constitutionally required.

f) Are There Any Other Stigma Offences?

Since most of the serious offences in the *Criminal Code* are in any event defined, or interpreted, to require proof of subjective fault, there have been relatively few constitutional challenges based on the stigma analysis. The terrorism offences, for example, are certainly stigma offences, but since they require proof of subjective fault in relation to the

---

that is aided or abetted, etc; if the Crown cannot show that someone committed an offence, there is nothing to be a party to.

258 *R v Rodney*, [1990] 2 SCR 687 at 692–93 (it would be contrary to the principles of fundamental justice to convict the accused of murder via s 21(2) where "the jury . . . entertained a reasonable doubt that the [accused] had subjective foresight that the murder would be a probable consequence" of the unlawful purpose).

259 *Logan*, above note 231 at 748.

260 *R v Chenier* (2006), 205 CCC (3d) 333 at 356–59 (Ont CA).

elements of terrorism, they already comply with the stigma principle. The specific offences of participating in, contributing to, or facilitating the activities of a terrorist group[261] must be read as requiring proof that "the accused knowingly participated or contributed and knew that the group was a terrorist group."[262] Similarly, a conviction for high treason or treason would mean that the accused was a "traitor," a label surely requiring proof of some form of subjective fault in relation to the *actus reus* of the offence; but to the extent that the definition of these offences does not already require proof of subjective fault, they would surely be so interpreted.[263]

Stigma-based challenges to the definitions of manslaughter and of sexual assault have failed, though for interestingly different reasons.

As noted above, the *Criminal Code* defines the offence of manslaughter indirectly, as a culpable homicide that is neither infanticide nor murder. Culpable homicide requires proof of criminal negligence or an unlawful act.[264] Thus, manslaughter is any homicide (other than infanticide), where the accused unintentionally caused death by an unlawful act or by criminal negligence. But that generalization merely tells us what manslaughter is not; it does not define a fault element, or specify a constitutionally sufficient fault element, for the offence. In *Creighton*,[265] the Supreme Court of Canada considered these questions. The accused had injected his girlfriend with cocaine. She went into convulsions and died a short time later. He was charged with manslaughter by means of an unlawful act (the injection, though consensual, was an act of trafficking in narcotics) or by criminal negligence.

---

261 *Criminal Code*, above note 24, ss 83.18 & 83.19.

262 Kent Roach, "The New Terrorism Offences in Canadian Criminal Law" in David Daubney, ed, *Terrorism, Law, and Democracy* (Montreal: Thémis, 2002) 113 at 136, quoted with approval (though incorrectly cited) in *R v Khawaja*, above note 35 at paras 37–38.

263 Consider, for example, s 46(1)(*a*) of the *Criminal Code*, above note 24, which states that "Every one commits high treason who, in Canada, . . . kills or attempts to kill Her Majesty . . . ." Suppose a person unlawfully but unintentionally killed the Queen, thereby committing manslaughter, despite the lack of any fault element relating to treason or despite not knowing that the victim was the Queen. Section 46(1)(*a*), read literally, would make that person guilty of high treason. If treason and high treason are stigma offences, the offence would have to be read up to ensure an appropriate subjective fault element.

264 *Criminal Code*, ibid, ss 222(5)(*a*) & (*b*). The section in fact defines two additional kinds of culpable homicide: (*c*) causing a person "by threats or fear of violence or by deception, to do anything that causes his death" and (*d*) "wilfully frightening . . . a child or sick person." I am not aware of any recent prosecutions under these branches of s 222(5).

265 *Creighton*, above note 201.

McLachlin J, for the majority,[266] held that the fault element for unlawful act manslaughter, as worked out at common law, was "objective foreseeability of the risk of bodily harm which is neither trivial nor transitory, in the context of a dangerous act,"[267] subject to the proviso that an accused who was incapable of perceiving the risk would not be culpable.[268] She then held that this fault element was constitutionally adequate, indeed that it was entirely "appropriate" to the stigma associated with a conviction for manslaughter, the essence of which was unlawful but unintentional killing.[269]

Apart from murder and theft, the most plausible candidate for special stigma offences would be the sexual offences: sexual assault and the sexual offences against children and young persons (sexual interference and sexual exploitation). If they are stigma offences, then the Crown must prove a special subjective mental element related to the nature of the crime. In the case of sexual assault, that mental element would relate to the complainant's lack of consent: sexual assault is a crime because it is non-consensual. In the case of offences against children, that mental element would relate to the age of the complainant: these offences are criminal because of the complainant's immaturity, not because of lack of consent (which is not an element of these offences). There might also be an argument that there should be a special mental element relating to the sexual nature of the contact, which is the principal element converting assault into the much more serious offence of sexual assault.

The *actus reus* of sexual assault is the non-consensual application of force "in circumstances of a sexual nature, such that the sexual integrity of the victim is violated."[270] The element of non-consent is established by proof that the complainant did not want the touching to occur.[271] The violation of the victim's sexual integrity is determined by

---

266 Justices L'Heureux-Dubé, Gonther, and Cory concurred; La Forest J concurred in separate reasons. Justice McLachlin's reasons are written in the style of a minority opinion, suggesting that the majority formed at the last minute: compare Stuart, above note 162 at 271–72.

267 *Creighton*, above note 201 at 45.

268 *Ibid* at 58–74.

269 *Ibid* at 47. Chief Justice Lamer, for the minority, took the view that the stigma associated with manslaughter was sufficiently great to require proof of objective foresight of *death* (not just of serious bodily harm).

270 *R v Ewanchuk*, [1999] 1 SCR 330 at para 24 [*Ewanchuk*].

271 *Ibid* at para 26.

an objective consideration of all the circumstances in which the assault occurred.[272]

Each element of the *actus reus* should, in principle, have a corresponding *mens rea*. According to the *Criminal Code*, the touching has to be intentional,[273] though the Supreme Court of Canada has held that there is no fault requirement for the violation of the victim's sexual integrity.[274] But there are few if any cases where these *mens rea* elements are in issue. In many sexual assault prosecutions, the crucial *mens rea* involves the accused's state of mind in relation to the complainant's consent. In *R v Pappajohn* (*Pappajohn*), the Supreme Court held that if the accused mistakenly believed that the complainant consented, he lacked the *mens rea* for non-consent and so must be acquitted.[275] So the Crown could prove *mens rea* by proving that the accused knew of, or was reckless about, the complainant's lack of consent. Subsequent cases established that proof of wilful blindness would also suffice.[276] But the fault element for sexual assault has become much more complex since *Pappajohn*. The two major changes are the reinterpretation of the meaning of "consent" in *R v Ewanchuk* (*Ewanchuk*) and the statutory imposition of a "reasonable steps" requirement. In *Ewanchuk*, the Court held that the accused must believe the complainant "had affirmatively communicated by words or conduct her agreement to engage in sexual activity with the accused."[277] Moreover, section 273.2(*b*) of the *Criminal Code* provides that mistaken belief in consent is not a defence where "the accused did not take reasonable steps, in the circumstances known to the accused at the time, to ascertain that the complainant was consenting." In light of *Ewanchuk*, the complainant's "consent" here means her "communicated" consent.

In light of all these developments, there are four ways in which the Crown can prove the *mens rea* relating to consent for sexual assault:

(1) The accused knew that the complainant had not communicated consent; or

---

272 *R v Chase*, [1987] 2 SCR 293; see also Stewart, *Sexual Offences*, above note 170 at 3:400.

273 *Criminal Code*, above note 24, s 265(1)(*a*); see also Stewart, *Sexual Offences*, *ibid* at 3:600.10.

274 *Ewanchuk*, above note 270 at para 25.

275 *R v Pappajohn*, [1980] 2 SCR 120, though the accused's rape conviction was upheld on the facts. The *Pappajohn* rule originally applied to the offence of sexual assault as well: Stewart, *Sexual Offences*, above note 170 at 3:600.30.20.

276 *R v Sansregret*, [1985] 1 SCR 570; for a statutory restatement, see *Criminal Code*, above note 24, s 273.2(*a*)(ii).

277 *Ewanchuk*, above note 270 at para 49.

(2) The accused was reckless as to the complainant's non-communication of consent; or

(3) The accused was wilfully blind to the fact that the complainant had not communicated consent; or

(4) The accused, though honestly believing that the complainant had communicated consent, had not taken reasonable steps, in the circumstances known to him at the time, to ascertain her communicated consent.

The fourth of these possible *mens rea* elements is a mixed subjective/objective standard: it depends both on what the accused knew ("the circumstances known to him") and on what a reasonable person would do in those circumstances ("reasonable steps").

In *R v Darrach*,[278] the accused challenged the "reasonable steps" requirement on the ground that sexual assault was a stigma offence requiring proof of a purely subjective fault element. The court was not persuaded that sexual assault was a stigma offence in the *Martineau* sense;[279] however, the true *ratio* of the decision is that even if sexual assault "carried with it a sufficient social stigma as to require . . . subjective fault . . . , notwithstanding s. 273.2(*b*), the offence is still largely one based on subjective fault—at least to a level that would satisfy constitutional requirements."[280] The court emphasized that the "reasonable steps" requirement, though "introducing an objective component into the mental element of the offence," is "personalized according to the subjective awareness of the accused at the time."[281]

The Supreme Court of Canada has never squarely addressed the question of whether sexual assault is a stigma offence. In *Daviault*, Sopinka J dissenting held that "sexual assault does not fall into the category of offences for which either the stigma or the available penalties

---

278 *R v Darrach* (1998), 122 CCC (3d) 225 (Ont CA), aff'd on other grounds, 2000 SCC 46 [*Darrach*].

279 *Ibid* at paras 85–87. For criticism of the court's reasoning on this point, see Stewart, "Step Forward," above note 238 at 17–19.

280 *Darrach, ibid* at para 87 (Ont CA).

281 *Ibid* at para 88. I expand on this aspect of the court's reasons in Stewart, "Step Forward," above note 238 at 19–22. The court added that "Were a person to take reasonable steps, and nonetheless make an unreasonable mistake about the presence of consent, he or she would be entitled to ask the trier of fact to acquit on this basis": *Darrach, ibid* at para 90. I do not think this understanding of the reasonable steps requirement can be correct, as the idea of taking reasonable steps to ascertain a fact must include not just gathering of information but also taking account of that information in deciding what to do: see Stewart, *Sexual Offences*, above note 170 at 3:600.30.20.

demand as a constitutional requirement subjective intent to commit the *actus reus*." He then went on to observe:

> Sexual assault is a heinous crime of violence. Those found guilty of committing the offence are rightfully submitted to a significant degree of moral opprobrium.[282]

It is difficult to see why these observations do not support the conclusion that sexual assault *is* a stigma offence requiring proof of subjective intent.[283] The other members of the Court did not consider this particular constitutional issue, and the Court has never revisited it.

Offences that have been held not to be special stigma offences requiring proof of subjective fault include, in addition to manslaughter, unlawfully causing bodily harm,[284] dangerous driving,[285] and careless storage of a firearm.[286]

g) What Is "Stigma"?

The Supreme Court's "stigma" analysis has frequently been criticized by commentators on grounds of uncertainty and judicial usurpation of the legislative role.[287] And, if we understand "stigma" as reflecting "the public opprobrium empirically incurred by the commission of an

---

282 *Daviault*, above note 163 at 119–20, Sopinka J dissenting, Gonthier and Major JJ concurring in the dissent.

283 This incoherence in Sopinka J's reasoning arose because *Daviault* concerns the notoriously difficult problem of the criminal responsibility of the intoxicated accused. The trial judge found that the accused had somehow managed to rape the complainant while so severely intoxicated that he was in a state of automatism, and acquitted him for lack of voluntariness. Justice Sopinka would have maintained the traditional rule that intoxication was not a defence to offences of "general intent," such as sexual assault; he therefore considered, and rejected, the possibility that there might be an exception to that rule for stigma offences. His underlying point was that a person who committed a sexual assault after voluntarily putting himself into a state of extreme intoxication akin to automatism deserved the stigma of a sexual assault conviction. *Daviault* is also discussed in Section C(1), above in this chapter; on intoxication and sexual assault more generally, see also Stewart, *Sexual Offences*, above note 170 at §3:200.20.20.

284 *R v DeSousa*, [1992] 2 SCR 944 [*DeSousa*].

285 *R v Hundal*, [1993] 1 SCR 867 [*Hundal*].

286 *R v Finlay*, [1993] 3 SCR 103 at 118–19.

287 See, for example, Rosemary Cairns Way, "The *Charter*, the Supreme Court and the Invisible Politics of Fault" (1992) 12 Windsor YB Access Just 128 at 163–67; Dennis Klinck, "The *Charter* and Substantive Criminal 'Justice'" (1993) 42 UNBLJ 191 at 200–2. Stuart welcomed the abolition of constructive murder occasioned by *Vaillancourt* and *Martineau*, but did not defend the stigma concept: Stuart, above note 162 at 207–13.

offence,"[288] a measure of public opinion, it cannot be defended as a constitutional standard. It would be difficult to conclude what the general public thinks when it hears that a person has been convicted of a particular offence, and no evidence of this fact has ever influenced the Court's stigma analysis. But even if it was possible to determine the general public's understanding of the elements of "murder" or "theft," and to compare them with the legal elements, there seems to be no good reason why the Court should judicially amend offence definitions to bring them in line with the general public's view of what the offence is. The proper remedy for such a discrepancy would be to instruct the public as to the elements of the offence, so that they would no longer assume that a person convicted of, say, murder under section 230 had intentionally killed the victim.[289]

The stigma analysis can be defended if offenders have, in some sense, a right to have their offences fairly labeled; that is, an offender has the right not to be stigmatized as "murderer" unless he has in fact committed a "murder."[290] But what does it mean for a person to have committed a "murder" other than to have engaged in the conduct, with the appropriate mental state, that Parliament and the courts (exercising their power of statutory interpretation) define as "murder"? The stigma analysis depends entirely on the Court's ability to define the essence of an offence apart from the legislative definition of the offence. In this vein, Brudner argues in favour of understanding "stigma as blame," where the blameworthiness of an act would be "determined . . . both by the importance to human well-being of the interest harmed by the wrongdoer and by the degree to which the harm is imputable to his agency as distinct from chance."[291] On this approach, the importance of *Martineau* was not just that it required proof of subjective foresight of death for a murder conviction, but that it required the law of homicide to distinguish between intentional and negligent killings.[292] This version of the stigma analysis is more satisfactory than an appeal to the general public's understanding of the meaning of the word "murder." But it depends less on the label attached to an offence than on the dif-

---

288 Alan Brudner, "Proportionality, Stigma, and Discretion" (1996) 38 Crim LQ 302 at 304.

289 *Ibid* at 304–5.

290 To take a fanciful example once offered by a student, it would surely be unjust for Parliament to define murder as "intentional unlawful killing or intentional unlawful parking" and thus to stigmatize people who intentionally parked in no-parking zones as "murderers."

291 Brudner, above note 288 at 309.

292 *Ibid* at 313.

ferentiation of offences by levels of fault—a principle that might have even more far-reaching consequences for Canadian criminal law than Lamer CJC's original conception of special stigma offences. An account of justice requiring that certain offences have subjective fault elements, for the purpose of fair labeling, is required to make sense of the Supreme Court of Canada's stigma approach.

h) Some Rejected Principles Concerning Fault

In *Vaillancourt*, Lamer J suggested that the principles of fundamental justice might require proof of subjective fault for all criminal offences; in other words, he suggested that the presumption established in *R v Sault Ste Marie (City)* that criminal offences should be interpreted as having subjective fault elements might have become a constitutional requirement under the *Charter*.[293] However, it is clear from *Creighton*,[294] *R v De Sousa (De Sousa)*,[295] and *R v Hundal (Hundal)*[296] that a principle requiring proof of subjective fault for all the elements of all true crimes is not a principle of fundamental justice. In *Creighton*,[297] the Court upheld an objective fault element for the offence of manslaughter; in *De Sousa*, the Court rejected the proposition that the Crown had to establish subjective foresight of bodily harm to prove the offence of unlawfully causing bodily harm; and in *Hundal*, the Court held that proof of a marked departure from the standard of conduct expected of the reasonable person was a constitutionally sufficient fault element for the offence of dangerous driving. Indeed, in *De Sousa*, the Court expressly held that there was "no constitutional requirement that intention, either on an objective or a subjective basis, extend to the consequences of unlawful acts in general."[298] Similarly, in *Hundal*, Cory J held that "[i]n the appropriate context, negligence can be an acceptable basis of liability which meets the fault requirement of s. 7."[299] He cited *Wholesale Travel Group*, a case dealing with a regulatory offence, in support of this proposition; but *Hundal* itself dealt with a serious *Criminal Code* offence—dangerous driving—and the Court had no difficulty

---

293 *Vaillancourt*, above note 219 at 653; according to *Sault Ste Marie*, above note 161 at 1325–326, criminal offenes should be interpreted as requiring proof of subjective fault unless it is clear that Parliament intended to require only proof of a lesser fault element.

294 Above note 201.

295 Above note 284.

296 Above note 285.

297 As discussed in Section C(3), above in this chapter.

298 *DeSousa*, above note 284 at 965.

299 *Hundal*, above note 285 at 882.

in finding that the context of that offence—the regulated activity of driving—supported the holding that an objective fault element was appropriate and constitutionally adequate.

In *Creighton*,[300] the majority held that the principles of fundamental justice required proportionality between the seriousness of an offence and its fault element; however, the majority rejected the proposition that the principles of fundamental justice required "absolute symmetry between *mens rea* and each consequence of a offence."[301] A requirement of "symmetry" would mean that the Crown would have to prove actual or imputed knowledge (the accused knew or ought to have known) of every element of the *actus reus*; so, for example, if causing death was an element of the *actus reus*, the Crown would have to prove either subjective or objective foresight (that is, the accused knew or ought to have known) that his conduct would cause death or, depending on the offence, created a risk of death; if property damage was an element of the *actus reus*, the Crown would have to prove either objective or subjective foresight of at least a risk that his conduct created a risk of damage to property. In the absence of this requirement, it may be constitutionally permissible for Parliament to define an offence with a consequential element but without proof that the accused knew or ought to have foreseen that consequence. Proof of subjective or objective foresight of another fact may suffice, as in the case of manslaughter where the Crown must prove that the accused ought to have been aware of a risk of serious bodily harm (not death); in some cases, it has been held that as long as there is a constitutionally acceptable level of fault for the unlawful act itself, the *Charter* requires no proof of fault at all in relation to the consequence.[302]

As noted above, in *Logan*, the Court held that the "stigma" doctrine has an implication for party liability: no-one can be convicted of a stigma offence without proof of the constitutionally required level of fault for the offence, regardless of their form of participation in that offence. But the Court in *Logan* also held that there is no principle of fundamental justice requiring all parties to an offence to have the same level of fault.[303] Consider, for example, the offence of assault. This is an offence requiring proof of subjective fault. The principal offender—the

---

300 See also Section C(3), above in this chapter.

301 *Creighton*, above note 201 at 50.

302 *DeSousa*, above note 284 at 967. But the Court held that, as a matter of statutory interpretation, the offence at issue (unlawfully causing bodily harm under s 269 of the *Criminal Code*, above note 24) required proof of objective foresight of a risk of bodily harm: *ibid* at 962–66.

303 *Logan*, above note 231 at 740.

person who, in the words of section 21(1)(*a*), "actually commits" an assault—must be shown to have intentionally applied force with some degree of subjective awareness of the complainant's lack of consent.[304] However, pursuant to section 21(2), an accused can be a party to an assault on the basis of objective foresight if she "ought to have known" that the assault would be the probable consequence of her carrying out an unlawful intention in common with the principal offender. This result is constitutionally permissible—unless assault is itself a special stigma offence requiring proof of subjective fault, a proposition that has not yet been tested in the case law.

5) Fault and Self-Induced Intoxication

Canadian criminal law, like the criminal law of other Anglo-American jurisdictions, deals with intoxicated offenders by using the somewhat *ad hoc* distinction between crimes of "general intent" and crimes of "specific intent." Where a crime is characterized as one of "general intent," the trier of fact is not allowed to consider evidence of the accused's intoxication in deciding whether the Crown has proved *mens rea*. Where the crime is characterized as one of "specific intent," the trier of fact may consider such evidence. Finally, there is one very important class of crimes of which intoxication is itself an element: the offences related to impaired driving.

These rules concerning the effect of self-induced intoxication on criminal liability raise a number of section 7 issues, as discussed below. First, the category of general intent offences has itself been unsuccessfully challenged under section 7. Second, the common law rule that the issue in specific intent offences was capacity rather than intent has been successfully challenged. Finally, the existence of offences having intoxication itself as an element does not violate section 7.

a) General Intent and Proof of Fault

Where an offence, such as assault or sexual assault, is characterized as an offence of general intent, the Crown must still prove the fault element beyond a reasonable doubt—but the accused may not lead evidence of self-induced intoxication to raise a reasonable doubt about the fault element. Thus, if the accused's self-induced intoxication ac-

---

304 Section 265(1)(*a*) expressly requires the intentional application of force. The fault requirement in relation to the complainant's lack of consent to a non-sexual assault derives from the caselaw: see Hamish Stewart, "When Does Fraud Vitiate Consent? A Comment on *R v Williams*" (2004) 49 Crim LQ 144 at 145 n 5.

tually did negate the fault element, it is entirely possible that the trier of fact will convict even though it would have acquitted had it heard the evidence concerning intoxication. This outcome seems to be a straight-forward violation of sections 7 and 11(d) of the *Charter*. But in *R v Bernard*,[305] the Supreme Court of Canada held that the common law category of general intent offences did not violate section 7.

The accused Bernard was charged with sexual assault causing bodily harm, and asserted that he lacked the intent to apply force to the complaint because he was very intoxicated. The trial judge instructed the jury, in accordance with the *Leary* rule that sexual assault was an offence of general intent;[306] thus, they could not consider the accused's intoxication in deciding whether the Crown had proved intent. The accused was convicted. In the Supreme Court, the accused challenged the constitutionality of the *Leary* rule. Dickson CJC and Lamer J, dissenting, agreed that the *Leary* rule offended sections 7 and 11(d) for the straightforward reason that it "imposes a form of absolute liability on intoxicated offenders, which is entirely inconsistent with the basic requirement for a blameworthy state of mind mandated by [s. 7]."[307] But the majority, *per* McIntyre J,[308] held that the *Leary* rule and the existence of general intent offences did not offend section 7. He characterized the general/specific intent distinction as follows:

> The general intent offence is one in which the only intent involved relates solely to the performance of the act in question with no further ulterior intent or purpose. The minimal intent to apply force in the offence of common assault affords an example. A specific intent offence is one which involves the performance of the *actus reus*, coupled with an intent or purpose going beyond the mere performance of the questioned act. Striking a blow or administering poison

---

305 Above note 170.

306 See *ibid*.

307 *Ibid* at 852, Dickson CJC dissenting. Justice La Forest indicated his "general agreement" with Dickson CJC's reasons, but would have upheld the guilty verdict under s 686(1)(*b*)(iii) of the *Criminal Code*, above note 24 (the trial judge's error occasioned no substantial wrong or miscarriage of justice): *ibid* at 892.

308 Justice Beetz concurred with McIntyre J. Justice Wilson, L'Heureux-Dubé J concurring, agreed that the *Leary* rule should survive, but expressed some doubts about McIntyre J's reasons, and, in particular, with his view that proof of intent to become intoxicated could be a constitutionally acceptable substitute for proof of the mental element of the crime: *ibid* at 882–86. Six years later, in *Daviault*, above note 163, the majority generally accepted McIntyre J's approach.

with intent to kill, or assault with intent to maim or wound, are examples of such offences.[309]

He noted that the Crown still has to prove the mental element of a general intent offence:

> The effect of excluding the drunkenness defence from such [general intent] offences is merely to prevent the accused from relying on his self-imposed drunkenness as a factor showing an absence of any intent.[310]

This rule did not offend section 7 because those who committed crimes after becoming voluntarily intoxicated were not "morally innocent":[311]

> If [accused persons] managed to get themselves so drunk that the did not know what the were doing, the reckless behaviour in attaining that level of intoxication affords the necessary evidence of the culpable mental condition. Hence, it is logically impossible for an accused person to throw up his voluntary drunkenness as a defence to a charge of general intent. Proof of his voluntary drunkenness can be proof of his guilty mind.[312]

The Court, in effect, accepted the proposition that proof of the accused's decision to become voluntarily intoxicated was a constitutionally acceptable substitute for proof of the mental element of the offence.

b) Specific Intent and Stigma

Even where the offence was one of "specific intent," the factual issue in pre-*Charter* law was not whether the accused's intoxication negated her intent, but whether it negated her capacity to form the intent ("the *MacAskill* rule"[313]). In R v Robinson (*Robinson*),[314] the Supreme Court of Canada held that this rule offended section 7. The accused was charged with murder, a specific intent offence, and raised a defence of intoxication. The trial judge instructed the jury in accordance with the *MacAskill* rule and the accused was convicted. Lamer CJC, speaking for the majority, saw the issue as a straightforward application of *Vaillancourt* and *Martineau*: under the *MacAskill* rule, "if the jury is satisfied that the accused's voluntary intoxication did not render the accused incapable

---

309 *Ibid* at 863.
310 *Ibid* at 871.
311 *Ibid* at 880; compare 871.
312 *Ibid* at 879.
313 *R v MacAskill*, [1931] SCR 330.
314 *R v Robinson*, [1996] 1 SCR 683.

of forming the intent, then they would be compelled to convict, despite the fact that the evidence raised a reasonable doubt as to whether the accused possessed the requisite intent."[315] The *MacAskill* rule could not be justified under section 1.[316] In the future, jury instructions in cases of specific intent offences, though they might refer to capacity, should make it clear that the accused could not be convicted unless the Crown had proved the requisite intent beyond a reasonable doubt.

The reasoning in *Robinson* is not expressly connected to the fact that murder is a special stigma offence (see Section C(4)(a), above in this chapter) and does not refer to other stigma offences. But since only those offences are constitutionally required to have a special subjective mental element, it is likely that the reasoning applies to all stigma offences—but only to stigma offences. This reasoning implies, in turn, that a stigma offence cannot be an offence of general intent, because it is the essence of those offences that the trier of fact can convict even though evidence of the accused's intoxication might have raised a reasonable doubt about the fault element.[317]

c) Intoxication as an Element

In *R v Penno*,[318] the Court considered the argument that intoxication should be a defence to the offence of having care or control of a motor vehicle while impaired,[319] or more particularly, that failing to allow evidence of intoxication to negate the *mens rea* of the "care or control" element was contrary to the principles of fundamental justice. The claim, in essence, was that if the accused was so intoxicated that he did not realize he was taking care or control of a motor vehicle, he should not be convicted of this offence. All seven members of the panel hearing the case rejected this argument, though on different grounds. Six of the judges agreed that the care or control offence was one of general intent, though Wilson J and McLachlin J both offered important qualifications to what might otherwise appear to be a circular holding. Wilson J held that "the *actus reus* requires the voluntary consumption of alcohol *to the point of impairment*" and that the *mens rea* of intent to assume care or control was one of general intent, meaning that the accused could not rely on evidence of intoxication to negate it.[320] Imposing liability on

---

315 *Ibid* at para 41.

316 *Ibid* at paras 42–45.

317 This conclusion is supported by Sopinka J's dissenting reasons in *Daviault*, as discussed in note 283 above.

318 *R v Penno*, [1990] 2 SCR 865 [*Penno*].

319 *Criminal Code*, RSC 1970, above note 181, s 234(1); see now s 253(1).

320 *Penno*, above note 318 at 890–91 [emphasis in original].

this basis might seem straightforwardly contrary to section 7, but Wilson J held that "crimes in which intoxication is made an element of the offence . . . are in a different category from crimes in which intoxication is relevant to the mental element only."[321] McLachlin J, whose views apparently constitute the majority,[322] held that while the offence might be characterized as one of general intent, the common law dichotomy between general and specific intent was not really relevant where Parliament had made intoxication an element of the crime: "Impairment being an essential element of the crime, it is illogical and contradictory to suppose that Parliament intended that its express aim of making such impairment criminal should be defeated by an unexpressed implication of law that the same impairment may provide an effective defence."[323] The *mens rea* of the offence was simply "voluntarily becoming intoxicated";[324] since there was no *mens rea* in relation to assuming care or control, it was not a violation of section 7 to deny the defence of intoxication in relation to that element.[325] Moreover, nothing in section 7 prevented Parliament from creating an offence of this kind.[326] Thus, where the very purpose of the offence is to criminalize a form of intoxicated conduct, there is no purchase for the argument that voluntary intoxication can negate fault, so refusing to recognize voluntary intoxication as going to fault does not violate section 7.

D. PRINCIPLES OF PENAL RESPONSIBILITY: DEFENCES

If the word "defence" is used loosely, one can say that there are several types of defences in Canadian criminal law. The denial of an element of the offence is a defence in this broad sense; for example, the accused's claim that she mistakenly believed in facts that would make her conduct innocent is often referred to as "the defence of mistake of fact"; the denial of the element of voluntariness that is always an element of the *actus reus* is often referred to as "the defence of automatism." Any

---

321 *Ibid* at 892.
322 Justices Sopinka and Gonthier concurred with McLachlin J. Justice La Forest wrote for himself, but his reasons are very similar to those of McLachlin J: see particularly *ibid* at 894.
323 *Ibid* at 899.
324 *Ibid* at 896.
325 *Ibid* at 904.
326 *Ibid* at 903–4. Chief Justice Lamer, speaking for himself, found a s 7 violation but would have justified it under s 1.

principles of fundamental justice that are relevant to the elements of offences are therefore applicable to "defences" in this broad sense.[327]

But in a narrower sense, a "defence" arises only when the Crown has proved all the elements of the offence and the accused points to facts that would justify or excuse his conduct. If the defence has an air of reality on the evidence, then the Crown must disprove it beyond a reasonable doubt.[328] The defence of necessity, for example, arises only if the Crown has proved the elements of the offence charged beyond a reasonable doubt; if the defence has an air of reality, the Crown then has to disprove one or more elements of that defence beyond a reasonable doubt.[329] Similarly, in a homicide case, the jury would only need to consider the defence of self-defence if satisfied that the Crown had proved the elements of murder (or manslaughter) beyond a reasonable doubt.

The presence or absence of a defence, in the narrow sense, can make the difference between acquittal and conviction. The definition of a defence therefore engages the liberty interest in section 7 of the *Charter*. Many defences in Canadian criminal law exist by virtue of the common law;[330] others are defined by the *Criminal Code*.[331] But in either case, the definition of the defence must comply with the principles of fundamental justice.[332] The Supreme Court of Canada has recognized several such principles in connection with defences in the narrow sense.

---

327 Compare the discussion of sexual assault and mistake of fact in Section C(4)(f), above in this chapter.

328 *R v Cinous*, 2002 SCC 29 [*Cinous*].

329 Compare *R v Latimer*, 2001 SCC 1 [*Latimer*], where the Court held that none of the elements of the defence had an air of reality on the evidence; the trial judge was therefore correct not to allow the jury to consider it.

330 Section 8(3) of the *Criminal Code*, above note 24, expressly preserved the common law defences and permits courts to recognize new ones. The common law defences in Canada include necessity (*Latimer*, ibid); entrapment (*R v Mack*, [1988] 2 SCR 903); and officially induced error (*Lévis (City) v Tétreault; Lévis (City) v 2629-4470 Québec Inc*, 2006 SCC 12).

331 Statutory defences include self-defence (*Criminal Code*, ibid, ss 34–36); defence of property (ss 38–42); correction of a child (s 43); and duress (s 17, and see also Section D(1), below in this chapter).

332 In *R v Ruzic*, 2001 SCC 24 [*Ruzic*], the Crown argued that statutory defences were entitled to special deference in constitutional review. Justice LeBel rejected this argument, commenting at para 25 that "statutory defences do not warrant more deference simply because they are the product of difficult moral judgments. The entire body of criminal law expresses a myriad of policy choices."

1) Penal Liability Requires Proof of Morally Voluntary Behaviour

It is a principle of fundamental justice that to be punishable, conduct must be morally voluntary, or that "society refrain from punishing morally involuntary action."[333]

This principle was developed in *R v Ruzic* (*Ruzic*) by analogy with the more familiar principle that to be punishable, conduct must be physically voluntary (see Section C(1), above in this chapter). Justice LeBel, for the Court, illustrated the analogy as follows:

> Suppose someone puts a knife in the accused's hand and forces it into the victim's chest. The accused's body is literally overpowered, as is her will. Consider next the situation of someone who gives the accused a knife and orders her to stab the victim or else be killed herself. Unlike the first scenario, moral voluntariness is not a matter of physical dimension. The accused here retains conscious control over her bodily movements. Yet, like the first actor, her will is overborne, this time by the threats of another. Her conduct is not, in a realistic way, freely chosen.[334]

The idea of moral involuntariness, then, is not to be equated with the idea that the accused had no physical control over his movements, or even that he had no choice in the matter. The accused's action is morally involuntary where the choice he makes is so constrained that it can no longer be recognized as *his* choice: he is said to have "acted in a morally involuntary fashion . . . because his acts cannot realistically be attributed to him, as his will was constrained by some external force."[335] Since every choice is made and every act is performed subject to constraints, the challenge in applying this principle is to identify those situations in which a court ought to say that the accused's act, though physically voluntary, was unpunishable because it was imposed on him by a natural event or the will of another.[336]

---

333 *Ibid* at para 48.
334 *Ibid* at para 44.
335 *Ibid* at para 46.
336 There is substantial scholarly literature on this problem; some sense of the different strands may be gleaned from George Fletcher, *Rethinking Criminal Law* (Boston: Little, Brown, 1978) ch 10; Martha Shaffer, "Scrutinizing Duress: The Constitutional Validity of s 17 of the *Criminal Code*" (1998) 40 Crim LQ 444; Dennis Klimchuk, "Necessity, Deterrence, and Standing" (2002) 8 Legal Theory 339; John Gardner, *Offences and Defences* (Oxford: Oxford University Press, 2007) ch 4–7.

This principle of fundamental justice requires that all defences in penal law, whether they are available by statute or at common law, be defined so as to ensure that morally involuntary behaviour is not punishable. In *Ruzic* itself, the accused challenged the statutory version of the defence of duress defined by section 17 of the *Criminal Code*:

> A person who commits an offence under compulsion by threats of immediate death or bodily harm from a person who is present when the offence is committed is excused for committing the offence if the person believes that the threats will be carried out and if the person is not a party to a conspiracy or association whereby the person is subject to compulsion . . . .

The cases had established that the words "immediate" and "present" were to be interpreted quite literally, so that a threat to harm the accused at a later time, or a threat to which the accused responded by committing an offence at a later time, could not form the basis for a defence of duress.[337] Moreover, section 17 does not recognize threats to third parties. Under this interpretation, the defence was not available to the accused Ruzic. She had imported a substantial amount of heroin into Canada, but testified that she had done so in response to threats against her and her mother made by a man in Yugoslavia.[338] Since the threats were not of "immediate" harm and since the man was not present when the accused imported the heroin into Canada, she could not rely on the defence as defined by section 17. The trial judge accepted her argument that section 17 was unconstitutional, and so charged the jury on the common law defence of duress, which is in most respects more generous than section 17. The accused was acquitted. The Crown's appeal to the Court of Appeal and its further appeal to the Supreme Court of Canada were dismissed. Justice LeBel, for the Court, held that section 17 offended the principle of fundamental justice requiring proof of morally voluntary behaviour because it permitted a conviction where the accused, on account of threats of future harm, threats to third parties, or threats by a person who is not present, behaves in a morally involuntary manner.[339] The Crown did not attempt to justify the infringement of section 7 under section 1, and LeBel J held that the infringement could not be justified in any event because the accused's rights were more than minimally impaired.[340] Section 17

---

337 See especially *R v Carker*, [1967] SCR 114.
338 *Ruzic*, above note 332 at paras 2–7.
339 *Ibid* at paras 87–88.
340 *Ibid* at paras 91–92.

was struck down to the extent that it required immediate threats from a person who was present when the offence was committed.

Section 17 also prevents an accused from asserting duress as a defence to a lengthy list of offences, ranging in seriousness from treason to unlawfully causing bodily harm.[341] The decision in *Ruzic* did not directly affect that part of section 17. However, the principle that there can be no liability for morally involuntary behaviour would seem to apply regardless of the offence committed, so it is difficult to see how these exclusions can be constitutionally permissible.

2) The Relationship between Principles of Fault and Defences

As noted above, the word "defence" in the broadest sense can refer to any fact which would result in the accused's acquittal, while "defence" in the narrow sense refers to those facts that result in acquittal even though the Crown has proved the elements of the offence. The Crown's failure to prove the required fault element is a defence in the broad sense but not in the narrow sense, while self-defence is a defence only in the narrow sense. But defences, like offence definitions, generally have mental states associated with them: the justification of self-defence, for example, is typically available only if the accused is aware of, or reasonably believes in, the facts that give rise to the justification.[342] As discussed in Sections C(1) through C(4), above in this chapter, section 7 requires proof of some form of fault for all offences for which imprisonment is a possible penalty, and proof of subjective fault for the special "stigma" offences. Since the presence or absence of the mental element of a defence, like the absence or presence of the fault element, makes the difference between acquittal and conviction, do the doctrines of section 7 concerning fault elements also apply to the mental elements of defences? Do the statutory or common law definitions of the mental elements of defences comply with section 7?

---

341 Specifically, s 17 of the *Criminal Code*, above note 24, provides that "this section does not apply where the offence that is committed is high treason or treason, murder, piracy, attempted murder, sexual assault, sexual assault with a weapon, threats to a third party or causing bodily harm, aggravated sexual assault, forcible abduction, hostage taking, robbery, assault with a weapon or causing bodily harm, aggravated assault, unlawfully causing bodily harm, arson or an offence under sections 280 to 283 (abduction and detention of young persons)."

342 See, for example, *Criminal Code*, ibid, s 34(2), requiring the accused to have a "reasonable apprehension" of death or grievous bodily harm, and a belief "on reasonable grounds" that the force used was necessary.

There are two ways in which this question could be posed. The first would be in the exotic scenario where the justifying or excusing conditions exist in fact, but the accused is unaware of them. In Canadian criminal law as it stands, the accused would be convicted in this scenario because the law requires that the accused know of (or reasonably believe in) the justifying or excusing circumstances before he is entitled to the justification (or excuse) in question. I will call this principle "the *Dadson* rule."[343] Is the *Dadson* rule consistent with the principles of fundamental justice? Is it right to convict a person whose conduct was in fact justified (or excused) even though he was unaware of the justifying (or excusing) circumstances? The *Dadson* rule is prevalent in the positive law of free and democratic societies and is supported by a substantial scholarly consensus.[344] A person who commits an offence *without* awareness of the conditions that would justify or excuse the act has, like a person who commits an impossible attempt,[345] amply demonstrated his willingness to violate the criminal law, so it does not appear unjust to convict him. An accused person would be hard pressed to show that the *Dadson* rule was *not* a fundamental tenet of our system of criminal justice.

The second way of posing the question is in connection with the objective component of the mental element of defences. Generally speaking, for a defence to succeed, the accused's belief that the conditions for the defence are present has to be reasonable. So an accused charged with murder who asserts self-defence would be convicted where he believed that his life was in danger, or where he believed he needed to use deadly force to defend himself, but one (or both) of those beliefs was not reasonable.[346] But murder is a stigma offence, so on the basis of

---

343   *R v Dadson* (1850), 4 Cox CC 358. The accused police officer shot and wounded a man who fled the scene after stealing wood. The victim had been twice convicted of stealing wood; the third theft would be a felony; the shooting would be justified under the "fleeing felon" rule. But the accused was not aware of the victim's prior convictions and therefore did not know that the victim was a fleeing felon. In these circumstances, the accused could not assert the justification. The *Dadson* rule is reflected in the statutory and common law definitions of Canadian criminal law defences.

344   See, among others, Gardner, above note 336; Fletcher, above note 336. The leading proponent of abandoning the *Dadson* rule has been Paul H Robinson; see, for instance, his "Competing Theories of Justification: Deeds vs Reasons" in AP Simester & ATH Smith, eds, *Harm and Culpability* (Oxford: Clarendon Press, 1996) 45; see also Williams, above note 162, §12.

345   Compare *Dynar*, above note 233.

346   Compare *Cinous*, above note 328 at paras 117–25 (the accused believed that he had to use deadly force, but there was no air of reality to his claim that there

Martineau,[347] it might be argued that the mental elements of the available defences, like the mental element of the offence itself, should be entirely subjective.

This argument has been raised, without success, in relation to the partial excuse of provocation. Under section 232 of the *Criminal Code*, murder is reduced to manslaughter where the accused committed it "in the heat of passion caused by sudden provocation";[348] a "wrongful act or insult" is "provocation" if it "is of such a nature as to be sufficient to deprive the ordinary person of the power of self-control . . . if the accused acted on it on the sudden and before there was time for his passion to cool."[349] The defence of provocation thus has objective and subjective elements: the wrongful act or insult must have been sufficient to provoke the ordinary person (objective element) and the accused must have been provoked (subjective element). In *R v Cameron*,[350] the Ontario Court of Appeal rejected the accused's claim that the objective element of the partial excuse of provocation was contrary to the principles of fundamental justice. The court reasoned that before the defence of provocation came into play, the Crown had to prove the full subjective *mens rea* of murder; thus, under section 232, no-one could be convicted of murder without proof of the constitutionally required level of fault. Conditioning the partial excuse of provocation on an objective element was not contrary to any principle of fundamental justice.[351] The court's reasoning is sound. Provocation does not justify conduct or negate blameworthiness; it operates as a partial excuse mitigating blameworthiness. Conditioning the defence on the response of the ordinary person serves merely to prevent those who are more sensitive than the ordinary person from taking advantage of the partial excuse.

The objective elements of the defence of self-defence would appear to be more vulnerable to a challenge along these lines. Consider the branch of self-defence in section 34(2) of the *Criminal Code*, where the accused "causes death or grievous bodily harm." There are three elements to this defence: (1) the accused reasonably believed he was being unlawfully assaulted; (2) the accused caused the death or grievous bodily harm "under reasonable apprehension of death or grievous bodily harm"; and (3) the accused believed "on reasonable grounds" that

---

were reasonable grounds for this belief; therefore, there was no air of reality to the claim of self-defence).

347 *Martineau*, above note 223.

348 *Criminal Code*, above note 24, s 232(1).

349 *Ibid*, s 232(2).

350 *R v Cameron* (1992), 71 CCC (3d) 272 (Ont CA).

351 *Ibid* at 273–74.

he could not "otherwise preserve himself from death or grievous bodily harm."[352] Each of these elements has an objective component; put another way, while the section permits reasonable mistake about the presence of an element, an unreasonable mistake about the presence of an element will deprive the accused of the defence. Yet when an accused acts under an honest though unreasonable belief that his life is endangered by an assault, he subjectively believes that he is not acting wrongfully—just as an accused who kills without *mens rea* subjectively believes that he is not committing murder.

It is likely that the Supreme Court of Canada would reject these challenges to the objective elements of defences by invoking the principle that morally involuntary behaviour is not punishable (see Section D(1), above in this chapter) and by holding that unreasonable responses to insults and threats are not morally involuntary. The Court has conditioned the elements of the common law defences of necessity and duress on the reasonableness of the accused's belief in the excusing conditions,[353] and it is unlikely that the Court would have defined the defences in this way if the Court believed that they would permit the conviction of one whose conduct is morally involuntary.

3) Mentally Disordered Offenders Are Not Penally Liable

Ever since *M'Naghten's Case*,[354] if not before, the criminal law of the common law world has recognized that certain forms of mental disorder interfere so seriously with a person's practical reasoning—that is, her ability to reason about the moral quality and the consequences of her conduct—that she should not be held criminally liable for the prohibited acts that she commits. The Supreme Court of Canada has used the *Charter*, and section 7 in particular, both to constitutionally entrench certain aspects of the common law approach to mental disorder and to require very substantial changes to the procedures for dealing with mentally disordered offenders. The impact of the Court's decisions in this area is best assessed through a chronological reading of the cases, against the background of the law as it stood when the *Charter* came into force.

---

352 Compare *R v Pétel*, [1994] 1 SCR 3.
353 Compare *Latimer*, above note 329 at paras 32–34 (necessity); *R v Hibbert*, [1995] 2 SCR 973 at paras 56–61.
354 *M'Naghten's Case* (1843), 8 ER 718 (HL).

a) Background: The Defence of Insanity and Fitness to Stand Trial before the *Charter*

In 1982, when the *Charter* came into force, the *Criminal Code* restated the *M'Naghten* rules as follows:[355]

> 16 (1) No person shall be convicted of an offence in respect of an act or omission on his part while he was insane.
>
> (2) For the purposes of this section a person is insane when he is in a state of natural imbecility or has disease of the mind to an extent that renders him incapable of appreciating the nature and quality of an act or omission or of knowing that an act or omission is wrong.
>
> (3) A person who has specific delusions, but is in other respects sane, shall not be acquitted on the ground of insanity unless the delusions caused him to believe in the existence of a state or things that, if it existed, would have justified or excused his act or omission.
>
> (4) Every one shall, until the contrary is proved, be presumed to be and to have been sane.

A person was insane for criminal law purposes when she had a "disease of the mind" which had one of two effects on her ability to reason practically: it rendered her "incapable of appreciating the nature and quality" of her conduct, or it rendered her "incapable . . . of knowing" that the conduct was "wrong."[356] Whether a particular disorder amounted to a "disease of the mind" was a legal question, not a medical question, though its determination was of course affected by medical opinion; a disease of the mind could be "any illness, disorder or abnormal condition which impairs the human mind and its functioning, excluding however, self-induced states caused by alcohol or drugs . . . ."[357] To "appreciate the nature and quality of an act" referred not just to "mere knowledge of the act" but also "an ability to perceive the consequences, impact, and results of a physical act."[358] The accused was incapable of

---

355 *Criminal Code*, RSC 1970, above note 181, s 16. On the differences between the *M'Naghten* rules and former s 16 of the *Criminal Code*, above note 24, see Stuart, above note 162 at 396–98.

356 There were few cases dealing with "natural imbecility" or "specific delusions."

357 *R v Cooper*, [1980] 1 SCR 1149 at 1159; see also *Parks*, above note 167, and *Stone*, above note 163, for the evolution of the Court's approach to determining whether a particular condition amounts to a disease of the mind.

358 *Cooper, ibid* at 1162. The "consequences" did not, however, include the penal consequences that would flow from conviction: *R v Abbey*, [1982] 2 SCR 24.

knowing that his act was "wrong" only if he was incapable of knowing that it was legally wrong.[359]

The defence of insanity could be asserted either by the accused or by the prosecution and, once asserted, had to be proved on a balance of probabilities.

Where a person was found not guilty by reason of insanity, the trial judge was required to "make an order that he be kept in strict custody in the place and in the manner that the [judge] directs, until the pleasure of the lieutenant governor of the province is known."[360] Under the *Criminal Code*, the executive had considerable discretion in dealing with the insane offender;[361] however, every province established a "review board,"[362] which examined the insane offender's case and advised the executive on whether to detain or to release him.

Former section 543 of the *Criminal Code* provided that "where it appears that there is sufficient reason to doubt that the accused is, on account of insanity, capable of conducting his defence," the court should "direct that an issue be tried whether the accused is then, on account of insanity, unfit to stand trial."[363] The word "insanity" had a different meaning here than in section 16, as the issue was whether the accused's mental disorder affected his ability to conduct a defence; for example, by making him incapable of communicating rationally with counsel.[364] However, if the accused was unfit to stand trial, he was subject to the same regime of detention as an insane acquittee.[365]

b) *Chaulk* and *Landry*

In *R v Chaulk* (*Chaulk*),[366] the Supreme Court of Canada considered several constitutional aspects of the pre-*Charter* defence of insanity. Though not expressly decided under section 7, *Chaulk* forms an important part of the background to the section 7 issues.

Two accused were charged with first degree murder. The only defence asserted was that of insanity, based on expert opinion evidence that they "suffered from a paranoid psychosis which made them believe that they had the power to rule the world and that the killing was a necessary means to that end . . . that they were above the ordinary

---

359 *R v Schwartz*, [1977] 1 SCR 673.
360 *Criminal Code*, RSC 1970, above note 181, s 542(2).
361 *Ibid*, s 546.
362 *Ibid*, s 547.
363 *Ibid*, s 615.
364 See, for example, *R v Steele* (1991), 63 CCC (3d) 149 (Que CA).
365 *Criminal Code*, above note 24, s 543(6).
366 *R v Chaulk*, [1990] 3 SCR 1303.

law . . . [and that] they had a right to kill the victim because he was 'a loser.'"[367] They were convicted at trial. A majority of the Supreme Court ordered a new trial on the ground that the trial judge had erroneously (though in compliance with previous authority) instructed the jury that the defence of insanity could succeed only if the accused's disease of the mind prevented them from knowing that their conduct was legally wrong. Lamer CJC, for the majority, held that the defence should be available even if the accused was capable of knowing that his conduct was legally wrong but incapable of knowing that it was morally wrong (and vice versa);[368] this reading of section 16(2) was not based on the *Charter* but on Lamer CJC's understanding of generally applicable principles of penal liability.

The accused also argued that the reverse onus in section 16(4) was unconstitutional. The majority agreed that the reverse onus infringed section 11(*d*) of the *Charter*, but held that this infringement was justified under section 1.[369] McLachlin J, dissenting in the result on other grounds,[370] held that section 16(4) did not violate section 11(*d*), and drew a link between section 11(*d*) and section 7: she held that the presumption of sanity embodied in section 16(4) "reflects the dignity which the law accords to each human being, and avoids the practical difficulties associated with requiring the Crown to prove in each case that the accused was sufficiently sane . . . [s. 16(4)], far from violating a fundamental principle of justice, reflects the fundamental precepts upon which our legal system and our *Charter* is based."[371] The majority, though disagreeing with the particulars of her analysis, agreed that imposing criminal liability on the insane is contrary to the principles of fundamental justice. As Lamer CJC put it, where an accused establishes the defence of insanity, he has refuted "one of the basic assumptions of our criminal law model: that the accused is a rational autonomous being who is capable of appreciating the nature and quality of an act and of knowing right from wrong."[372]

In *R v Landry* (*Landry*),[373] the Supreme Court indicated that section 7 of the *Charter* had not affected the content of the test for insanity. The accused was charged with first degree murder and offered a defence of insanity, based on uncontradicted evidence that he "suffered from a

---

367 *Ibid* at 1314.
368 *Ibid* at 1345–58.
369 *Ibid* at 1317–45.
370 She disagreed with Lamer CJC's interpretation of s 16(2): *ibid* at 1407–14.
371 *Ibid* at 1404–405.
372 *Ibid* at 1320.
373 *R v Landry*, [1991] 1 SCR 99.

severe psychosis that made him believe that he was God and had a mission to destroy all forces of evil on Earth." He killed the victim because he believed the victim to be Satan, though he knew he was killing the victim and that it was legally wrong do to so.[374] He was convicted at trial. The Quebec Court of Appeal ordered a new trial, reasoning that section 7 of the *Charter* required the test for "appreciating the nature and quality of the act" to be extended to include the incapacity to appreciate that it was wrong; a verdict of not guilty by reason of insanity was substituted.[375] The Supreme Court held that the Court of Appeal had erred in using the *Charter* to modify the established meaning of the phrase "nature and quality of the act"; however, the verdict of insanity was upheld on the ground that the evidence showed that the accused, though capable of appreciating the nature and quality of his act, was incapable of knowing that it was wrong.[376] Since *Landry*, the Court has not suggested that section 7 requires any modification of the established meaning of the two branches of the test for insanity.

c)   Swain

In *R v Swain* (*Swain*),[377] the majority[378] recognized, or applied, at least three distinct principles of fundamental justice:

- "it is a principle of fundamental justice that the criminal justice system not convict a person who was insane at the time of the offence."[379]
- it is a principle of fundamental justice that "an accused person have the right to control his or her own defence."[380]
- it is a principle of fundamental justice that a person deprived of liberty have a fair hearing.[381]

---

374   *Ibid* at 103.
375   See *ibid* at 106.
376   *Ibid* at 109.
377   *R v Swain*, [1991] 1 SCR 933 [*Swain*].
378   Chief Justice Lamer, Sopinka and Cory JJ concurring. Justice Gonthier, La Forest J concurring, stated at 1038 that he "substantially agree[d]" with Lamer CJC's reasons. Justice Wilson, concurring in the result, agreed with Lamer CJC as to the defects of the existing scheme, but had a somewhat different view of the rule that should replace the impugned common law rule. Justice L'Heureux-Dubé dissented on all the *Charter* issues.
379   *Swain, ibid* at 976.
380   *Ibid* at 972. See also Chapter 5, Section B(4)(d).
381   *Ibid* at 1009. See also Chapter 5, Section A.

Moreover, the majority held that the procedures then in place for dealing with mentally disordered offenders did not fully comply with those principles.

The accused was charged with assault and aggravated assault. At trial, the Crown, over his objection, led evidence supporting the defence of insanity; the trial judge accepted the defence, and found him not guilty by reason of insanity. The accused then challenged the constitutional validity of section 542(2) of the Code, which required the trial judge to commit him to await the pleasure of the lieutenant governor. The trial judge rejected the challenge, and the accused was committed into safe custody for some fourteen months. The accused's appeal eventually reached the Supreme Court of Canada. The majority held that the common law rule permitting the Crown to assert the accused's insanity violated section 7 and that section 542(2) violated sections 7 and 9.

As noted above, at common law, the Crown was entitled to lead evidence that the accused was insane, and thus in effect raise the defence of insanity even where the accused did not wish to. The accused's motivation for not asserting a possible defence of insanity would be to avoid being held until the pleasure of the lieutenant governor was known. The Crown's motivation for alleging insanity would usually be to protect the public from the danger posed by a mentally disordered offender who would otherwise be acquitted outright. There were typically two situations in which the Crown would try and assert that the accused was insane. First, the accused raised a defence of involuntariness (or non-insane automatism), and the Crown wished to argue that the condition giving rise to the accused's involuntary behaviour was properly characterized as a disease of the mind and therefore as insane automatism. Second—and this appears to have been the situation in *Swain* itself—the accused preferred to take the chance of being convicted of a minor offence such as assault and serving a definite term of imprisonment, rather than being committed to a psychiatric institution for an indefinite period, but the Crown's position was that the protection of the public required a finding of insanity followed by confinement.

Lamer CJC held that "the principles of fundamental justice require that an accused person have the right to control his or her own defence." This principle of fundamental justice, like other aspects of the adversarial trial process, was based on "respect for the autonomy and dignity of human beings"; the accused is not just the object of the proceedings but a participant with control over several decisions: "whether to have counsel, whether to testify on his or her own behalf, and what witnesses to call." The decision to seek an exemption from criminal responsibility on the basis of insanity was such a decision.[382] The common law rule therefore violated the principles of fundamental justice. Rather than subjecting that rule to a full section 1 analysis, Lamer CJC articulated a new common law rule which, he held, would achieve its objectives without limiting the accused's rights under section 7. According to the new rule, the Crown may lead evidence of the accused's insanity in two situations: first, where the accused has otherwise been found guilty; second, where "the accused's own defence has (in the view of the trial judge) put the accused's capacity for criminal intent in issue."[383] In these situations, the right to control the conduct of one's defence would not be violated; in the first, because the accused would have already been found guilty, and in the second, "because the very issue [of insanity] has been raised by the accused's conduct of his or her own defence."[384]

But the most significant effect of *Swain* flowed from the holdings concerning section 542(2) and the whole system for dealing with insane acquittees. As noted above, section 542(2) required the trial judge to commit the insane acquittee into custody until the pleasure of the lieutenant governor was known. Since the section provided "no hearing or other procedural safeguards whatsoever," it was procedurally unfair and contrary to section 7.[385] There was no possibility of reading procedural safeguards into the section because the section was mandatory and conferred no discretion.[386] The substantive defect of the section—detention "without any rational standard for determining which individual insanity acquittees should be detained and which should be released"—amounted to arbitrary detention under section 9 of the *Charter*, though Lamer CJC was clearly of the view that this arbitrary detention also violated section 7.[387] The violations of sections 7 and 9 could not be justified under section 1.[388]

If section 542(2) had simply been struck down, the detention of all insane acquittees would have been unlawful and they have been entitled to immediate release. To avoid the chaos and danger this would have produced, the Court declared section 542(2) invalid but sus-

---

382 *Ibid* at 972.
383 *Ibid* at 987–88.
384 *Ibid* at 988.
385 *Ibid* at 1009.
386 *Ibid* at 1010–12.
387 *Ibid* at 1012.
388 *Ibid* at 1013–19.

pended the declaration of invalidity for six months (later extended)[389] to allow Parliament an opportunity to create a new scheme.

d) After *Swain*

Parliament responded to *Swain* by restating and renaming the defence of insanity, and by modifying the procedures for dealing with a person acquitted on this ground or found unfit to stand trial. Section 16(1) of the *Criminal Code* now states the defence of "mental disorder" as follows:

> 16(1) No person is criminally responsible for an act or omission made while suffering from a mental disorder that rendered the person incapable of appreciating the nature and quality of the act or omission or of knowing that it was wrong.

"Mental disorder" is defined in section 2 as "a disease of the mind." Section 16(2) restates the presumption of sanity, and section 16(3) places the burden of proof on the issue of mental disorder "on the party that raises the issue." Thus, section 16(1) essentially restates the former defence of insanity under the new name "not criminally responsible on account of mental disorder" (NCRMD),[390] subject to the procedural rule in *Swain*[391] which permits the Crown to raise the issue only when the accused has otherwise been acquitted or has raised a defence putting his mental capacity in issue.[392]

The new section 16 has not been subjected to any fresh challenges under section 7, or indeed under any other section of the *Charter*, and in light of the earlier cases would likely survive any such challenge.

The revisions to the *Criminal Code* prompted by *Swain* also addressed the situation of the person unfit to stand trial, now defined in section 2 as "unable on account of mental disorder to conduct a defence," and in particular unable to understand the nature, object, or consequences of the proceeding, or to communicate with counsel. As before, the judge can order a trial of the issue of fitness to stand trial.[393]

The new procedures for dealing with the NCRMD accused and those unfit to stand trial are found in Part XX.1 of the *Criminal Code*. In essence, where the accused is found NCRMD or unfit to stand trial,

---

389 See [1991] Supreme Court Bulletin of Proceedings 2516.
390 See *Criminal Code*, above note 24, s 672.34.
391 Codified in *ibid*, s 672.12(3).
392 For an overview of the new s 16 and its relationship to its predecessor, see Stuart, above note 162 at 397–98.
393 *Criminal Code*, above note 24, s 672.23(1).

the trial judge or a provincial Review Board[394] must hold a disposition hearing.[395] The possible dispositions are defined by section 672.54:

> Where a court or Review Board makes a disposition pursuant to sub-section 672.45(2) or section 672.47 or section 672.83, it shall, taking into consideration the need to protect the public from dangerous persons, the mental condition of the accused, the reintegration of the accused into society and the other needs of the accused, make one of the following dispositions that is the least onerous and least restrictive to the accused:
>
> (a) where a verdict of not criminally responsible on account of mental disorder has been rendered in respect of the accused and, in the opinion of the court or Review Board, the accused is not a significant threat to the safety of the public, by order, direct that the accused be discharged absolutely;
> (b) by order, direct that the accused be discharged subject to such conditions as the court or Review Board considers appropriate; or
> (c) by order, direct that the accused be detained in custody in a hospital, subject to such conditions as the court or Review Board considers appropriate.

If the person is detained under section 672.54(c) or discharged on conditions under section 672.54(b), the disposition must be reviewed every twelve months (or every twenty-four months on consent of both parties where the person is represented by counsel).[396]

Various aspects of this scheme have been challenged under section 7. In *Winko v Forensic Psychiatric Institute*,[397] the Supreme Court of Canada upheld the constitutionality of Part XX.1. The section 7 challenge focused on the criteria for detention in section 672.54. The Court held that the phrase "significant threat to the safety of the public" in section 672.54(b) was not unconstitutionally vague[398] and that section 672.54 was not overbroad in light of its goals of protecting the public and "safeguarding the NCR accused's liberty to the maximum extent possible."[399] The Court also read section 672.54 as not imposing any particular onus on the NCRMD accused, but as requiring the court or Review Board to

---

394 *Ibid*, s 672.38.
395 *Ibid*, ss 672.45 and 672.47.
396 *Ibid*, s 672.81.
397 *Winko v Forensic Psychiatric Institute*, [1999] 2 SCR 625.
398 *Ibid* at paras 68–69.
399 *Ibid* at para 71.

determine whether she posed a threat to public safety, and in light of that finding to "make the disposition that is the least restrictive of the NCR accused's liberty possible." On this reading, the section did not offend the principles of fundamental justice.[400]

In *Penetanguishene Mental Health Centre v Ontario (AG)*,[401] the Ontario Review Board ordered the transfer of an NCRMD accused from a maximum-security to a medium-security hospital, on the basis that this disposition was the "least onerous and least restrictive to the accused" in his circumstances. The Ontario Court of Appeal set aside the decision and ordered a new hearing, on the ground that the "least onerous and least restrictive to the accused" test applied only to the choice among paragraphs (*a*), (*b*) and (*c*) of section 672.54; since the accused would be detained under section 672.54(*c*) regardless of which hospital he was in, it was an error to apply that test to the question of where he was detained. The accused appealed to the Supreme Court of Canada, arguing that the section as interpreted by the Court of Appeal violated section 7 because it affected the accused's liberty more than necessary to achieve the section's objectives.[402] The Court held that the conditions under which an accused was detained pursuant to section 672.54(*c*) had a very significant effect on his liberty interest; accordingly, the phrase "such conditions as the court or Review Board considers appropriate" should be read as incorporating the "least onerous and least restrictive to the accused" standard.[403] Put another way, every disposition hearing or periodic review should seek the disposition that was "least onerous and least restrictive to the accused," whether or not the disposition resulted in a change between the three categories of disposition, a change in the conditions of detention, or a change in the conditions of discharge:

> Parliament intended the Review Board to consider at every step of s. 672.54 "the need to protect the public from dangerous persons, the mental condition of the accused, the reintegration of the accused into society and the other needs of the accused," and there is no textual or contextual reason to isolate the governing requirement of s. 672.54 ("the least onerous and least restrictive") from the preceding list and

---

400 *Ibid* at para 70.

401 *Penetanguishene Mental Health Centre v Ontario (AG)*, 2004 SCC 20.

402 It would, in other words, be overbroad, though the Court does not use that word: compare *ibid* at paras 3, 21–22.

403 *Ibid* at paras 48–56.

hold that it alone does not apply to the formulation of conditions that constitute part of the *décision* or disposition order.[404]

On this interpretation, section 672.54 was consistent with section 7 of the *Charter.*[405]

In *Demers*, as noted above,[406] the Court held that the procedure for dealing with an accused who was found unfit to stand trial was overbroad because it did not permit the person to be discharged absolutely. Parliament remedied this constitutional deficiency by enacting section 672.851, which enables a court, on its own motion or following the recommendation of a review board, to hold an inquiry and decide whether to stay the proceedings against the unfit accused where she "is not likely to ever become fit to stand trial" and "does not pose a significant threat to the safety of the public" and where "a stay is in the interests of the proper administration of justice."[407]

4) Youthful Offenders

It is a principle of fundamental justice that "young people are entitled to a presumption of diminished moral culpability throughout any proceedings against them."[408] This principle arises because "young people have heightened vulnerability, less maturity and a reduced capacity for moral judgment."[409]

It is difficult to characterize this principle as procedural or substantive. It might be characterized as procedural for the following reasons. While young offenders are subject to the same substantive criteria of criminal responsibility as adult offenders, they are entitled to special procedures that reflect their reduced maturity and heightened vulnerability. But it might be characterized as substantive in that it is, like the defence of mental disorder, connected with the capacity to commit crime, and in particular with the young person's transition from being a person under twelve and exempt from criminal liability to being a person over eighteen and subject to the full weight of the criminal justice system. Fortunately, since the principles of fundamental justice can be either procedural or substantive, it is unnecessary to decide how best to characterize the principle.

---

404 *Ibid* at para 45.
405 *Ibid* at para 74.
406 *Demers*, above note 52; see Section B(2), above in this chapter.
407 *Criminal Code*, above note 24, s 672.851(7).
408 R v B(D), 2008 SCC 25 at para 69 [B(D)], Abella J; compare *ibid* at para 106, Rothstein J dissenting.
409 *Ibid* at para 41.

In 2003, a new *Youth Criminal Justice Act* (*YCJA*),[410] replacing a *Young Offenders Act* (*YOA*),[411] came into force.[412] The *YCJA* is in certain respects harsher than the *YOA*; in particular, a young person convicted under the *YCJA* is likely to face a longer sentence, particularly for serious offences, than if she had been convicted under the *YOA*. In *R v B(D)* (*B(D)*), the Supreme Court of Canada unanimously accepted the principle that young persons are entitled to a presumption of diminished moral responsibility,[413] but the members of the Court differed sharply about its application to the *YCJA*. The accused challenged the provisions of the Act defining a category of "presumptive offences" for which a young person was to be sentenced as an adult unless he successfully applied for an order that he be sentenced as a youth.[414] The majority, *per* Abella J, held that the category of presumptive offences was contrary to the principle of presumed diminished responsibility because it amounted to an impermissible reverse onus on the issue of whether the youth should be sentenced as an adult.[415]

E. PRINCIPLES GOVERNING PENAL INVESTIGATIONS

The specific guarantees in sections 8, 9, and 10 of the *Charter* have had a very significant impact on the investigative process and on the trial of criminal and other penal offences. But the courts have recognized a number of additional norms governing the investigative process as principles of fundamental justice under section 7. Many of them flow from the principle against self-incrimination, which the Court has (in

---

410 *Youth Criminal Justice Act*, SC 2002, c 1 [*YCJA*].

411 *Young Offenders Act*, RSC 1985, c Y-1.

412 The government of Quebec referred the question of the constitutionality of the new *YCJA* to the Quebec Court of Appeal. The court found most of the *YCJA* to be constitutionally valid: see *Quebec (Minister of Justice) v Canada (Minister of Justice)* (2003), 175 CCC (3d) 321 (Que CA). See now *B(D)*, above note 408.

413 *B(D)*, *ibid* at paras 37–69, Abella J for the majority; and at para 124, Rothstein J for the minority.

414 *Criminal Code*, above note 24, s 63.

415 *B(D)*, *ibid* at paras 70–87, Abella J. Justice Rothstein, speaking for the minority, accepted the principle, but argued that Abella J's reasoning contained an unarticulated assumption: that the principle of presumed diminished responsibility implied a presumption that a youth sentence should be imposed. He held that for the applicant's challenge to succeed, this second presumption had to be shown to be a principle of fundamental justice in its own right; and he held that it was not: *ibid* at paras 128–38.

a non-constitutional case) described as "the single most important organizing principle in criminal law."[416]

1) The Pre-trial Right to Silence

It is a principle of fundamental justice that a person in detention has
the right to silence; that is, the right to make an informed decision
about whether to speak to a person in authority.[417]

That right was recognized as a principle of fundamental justice
as early as 1990. In *R v Hebert* (*Hebert*),[418] the Crown and the defence
agreed that there was a right to silence under section 7; while the Court
has been criticized for accepting the agreement of the parties as a basis
for recognizing such an important proposition of law, the reasons for
judgment leave no doubt that the Court would have recognized the
right even if the parties had not agreed. As noted above, McLachlin J,
for the majority, invoked a number of common law and statutory doctrines, as well as other *Charter* rights, to support the proposition that
the right to silence was a basic tenet of the Canadian legal system.

The Supreme Court of Canada has often said that the section 7
right to silence arises only on detention, so that a suspect who is not
detained does not have this right.[419] However, a person who is not detained retains the general liberty to decide whether or not to speak to
a police officer or another agent of the state.[420] A statute that interfered
with this general liberty might well raise an issue about whether the
section 7 right to silence extended beyond the context of detention.
Moreover, if a person who decides not to speak to the police is charged
with an offence, the use of that person's silence as the source for an
adverse inference about her guilt at trial violates the right to silence.[421]

The section 7 right to silence is a right to choose whether to speak
to an agent of the state. This way of conceiving of the right is the key to
understanding two aspects of its content.

First, the section 7 right to silence applies when a detainee is speaking to an agent of the state. It does not apply when the detainee is

---

416   *R v P(MB)*, [1994] 1 SCR 555 at 577.
417   *R v Hebert*, [1990] 2 SCR 151 [*Hebert*]; *R v Broyles*, [1991] 3 SCR 595 [*Broyles*]; *R
      v Singh*, 2007 SCC 48 [*Singh*].
418   *Ibid.*
419   *Hebert*, *ibid* at 184; *Singh*, above note 417 at para 32; *R v Hicks*, [1990] 1 SCR 120,
      aff'g (1988), 42 CCC (3d) 394 (Ont CA).
420   See *R v Grant*, 2009 SCC 32 at paras 37–38 [*Grant*].
421   *R v Chambers*, [1990] 2 SCR 1293; *R v Turcotte*, [2005] 2 SCR 519; *R v Rohde*,
      2009 ONCA 463.

speaking to another detainee who is not an agent of the state.[422] But the right does not entirely prevent the police from using deception to obtain statements. In the common scenario where an undercover officer or other state agent is placed in a cell with a detainee and the detainee speaks, the section 7 right to silence is not always violated. Using undercover officers to "observe" the detainee does not violate section 7; but where "the police use subterfuge to interrogate an accused after he has advised them that he does not wish to speak to them, they are improperly eliciting information that they were unable to obtain by respecting the suspect's constitutional right to silence." In *Hebert* itself, the accused told the police he did not want to make a statement. He was placed in a cell with an undercover officer who, in the words of the agreed statement of fact, "engaged the accused in conversation."[423] This method of obtaining a statement was unobjectionable at common law,[424] but it violated section 7 because the police used "a trick to negate his decision not to speak."[425] This holding might appear to imply that all undercover operations directed at obtaining statements from detainees would violate section 7, but in *R v Broyles* (*Broyles*),[426] the Court held that that was not the case. The accused was arrested and charged with murder, and declined to make a statement. The police persuaded a friend of his to visit him in his cell wearing a recording device, and their conversation was recorded. The Supreme Court held that where the police used a trick of this kind to obtain a statement from a detainee, two questions had to be asked:

> First, as a threshold question, was the evidence obtained by an agent of the state? Second, was the evidence elicited? Only if the answer to both questions is in the affirmative will there be a violation of the right to silence in s. 7.[427]

On the facts of the case, the accused's friend was an agent of the state, and he had elicited the statement; the accused's section 7 right to silence was therefore violated.[428] The *Broyles* approach to statements ob-

---

422 *Hebert*, above note 417 at 184.

423 *Ibid* at 159, quoting from the agreed statement of facts.

424 See *R v Rothman*, [1981] 1 SCR 640.

425 *Hebert*, above note 417 at 187. The statement was excluded under s 24(2) of the *Charter*. See also *R v Liew*, [1999] 3 SCR 227, where the statement was found not to have been elicited.

426 Above note 417.

427 *Ibid* at 607.

428 *Ibid* at 612–16. The accused's statement to his friend was excluded under s 24(2) of the *Charter*: *ibid* at 616–20.

tained by undercover agents reflects the idea that the right to silence is a right to choose. If the accused decides to speak to a fellow detainee, he has chosen to speak and his right to silence has not been violated, even if that detainee turns out to be an undercover agent of the police. But if a state agent "elicits" a statement from the accused, then he has not chosen to speak, and his right to silence has been violated.

Second, the section 7 right to silence is not a right against being questioned. Once the detainee has spoken to counsel, who will advise her of her right to silence, the police may question the detainee in the absence of counsel.[429] The police may continue questioning the detainee even where she re-asserts the right to silence and says that she does not want to answer any more questions. In *R v Singh* (*Singh*),[430] the police disregarded eighteen assertions by the accused of his right to silence; nonetheless, a majority of the Supreme Court held that his right to silence has been respected. Only where police questioning or other police tactics amount to "denying the suspect the right to choose or depriving him of an operating mind"[431] or to depriving the detainee of "a free will to speak to the authorities"[432] will police questioning violate the right to silence.

2) The Right to Silence and the Common Law Confessions Rule

It is probably a principle of fundamental justice that if an accused person's statement would be involuntary at common law, it will be inadmissible at trial for any purpose.

Under the common law confessions rule, a statement made by an accused person to a person in authority is inadmissible for any purpose unless the Crown can prove beyond a reasonable doubt that it was voluntary. To be voluntary, the statement must be untainted by any inducement (fear of prejudice or hope of advantage) or by any oppressive questioning or conduct by the police, and must be the product of the accused's operating mind. As noted above, the common law confessions rule was one of the sources invoked in *Hebert* to support the conclusion that the right to silence was a principle of fundamental justice. But after *Hebert*, the Court was cautious about identifying the confessions rule itself as a principle of fundamental justice;[433] there are

---

429 *Hebert*, above note 417 at 184.
430 Above note 417.
431 *Hebert*, above note 417 at 184.
432 *Singh*, above note 417 at para 47.
433 See particularly *R v Oickle*, 2000 SCC 38.

several procedural and substantive differences between the common law rule and the *Charter* right, particularly as regards the burden and quantum of proof. At common law the Crown must establish voluntariness beyond a reasonable doubt and exclusion of evidence is automatic, while under the *Charter* the accused must establish a breach of a *Charter* right on a balance of probabilities and must then argue for exclusion of evidence under section 24(2).

Notwithstanding this caution, two cases point towards recognition of the common law confessions rule as a principle of fundamental justice. In *R v G(B)*,[434] the Court effectively read down a provision of the *Criminal Code* that was inconsistent with the common law rule. The statements that the accused makes while being assessed for purposes of fitness to stand trial or disposition following a verdict of NCRMD are normally inadmissible pursuant to section 672.21(1) and (2); however, section 672.21(3) defines a number of exceptions, including use of the statement to impeach the accused's credibility if his testimony at trial is inconsistent with the statement.[435] The Supreme Court of Canada held that this section had to be read as inapplicable to involuntarily obtained statements, thus rendering it compatible with the common law rule. The majority commented that "Parliament could not make it [the involuntary statement] admissible for any purpose whatsoever without violation section 7 of the *Charter*,"[436] clearly signaling that any statute conflicting with the confessions rule—for example, by purporting to make involuntary statements admissible at trial—would be inconsistent with the principles of fundamental justice. The easiest way to explain this holding is to treat the confessions rule, in its guise as a rule of evidence at trial, as a principle of fundamental justice.

In *Singh*, the Court took a different approach, emphasizing the conduct of the police in obtaining the statement rather than the use of the statement at trial. The accused made an incriminating statement after having asserted his right to silence some eighteen times. The Court found no violation of the section 7 right to silence, and went on to comment (unnecessarily for the resolution of the issues before it) on the common law confessions rule. The Court held that in some situations "the confessions rule effectively subsumes the constitutional right to silence";[437] in particular, where the accused person is detained and has been advised of her right to counsel, it will be impossible for her to show that a voluntary statement was obtained in violation of the right

---

434 *R v G(B)*, [1999] 2 SCR 475 [*G(B)*].
435 *Criminal Code*, above note 24, s 673.21(3)(*f*).
436 *G(B)*, above note 434 at para 44.
437 *Singh*, above note 417 at para 39.

to silence, and it will also be impossible for the Crown to show that a statement obtained through a violation of the right to silence was voluntary.[438]

Singh leaves unresolved many issues about the relationship between the common law confessions rule and section 7 of the *Charter*. In particular, it is not clear whether all the ways of making a statement involuntary will also amount to a breach of section 7, and whether evidence derived from an involuntary statement, which was straightforwardly admissible at common law,[439] will now be subject to an argument for exclusion under section 24(2).[440] But *Singh* clearly gives some constitutional status to the common law confessions rule.[441]

3) The Right against Self-Incrimination

It is a principle of fundamental justice that the Crown may not use a witness's compelled self-incriminatory testimony, or undiscoverable evidence derived from self-incriminatory testimony, against him in subsequent proceedings. It is also a principle of fundamental justice that a person cannot be compelled to testify where the predominant purpose of calling him as a witness is to obtain evidence against him.

There are many situations in which a person might be required to give self-incriminatory evidence in a proceeding in which she is not the accused person. A person might be a witness at someone else's criminal trial and her testimony might disclose some involvement in the crime.[442] Two persons charged with the same offence might be tried separately, so that they would be compellable Crown witnesses at each other's preliminary inquiry or trial.[443] A person might be required to testify at a judicial inquiry into a situation and might give testimony implicating

---

438 *Ibid.*

439 *R v St Lawrence* (1949), 93 CCC 376 (Ont HCJ); *R v Wray*, [1971] SCR 272.

440 On this issue, see the discussion in *R v Sweeney* (2000), 148 CCC (3d) 247 (Ont CA). The somewhat elliptical comments of McLachlin CJC and Charron J in *Grant*, above note 420 at para 90, suggest that the accused would have to show a violation of another *Charter* right before being able to argue for exclusion of derivative evidence; but compare *Grant* at para 80.

441 For further discussion of the issues raised by *G(B)* and *Singh*, see Hamish Stewart, "The Confessions Rule and the *Charter*" (2009) 54 McGill LJ 517.

442 See, for example, *R v Noël*, 2002 SCC 67. The accused's brother had previously been charged with murder; the accused was a witness at his brother's trial and admitted that he had committed the offence.

443 As in *R v S(RJ)*, [1995] 1 SCR 451 [*S(RJ)*] and *R v Primeau*, [1995] 2 SCR 60.

himself in a crime.[444] In these circumstances, the witness's right against self-incrimination is protected by both sections 13 and 7 of the *Charter*.

Section 13 of the *Charter* provides a right against self-incrimination in the following terms:

> A witness who testifies in any proceedings has the right not to have any incriminating evidence so given used to incriminate that witness in any other proceedings, except in a prosecution for perjury or for the giving of contradictory evidence.

Section 13, like its statutory cousin,[445] does not protect a person from having to provide self-incriminatory testimony in proceedings where she is not the accused. Rather, it proves "use immunity"; the testimony must be given, but cannot be used against the accused in subsequent proceedings. It is now well established that this use immunity applies both to the direct use of the evidence—the Crown cannot lead the evidence as part of its case in chief—and to use of the evidence to undermine the accused's credibility—the Crown cannot cross-examine the accused on the prior testimony if it is inconsistent with his testimony at trial.[446] It is very likely that if section 13 had not been included in the *Charter*, the right it defines would have been recognized as a principle of fundamental justice under section 7.

Section 13 does not, however, prevent the Crown from using evidence derived from self-incriminatory testimony, nor does it provide any mechanism by which a person can avoid the compulsion to testify. The Supreme Court of Canada has recognized both of these protections as principles of fundamental justice under section 7. In *R v S(RJ)* (*S(RJ)*), the accused and another were charged with the same offence but were tried separately. The Crown sought to compel the accused to testify at the preliminary inquiry of the other alleged offender. The Court held that the accused could be compelled to testify, but that in addition to the use immunity conferred by section 13, he was entitled under section 7 to "derivative use immunity"; that is, at his trial, the Crown could not use any evidence that "could not have been obtained, or the significance of which could not be appreciated, but for [his] testimony" at the preliminary inquiry.[447] The Court has also held that while a wit-

---

444 As might have occurred in *Phillips v Nova Scotia* (*Commission of Inquiry into the Westray Mine Tragedy*), [1995] 2 SCR 97.

445 *Canada Evidence Act*, RSC 1985, c C-5, s 5.

446 *R v Henry*, 2005 SCC 76.

447 *S(RJ)*, above note 443 at para 191; see also *Re Application under s 83.28 of the Criminal Code*, 2004 SCC 42 at para 71 ("derivative use protection insulates the individual from having the compelled incriminating testimony used to

ness will be compelled to testify, with use immunity and derivative use immunity, where the proceedings have a "legitimate public purpose," she will be exempted from the obligation to testify where "the predominant purpose for seeking the evidence is to obtain incriminating evidence against the person compelled to testify."[448] However, the Supreme Court of Canada has never exempted a witness from testifying on this basis.

Other legal obligations can also create self-incriminatory statements, which may or may not be admissible in a criminal trial, depending on the context. In *R v White* (*White*),[449] the accused, while driving her motor vehicle, struck and killed a man who was changing a tire at the side of the road. Under provincial law, she was required to report the accident and to give the police information about it; and she did so. She was charged with failing to remain at the scene of an accident with intent to avoid liability, contrary to section 252(1)(*a*) of the *Criminal Code*. The trial judge excluded her statements to the police on the ground that their use against her at trial would offend section 7. The accused was acquitted. The Crown's appeals to the British Columbia Court of Appeal and to the Supreme Court of Canada were dismissed. The accused found herself in an adversarial relationship with the police and she honestly and reasonable believed that she was required to make the statements under provincial law. In this context, the Crown's use of the statements at trial would infringe the right against self-incrimination.[450] The court contrasted this situation with *R v Fitzpatrick* (*Fitzpatrick*),[451] where the prosecution of the accused for violating fishing quotas was based on records that he was required to keep under the *Fisheries Act*.[452] In that context, there was no adversarial relationship between the accused and the state when the records were created, and the accused had voluntarily chosen to enter a regulated area of conduct and to comply with the applicable law, including the reporting obligation.[453] The

---

obtain other evidence, unless that evidence is discoverable through alternative means").

448 *British Columbia Securities Commission v Branch*, [1995] 2 SCR 3 at para 7; see also *Re Application under s 83.28 of the Criminal Code*, ibid at para 71 (s 7 provides "a complete exemption from testifying where proceedings are undertaken or predominately [sic] used to obtain evidence for the prosecution of the witness").

449 *R v White*, [1999] 2 SCR 417.

450 *Ibid* at paras 52–68.

451 *R v Fitzpatrick*, [1995] 4 SCR 154 [*Fitzpatrick*]; compare *R v Rice*, 2009 BCCA 569 at paras 55–65 (compelled statement under wildlife protection statute).

452 *Fisheries Act*, RSC 1985, c F-14, s 61.

453 *Fitzpatrick*, above note 451 at paras 35–42.

contrast between *White* and *Fitzpatrick* indicates that whether use of a statutorily-compelled statement will infringe the principle against self-incrimination will depend on a number of contextual factors, but particularly on whether the statement was produced in the context of a regulated activity that the accused voluntarily chose to enter into and, even if not, whether there was an adversarial relationship between the accused and the state at the time the statement was originally made.

The right against self-incrimination may also limit the state's ability to use certain procedures to obtain statements from individuals. In *R v Jarvis* and *R v Ling*,[454] the Supreme Court of Canada considered tax officials' use of their audit powers to further a prosecution for tax offences. It is clear that the Crown could use any statements made by a taxpayer in, for example, an income tax return or other document routinely required in the administration of a taxation scheme; the use of such statements at trial does not infringe the right against self-incrimination because the relationship between the taxpayer and the state is not at that point adversarial. Tax officials may also use their audit powers to ensure compliance with the tax system without infringing the principle against self-incrimination. However, once "the predominant purpose of a particular inquiry is the determination of penal liability," tax officials can no longer rely on their statutory powers to compel statements;[455] from that point onward the investigation must rely on tools such as search warrants, and the target of the investigation is entitled to the procedural protections appropriate to criminal investigation.[456] The Court listed a number of factors to be considered in deciding whether the predominant purpose of an investigation had changed from ensuring compliance to determining penal liability.[457] Evidence obtained in violation of these principles would be subject to exclusion under section 24(2) of the *Charter*, as the accused's *Charter* rights would be violated.[458]

F. PRINCIPLES OF SENTENCING

There is no doubt that section 7 of the *Charter* remains engaged during the sentencing process. Even though the accused person has at this

---

454 *R v Jarvis*, 2002 SCC 73 [*Jarvis*]; *R v Ling*, 2002 SCC 74 [*Ling*].

455 *Jarvis*, *ibid* at para 88.

456 *Ibid* at para 96.

457 *Ibid* at para 94.

458 *Ling*, above note 454 at para 32.

point been found guilty beyond a reasonable doubt and is therefore no longer entitled to the presumption of innocence, her liberty interests are still at stake. The Court has recognized relatively few substantive principles of fundamental justice that apply in sentencing. The Crown must prove aggravating factors beyond a reasonable doubt; beyond that, the most that can be said is that young persons may be constitutionally entitled to a separate sentencing regime and that there may be a principle favouring the preservation of judicial discretion in sentencing. These principles are discussed below.

1)   Burden and Quantum of Proof in Sentencing Proceedings

In the criminal trial, both at common law and under the *Charter*, the Crown has the burden of proof to establish all the elements of the offence, and to disprove any defence that has an air of reality, beyond a reasonable doubt. Because proof beyond a reasonable doubt has been recognized as a constitutional requirement under section 11(*d*), [459] it has not been necessary to consider whether it is also a principle of fundamental justice under section 7. [460] However, the Supreme Court of Canada has unanimously recognized the following related principle of fundamental justice: in sentencing proceedings, the Crown must prove all aggravating factors beyond a reasonable doubt. [461] As noted above, provisions of the *Youth Criminal Justice Act* created a category of offences for which the accused would be sentenced as an adult unless she could establish that she should be sentenced as a youth. In *B(D)*, the accused challenged these provisions. The majority understood the displacement of the usual youth sentencing regime as an aggravating factor in sentencing. Since the statute presumed that a youth would be sentenced as an adult if found guilty of a presumptive offence, the statute in effect reversed the onus of proof with respect to this aggravating factor. The statute was therefore inconsistent with the constitutional requirement that the Crown prove all aggravating factors beyond a reasonable doubt. [462] The minority, in contrast, held that the category of presumptive offences did not impose any sort of persuasive burden on

---

459   *R v Oakes*, above note 48; see also *R v Whyte*, [1988] 2 SCR 3.
460   But compare *Pearson*, above note 28 at 686.
461   *B(D)*, above note 408 at para 78, Abella J. This holding amounts to constitutionalizing the pre-*Charter* rule to the same effect: *R v Gardiner*, [1982] 2 SCR 368.
462   *B(D)*, *ibid* at paras 70–82.

the accused and so did not offend the relevant principle of fundamental justice.[463]

2) Sentencing Regime for Young Offenders

B(D),[464] discussed in greater detail in Section D(4), above in this chapter, appears to imply the following principle of fundamental justice: youthful offenders are entitled to a sentencing regime that is separate or distinct from the sentencing regime applicable to adults. The Court unanimously held that the principles of fundamental justice entitle young persons to a presumption of diminished moral responsibility. It is difficult to see how this principle could be implemented without an entirely separate sentencing regime for young persons; or, at least, without certain distinct principles of sentencing that were applicable to young persons but not to adults.

3) Judicial Discretion in Sentencing

There is some support in the caselaw for the following principle of fundamental justice: sentencing is a judicial function, not a prosecutorial function. This principle has been recognized in circumstances where the imposition of a minimum sentence depends on an exercise of prosecutorial discretion. Consider, in particular, the following specific circumstance. Under section 255(1)(*a*)(ii) of the *Criminal Code*, a person convicted of a second impaired driving or "over eighty" offence is liable to a minimum term of imprisonment. Section 665(1) of the Code provides that "where an accused . . . is convicted of an offence for which a greater punishment may be imposed by reason of previous convictions, no greater punishment shall be imposed on him by reason thereof unless the prosecutor satisfies the court that the accused . . . , before making his plea, was notified that a greater punishment would be sought by reason thereof." Section 665(2) provided for proof of the prior conviction at the sentencing hearing (see now section 727(1)). Thus, the minimum term of imprisonment under section 255(1)(*a*)(ii) is available only where the Crown complies with section 665 (now section 727); if the Crown notifies the accused of its intention to seek the minimum term, the minimun term must be imposed; but if, for whatever reason, the Crown does not notify the accused, the sentencing judge would not be required to impose it.

---

463 *Ibid* at paras 161–70.
464 *Ibid*.

In *R v Kumar* (*Kumar*), the British Columbia Court of Appeal held that this process offended the principles of fundamental justice because the Crown, rather than the court, effectively controlled the decision whether to impose the minimum term under section 255(1)(a)(ii).[465] The majority held that this infringement of section 7 was justified under section 1 because the sentencing judge could grant a constitutional exemption from section 255(1)(a)(ii);[466] however, this solution is no longer available owing to the Supreme Court of Canada's subsequent rejection of constitutional exemptions in sentencing.[467] Some courts have continued to follow *Kumar* in holding that the interaction between sections 255(1)(a)(ii) and 665(1) would offend section 7 if it effectively left the decision to impose the minimum sentence in the hands of the Crown, but have interpreted the provisions to permit the trial judge to review the Crown's decision to give notice. On this interpretation, the provisions do not offend section 7 because they preserve the sentencing judge's role in sentencing.[468]

If the principle that sentencing is a judicial rather than a prosecutorial function is a principle of fundamental justice under section 7, it does not affect the constitutionality of minimum sentence provisions in the *Criminal Code* if the imposition of the minimum sentence does not depend on prosecutorial discretion. If the minimum sentence depends on a legislative judgment about the just penalty for the crime, it may be challenged as cruel and unusual under section 12 of the *Charter*,[469] but does not otherwise violate section 7.

---

465 *R v Kumar* (1993), 85 CCC (3d) 417 at 451–52 (BCCA); see also *R v Lonegren*, 2009 BCSC 1678 [*Lonegren*], holding that a section of the Code imposing different minimum sentences depending on whether the Crown chose to proceed summarily or by way of indictment was arbitrary under s 9 (and, it appears, therefore also violated s 7) because the Crown could make the choice for reasons unrelated to the principles of sentencing.

466 As in *R v Luc* (2007), 222 CCC (3d) 299 (Ont Ct J).

467 *R v Ferguson*, 2008 SCC 6 [*Ferguson*].

468 *R v Gill*, 2008 ONCJ 502; *R v Mohla*, 2008 ONCJ 675; see also *Lonegren*, above note 465, and compare *R v King*, 2007 ONCJ 238. Contrast *R v Martin*, 2005 MBQB 185.

469 The standard for a s 12 violation is gross disproportionality between the offence and the sentence: see *Smith*, above note 137; *R v Goltz*, [1991] 3 SCR 485; *Ferguson*, above note 467.

G. SOME POSSIBLE PRINCIPLES

In this section, I briefly note two legal principles that have been identified as principles of fundamental justice in *obiter dicta* or by minorities of the Supreme Court of Canada or provincial Courts of Appeal, but have never been expressly accepted or rejected by a majority of the Supreme Court.

1) Statutory Defences Must Not Be Illusory

In the view of two judges of the Supreme Court, it is a principle of fundamental justice that a statutory defence must not be impossible, or practically impossible, to attain.

In *Morgentaler*,[470] as noted above, the accused physicians challenged section 251 (now section 287) of the *Criminal Code*, which criminalized abortions subject to an exception for an abortion performed by a physician in an accredited hospital where the hospital's "therapeutic abortion committee" had issued a certificate in writing stating that "in its opinion the continuation of the pregnancy . . . would or would be likely to endanger [a woman's] life or health."[471] Chief Justice Dickson, Lamer J concurring, held that it was a principle of fundamental justice "that when Parliament creates a defence to a criminal charge, the defence should not be illusory or so difficult to attain as to be practically illusory." This principle was based on the nature of the criminal law and of criminal defences:

> The criminal law is a very special form of governmental regulation, for it seeks to express our society's collective disapproval of certain acts and omissions. When a defence is provided, especially a specifically-tailored defence to a particular charge, it is because the legislator has determined that the disapprobation of society is not warranted when the conditions of the defence are met.[472]

Dickson CJC went on to consider the many practical difficulties that women faced in accessing this defence, and concluded that the procedure established by section 251 did not comply with the principles of fundamental justice. In light of this reading of the principle, it might be read as a more specific application of the principle against laws that are arbitrary or "manifestly unfair" (see Section B(3), above in this

---

470 *Morgentaler*, above note 74.
471 *Criminal Code*, above note 24, s 287(4).
472 *Morgentaler*, above note 74 at 70.

chapter), in that it is manifestly unfair for the legislature to recognize an exemption to criminal liability that, in practice, cannot be invoked, even where the policy behind the exemption suggests that it should be available.

2) No Punishment without Law

It is probably a principle of fundamental justice that no-one may be punished for conduct that was not an offence at the time it occurred (*nulla poena sine lege*). Most fact situations in which such an argument might arise are covered by the ordinary rules of criminal law and procedure or by section 11(g) of the *Charter*, which provides:

> Any person charged with an offence has the right . . . not to be found guilty on account of any act or omission unless, at the time of the act or omission, it constituted an offence under Canadian or international law or was criminal according to the general principles of law recognized by the community of nations . . .

There may be a few situations that do not fall under section 11(g) because the *Charter* claimant is not a person "charged with an offence," as section 11 requires. In *R v Lyons*, an offender argued that the dangerous offender provisions of the *Criminal Code* were contrary to the principles of fundamental justice because they permitted imprisonment on the ground of dangerousness rather than for the commission of an offence. La Forest J, speaking for the Court on this point, rejected that argument because the dangerous offender designation and the associated period of incarceration is a form of sentencing for the offence that the offender has been found guilty of. But he commented that if the legislation permitted "an individual to be sentenced for crimes he or she has not committed or for crimes for which he or she has already been punished . . . it would, indeed, constitute a violation of s. 7."[473] This comment, though *obiter dicta*, indicates a commitment to the principle of legality in punishment. In *United States v Budd*, the United States sought a person's extradition for conduct that was an offence in the United States, but arguably not in Canada, at the time it occurred; by the time the Minister of Justice issued the authority to proceed, the conduct was criminal in Canada as well. The Ontario Court of Appeal rejected the argument that extradition in these circumstances would violate any provision of the *Charter*;[474] although the holding is sketchy

---

473 *R v Lyons*, [1987] 2 SCR 309 at 327–28.
474 *United States of America v Budd* (2006), 210 CCC (3d) 189 at para 16 (Ont CA).

and in *obiter dicta*, there would surely have been an arguable *Charter* issue from the principle of legality if the conduct had never become a crime in Canada.

FURTHER READINGS

CAMERON, JAMIE. "Fault and Punishment under Sections 7 and 12 of the *Charter*" (2008) 40 Sup Ct L Rev (2d) 553.

MANNING, MORRIS, & PETER SANKOFF. *Manning, Mewett & Sankoff: Criminal Law*, 4th ed (Markham, ON: LexisNexis, 2009) ch 2.III.

ROACH, KENT. "Mind the Gap: Canada's Different and Constitutional Standards of Fault" (2011) 61 UTLJ 545.

SHARPE, ROBERT J, & KENT ROACH. *The Canadian Charter of Rights and Freedoms*, 4th ed (Toronto: Irwin Law, 2009) ch 13.A and 14.A.

STUART, DON. *Charter Justice in Canadian Criminal Law*, 4th ed (Toronto: Thomson Carswell, 2005) ch 2.5.

THOMPSON, ROLLIE. "Rounding Up the Usual Criminal Suspects and a Few More Civil Ones: Section 7 after *Chaoulli*" (2007) 20 NJCL 129.

YOUNG, ALAN N. "Done Nothing Wrong: Fundamental Justice and the Minimum Content of Criminal Law" (2008) 40 Sup Ct L Rev (2d) 441.

CHAPTER 5

PROCEDURAL FAIRNESS AS A PRINCIPLE OF FUNDAMENTAL JUSTICE

A. GENERAL PRINCIPLES

1) Fundamental Justice Requires a Fair Process

It is a principle of fundamental justice that the procedure for making a decision that affects a person's life, liberty, and security of the person must be procedurally fair. This principle has been widely accepted from the beginning of the *Charter* era.[1] If the process is "fundamentally unfair to the affected person," then section 7 is violated.[2]

For a process to be fair, it must at a minimum satisfy the administrative law principles of natural justice.[3] But, as in the administrative law doctrine on which the constitutional concept of procedural fairness draws, the content of the requirement of procedural fairness varies with the context and the nature of the interest affected.[4] In *Baker v Canada (Minister of Citizenship and Immigration)* (*Baker*), the leading

---

1   See, for example, *Singh v Canada (Minister of Employment and Immigration)*, [1985] 1 SCR 177 at 212–13 [*Singh*], and the discussion in Chapter 3, Section B.

2   *Charkaoui v Canada (Citizenship and Immigration)*, 2007 SCC 9 at para 22 [*Charkaoui*].

3   *Pearlman v Manitoba Law Society Judicial Committee*, [1991] 2 SCR 869 at 883 [*Pearlman*]; *Mooring v Canada (National Parole Board)*, [1996] 1 SCR 75 at para 38 [*Mooring*].

4   *R v Lyons*, [1987] 2 SCR 309 at 361; *Mooring, ibid* at para 39; *Pearlman, ibid* at 884–85.

case on the duty of fairness in administrative law, the Supreme Court of Canada provided a non-exhaustive list of factors relevant to the content of the duty:

- "the nature of the decision being made and the process followed in making it";
- "the nature of the statutory scheme and the 'terms of the statute pursuant to which the body operates'";
- "the importance of the decision to the individual or individuals affected";
- "the legitimate expectations of the person challenging the decision";
- "the choices of procedure made by the [decision maker] itself, particularly when the statute leaves to the decision-maker the ability to choose its own procedures, or when the [decision-maker] has an expertise in determining what procedures are appropriate in the circumstances."[5]

In *Suresh v Canada (Minister of Citizenship and Immigration)* (*Suresh*), the Court held that these factors were equally relevant to determining the content of the duty of fairness under section 7 of the *Charter*:

> What is required by the duty of fairness—and therefore the principles of fundamental justice—is that the issue at hand be decided in the context of the statute involved and the rights affected . . . . More specifically, deciding what procedural protections must be provided involves consideration of the following factors: (1) the nature of the decision made and the procedures followed in making it, that is, "the closeness of the administrative process to the judicial process"; (2) the role of the particular decision within the statutory scheme; (3) the importance of the decision to the individual affected; (4) the legitimate expectations of the person challenging the decision where undertakings were made concerning the procedure to be followed; and (5) the choice of procedure made by the agency itself: *Baker, supra*, at paras. 23–27. This is not to say that other factors or considerations may not be involved. This list of factors is non-exhaustive in determining the common law duty of fairness: *Baker, supra*, at para. 28. It must necessarily be so in determining the procedures demanded by the principles of fundamental justice.[6]

---

5   *Baker v Canada (Minister of Citizenship and Immigration)*, [1999] 2 SCR 817, 174 DLR (4th) 193 at paras 23–27 [*Baker*].

6   *Suresh v Canada (Minister of Citizenship and Immigration)*, 2002 SCC 1 at para 115 [*Suresh*].

Thus, as a general rule, the considerations relevant to determining the content of the duty of fairness are the same whether or not the person affected has a constitutionally-protected interest at stake. But the constitutional duty of fairness cannot (in the absence of a section 1 justification or section 33 override) be ousted by express statutory language, whereas the common law duty can.[7]

The principle of procedural fairness, and even the five specific factors identified in *Baker* and *Suresh*, are very general and abstract. The rest of this chapter explains how they have been made more specific in particular contexts.

2) Fundamental Justice Sometimes Requires an Oral Hearing

The principles of fundamental justice do not necessarily require an oral hearing. In extradition matters, for example, the Minister of Justice's surrender decision affects the liberty interest and must therefore comply with the principles of fundamental justice; but the Minister's decision is typically made on the basis of a paper record, with the benefit of written advice of lawyers from the Department of Justice and written submissions from the person sought. This procedure has been held to comply with section 7 (see Section C(1)(c), below in this chapter). But the principles of fundamental justice do require an oral hearing in certain circumstances; for example, "where a serious issue of credibility is involved" in making the decision,[8] or where the person affected will be detained for a significant period of time.[9] To comply with section 7, the hearing must be procedurally fair and must be held before an impartial decision maker. These requirements may be spelled out further as follows:

- the hearing must be held "before an independent and impartial magistrate" (that is, a person capable of acting judicially who is and

---

7   Compare *Ocean Port Hotel Ltd v British Columbia (General Manager, Liquor Control and Licensing Branch)*, 2001 SCC 52. The decision maker's degree of independence did not have to satisfy the constitutional standard for procedural fairness because the applicant's constitutionally protected interests were not at stake and because the statute clearly did not require the decision maker to be independent.

On the question of whether the standard of review is affected by the fact that constitutional interests are at stake, see Chapter 2, Section B(3).

8   *Singh*, above note 1 at 213–14.

9   *Charkaoui*, above note 2 at para 28.

who appears to be independent of and impartial as between the parties);

- the magistrate must decide the matter "on the facts and the law";
- the person affected must have "the right to know the case put against one and the right to answer that case."[10]

The stringency with which these criteria apply varies with the context. In *Re Charkaoui* (*Charkaoui*),[11] where the interest at stake was a lengthy period of detention without trial, they were applied very stringently. Under the *Immigration and Refugee Protection Act* (*IRPA*) as it then read,[12] two federal ministers could issue a certificate declaring that a foreign national or permanent resident is inadmissible on the ground of security.[13] Inadmissibility to Canada on security grounds is established where "there are reasonable grounds to believe [that the person] engages, has engaged or will engage" in acts of terrorism.[14] The certificate was referred to a designated judge of the trial division of the Federal Court, who determined whether the certificate was reasonable.[15] There was no appeal from the determination of reasonableness.[16] Meanwhile, the person named in the certificate was detained;[17] under the statute, permanent residents were entitled to periodic reviews of their detention,[18] but foreign nationals were not entitled to review for six months after the certificate was determined to be reasonable.[19]

The process for determining the reasonableness of the certificate, and for reviewing detention, was to a large extent secret and *ex parte*. In particular, the designated judge was *required* to "ensure the confidentiality of the information on which the certificate is based . . . if, in the opinion of the judge, its disclosure would be injurious to national security or to the safety of any person."[20] Thus, while the detainee was entitled to a summary of the information, that summary could not include any of the information that the designated judge is required to

---

10   Quoted portions from *Charkaoui*, above note 2 at para 29, emphasis removed; see also *Singh*, above note 1 at 212–13; *Pearlman*, above note 3 at 882–83; *United States v Ferras; United States v Latty*, 2006 SCC 33 at para 22 [*Ferras*].

11   *Ibid*.

12   *Immigration and Refugee Protection Act*, SC 2001, c 27 [*IRPA*].

13   *Ibid*, s 77(1).

14   *Ibid*, s 34(1)(*f*).

15   *Ibid*, s 80(1).

16   *Ibid*, s 80(3).

17   *Ibid*, s 82.

18   *Ibid*, s 83.

19   *Ibid*, s 84(2).

20   *Ibid*, s 78(*b*).

keep confidential. Only the government's lawyer and the designated judge were able to see this information.

Charkaoui and two other detainees brought a wide-ranging constitutional challenge to several aspects of the security certificate scheme. The Supreme Court of Canada rejected most of these challenges, but accepted the argument that the process for determining the reasonableness of the certificate was unconstitutional because it was procedurally unfair. The Court agreed that *IRPA* provided for a hearing before an independent and impartial decision maker,[21] but held that the hearing did not comply with the requirement that the decision be made on the facts and the law, or with the requirement that the person affected know the case against him. These failures resulted from the statutory provisions deigned to prevent the detainee from having access to much of the information on which the designated judge based her decision. The Court held that without knowledge of this information or a "substantial substitute" for it,[22] the detainee could not respond to the allegations against him,[23] and the designated judge, despite her best efforts, might not be able to make a decision on the facts and the law:[24]

> . . . the secrecy required by the scheme denies the named person the opportunity to know the case put against him or her, and hence to challenge the government's case. This, in turn undermines the judges' ability to come to a decision based on all the relevant facts and law. Despite the best efforts of judges of the Federal Court to breathe judicial life into the *IRPA* procedure, it fails to assure the fair hearing that s. 7 of the *Charter* requires before the state deprives a person of life, liberty and security of the person.[25]

This violation of section 7 was not justified under section 1, and so the *IRPA* scheme for determining the reasonableness of security certificates was unconstitutional.

The declaration of invalidity in *Charkaoui* was suspended for one year to allow Parliament an opportunity to enact a new scheme that would satisfy the *Charter*.[26] Shortly before the suspension expired, Parliament substantially amended the *IRPA* to provide for a system of "special advocates" on the British model. The role of the special advocate "is to protect the interests of the permanent resident or foreign

---

21   *Charkaoui*, above note 2 at paras 32–47.
22   *Ibid* at para 61.
23   *Ibid* at paras 53–64.
24   *Ibid* at paras 48–52.
25   *Ibid* at para 65.
26   *Ibid* at para 140.

national in a proceeding [concerning a security certificate] when information or other evidence is heard in the absence of the public and of the permanent resident or foreign national and their counsel."[27] The special advocate is to be provided with "a copy of all information and other evidence that is provided to the judge but that is not disclosed to the permanent resident or foreign national and their counsel,"[28] but is prohibited from disclosing the information to anyone and from communicating with anyone about the proceeding except with the judge's authorization.[29]

The Federal Court has upheld the special advocate system, holding that it responds to the problems identified in *Charkaoui*, because it provides the named person with sufficient notice of the case against him and, just as importantly, because it enables the designated judge to decide the case on the fact and the law in light of the submissions made by the special advocate.[30] The court also rejected the argument that the special advocate system is unconstitutional because, in contrast to the procedure under the *Canada Evidence Act*,[31] it does not permit the judge to balance the interests in disclosure with the interests in non-disclosure. The designated judge must "ensure the confidentiality of information and other evidence" if "disclosure could be injurious to national security or endanger the safety of any person";[32] while such information must be disclosed to the special advocate, it cannot be disclosed to the named person. Justice Noël held that the provisions in question "strike a proper balance between the need for protection of confidential information and the rights of the named person."[33] This conclusion flows naturally from the holding that the new statutory scheme meets the requirements of procedural fairness. There is no free-standing principle of fundamental justice requiring a proper balancing of interests in general,[34] or requiring the balancing of interests in decisions about disclosure; the question is rather whether a given set of procedures is fair in its context.

---

27   *IRPA*, above note 12, s 85.1.
28   *Ibid*, s 85.4(1).
29   *Ibid*, ss 85.4, 85.5.
30   *Re Harkat*, 2010 FC 1242 at paras 127–43 [*Harkat*].
31   This procedure is described in *R v Ahmad*, 2011 SCC 6 [*Ahmad* 2011], discussed in Section B(4)(a)(ii), below in this chapter.
32   *IRPA*, above note 12, s 83(1)(c); compare (d) & (e).
33   *Harkat*, above note 30 at para 162.
34   Compare Chapter 3, Section B(4).

The importance of context can be seen by contrasting *Charkaoui* with *Pearlman v Manitoba Law Society Judicial Committee*,[35] where the interest at stake was quite different. The applicant, a lawyer, challenged the fairness of the Manitoba Law Society's disciplinary procedure on the ground of reasonable apprehension of bias. The Law Society's Judicial Committee had the power to require a lawyer found guilty of professional misconduct to pay the costs of the investigation and hearing. The members of the Judicial Committee were themselves fee-paying members of the Law Society. So, the applicant argued, a reasonable person would apprehend that the committee had an interest in finding him guilty, since any revenue derived from the costs recouped from a member could potentially reduce the fees paid by the committee members. The Supreme Court of Canada rejected this argument, holding *inter alia* that the committee members' pecuniary interest in the outcome was "far too attenuated and remote to give rise to a reasonable apprehension of bias."[36] But the context of the decision was also important: the Court emphasized the importance of self-governance in disciplinary matters and rejected as unrealistic the thought that some body other than the Judicial Committee would be appropriate to decide questions of professional misconduct.[37] In a different context, for example a judicial proceeding in which a person's liberty was at stake, even a remote and attenuated pecuniary interest in the outcome might raise a reasonable apprehension of bias, and conflict with the principles of fundamental justice.

3) Fundamental Justice Requires Solicitor-Client Privilege

It is a principle of fundamental justice that confidential communications between a lawyer and a client for the purpose of giving or receiving legal advice are protected from disclosure; or, more simply put, solicitor-client privilege is a principle of fundamental justice.[38]

Solicitor-client privilege applies where there is "(i) a communication between solicitor and client; (ii) which entails the seeking or giving of legal advice; and (iii) which is intended to be confidential by the parties."[39] All three elements must be present. If the communication

---

35   *Pearlman*, above note 3.

36   *Ibid* at 891.

37   *Ibid* at 886–90.

38   *R v McClure*, 2001 SCC 14 at para 41 [*McClure*]; *Lavallée, Rackel and Heintz v Canada (AG)*, 2002 SCC 61 at para 21 [*Lavallée, Rackel and Heintz*].

39   *Solosky v Canada*, [1980] 1 SCR 821 at 837. These conditions have often been reiterated; see, for instance, *Pritchard v Ontario (Human Rights Commission)*, 2004

is for the purpose of obtaining legal advice, but the person providing the advice is not a solicitor, the communication is not privileged. If the communication is between a solicitor and client, but the conversation is concerned with, for example, personal matters or business strategy rather than with legal advice, the communication is not privileged. If the first two elements are satisfied, but the client does not intend the communication to be confidential, the communication is not privileged.

Since the privilege applies whether or not the client is involved in litigation, it can be conceived of not merely an aspect of procedural fairness, but also as a substantive right.[40] The privilege applies both when the solicitor is in private practice and is retained by the client and when the solicitor is an employee of the client. Moreover, the privilege is available both to private clients and to government officials and agencies that retain or employ solicitors.

Unless one of the exceptions noted below applies, where a communication is protected by solicitor-client privilege, neither the solicitor nor the client can be compelled to disclose it. The privilege can be waived, expressly or by implication, but only by the client; the solicitor cannot choose, or be compelled, to disclose a privileged communication unless and until the client waives the privilege.

There are three common law exceptions to solicitor-client privilege. First, the privilege does not apply where the purpose of the communication is to facilitate the commission of a crime (or possibly an intentional civil wrong).[41] Second, the privilege does not apply where breaching it is necessary in the interest of public safety; under this exception, there must be a clear and imminent risk of death or serious bodily harm to an identifiable person or group of persons.[42] Third, the privilege does not apply where the innocence of another person is at stake. The procedure for invoking this exception has two stages, designed to protect the privilege as far as possible. At the first stage, the accused person who seeks to invade another's privilege must satisfy the trial judge that there is "some evidentiary basis upon which to conclude that there exists a communication that could raise a reasonable doubt

---

SCC 31 at para 15 [*Pritchard*]; and compare *Geffen v Goodman Estate*, [1991] 2 SCR 353 at 383.

40   *Canada (Privacy Commissioner) v Blood Tribe Department of Health*, 2008 SCC 44 at para 10 [*Blood Tribe Department of Health*].

41   *Descôteaux v Mierzwinksi*, [1982] 1 SCR 860 at 881 (crime exception); *Dublin v Montessori Jewish Day School of Toronto* (2007), 281 DLR (4th) 366 (Ont SCJ) (intentional civil wrong).

42   *Smith v Jones*, [1999] 1 SCR 455 at para 77.

as to his guilt."[43] This is a significant hurdle in itself; if the accused does not so satisfy the trial judge, the application must be dismissed. If the first stage is satisfied, the privileged material is produced to the trial judge. At the second stage, the trial judge examines the material to determine whether it contains any communication that could raise a reasonable doubt as to the accused's factual guilt.[44] To meet this standard, the material must usually go "directly to one of the elements of the offence"; material casting doubt on a witness's credibility or suggesting that evidence was obtained unconstitutionally does not normally meet the standard.[45]

The fundamental status of solicitor-client privilege is justified by its role in the legal system: the ability of individuals to be completely candid while obtaining the necessary professional assistance to vindicate their rights or resist an allegation of wrong-doing is essential to the proper operation of the justice system.[46]

Direct statutory intrusions on solicitor-client privilege are rare; consequently, in very few cases has it been necessary to rely on the constitutional status of the privilege to invalidate a statute.[47] More commonly, the fundamental status of the privilege has been invoked in the construction of statutes and common law rules that could be interpreted as trenching on it, so as to preserve its "all but absolute"[48] status. The Supreme Court of Canada has interpreted access to information statutes so that they do not require disclosure of material protected by solicitor-client privilege.[49] Similarly, the three common law exceptions are construed narrowly in substance and are difficult to establish procedurally, again to preserve the privilege as far as possible.[50]

---

43 *McClure*, above note 38 at paras 52–56.

44 *Ibid* at paras 57*ff*.

45 *Ibid* at para 58.

46 *Ibid* at paras 31–33; *Smith v Jones*, above note 42 at para 45.

47 But see *Lavallée, Rackel and Heintz*, above note 38, as discussed in Chapter 1, Section C(3)(a).

48 *Ontario (Public Safety and Security) v Criminal Lawyers' Association*, 2010 SCC 23 at para 53 [*Ontario (Public Safety and Security)*].

49 *Blood Tribe Department of Health*, above note 40 at para 11; *Ontario (Public Safety and Security)*, *ibid*.

50 Solicitor-client privilege and the exceptions to it are discussed in much greater detail in many sources, including: Sidney Lederman, Alan W Bryant, & Michelle Fuerst, *The Law of Evidence in Canada*, 3d ed, (Markham: LexisNexis, 2009) ch 14C; Robert W Hubbard, Susan Magotiaux, & Suzanne M Duncan, *The Law of Privilege in Canada*, loose-leaf (Aurora, ON: Canada Law Book, 2006–).

Other intrusions on solicitor-client privilege may result in quite significant remedies, either at common law[51] or under the *Charter. R v Bruce Power Inc*[52] is a good example. Following a serious accident at a power plant, an investigative team including management and union representatives prepared a report. It was always intended that the report was to be confidential and to be used in defending the corporation against possible charges. The inspector in charge of the Ministry of Labour's investigation of the accident sought production of the report, but the corporation that operated the plant asserted privilege. The ministry conducted its own investigation, and the corporation and two individuals were charged with offences under provincial occupational health and safety legislation. In a further investigation, the inspector obtained a copy of the report. The justice of the peace presiding over the trial found that the report was protected by both solicitor-client and litigation privilege, and stayed the proceedings on the ground that the violation of privilege had irretrievably prejudiced the accused's right to a fair trial. The prosecution's appeal to the provincial court was allowed, but the Ontario Court of Appeal restored the stay of proceedings. The court held that there was no justification for the inspector's taking the copy of the report, that the breach of privilege gave rise to a rebuttable presumption of prejudice to the accused, and that the presumption had not been rebutted.[53] Finally, although the remedy of a stay is quite drastic (see Section A(4), below in this chapter), the court found that the justice of the peace had made no error in granting one, in light of the nature of the privileged document and the failure of the Crown to rebut the presumption of prejudice.[54]

4) Abuse of Process Is Contrary to the Principles of Fundamental Justice

It is a principle of fundamental justice that adjudicative processes should not be abused. Proceedings are abusive where they would "violate those fundamental principles of justice which underlie the community's sense of fair play and decency" or where they would be

---

51   For the effect of breaches of privilege, or possible breaches of privilege, in cases where s 7 did not apply, see *MacDonald Estate v Martin*, [1990] 3 SCR 1235; *Celanese Canada Inc v Murray Demolition Corp*, 2006 SCC 36.

52   *R v Bruce Power Inc*, 2009 ONCA 573.

53   *Ibid* at paras 49–55.

54   *Ibid* at paras 60–65; compare paras 31–33 and 48.

"oppressive or vexatious."[55] The standard for abuse of process has also been described as "conduct which shocks the conscience of the community and is so detrimental to the proper administration of justice that it warrants judicial intervention."[56]

The power to stay proceedings for abuse of process has its origin in the common law jurisdiction of the court to control its own processes. But the doctrine of abuse of process also has a constitutional dimension. Proceedings that amount to abuse of process are inconsistent with the principles of fundamental justice and so, if they engage one of the section 7 interests, are contrary to section 7 of the *Charter*.[57] Apart from the interests at stake, there is no essential difference between the common law doctrine and the constitutional doctrines of abuse of process. Whether at common law or under the *Charter*, a Canadian court has the power to grant a remedy where the proceedings before the court are an abuse of the court's process.

Two categories of state conduct may amount to abuse of process. The first category consists of conduct that will cause unfairness in the trial. The second, or residual, category is intended to address "the panoply of diverse and sometimes unforeseeable circumstances in which the prosecution is conducted in such a manner as to connote unfairness or vexatiousness of such a degree that it contravenes fundamental notions of justice and thus undermines the integrity of the judicial process."[58] State conduct in the second category does not necessarily affect the fairness of the trial as such, but affects the fairness of the proceedings as a whole.

The early cases on point could be read as holding that a stay of proceedings was the only remedy for an abuse of process, and conversely that proceedings could not be stayed unless they were abusive. In *R v Young*, for example, the Ontario Court of Appeal appeared to forge a tight link between the wrong of an abuse of process and the remedy of a stay:

> . . . there is a residual discretion in a trial court judge to stay proceedings where compelling an accused to stand trial would violate those fundamental principles of justice which underlie the community's

55   *R v O'Connor*, [1995] 4 SCR 411 at para 59 [*O'Connor*], quoting from *R v Young* (1984), 13 CCC (3d) 1 at 13 (Ont CA) [*Young*]; see also *R v Jewitt*, [1985] 2 SCR 128 at 136–37.

56   *R v Power*, [1994] 1 SCR 601 at 615.

57   The common law doctrine of abuse of process might apply where the s 7 interests were not engaged: see *O'Connor*, above note 55 at para 70.

58   *O'Connor*, ibid at para 73; see also *Canada (Minister of Citizenship and Immigration) v Tobiass*, [1997] 3 SCR 391 at para 89 [*Tobiass*].

sense of fair play and decency and to prevent the abuse of a court's process through oppressive or vexatious proceedings.[59]

But it is clear from subsequent cases that a finding of abuse of process does not inexorably lead to a stay of proceedings. Instead, the remedy for the abuse should respond to the nature of the abuse. The remedy of a stay is prospective: it is intended "to prevent the perpetuation of a wrong that, if left alone, will continue to trouble the parties and the community as a whole."[60] If a lesser remedy can achieve this result, then that lesser remedy should be granted. A stay of proceedings should be granted only "in the clearest of cases,"[61] where

(1) the prejudice caused by the abuse in question will be manifested, perpetuated or aggravated through the conduct of the trial, or by its outcome; and

(2) no other remedy is reasonably capable of removing that prejudice.[62]

In cases of uncertainty as to whether the stay is required to remedy the prejudice, a trial judge should balance "the interests in granting a stay against society's interest in having a trial on the merits."[63]

Given the high standard for a finding of abuse of process and for granting the remedy of a stay, it is unsurprising that stays of proceedings for abuse of process are rarely granted. In *Charkaoui v Canada (Citizenship and Immigration)*,[64] for example, the federal government breached its duty of fairness to the *Charter* applicant by destroying evidence that should have been preserved and disclosed in proceedings to determine the reasonableness of a security certificate; that is, in a context where the applicant's ability to challenge the case put against him was vital to his liberty and security interests. Nonetheless, the Supreme Court of Canada declined to stay the proceedings, largely because the case before it was an appeal from an interlocutory decision concerning disclosure. The designated judge had yet to rule on the merits: the question of a stay was left for him to decide at a later stage. The Supreme Court of Canada's remedy was limited to confirming the duty to disclose.[65]

---

59   *Young*, above note 55 at 31.
60   *Tobiass*, above note 58 at para 91.
61   *Young*, above note 55 at 31.
62   *O'Connor*, above note 55 at para 75; *R v Regan*, 2002 SCC 12 at para 54 [*Regan*].
63   *R v Zarinchang*, 2010 ONCA 286 at para 57 [*Zarinchang*].
64   *Charkaoui v Canada (Citizenship and Immigration)*, 2008 SCC 38.
65   *Ibid* at para 77. Some further examples are noted at Sections B(4)(a) and C(1)(b), below in this chapter.

B. PROCEDURAL FAIRNESS IN CRIMINAL PROCEEDINGS

The procedural aspects of the principles of fundamental justice apply fully in criminal proceedings because the accused always faces the possibility of a deprivation of liberty. Much of the statutory and common law apparatus of the criminal trial as it existed both before and after the *Charter* came into force, is certainly also required by the principles of fundamental justice. The right to a hearing before an independent and impartial court; the right to be present throughout the hearing; the right to a trial conducted in accordance with the rules of evidence; the right to know the prosecution's case before responding to it; the right to make full answer and defence (including the right to cross-examine the prosecution witness and the right to call evidence); the right to make submissions to the presiding judge and to the trier of fact: all of these rights existed before the *Charter* and continue to exist in the *Charter* era. Some of them are guaranteed by statute,[66] others by the common law rules of evidence and procedure; a statutory attempt to remove any of them would no doubt violate the principles of fundamental justice.

The enactment of the *Charter*, and section 7 in particular, nonetheless had a significant impact on the conduct of criminal trials. The right to a fair trial is a principle of fundamental justice, but a very abstract one; in the *Charter* era, Canadian courts have made the right more concrete by recognizing several specific rights as aspects or branches of the right to a fair trial.

1) Right to Counsel at Trial

There is no doubt that the accused's right to be represented by counsel at trial is a principle of fundamental justice. The right to counsel at trial includes the right to retain counsel of one's choosing.[67] Thus, where the Crown, or a co-accused, applies to remove the accused's counsel, for example on the ground of conflict of interest and duty, the trial judge's power to remove counsel should be "exercised cautiously and only for

---

66   Compare *Criminal Code*, RSC 1985, c C-46, s 650(3) (the right to make full answer and defence); s 650(1) (the right to be present during the trial); s 651 (the right to address the jury).

67   *R v Robillard* (1986), 28 CCC (3d) 22 at 26 (Ont CA).

compelling reasons,"[68] so as to preserve the accused's choice of counsel as far as possible.

Where the accused cannot afford to retain counsel privately and does not qualify for legal aid, the principles of fundamental justice do not require the state to pay for defence counsel, unless the accused cannot afford counsel and representation by counsel is essential to a fair trial.[69] Where these conditions are satisfied, the trial judge may make a "*Rowbotham* order" staying the proceedings until an appropriate arrangement to fund counsel has been worked out; usually, this arrangement will involve the Crown paying for privately retained counsel.[70]

The right to counsel at trial also includes the right to effective assistance of counsel.[71] As Doherty JA put it in *R v Joanisse* (*Joanisse*), the leading case, "Where counsel fails to provide effective representation, the fairness of the trial, measured both by reference to the reliability of the verdict and the adjudicative fairness of the process used to arrive at the verdict, suffers."[72] A claim of ineffective assistance of counsel can only be made on appeal from conviction. The appellant must show that trial counsel's conduct of the trial was incompetent in the sense of falling below the standard of providing "reasonable professional assistance" and that trial counsel's incompetence caused a miscarriage of justice, in the sense of leading to an unreliable verdict or an unfair trial.[73] If the appellate court is satisfied that the appellant was not prejudiced,

---

68   *R v Bogiatzis* (2002), 162 CCC (3d) 374 at para 8 (Ont SCJ); see also *R v Desmond*, 2010 ONSC 2945.

69   *R v Rowbotham* (1988), 41 CCC (3d) 1 at 66 (Ont CA) [*Rowbotham*]. In *R v Martell*, 2009 ONCA 46, a *Rowbotham* order was set aside on the ground that the accused had actually been granted legal aid but had refused to accept it (he did not believe he could make the monthly payments that legal aid required of him).

70   *Rowbotham, ibid* at 69. The court (at 70) left open the question whether a trial judge could order the Crown or the legal aid plan to pay for counsel; more recent authority holds that the trial judge has no jurisdiction to order the legal aid plan to fund the accused's defence: *R v Ahmad* (2007), 222 CCC (3d) 77 (Ont SCJ).

71   Where the accused is represented by an agent who is not a lawyer, the accused is deemed to have foregone the right to effective assistance of counsel; on appeal, he can allege a miscarriage of justice, but not on the ground that his agent did not meet the standard expected of counsel: *R v Romanowicz* (1999), 138 CCC (3d) 225 (Ont CA). Similarly, self-represented accused cannot complain on appeal that their self-representation did not meet the standard expected of counsel: *R v Peepeetch*, 2003 SKCA 76.

72   *R v Joanisse* (1995), 102 CCC (3d) 35 at 57 (Ont CA) [*Joanisse*].

73   *Ibid* at 57–58; *R v GDB*, 2000 SCC 22 at paras 26–28 [*GDB*].

it is not necessary and "will usually be undesirable" to consider whether trial counsel was incompetent.[74]

Successful assertions of ineffective assistance of counsel are rare
because it is often difficult to demonstrate both incompetence of trial
counsel and a miscarriage of justice. In *Joanisse* itself, the Ontario Court
of Appeal concluded that defence counsel's handling of the accused's
decision not to testify, where testifying represented his only realistic
chance of acquittal, fell within the standard of competence;[75] in *R v
GDB*, defence counsel's tactical decision not to use a piece of evidence
that might have undermined the credibility of a crucial Crown witness
was found not to have affected the outcome of the trial; it was therefore
unnecessary to determine whether the decision fell below the standard
of competence.[76] Ineffective representation has, however, been found
to affect the outcome and to require a new trial in cases where in a
voir dire to determine voluntariness counsel failed to call a physician
who would have given evidence supporting the claim that the accused
lacked an operating mind;[77] where counsel failed to call evidence suggesting that a complainant's identification of the accused who sexually
abused her was false;[78] where counsel misunderstood the applicable
substantive law and failed to prepare properly to cross-examine a
complainant on his prior inconsistent testimony from the preliminary inquiry;[79] and where inexperienced counsel had inadequately conducted a *Charter* challenge to the admissibility of evidence.[80]

---

74   *GDB, ibid* at para 29; and see, for example, *R v Walsh* (2006), 206 CCC (3d) 543
     (Ont CA).
75   *Joanisse*, above note 72 at 77–79. Doherty JA, concurring in the result, found
     that defence counsel fell below the standard of competence in this respect, but
     that there was no reasonable possibility that the result would have been differ-
     ent: *ibid* at 72–76. See also *R v W(R)* (2006), 207 CCC (3d) 137 at para 94 (Ont
     CA), where the court found that defence counsel's cross-examination of a wit-
     ness had in one respect fallen below the standard of competence, but that this
     incompetence could not have affected the outcome.
76   *GDB*, above note 73 at paras 37–41. See also the following cases where the asser-
     tion of ineffective assistance was rejected on the ground that counsel's conduct
     of the case came within the standard of competence: *R v R(P)* (1998), 132 CCC
     (3d) 72 (Que CA); *R v Canhoto* (1999), 140 CCC (3d) 321 (Ont CA); *R v Tran*,
     2004 BCCA 550.
77   *R v Carr*, 2010 ABCA 386.
78   *R v C(L)* (1999), 138 CCC (3d) 356 (Ont CA).
79   *R v P(T)* (2002), 281 CCC (3d) 165 (Ont CA).
80   *R v Smith*, 2007 SKCA 71.

2) Jury Selection

The process of selecting a jury established by the *Criminal Code*[81] clear-ly affects the accused's liberty interest and so must comply with the principles of fundamental justice. The right to trial by jury where the maximum punishment for the offence is five years' imprisonment or more is expressly guaranteed by section 11(*f*) of the *Charter*. That right, combined with the right to a fair trial in section 11(*d*), requires the jury to be representative of the community and, as the trier of the facts, to be impartial.[82] Thus, the jury selection provisions of the Code "should be read in light of the fundamental rights to a fair trial by an impartial jury and to equality before and under the law."[83] This reading has led the Court to develop a more robust right to challenge potential jurors for cause than was available in the pre-*Charter* era.[84] These principles have been developed in the context of interpreting the right to trial by jury in section 11(*f*), but might well have been recognized under section 7.

3) The Rules of Evidence in Criminal Proceedings

Section 7 of the *Charter* has had a significant effect on the rules of evi-dence in criminal proceedings. Although few common law or statutory rules of evidence have been invalidated as contrary to the principles of fundamental justice, there is a distinct tendency to interpret those rules as preserving a discretionary exclusionary power to ensure that criminal proceedings meet the constitutional requirement of a fair trial.

a) The Evidentiary Balancing Principle

There are two principles of fundamental justice connected with a trial judge's power to exclude excessively prejudicial evidence. First, it is a principle of fundamental justice that evidence tendered by the prosecu-tion should be excluded where its probative value is outweighed by its prejudicial effect. Second, it is a principle of fundamental justice that evidence tendered by the defence should not be excluded unless its probative value is significantly outweighed by its prejudicial effect.[85]

For the purposes of this chapter, I will refer to the trial judge's power to exclude excessively prejudicial evidence as the "evidentiary

---

81   *Criminal Code*, above note 66, ss 626–44.
82   *R v Sherratt*, [1991] 1 SCR 509.
83   *R v Williams*, [1998] 1 SCR 1128 at para 49.
84   *Ibid*; *R v Spence*, 2005 SCC 71.
85   *R v Seaboyer*, [1991] 2 SCR 577 at 611 [*Seaboyer*].

balancing principle."[86] In the immediate pre-*Charter* period, this principle was framed in stringent terms[87] and was said not to apply at all to evidence led by the defence.[88] But in *R v Seaboyer* (*Seaboyer*),[89] the Supreme Court of Canada reformulated the common law evidentiary balancing principle and treated it as the source of the two principles of fundamental justice just noted.

Since the law of evidence is for the most part governed by the common law, it is usually simple to ensure that the rules of evidence are consistent with the evidentiary balancing principle: the principle is either built into, or is applied subsequent to, any other exclusionary rule. For example, the principle is built into the rule governing the admissibility of the accused's other bad acts (so-called "similar fact" evidence)[90] and is, in theory at least, applicable subsequent to other admissibility decisions.[91] However, statutes that modify the common law of evidence must comply with the evidentiary balancing principle. Thus, a statute that purported to make Crown evidence admissible without any assessment of its prejudicial effect would not comply with the principles of fundamental justice. The Supreme Court of Canada has generally avoided invalidating evidentiary statutes on this ground by reading them as preserving the evidentiary balancing principle. So, for example, section 12 of the *Canada Evidence Act*,[92] which provides

---

86   The phrase "evidentiary balancing principle" is somewhat cumbersome but is meant to highlight the requirement of "balancing" probative value and prejudicial effect; that is, of assessing the beneficial and detrimental effects of the evidence on the trial process. I have previously used the phrase "discretionary exclusionary power": see Hamish Stewart, "Section 7 of the *Charter* and the Common Law Rules of Evidence" (2008) 40 Sup Ct L Rev (2d) 415 [Stewart, "Common Law Rules"]. But this phrase may suggest, incorrectly, that the trial judge has a discretion to exclude excessively prejudicial evidence. While the power to exclude is discretionary in the limited sense that its exercise is entitled to appellate deference, a trial judge has no discretion to admit evidence after having concluded that it is excessively prejudicial: Stewart, *ibid* at 419–20.

87   In *R v Wray*, [1971] SCR 272 at 293, the discretion was said to extend only to "evidence gravely prejudicial to the accused, the admissibility of which is tenuous, and whose probative force in relation to the main issue before the court is trifling."

88   *R v Valley* (1986), 26 CCC (3d) 207 at 239, leave to appeal to SCC refused, [1986] 1 SCR xiii.

89   Above note 85.

90   See *R v Handy*, 2002 SCC 56 [*Handy*]. At the heart of the test for admissibility of similar fact evidence is the question whether its probative value on a permissible line of reasoning outweighs its prejudicial effects on the trial process.

91   See, for example, *R v Starr*, 2000 SCC 40 at paras 187–89 [*Starr*].

92   RSC 1985, c C-5.

that witnesses, including the accused, "may be questioned" as to their criminal records to assess their credibility, was read as preserving the trial judge's discretion to edit the accused's criminal record and exclude convictions with little probative value on credibility and substantial prejudicial effect.[93]

Seaboyer itself concerned Parliament's attempt to limit the admissibility of evidence of a complainant's sexual history in the trial of sexual offences. The provision at issue, a predecessor of the current section 276 of the *Criminal Code*, provided that such evidence was inadmissible except in very narrowly defined circumstances. To the extent that the provision prevented the trier of fact from engaging in impermissible reasoning about the complainant's credibility or propensity to consent, based on her previous sexual conduct, it was unobjectionable.[94] But the majority, *per* McLachlin J, held that this provision might require exclusion of defence evidence even where the probative value of the evidence to a live issue in the case was not substantially outweighed by its prejudicial effect. Accordingly, it failed to comply with the principles of fundamental justice and offended section 7.[95]

Rather than allowing the common law rule to reassert itself, the Court enunciated a new common law rule governing the admissibility of evidence of the complainant's sexual history, making it clear that such evidence could not found inferences concerning credibility or consent and was admissible for another purpose only if its probative value on a legitimate inference was not substantially outweighed by its prejudicial effect.[96] The new common law rule is substantially reproduced in section 276 of the *Criminal Code*, which was subsequently held to be constitutionally valid.[97] The statute restates the discretionary exclusionary power as a power to admit evidence which "has *significant* probative value that is not substantially outweighed by the danger of prejudice to the proper administration of justice."[98] The Court held that this wording did not represent any real departure from the constitutional standard established in *Seaboyer*, particularly since there is no

---

93   *R v Corbett*, [1988] 1 SCR 670; more examples are discussed in Stewart, "Common Law Rules," above note 86.

94   *Seaboyer*, above note 85 at 612–21.

95   It could not be justified under s 1 and was invalid: *ibid* at 626–27.

96   *Ibid* at 632–33.

97   *R v Darrach*, 2000 SCC 46 [*Darrach*].

98   *Criminal Code*, above note 66, s 276(2)(*c*) [emphasis added].

word corresponding to "significant" in the equally authoritative French version of section 276.[99]

b) Exclusion of Evidence

It is a principle of fundamental justice that otherwise admissible evidence should be excluded if its exclusion is necessary to preserve the fairness of the trial.[100]

The principal vehicle for exclusion of evidence under the *Charter* is not section 7 but section 24(2), which provides that where "evidence was obtained in a manner that infringed or denied any rights or freedoms guaranteed by this *Charter*, the evidence shall be excluded if it is established that, having regard to all the circumstances, the admission of it in the proceedings would bring the administration of justice into disrepute."[101] However, where evidence was *not* obtained in a manner that violates a *Charter* right, exclusion is possible under section 7 to protect the fairness of the trial. A typical scenario for exclusion on this ground is as follows: the evidence in question was obtained in a situation where the *Charter* did not apply, but would arguably have been violated if it had applied. In *R v Harrer*,[102] for example, the accused made a statement in the United States to American authorities; the warnings that the authorities gave her complied with US law but would not have complied with the *Charter* had they been given in Canada. She could not argue for exclusion under section 24(2) of the *Charter* because the *Charter* did not apply to the American authorities and therefore was not violated; instead, she could argue for exclusion on the ground that the admission of the evidence itself would violate the principles of fundamental justice or the right to a fair trial. The argument was, however, rejected and the evidence was admitted; exclusion on this ground has been rare.[103]

---

99   *Darrach*, above note 97 at paras 38–43. The French version refers simply to the "valeur probante" of the evidence.

100 *R v Harrer*, [1995] 3 SCR 562 at para 15; *R v Terry*, [1996] 2 SCR 207 at para 25 [*Terry*]. See also *Schreiber v Canada (AG)*, [1998] 1 SCR 841 at para 35; *R v Cook*, [1998] 2 SCR 597.

101 *Canadian Charter of Rights and Freedoms*, Part I of the *Constitution Act, 1982*, being Schedule B to the *Canada Act 1982* (UK), 1982, c 11, s 24(2) [*Charter*]. See *R v Grant*, 2009 SCC 32, for the Supreme Court of Canada's most recent interpretation of s 24(2).

102 Above note 100.

103 See also *Terry*, above note 100; *R v Thomas*, 2005 QCCA 628. Both cases involve the admissibility of a statement taken abroad in compliance with foreign law but in circumstances that would have amounted to a *Charter* violation in Canada.

c) Cross-Examination of Crown Witnesses

The accused's right to cross-examine the witnesses for the Crown, personally or by counsel, was well established before the *Charter* and has been reinforced by section 7 of the *Charter*. In *R v Lyttle*, the Supreme Court of Canada, *per* Fish J, commented that "the right of an accused to cross-examine prosecution witnesses without significant and unwarranted constraint is an essential component of the right to make a full answer and defence"[104] and that this right was protected by sections 7 and 11(*d*) of the *Charter*.[105] The issue in the case was whether counsel, before putting a question in cross-examination, had to be in a position to independently prove the factual basis of the question. The Court rejected this proposition. Although cross-examination cannot be based on inadmissible evidence, it does not have to be based only on facts that can be independently proved. The Court held that "a question can be put to a witness in cross-examination regarding matters that need not be proved independently, provided that counsel has a good faith basis for putting the question." It was necessary to allow such a wide scope for cross-examination because it may be the only way to prove certain facts.[106] This generous rule is likely required by section 7 of the *Charter*.

Section 486.3 of the *Criminal Code* limits the right of personal cross-examination. Section 486.3(1) provides that the accused "shall not personally cross-examine" a witness under eighteen years of age, and that counsel shall be appointed to conduct the cross-examination, unless the trial judge "is of the opinion that the proper administration of justice requires the accused to personally conduct the cross-examination." Section 486.3(2) extends this limit to any witness where, on application by the prosecution or the witness, the judge "is of the opinion that, in order to obtain a full and candid account from the witness of the acts complained of, the accused should not personally cross-examine the witness." These limits do not appear to have been subject to any challenge under section 7 of the *Charter*, but it is likely that the provision for appointment of counsel to conduct the cross-examination, though it impinges on the right of the accused to control his own defence (see Section B(4)(c), below in this chapter) would satisfy the section 7 right to a fair trial because that right is construed in light of the societal interest in determining the truth of the allegations against

---

104 *R v Lyttle*, 2004 SCC 5 at para 41.

105 *Ibid* at para 43. "The cross-examiner may pursue any hypothesis that is honestly advanced on the strength of reasonable inference, experience or intuition": *ibid* at para 48.

106 *Ibid* at para 47.

the accused. Where the statutory condition that preventing personal cross-examination is necessary "to obtain a full and candid account" from the witness, and where cross-examination can be effectively conducted by counsel appointed for that purpose, the right to a fair trial would be protected.

d) Hearsay Exceptions and Fundamental Justice

It is not a principle of fundamental justice that the accused has the right to cross-examine any person who made a statement that is to be used against him; put another way, the fact that there are exceptions to the rule against hearsay does not offend the principles of fundamental justice.[107] But it is likely that extensive departures from the rule against hearsay, or excessively broad exceptions to it, would offend the principles of fundamental justice. In a number of cases, the Supreme Court of Canada has suggested that some control on the reliability of hearsay evidence, either in the form of an opportunity to cross-examine the declarant at some stage or in the form of a demonstration that the evidence is likely to be true, is necessary for exceptions to the rule against hearsay to comply with section 7. In *R v Potvin (Potvin)*,[108] the Court considered a constitutional challenge to the predecessor of section 715 of the *Criminal Code*, which permits the Crown to put into evidence the transcript of a witness's evidence from a previous proceeding where the witness is, for certain specified reasons, unavailable and provided that the accused had a "full opportunity to cross-examine the witness." The section is often used where, for example, a witness has testified for the Crown at the preliminary inquiry but has died before trial; in *Potvin* itself, the witnesses in question had testified at the preliminary inquiry but refused to testify at trial. The Court rejected the accused's argument that it was a principle of fundamental justice that he must be given the opportunity "to cross-examine all adverse witnesses at trial before the trier of fact."[109] However, the Court accepted a less demanding rule; the accused must have "a full opportunity to cross-examine the witnesses when the previous testimony was taken if a transcript of such testimony is to be introduced as evidence in a criminal trial for the purpose of convicting the accused."[110] Moreover, the trial judge has a discretion to refuse to admit the transcript where its admission

---

107   *R v Potvin*, [1989] 1 SCR 525.
108   *Ibid.*
109   *Ibid* at 540.
110   *Ibid* at 543.

would be excessively prejudicial.[111] Section 715 complies with these principles.

Similarly, in *R v L(DO)*,[112] the Court considered the predecessor of section 715.1 of the *Criminal Code*, which made the video-recorded statement of a child complainant in a sexual case, describing the sexual conduct complained of, admissible if the video-recording was made within a reasonable time and if the child adopted it while testifying.[113] The hearsay exception thus created was held not to violate section 7 of the *Charter* because the statutory requirements for admissibility ensured the necessity and reliability of the statement and because the statute preserved the evidentiary balancing principle.[114]

The Supreme Court has also held that its common law development of the exceptions to the rule against hearsay must comply with section 7 of the *Charter*.[115] Since 1990, the Court has articulated a principled approach to hearsay: hearsay evidence, even though inadmissible under any statutory or traditional common law exception to the rule, may be admitted if it is necessary and reliable.[116] In its most recent restatement of the governing principles, the Court held that there were two main ways for the proponent of hearsay evidence to demonstrate its reliability[117]: first, where the circumstances in which the statement was made indicate that it is probably reliable or even true; second, where the opponent has another opportunity to test the reliability of the statement; for example, by cross-examining the declarant at trial. These methods of demonstrating reliability have a "constitutional dimension" because in the criminal trial, "difficulties in testing the evidence, or conversely the inability to present reliable evidence, may impact on an accused's

---

111   *Ibid* at 547–55, and compare the discussion of the evidentiary balancing principle in Stewart, "Common Law Rules," above note 86.

112   *R v L(DO)*, [1993] 4 SCR 419 [*L(DO)*].

113   The current version of s 715.1 is broader and applies to witnesses under the age of eighteen generally, not just to young complainants in sexual cases. See also *Criminal Code*, above note 66, s 715.2.

114   *L(DO)*, above note 112 at 455–61. For further discussion of *L(DO)*, including the question of whether it actually creates a hearsay exception, see Hamish Stewart, *Sexual Offences in Canadian Law*, loose-leaf (Aurora, ON: Canada Law Book, 2004) at §§:400.

115   See also *R v Arp*, [1998] 3 SCR 339 at paras 68–75, holding that the similar fact rule in its present common-law form does not offend the principles of fundamental justice, and compare *Handy*, above note 90 at para 139.

116   The major cases in the development of the principled approach were *R v Khan*, [1990] 2 SCR 531; *R v Smith*, [1992] 2 SCR 915; *R v B(KG)*, [1993] 1 SCR 740; *R v Hawkins*, [1996] 3 SCR 1043; *Starr*, above note 91; *R v Mapara*, 2005 SCC 23 ; *R v Khelawon*, 2006 SCC 57 [*Khelawon*].

117   *Khelawon*, *ibid* at para 49; see also paras 61–64.

ability to make full answer and defence, a right protected by s. 7 of the (*Charter*)."[118] A statute that purported to make hearsay admissible without a demonstration of reliability in one of these two ways would likely offend the principles of fundamental justice, unless it could be read so as to preserve the discretionary exclusionary power.

e)   No General Right against Unreliable Evidence

The cases reviewed in this section so far show that section 7 of the *Charter* has had an important impact on the common law of evidence, not because any common law rules have been invalidated on *Charter* grounds, but because the *Charter* guarantee of a fair trial has encouraged the courts to develop the common law of evidence in light of that guarantee. These cases might be read as suggesting that an accused person has, as an adjunct of the right to a fair trial, a right to exclusion of unreliable evidence in general.[119] But Canadian courts have stopped short of identifying such a right at common law or under section 7. In *R v Buric*, the Ontario Court of Appeal commented that "The admission of evidence which *may* be unreliable does not *per se* render a trial unfair,"[120] and other courts have generally taken the same view.[121]

The rise of the principled approach to admissibility at common law, and its constitutional dimension (see Section B(3)(d), above in this chapter), should support the recognition of a right against the admission of extremely unreliable evidence. Where it has been demonstrated that a particular type of evidence is unreliable, and where appellate courts often set aside verdicts based on such evidence as unreasonable, there is no principled reason why an accused person should have to respond to such evidence—just as there is no principled reason why she should have to respond to inadmissible hearsay.

f)   The Right to Silence at Trial

Except to the extent that the accused cannot be compelled to be a witness,[122] the *Charter* does not expressly guarantee a right to silence. But, as noted in Chapter 4, Section E(1), the Supreme Court of Canada

---

118 *Ibid* at para 47.

119 Compare Stewart, "Common Law Rules," above note 86; Kent Roach, "Unreliable Evidence and Wrongful Convictions: The Case for Excluding Tainted Identification Evidence and Jailhouse and Coerced Confessions" (2007) 52 Crim LQ 210.

120 *R v Buric* (1996), 28 OR (3d) 737 at 750, aff'd [1997] 1 SCR 535.

121 See, for instance, *R v Osmar*, 2007 ONCA 50; *R v Duguay*, 2007 NBCA 65; *R v Brooks*, 2000 SCC 11.

122 *Criminal Code*, above note 66, s 11(*c*).

has recognized a pre-trial right to silence under section 7. The general principle against self-incrimination expressed in section 11(c) and the section 7 right to silence also prevent the Crown from arguing before the trier of fact that an adverse inference should be drawn from the accused's pre-trial silence.[123] In *R v Chambers* (*Chambers*), cross-examination of the accused on his failure to advance his defence before he testified at trial was held to be objectionable, apparently because it violated section 7 of the *Charter*.[124] More recently, in *R v Turcotte* (*Turcotte*),[125] the trial judge told the jury that the accused's refusal to answer any police questions before he was arrested was "post-offence conduct" from which they could draw inferences about his state of mind. The Supreme Court of Canada held unanimously, *per* Abella J, that the instruction was erroneous because the accused's silence, being merely the exercise of a liberty not to speak to the police, was not probative of guilt.[126] As in *Chambers*, the Court appears to be of the view that the evidentiary use at trial of the accused's silence violated section 7 of the *Charter*: the pre-trial, pre-arrest right to silence "would be an illusory right if the decision not to speak to the police could be used by the Crown as evidence of guilt."[127]

In both *Chambers* and *Turcotte*, the Court was careful to recognize that in some situations cross-examination or other evidentiary use of the accused's pre-trial silence would not be objectionable, because the accused's strategic or tactical choices about the conduct of the trial would give his silence a relevance it would not normally have. For example "where the defence seeks to emphasize the accused's cooperation with the authorities . . . ; where the accused testified that he had denied the charges against him at the time he was arrested . . . ; or where silence is relevant to the defence theory of mistaken identity and a flawed police investigation,"[128] evidence of silence may be admissible. In this type of case, evidence of the accused's silence may be relevant to rebut one or more aspects of the accused's theory of the case, which is

---

123 For a similar result at common law, see *R v Eden*, [1970] 3 CCC 280 (Ont CA), though some commentators argued that the common law "right to silence" was merely correlative to the absence of a legal duty to speak: Ed Ratushny, "Is There a Right against Self-Incrimination in Canada?" (1973) 19 McGill LJ 1 at 11–14.

124 *R v Chambers*, [1990] 2 SCR 1293 at 1316.

125 *R v Turcotte*, 2005 SCC 50.

126 *Ibid* at para 55.

127 *Ibid* at para 44.

128 *Ibid* at para 49.

permissible, rather than to support the impermissible inference that an innocent person would have responded to an accusation.

Whether section 7 and section 11(*d*) actually forbid an adverse inference from silence, or merely forbid the Crown from arguing for it, is uncertain. However, caselaw suggests that the inference is prohibited. The decision in *Turcotte* rests on the twin holdings that the accused's silence is irrelevant and that evidentiary use of silence at trial would undermine the right to silence; these holdings suggest that the inference is forbidden.[129] Similarly, in *R v Noble (Noble)*,[130] a majority of the Supreme Court of Canada held that silence at trial could not be used as a positive piece of evidence in building the Crown's case against the accused.[131]

The view that inferring guilt from silence is improper suggests that, at least in certain cases, juries should be instructed not to do so, just as they are instructed to avoid other improper inferences. But section 4(6) of the *Canada Evidence Act* provides that the accused's failure to testify "shall not be made the subject of comment by the judge or by counsel for the prosecution."[132] The majority in *Noble* adopted a plain reading of section 4(6) and held that it prevented the trial judge from instructing the jury not to infer guilt from silence.[133] This *obiter dictum* suggests, oddly, that an adverse inference from the accused's silence, though forbidden in judge-alone trials, is unavoidably permitted in jury trials.[134] But the plain reading of section 4(6) is inconsistent with the Court's purposive pre-*Charter* holding that only *adverse* comments on the failure to testify are prohibited; an instruction to the effect that an inference should not be drawn from silence is consistent with the purpose of section 4(6) and is therefore not prohibited by it.[135] *Turcotte* and *Noble* both suggest that an adverse inference from silence is contrary to the principles of fundamental justice. Thus, to comply with section 7 of the *Charter*, section 4(6) should be read to permit a trial judge, in appropriate circumstances, to instruct the jury that they should not infer guilt from silence.[136] This approach would be consistent with the Ontario Court of Appeal's holding, on non-constitutional grounds, that

---

129 *R v Prokofiew*, 2010 ONCA 423 at para 34 [*Prokofiew*].

130 *R v Noble*, [1997] 1 SCR 874.

131 *Ibid* at paras 75–82.

132 *Canada Evidence Act*, above note 92, s 4(6).

133 *R v Noble*, above note 130 at para 96.

134 The holding was *obiter* because the accused, Noble, was tried by judge alone.

135 *R v McConnell*, [1968] SCR 802.

136 Hamish Stewart, "Nothing Can Come of Nothing: Three Implications of *Noble*" (1999) 42 Crim LQ 286 at 307–10 [Stewart, "Nothing Can Come of Nothing"].

the *Noble obiter dictum* is not binding because it is peripheral to the reasoning and inconsistent with prior binding authority.[137] Thus, at least in Ontario, a trial judge is permitted to instruct a jury not to draw an adverse inference from the accused's failure to testify.[138]

4) The Right to Make Full Answer and Defence

The right of the accused to make full answer and defence to the charge is explicitly recognized in the *Criminal Code*[139] and is a principle of fundamental justice under section 7 of the *Charter*.[140] This right "manifests itself in several more specific rights and principles, such as the right to full and timely disclosure, the right to know the case to be met before opening one's defence, the principles governing the re-opening of the Crown's case, as well as various rights of cross-examination, among others" and is "integrally linked to other principles of fundamental justice, such as the presumption of innocence, the right to a fair trial, and the principle against self-incrimination."[141]

a) Disclosure
As an aspect of the common law and constitutional right to make full answer and defence, the accused has a right to disclosure from the Crown. The Crown's duty of disclosure is justified by the avoidance of surprise at trial and by Crown counsel's role as a public official whose task is to ensure that justice is done. In *R v Stinchcombe* (*Stinchcombe*), where disclosure was first recognized as a constitutional obligation resting on the Crown, the court held that "failure to disclose impedes the ability of the accused to make full answer and defence."[142]

---

137 *Prokofiew*, above note 129 at paras 14–40.
138 Some appellate authority appears to hold that the inference is permissible and that it would be an error of law for the trial judge to give such an instruction: see, for example, *R v Miller* (1998), 131 CCC (3d) 141 at para 14 (Ont CA); *R v Sparvier*, 2006 SKCA 139 at para 35. This authority is surely inconsistent with *Noble* and certainly with *Prokofiew*. There is, however, an exception: where the accused offers an alibi defence, the adverse inference from silence is permitted: see *R v Vézeau*, [1977] 2 SCR 277. For a critique of the alibi exception, see Stewart, "Nothing Can Come of Nothing," above note 136 at 305–6.
139 *Criminal Code*, above note 66, s 650(3).
140 *R v Rose*, [1998] 3 SCR 262 at para 98 [*Rose*].
141 *Ibid.*
142 *R v Stinchcombe*, [1991] 3 SCR 326 at 336 [*Stinchcombe*].

i) The Crown's Disclosure Obligation

The Crown has an obligation to disclose all material in its possession relating to the investigation against the accused, unless the material is clearly irrelevant or privileged,[143] or unless disclosure of the material "is otherwise governed by law."[144] The concept of "relevance" means only that there is a reasonable possibility that the material in question might be used by the accused in making full answer and defence or in making decisions about the conduct of the case.[145] It does not matter whether the material in question is inculpatory or exculpatory[146] or whether the Crown intends to lead the material as evidence at trial.[147]

It appears that the Crown may assert any kind of privilege to justify a refusal to disclose. Informer privilege is the most common ground asserted; the disclosure obligation does not extend to material that would tend to identify a confidential informer, and given that the informer privilege belongs to both the Crown and the informer, the Crown cannot in any event exercise its discretion and disclose such material. Only where the accused's factual innocence is at stake would there be an exception to informer privilege requiring the Crown to disclose material tending to identify a confidential informer.[148]

It is relatively rare for the Crown to assert other forms of privilege. Solicitor-client privilege may be asserted in appropriate circumstances; for instance, where counsel has provided a legal opinion to a police force or to other Crown counsel,[149] but it is unclear whether this privilege can always be invoked to resist disclosure.[150] Since solicitor-client privilege protects only communications and not facts or evidence as such, and since the relevant facts or evidence have to be disclosed pursuant to the Crown's disclosure obligation, it is likely that the Crown or the police can invoke solicitor-client privilege over any communications that do not contain any facts or evidence otherwise subject to disclosure. Suppose, for example, that Crown counsel seeks an outside legal opinion concerning the prospect of successful prosecution on the basis of an assumed set of facts or a summary of the anticipated evi-

---

143 Ibid at 335–36.

144 R v McNeil, 2009 SCC 3 at para 18 [McNeil].

145 Stinchcombe, above note 142 at 340; R v Egger, [1993] 2 SCR 451 at 467.

146 Stinchcombe, ibid at 343.

147 Ibid at 345.

148 On the stringency of the informer privilege and the scope of the innocence-at-stake exception, see Named Person v Vancouver Sun, 2007 SCC 43; R v Leipert, [1997] 1 SCR 281.

149 R v Campbell, [1999] 1 SCR 565 at paras 49–54 [Campbell]. On the facts, the privilege was waived by the conduct of the litigation.

150 Ibid at paras 65–66.

dence. All factual information in the Crown's possession concerning those facts and evidence would have to be disclosed in any event; but outside counsel's opinion would likely be protected by solicitor-client privilege. Another possibility would be to consider whether the innocence-at-stake exception to solicitor-client privilege would apply to the opinion,[151] which would rarely be the case.

It has been held that the Crown can assert litigation or "work product" privilege,[152] but since the Crown's disclosure obligation clearly requires disclosing considerable material that might well be protected by litigation privilege in civil proceedings, this privilege would have to be applied very narrowly to respect the accused's constitutional right to know the case against her.

The executive branch of government is not considered to be "indivisible" for the purposes of the disclosure obligation; thus, the various parts of the government—Crown prosecutors, police forces, other investigative bodies, and other government agencies—are not all subject to the disclosure obligation.[153] Crown prosecutors are not deemed to be in possession of all the information that any other part of the government might have. Nonetheless, the Crown's disclosure obligation extends beyond the material actually in its possession. First, the investigating police force has an obligation to disclose all material that is not irrelevant or clearly privileged to the Crown, and the Crown is therefore deemed to be in possession of this material.[154] Second, the Crown is obliged "to make reasonable inquiries of other Crown entities and third parties" and is therefore also deemed to have any material that would be obtained from such inquiries in its possession.[155]

The Crown has a discretion in relation to the timing of disclosure, particularly for the purpose of protecting an ongoing investigation.[156] However, the Crown's obligation to disclose is a continuing one, extending to material obtained during the trial and throughout the appeal process.[157] The defence has a corresponding obligation to pursue disclosure diligently, and its failure to do so, though not relieving the

---

151 See *R v Chan* (2002), 164 CCC (3d) 24 at paras 72–89 (Alta QB) [*Chan*], considering whether the innocence-at-stake exception was applicable to material protected by solicitor-client privilege as asserted by the Crown.

152 *R v Trang*, 2002 ABQB 19 at paras 64–97; *Chan, ibid* at para 100.

153 *McNeil*, above note 144 at para 22.

154 *Ibid* at para 14.

155 *Ibid* at para 13.

156 *Stinchcombe*, above note 142 at 336.

157 *R v Trotta* (2004), 23 CR (6th) 261 (Ont CA); *McNeil*, above note 144 at para 17.

Crown of the obligation to disclose, may be relevant to the remedy for non-disclosure.[158]

The right to disclosure is an aspect of the right to a fair trial; more specifically, of the right to make full answer and defence. Thus, where the Crown has failed to comply with its disclosure obligation, the accused is entitled to a remedy that is, in the words of section 24(1) of the *Charter*, "appropriate and just in the circumstances." Indeed, non-disclosure does not in itself violate section 7; the Crown's failure to meet its disclosure obligation violates section 7 only where "it impairs the accused's right to full answer and defence."[159] Thus, the appropriate and just remedy depends on the impact of that failure on the right to make full answer and defence. The drastic remedy of a stay of proceedings is appropriate only where there is no other method of remedying the prejudice caused by the non-disclosure.[160] More commonly, an adjournment, the recall of witnesses, or a mistrial will be appropriate remedies for non-disclosure that affects the right to make full answer and defence.[161] Where the Crown's failure to disclose comes to light after the accused is convicted, the accused must on appeal show a reasonable possibility that the non-disclosure affected either the result or the fairness of the trial.[162]

The high threshold for a stay is well illustrated by *R v Taillefer*.[163] The two accused, Taillefer and Duguay, were charged with and convicted of first-degree murder. Taillefer's conviction appeal was dismissed, but Duguay's was allowed and a new trial was ordered on a charge of second-degree murder. Duguay pleaded guilty to manslaughter and was sentenced to twelve years' imprisonment. It subsequently emerged that the Crown had failed to disclose considerable material that could have been used to impeach the credibility of the Crown witness, or indeed to cast doubt on the Crown's entire theory of the case. Nonetheless, the Court of Appeal refused to grant Duguay leave to withdraw his guilty plea, and dismissed Taillefer's application for a review of the

---

158 *R v Dixon*, [1998] 1 SCR 244 at para 37 [*Dixon*].

159 *O'Connor*, above note 55 at para 76.

160 *Ibid* at para 77: for examples, see *R v Khela* (1998), 126 CCC (3d) 341 (Que CA), where the Crown failed to comply with its disclosure obligation after protracted proceedings, including an appeal to the Supreme Court of Canada; *R v Cassidy* (2004), 182 CCC (3d) 294 at para 23 (Ont CA), where the Crown "maintained a disclosure position that is clearly constitutionally inadequate for two years."

161 *O'Connor*, *ibid* at para 77; compare *R v Leboeuf* (2003), 190 CCC (3d) 104 (Que SC) (mistrial and costs award for aborted trial); *R v Leduc* (2003), 176 CCC (3d) 321 (Ont CA).

162 *Dixon*, above note 158 at para 34; *R v Illes*, 2008 SCC 57 at para 24.

163 *R v Taillefer*, 2003 SCC 70 [*Taillefer*].

trial.[164] The two accused appealed to the Supreme Court of Canada. The Court found a very serious breach of the Crown's disclosure obligations and of the accused's right to make full answer and defence. But Taillefer's remedy was limited to a new trial. The proceedings against Duguay were stayed, as he had already served eight years of his sentence: "Ordering a new trial when the accused has already served so much of his sentence would contribute to perpetuating an injustice and would tarnish the integrity of our judicial system."[165] Without the additional factor of the term of imprisonment, it appears that Duguay's remedy would also have been limited to a new trial.

ii) Interaction of Public Interest Immunity and Disclosure

Material protected by public interest immunity and on national security grounds is not privileged as such, but it is material whose disclosure "is otherwise governed by law." It is therefore neither exempted from disclosure nor necessarily to be disclosed; instead, it is subject to the procedure in sections 37 through 38.15 of the *Canada Evidence Act*.[166] An objection to disclosure on the ground of a specified public interest is determined by the trial judge, *per* section 37. But if the information in question is "sensitive information or potentially injurious information," as defined in section 38, then the anticipated disclosure of the information by any "participant" in a proceeding is governed by a complex procedure laid out in sections 38.01 through 38.15.[167] This procedure essentially involves the determination of the question of disclosure by a designated judge of the Federal Court, regardless of the forum in which the issue initially arose. Officials and the participants in any proceeding are obliged to give notice to the federal Attorney General if they anticipate that sensitive or potentially injurious information will be disclosed.[168] The Attorney General may, among other things, apply to the Federal Court for an order concerning disclosure;[169] the Federal Court judge "shall hear the representations of the Attorney General,"[170]

---

164 The application resulted from a reference by the Minister of Justice pursuant to s 690 of the *Criminal Code*, as it then stood.
165 *Taillefer*, above note 163 at para 128.
166 Above note 92.
167 For overviews of the scheme, see Hamish Stewart, "Public Interest Immunity after Bill C-36" (2003) 47 Crim LQ 249; Peter Rosenthal, "Disclosure to the Defence after September 11: Sections 37 and 38 of the *Canada Evidence Act*" (2004) 48 Crim LQ 186; *Ahmad* 2011, above note 31 at paras 16–26.
168 *Criminal Code*, above note 66, s 38.01.
169 *Ibid*, s 38.04(1).
170 *Ibid*, s 38.04(5)(*a*).

shall decide whether to hold a hearing,[171] and if a hearing is held, "shall . . . determine who should be given notice of the hearing."[172] The heart of the scheme is section 38.06(2), which provides that if disclosure would be "injurious" in the sense contemplated in section 38, the Federal Court judge must balance the interests in disclosure with the interests in non-disclosure; and if the balance of interests favour disclosure, must make an order concerning disclosure that is "most likely" to limit the injurious effects. The accused's right to a fair trial is protected by section 38.14, which gives the trial judge the power to "make any order that he or she considers appropriate in the circumstances to protect the right of the accused to a fair trial," including a stay of proceedings. So if the Crown fails to meet its usual disclosure obligations because the material in question cannot be disclosed under this statutory scheme, the trial judge would have the same remedial powers under section 38.14 that he would have under section 24(1) of the *Charter* for a breach of the disclosure obligation, as discussed below.

In *R v Ahmad*,[173] a number of persons charged with terrorism offences challenged the constitutionality of the section 38 procedure. The Supreme Court of Canada rejected the challenge and upheld the scheme. The heart of the Court's reasoning is its interpretation of the Federal Court judge's role under section 38.04 and the trial judge's role under section 38.14.

Although section 38.04 appears to grant the Federal Court judge a discretion to decide whom to apprise of the hearing, the Court held that section 38.04(5) should be read as requiring the Federal Court judge to give notice to the criminal trial court,[174] and, "absent compelling reasons to the contrary," to the accused person in the criminal trial.[175] Moreover, in order to assess the impact of non-disclosure on trial fairness, "the trial judge will require some information about the withheld information," perhaps in the form of a summary, perhaps in "more extensive" form.[176] Indeed, the Court commented that "[d]isclosure to the trial judge alone . . . for the sole purpose of determining the impact of non-disclosure on the fairness of the trial, will often be the most appropriate option."[177] The Court held that the section 38 scheme was flexible enough to permit the trial judge to adopt procedures designed

---

171 *Ibid*, s 38.04(5)(*b*).
172 *Ibid*, s 38.04(5)(*c*)(i).
173 Above note 31.
174 *Ibid* at para 39.
175 *Ibid* at para 40.
176 *Ibid* at para 42.
177 *Ibid* at para 45.

to protect the right to a fair trial without compromising the secrecy of the information in question, such as appointing a special advocate (compare Section A(2), above in this chapter) or, possibly, allowing a security-cleared defence counsel "access to the withheld material on an undertaking not to disclose it to the accused."[178] With access to the material and submissions made in an adversarial setting, the trial judge would be in a good position to assess the impact of non-disclosure on the right to a fair trial.

But because the disclosure decisions ultimately rest with the Attorney General and the Federal Court judge, the trial judge might nonetheless not have access to enough of the non-disclosed information to determine the impact of non-disclosure on the accused's right to a fair trial. In this situation, "the trial judge must presume that the non-disclosure order has adversely affected the fairness of the trial" and must inform the Crown so that the Attorney General can be given "an opportunity to make further and better disclosure." If that is not possible, "a stay of proceedings will be the presumptively appropriate remedy."[179]

Section 38.14 empowers the trial judge to make any order necessary to protect the accused's right to make full answer and defence. The Court interpreted the section as broadly as its wording suggests, and added that the power to order a stay under section 38.14 was not restricted to the "clearest of cases" as is usually the case (compare Section A(4) above) because it was a statutory remedy designed to protect the right to a fair trial where "the trial judge is simply unable to conclude affirmatively that the right to a fair trial, including the right of the accused to a full and fair defence, has not been compromised."[180]

Under this interpretation, particularly of sections 38.04 and 38.14, the section 38 scheme does not offend section 7 of the *Charter* because it ensures that the accused will either receive a fair trial or, if that is not possible given the Attorney General's decision not to disclose information, no trial at all.

iii) Lost or Destroyed Evidence

Correlative to the accused's right to disclosure is not only the Crown's obligation to disclose but also its obligation to preserve the evidence in its possession so that it may be disclosed when requested. The deliber-

---

178   *Ibid* at para 49; the successful operation of such a procedure is described in Michael Code, "Problems of Process in Litigating Claims of Privilege under the Flexible Wigmore Model" in The Law Society of Upper Canada, *Special Lectures 2003: The Law of Evidence* (Toronto: Irwin Law, 2004) 251.

179   *Ahmad* 2011, *ibid* at para 51.

180   *Ibid* at para 35.

ate destruction or negligent loss of evidence may violate the accused's right to disclosure, and to make full answer and defence, to such an extent as to require a remedy.[181]

iv) *Deliberate Destruction of Evidence*

"[S]erious departures from the Crown's duty to preserve material that is subject to [disclosure]," such as deliberate destruction or loss through unacceptable negligence, violates the accused's right to disclosure and may also amount to an abuse of process.[182] In such a case, it is not necessary for the accused to establish actual prejudice to her right to make full answer and defence to demonstrate a violation of her rights under section 7. However, the appropriate remedy depends on the circumstances, and the degree of prejudice will be relevant to that question. A stay of proceedings is appropriate only where it is the only way to cure any prejudice caused by the loss of evidence (compare Section B(4)(a)(iii), above in this chapter).

There are few examples of accused persons being granted remedies on the basis of deliberate destruction of evidence that is likely relevant. *R v Carosella (Carosella)*,[183] the most notorious case on point, involves destruction of evidence not by the Crown but by a third party, and its precedential force is not clear. The accused was charged with sexual offences alleged to have occurred in 1964. In 1992, the complainant had sought advice from a Sexual Assault Crisis Centre, where she spoke with a social worker for up to two hours. The social worker took notes of the interview. Immediately after the interview, the complainant went to the police, who laid the charges. The complainant continued to receive counseling from the Centre for several months after that. At trial, the accused applied for production of the Centre's file concerning the complainant; this application was granted on consent, but the file contained no notes of the interviews. The Centre had by that time shredded these notes, pursuant to a policy of destroying records that might be subpoenaed for use in criminal trials (though the policy also provided that files under subpoena or the subject of an application for production could not be shredded). The Centre's policy was founded on its belief that the routine production of its files in sexual assault trials contributed to the "further victimization [of] the clients it serves."[184] If the notes had been in the possession of the Crown, there is no doubt

---

181   See also the convenient statement of principles in *R v B(FC)*, 2000 NSCA 35 [*B(FC)*].

182   *R v La*, [1997] 2 SCR 680 at para 22 [*La*].

183   *R v Carosella*, [1997] 1 SCR 80, 112 CCC (3d) 289.

184   *Ibid* at para 9, quoting from the policy.

that they would have been disclosed; if the Crown had destroyed the notes, there is no doubt that the Crown would have seriously violated its disclosure obligations. The majority, *per* Sopinka J, took the view that these obligations applied equally to the Centre, stating that "The entitlement of an accused person to production either from the Crown or third parties is a constitutional right"[185] and noting that the Centre was in receipt of some government funding.[186] He went on to hold that the deliberate destruction of the evidence was a violation of the right to make full answer and defence,[187] a violation sufficiently serious to justify a stay of proceedings, particularly since there was no obvious alternative remedy.[188]

If the Centre truly was subject to the same stringent disclosure obligations as the Crown, Sopinka J's conclusion would follow fairly easily. But, as L'Heureux-Dubé J noted in a persuasive dissent, it is difficult to see why these obligations should have rested on the Centre. If the Centre had received the accused's application before shredding the notes, the shredding would arguably have amounted to obstruction of justice. But the Centre, as a private party that had not received a subpoena or a notice of the accused's application for production, was under no obvious legal obligation to preserve its records for use in litigation.[189] The suggestion that the disclosure obligation rests just as heavily on third parties as on the Crown was not repeated in *R v La*,[190] and is plainly inconsistent with the Court's reasoning in *R v McNeil* (*McNeil*) concerning the Crown's obligation to obtain evidence from third parties (discussed above). *McNeil* recognized that the Crown was required, as part of its disclosure obligation, "to make reasonable inquiries of other Crown entities and third parties";[191] but it would be unnecessary to impose this obligation on the Crown if those third parties were already obliged to disclose. Indeed, in *McNeil*, the Court expressly stated that "Third parties are under no obligation to come forth with relevant information to assist the accused in his defence."[192] *Carosella* thus stands as a very anomalous decision; its principles are applicable only in the highly unusual situation where the Crown, or another part of the

---

185 *Ibid* at para 26.
186 *Ibid* at paras 3, 56.
187 *Ibid* at paras 25–47.
188 *Ibid* at paras 48–56.
189 *Ibid* at para 66.
190 Compare Sopinka J's restatement of the *Carosella* principles in *La*, above note 182 at para 22.
191 *McNeil*, above note 144 at para 13.
192 *Ibid* at para 47.

government whose material is deemed to be in the Crown's possession for disclosure purposes, deliberately destroys evidence.

R v Bero[193] provides a rare example where the destruction of a central piece of evidence did amount to a violation of the Crown's disclosure obligation. The accused was charged with impaired driving causing bodily harm and "over eighty." The central issue at trial was whether it was the accused or the injured person (who was also the owner of the vehicle) who was driving. After the accident, the vehicle was examined by a police officer who was an expert in accident reconstruction. It was then sent to an auto wrecker and subsequently sold to another auto wrecker. The accused was charged after the vehicle was sent to the first auto wrecker. Shortly after receiving disclosure, the accused's counsel requested that the vehicle be examined; but the second auto wrecker had destroyed the vehicle three days earlier.[194] No-one had considered the possible relevance of the vehicle to the issues at trial, much less examined it for forensic evidence relating to the question of who was driving. In these circumstances, the destruction of the vehicle, though not a deliberate attempt to frustrate the accused's right to disclosure, was "a sufficiently serious departure from the Crown's duty to preserve evidence that it constitutes an abuse of process."[195] However, a stay of proceedings was not the appropriate remedy; instead, the trial judge should not have prevented defence counsel from cross-examining the reconstruction expert on what might have been learned from a forensic examination of the vehicle[196] and should have instructed the jury "that the Crown was under an obligation to preserve the evidence and failed to do so, and that the defence cannot be faulted for not gaining access to the evidence before it was destroyed."[197]

v) Satisfactorily-Explained Loss of Evidence

Where evidence that is likely relevant has been lost or destroyed, but the Crown can provide a satisfactory explanation, the accused's right to disclosure is not violated unless he or she can demonstrate actual preju-

---

193　*R v Bero* (2000), 151 CCC (3d) 545 (Ont CA).

194　*Ibid* at paras 19–24.

195　*Ibid* at para 39.

196　*Ibid* at paras 57–66.

197　*Ibid* at para 67. See also *R v Forster*, 2005 SKCA 107, where the police destroyed a computer disc containing information that was used to put together the Information to Obtain a search warrant. The destruction was either "bad faith" or "inexcusable negligence" on the part of the officer (para 31); a stay of proceedings was the only remedy capable of responding to the prejudice caused by the defence's inability to challenge the search (para 33).

dice to the right to make full answer and defence; it is anticipated that this actual prejudice will only arise "in extraordinary circumstances."[198] The remedy of a stay of proceedings should be granted only where no other remedy is capable of curing the prejudice;[199] it is generally preferable for the trial judge to have heard all the evidence before deciding on the remedy.[200]

Cases where the loss or destruction of evidence has been so significant as to impair the right to make full answer and defence are rare. In *R v B(FC)*,[201] for example, a police officer's handwritten statement summarizing his conversation with a complainant and signed by her was destroyed pursuant to a pre-*Stinchcombe* RCMP policy on document retention; however, a typed transcript of the statement was available. The hand-written statement would certainly have been disclosed had it been available; however, the Crown had provided a satisfactory explanation for its destruction,[202] and several factors — the availability of the typed transcript and, possibly, of other prior statements of the complainant — indicated that the accused's right to make full answer and defence had not been prejudiced.[203]

b) Access to Records Held by Third Parties

Sometimes evidence relevant to an accused person's defence is contained in, or may be discovered by examining, records held by persons and institutions other than the Crown. Often third parties, including complainants and other witnesses, have significant and constitutionally-protected privacy interests in those records. Under what conditions do the principles of fundamental justice require the accused to be granted access to these third party records, which lie "beyond the possession or control of the prosecuting Crown"?[204] Canadian law currently provides two related but distinct procedures: the first is the common law procedure established in *R v O'Connor (O'Connor)*,[205] and the second is a statutory procedure that supersedes *O'Connor* in trials of sexual offences.[206] Both procedures have been held to comply with the principles of fundamental justice.

---

198 *La*, above note 182 at para 24.
199 *Ibid* at para 27.
200 *Ibid*; see also *R v Sheng*, 2010 ONCA 296.
201 *B(FC)*, above note 181.
202 *Ibid* at 548–53.
203 *Ibid* at 554–56. See also *R v JP*, 2009 ONCA 850.
204 *McNeil*, above note 144 at para 11.
205 *O'Connor*, above note 55.
206 *Criminal Code*, above note 66, ss 278.1–278.91.

In *O'Connor*, the Court established the following procedure where the accused seeks production of third party records,[207] that is, records outside the control of the Crown in which third parties had a privacy interest.[208] The accused should cause a subpoena *duces tecum* pursuant to section 698 of the *Criminal Code* to be issued to the person holding the records and should give notice to any person whose privacy interests are affected.[209] The application for production should be made before the trial judge. On the application, the accused must first establish that the records are "likely relevant;" that is, that "information is logically probative to an issue at trial or the competence of a witness to testify."[210] Since the accused will not have seen the records, the burden of establishing likely relevance is not high.[211] If the accused's claim of likely relevance is not borne out on the trial judge's inspection of the records, then production should be refused.[212] If, on the other hand, there is no-one who has a reasonable expectation of privacy in the record, then "there is no balancing of interests left to perform" and the records should be produced to the accused.[213] In the intermediate case where the records do have some relevance but where their production would affect the privacy interests of third parties, the trial judge must balance the accused's right to make full answer and defence against the privacy interests of the third party. In *O'Connor*, the Court held that the following factors should be considered in assessing this balance:

(1) the extent to which the record is necessary for the accused to make full answer and defence;

(2) the probative value of the record in question;

(3) the nature and extent of the reasonable expectation of privacy vested in that record;

(4) whether production of the record would be premised upon any discriminatory belief or bias;

---

207 The Court in *O'Connor* was badly divided on the issues and in the result, but it is possible to identify a majority position on each of the points discussed in the text. The positions of the majority are largely restated, in the context of non-sexual cases, in *McNeil*, above note 144.

208 Such records include "records that are medical or therapeutic in nature, school records, private diaries, and activity logs prepared by social workers . . . .": *O'Connor*, above note 55 at para 99, L'Heureux-Dubé J. The entire Court agreed with these examples.

209 *McNeil*, above note 144 at para 27.

210 *O'Connor*, above note 55 at para 22, Lamer CJC and Sopinka J, dissenting on other grounds; *McNeil*, *ibid* at para 33.

211 *O'Connor*, *ibid* at paras 25–29; *McNeil*, *ibid* at para 29.

212 *McNeil*, *ibid* at para 40.

213 *Ibid* at para 37.

(5) the potential prejudice to the complainant's dignity, privacy or security of the person that would be occasioned by production of the record . . . .[214]

These factors were tailored to the context of third-party records in which a complainant in a sexual case had a privacy interest. The *O'Connor* regime is now both narrower and broader than it was when *O'Connor* itself was decided: it no longer applies to sexual cases at all, but in non-sexual cases it applies to any records held by third parties. Thus, while these five factors are still applicable, where likely relevance is established the balance in most cases will favour production to the accused, as if the record was part of the Crown's file and subject to the *Stinchcombe* disclosure obligation.[215] If any records are produced to the defence, the admissibility of any information contained within them depends on the usual rules of evidence; that is, an order for production is not an order concerning admissibility.

Parliament responded to the decision in *O'Connor* by enacting sections 278.1 through 278.91 of the *Criminal Code*, which replace the *O'Connor* regime for the trial of sexual offences.[216] Although these provisions preserve the two-stage structure from *O'Connor*—establishing likely relevance and balancing interests—the criteria applicable at each stage largely mirror the minority position in *O'Connor* rather than the majority; moreover, the second stage is divided into two: production to the judge and production to the accused. At the first stage, section 278.3(4) appears to impose a significant burden on the accused in establishing likely relevance,[217] as it states that "[a]ny one or more of the following assertions by the accused are not sufficient on their own" to establish likely relevance, and then lists eleven "assertions" that essentially cover all the possible reasons that the accused might have for asserting the relevance of records that he has not seen. At the second stage, the judge is required to balance the relevant interests twice, once in deciding whether to order production to herself, and again in deciding whether to order production to the accused. The test is the same at

---

214 *O'Connor*, above note 55, quoting from para 156 of L'Heureux-Dubé J's reasons but refusing to adopt two additional factors that she would have added: "(6) the extent to which production of records of this nature would frustrate society's interest in encouraging the reporting of sexual offences and the acquisition of treatment by victims; and (7) the effect on the integrity of the trial process of producing, or failing to produce, the record, having in mind the need to maintain consideration in the outcome." See also *McNeil, ibid* at paras 34–35.

215 *McNeil, ibid* at paras 41–42.

216 The specific offences are listed in s 278.2.

217 *McNeil*, above note 144 at paras 30–32.

both steps. Production shall be ordered if "necessary in the interests of justice,"[218] and in making this determination, "the judge shall consider the salutary and deleterious effects of the determination on the accused's right to make a full answer and defence and on the right to privacy and equality of the complainant or witness . . . and any other person to whom the record relates."[219] The factors to be considered include the five recognized by the majority in *O'Connor*, and three more, two of which the majority had specifically rejected: "(*f*) society's interest in encouraging the reporting of sexual offences; (*g*) society's interest in encouraging the obtaining of treatment by complainants of sexual offences; and (*h*) the effect of the determination on the integrity of the trial process."[220] Moreover, the *O'Connor* regime was inapplicable to records already in possession of the·Crown,[221] while section 278.1 does not contain this limitation and applies to records in which third parties have a privacy interest, even if they are already in the Crown's possession.

Since the majority in *O'Connor* had considered all of the constitutional interests at stake and had balanced them to reach what it considered to be the solution mandated by section 7, the argument that the new statutory regime applicable to sexual offences violated section 7 of the *Charter* appeared very strong. Nonetheless, in *R v Mills*,[222] the Supreme Court of Canada held, nearly unanimously,[223] that sections 278.1 through 278.91 of the *Criminal Code* did not offend the principles of fundamental justice. The Court reached this conclusion partly by recognizing that there may be more than one constitutionally sufficient solution to the problem of balancing section 7 interests,[224] and partly by construing the statutory provisions so that their effect on the section 7 right to make full answer and defence was minimal. Section 278.3(4), the "insufficient assertions" provision, was read as preventing the accused from merely "asserting" the matters listed, not as preventing a finding of likely relevance where there was a proper "evidentiary and

---

218 *Criminal Code*, above note 66, ss 278.5(1)(*c*) and 278.7(1).
219 *Ibid*, ss 278.5(2) and 278.7(2).
220 *Ibid*, s 278.5(2), and compare s 278.7(2). Compare also with note 214, above in this chapter.
221 *O'Connor*, above note 55 at para 19.
222 *R v Mills*, [1999] 3 SCR 668 [*Mills*].
223 Lamer CJC, dissenting in part, would have held that the scheme did not apply to records that were in the Crown's possession: *ibid* at paras 1–11.
224 *Ibid* at paras 20–22. This aspect of the decision is emphasized by those who advocate the dialogue theory of the legitimacy of constitutional adjudication: see, for example, Kent Roach, *The Supreme Court on Trial: Judicial Activism or Democratic Dialogue* (Toronto: Irwin Law, 2001) at 277–81.

informational" foundation for one or more of them.[225] Section 278.5(2), listing the factors to be considered in a production order, was read as giving priority to the right to make full answer and defence: "If the judge concludes that it is necessary to examine the documents at issue in order to determine whether they should be produced to make full answer and defence, then production to the judge is necessary in the interests of justice . . . ."[226] Indeed, "it can never be in the interests of justice for an accused to be denied the right to make full answer and defence."[227] And the same principle applies if and when the judge reaches the stage of considering production to the accused.[228]

As a result of *O'Connor* and the statutory response to it, there are two separate procedures for obtaining production of third party records (though the two procedures have much in common). First, where the accused is charged with one of the offences listed in section 278.2 of the *Criminal Code*, the statutory procedure in sections 278.1 through 278.91 applies. Second, where the accused is charged with any other offence, the common law procedure from *O'Connor* applies.

c) Right to Control the Conduct of the Defence

An aspect of the right to make full answer and defence is the accused's right to control the conduct of his defence. This right was recognized and applied in *R v Swain*[229] to limit the Crown's power to introduce evidence of mental disorder against the accused's wishes. But the right to control the conduct of the defence has other aspects as well. Although the proposition has never been tested, it is likely that the right guarantees the accused the right to refuse counsel and to represent herself.[230] The right also has implications where a new trial is ordered following an appeal from conviction or acquittal. In *R v Warsing (Warsing)*,[231] the accused was convicted at trial of two counts of first-degree murder and one count of attempted murder. The British Columbia Court of Appeal allowed his appeal on the basis of fresh evidence that could support a defence of not criminally responsible on account of mental disorder (NCRMD), but ordered that the new trial be restricted to the NCRMD issue; that is, the accused would not be permitted to argue for fac-

---

225 *Mills*, above note 222 at paras 117–20.

226 *Ibid* at para 132.

227 *Ibid* at para 138.

228 *Ibid* at paras 139–41.

229 *R v Swain*, [1991] 1 SCR 933; see discussion in Chapter 4, Section D(3)(c).

230 Compare *Rowbotham*, above note 69 at 63, citing the pre-*Charter* authority of *R v Vescio*, [1949] SCR 139.

231 *R v Warsing*, [1998] 3 SCR 579.

tual innocence on the basis of lack of *mens rea*. The Supreme Court of Canada dismissed the Crown's appeal and allowed the accused's cross-appeal, holding that the new trial could not be limited to the NCRMD issue as that would interfere with the accused's right to control the conduct of the defence: "The accused must be allowed to put forward whatever defence he has."[232] Similarly, in the companion case of *R v Thomas* (*Thomas*),[233] the accused was convicted of murder at trial; on his successful appeal from conviction, the Court of Appeal ordered a new trial limited to the issue of whether the accused had committed murder or manslaughter. The Supreme Court of Canada held that the new trial had to be unrestricted.

It is significant that the accused Warsing neither admitted killing the victims nor tried to plead guilty to a lesser offence; the defence theory at trial was that the offences had been committed by another person. Therefore, *Warsing* may be distinguishable in cases where the accused formally admits some form of liability or involvement in the crime, but contests his liability on the basis of mental disorder. In such cases, the accused's admissions then become part of his trial strategy, which is itself protected by the right to control the conduct of the defence. In those cases, a retrial may be limited to the mental disorder issue because the limit on the retrial does not violate the accused's right to control his own defence. In *R v Luedecke*,[234] for example, the accused was charged with sexual assault; he admitted the acts, but led evidence indicating that he had committed them while in a state of non-mental-disorder automatism. The judge at the first trial accepted this argument and therefore acquitted him. The Crown successfully appealed on the ground that the accused's condition should have been characterized as mental disorder automatism, and a new trial was ordered. The accused took the position that the new trial should be limited to the issue of the proper characterization of the accused's automatism, while the Crown sought an unrestricted new trial. The Court of Appeal accepted the accused's position, reasoning that a restriction on the new trial that was

---

232 *Ibid* at para 74, Major J, Cory, Iacobucci, and Binnie JJ concurring. Lamer CJC and Bastarache J agreed with this ruling, holding that although the appropriate course of action would have been for the Court of Appeal to accept the NCRMD defence and order a disposition hearing, the new trial could not be limited to the NCRMD issue. Justice L'Heureux-Dubé, Gonthier and McLachlin JJ concurring, held that the new trial could be limited to the NCRMD issue.

233 *R v Thomas*, [1998] 3 SCR 535 [*Thomas*].

234 *R v Luedecke*, 2008 ONCA 716.

to the accused's benefit was consistent with his right to control his own defence.[235]

It is, however, unlikely that similar reasoning would apply where the accused conceded liability for a lesser included offence, was convicted of the main offence, and successfully appealed. In *Thomas* itself, at the first trial, defence counsel conceded in his jury address that the accused had killed the victim, effectively admitting his guilt on the included offence; nonetheless, the Supreme Court held that the new trial had to be unrestricted and could not be limited to the issue of murder or manslaughter.[236] The accused could, of course, choose to admit liability for manslaughter at the new trial, as that would be an exercise of his right to control the conduct of his defence.[237]

d) Counsel's Address to the Jury

Section 651 of the *Criminal Code* gives both Crown and defence counsel the right to address the jury, but provides that where the accused has led evidence, defence counsel shall address the jury first, followed by Crown counsel, and that where the accused has not led evidence, Crown counsel shall address the jury first, followed by defence counsel. In other words, the accused has the right that his counsel address the jury last only where she has not led any evidence. In *R v Rose (Rose)*,[238] the accused argued that this provision was inconsistent with the section 7 right to a fair trial because it interfered with the right to make full answer and defence by requiring the accused who has led evidence to address the jury without knowing what Crown counsel would say to them. A 5:4 majority of the Supreme Court of Canada held that the statutory provision did not unfairly interfere with the right to make full answer and defence. The majority reasoned that it was unlikely that, at the end of the trial, defence counsel would not know the Crown's theory of the case and interpretation of the evidence, and that "the Crown's ability to take the defence by surprise is severely curtailed by the restrictions placed on the scope of the Crown's closing address to the jury."[239] If there were any improprieties in the Crown's closing address, the problem could be cured by the trial judge providing a jury instruction or, in the exercise of the court's inherent jurisdiction to ensure a fair trial, allowing defence counsel an opportunity to reply.[240]

---

235 *Ibid* at paras 120–41.

236 *Thomas*, above note 233.

237 See *R v MacDonald*, 2008 ONCA 572; *R v Miljevic*, 2010 ABCA 115.

238 *Rose*, above note 140.

239 *Ibid* at paras 106–7.

240 *Ibid* at paras 124–31.

Although the statute appears to exclude that possibility, four members of the Court reasoned that the inherent jurisdiction to ensure a fair trial could only be removed "by clear and precise statutory language," and that section 651 had not done so.[241] In effect, the Court interpreted the statute as permitting a right of reply where reply would be constitutionally required; *Rose* is in this respect similar to the cases, discussed in Section B(3), above in this chapter, that preserve a trial judge's power to apply the evidentiary balancing principle.

5)   Abuse of Process in Criminal Proceedings

a)   General

The Supreme Court of Canada's two leading decisions on abuse of process in criminal proceedings both involved prosecutions of well-known public figures for historical sexual offences. In neither case did the Court find misconduct by the Crown sufficient to require a stay of proceedings. In *O'Connor*, the accused was a Roman Catholic bishop who was charged with four sexual offences involving four complainants, alleged to have occurred in the 1960s. The Crown was ordered to make disclosure of considerable material, including but not limited to certain records held by third parties involving the complainants,[242] but by the third day of trial, months after the order had been made, disclosure was still incomplete. The trial judge stayed the proceedings. The Supreme Court of Canada lifted the stay. All members of the Court held that the Crown had not discharged its disclosure obligations and described the Crown's conduct with words such as "shoddy and inappropriate,"[243] "extremely high-handed and thoroughly reprehensible,"[244] "inexcusable,"[245] and in violation of "the fundamental principles which underlie the community's sense of fair play and decency."[246] Nonetheless, six of nine judges found that a stay was not an appropriate remedy. Four judges found that a stay was not appropriate because the Crown's conduct had not affected the accused's right to make full answer and defence, while the two who had described the

---

241 *Ibid* at para 133. Justice L'Heureux-Dubé disagreed on this point, holding that the statute did exclude the jurisdiction to permit a reply: *ibid* at para 59.

242 See Section B(4)(b), above in this chapter.

243 *O'Connor*, above note 55 at para 90, L'Heureux-Dubé J, La Forest, and Gonthier JJ concurring; McLachlin J concurred with L'Heureux-Dubé J in separate reasons: *ibid* at para 191.

244 *Ibid* at para 188, Cory and Iacobucci JJ.

245 *Ibid* at para 35, Lamer CJC and Sopinka J dissenting in the result.

246 *Ibid* at para 246, Major J dissenting in the result.

Crown's conduct as "reprehensible" found that "the drastic remedy of a stay" was not warranted.[247]

In *R v Regan*,[248] the accused was a former Premier of Nova Scotia. He was charged with numerous sexual offences alleged to have been committed over many years. The trial judge stayed some of these charges in response to conduct by the Crown and the police that he regarded, cumulatively, as abusive. Specifically, the trial judge found that the Crown had engaged in "judge-shopping," that the Crown had inappropriately interviewed witnesses before charges were laid, and that the RCMP had issued a premature press release regarding the investigation.[249] A closely divided Supreme Court of Canada lifted the stay, finding that there was no abuse of process. The Crown's apparent attempt at judge-shopping was "offensive" but was not acted on and was not determinative of the trial judge's finding of abuse.[250] The involvement of Crown counsel in interviewing witnesses before charges were laid, though it created a risk of blurring the distinct roles of the police and the Crown, was not "*per se* . . . an abuse of process."[251] Finally, the release of the accused's name to the media before charges had been laid "was in contravention of the express policy of law enforcement agencies" and was a "misstep," but was not done in bad faith and was not "egregious."[252] Significantly, the Court held that even if there had been an abuse of process, the remedy of a stay would not have been appropriate because its effects would not have been "manifested or perpetrated if the process continue[d]"[253] and because there were significant societal interests served by a trial on the merits.[254]

In some cases of abuse of process, a remedy less drastic than a stay has been found adequate.[255] In *R v Xenos*,[256] for example, the ac-

---

247   *Ibid* at para 188, Cory and Iacobucci JJ dissenting in the result.
248   *Regan*, above note 62.
249   *Ibid* at para 58.
250   *Ibid* at para 61.
251   *Ibid* at para 91.
252   *Ibid* at paras 92–95.
253   *Ibid* at para 107.
254   *Ibid* at para 116.
255   In *R v Felderhof* (2003), 180 CCC (3d) 498 at para 74 (Ont CA), Rosenberg JA suggests evidentiary remedies less drastic than a stay: exclusion of evidence and admission of otherwise inadmissible evidence. See also *R v C(G)*, 2010 ONSC 115, setting aside the decision of the Attorney General to direct a jury trial as a remedy for an abuse of process.
256   *R v Xenos* (1991), 70 CCC (3d) 362 (Que CA) [*Xenos*]. Subsequent authority suggests that the payment of a witness is not necessarily abuse of process: *R v Dikah* (1994), 89 CCC (3d) 321 (Ont CA), aff'd [1994] 3 SCR 1020.

cused was charged with arson. It emerged in cross-examination of a key Crown witness that the insurers of the destroyed property had agreed to pay the witness $50,000 on condition that the accused was convicted, and that the police were aware of this arrangement. The trial judge, sitting without a jury, said that he would not consider the witness's evidence, and convicted the accused on the remaining evidence. The Court of Appeal held that the calling of this witness in these circumstances was a "clear and manifest abuse,"[257] but held also that the trial judge was correct not to stay the proceedings because there was a less drastic remedy for the abuse: the trial judge should have declared a mistrial and withdrawn from the case.[258] The appropriate remedy on appeal was to order a new trial in which the witness in question would not be heard.[259] In *R v Zarinchang*, systemic problems resulting in an unacceptable delay of the accused's bail hearing was held to fall into the residual category of abuse of process, but a stay was not obviously the appropriate remedy; the trial judge should have balanced the interests in granting a stay against those in a trial on the merits.[260] A modest award of costs was, however, an appropriate remedy.[261]

b) Entrapment

In Canadian law, the defence of entrapment is a specific application of the doctrine of abuse of process.[262] The conviction of persons who have been entrapped into committing offences brings the administration of justice into disrepute.[263] So, where the Crown proceeds against an offender who was entrapped into committing the offence, it would be an abuse of process to punish the offender for that offence; the proceedings are judicially stayed following the finding of guilt and before sentencing.[264] A finding of entrapment is therefore not a defence that negates an element of the offence or that prevents a finding of

---

257 *Xenos, ibid* at 374.

258 The trial judge's reasons for judgment suggested that he had not succeeded in entirely disregarding the witness's evidence. There seems no reason in principle why the abuse would not have been remedied if he had in fact done what he set out to do.

259 *Xenos*, above note 256 at 375. Compare *R v McMillan*, [2003] OJ No 3489 (CA), excluding the evidence of a witness as a remedy for an abuse of process.

260 *Zarinchang*, above note 63 at paras 62–66.

261 *Ibid* at para 71.

262 *R v Mack*, [1988] 2 SCR 903 at 939–40 [*Mack*]; see also *Campbell*, above note 149 at para 21.

263 *Mack, ibid* at 940–42.

264 *Ibid* at 967–77.

culpability;[265] it is rather a finding that, in the circumstances, it would be fundamentally unfair to punish the offender.

To invoke the defence of entrapment, the accused must first be found guilty of the offence. She must then make a motion to the trial judge for a stay of proceedings on the basis of entrapment. On this motion, the burden of proof is on the offender to establish the elements of entrapment on a balance of probabilities. There are two alternative branches to the defence:

(a) the authorities provide a person with an opportunity to commit an offence without acting on a reasonable suspicion that this person is already engaged in criminal activity or pursuant to a *bona fide* inquiry; [or]

(b) although having such a reasonable suspicion or acting in the course of a *bona fide* inquiry, they go beyond providing an opportunity and induce the commission of an offence.[266]

A reasonable suspicion can be based on a variety of factors;[267] however, in contrast to the American approach, the accused's "predisposition" to commit the offence is irrelevant to the defence of entrapment.[268] A *bona fide* inquiry can relate to a defined geographical area where the criminal activity under investigation is likely to occur. In these circumstances, it is not necessary for the authorities to have a reasonable suspicion that the person investigated is engaging in criminal activity (for example, on a city street known to be a location where illegal drugs are bought and sold). It is sufficient that the person is "associated" with that location, for example by passing through it.[269] Situations where the police lack a reasonable suspicion of the person or location in question are sometimes referred to as cases of "random virtue testing," an inappropriate activity for the investigative authorities of a free and democratic society.[270]

The Ontario Court of Appeal has modified the doctrine of entrapment as it applies to the prosecution of certain provincial regulatory offences. In *R v Clothier*, the court considered the use of a "random test shopper," that being an underaged individual who attempts to pur-

---

265 *Ibid* at 942–51.

266 *Ibid* at 964–65; see also 959.

267 *Ibid* at 957–58.

268 *Ibid* at 953–56.

269 *R v Barnes*, [1991] 1 SCR 449 at 463.

270 ". . . the state does not have unlimited power to intrude into our lives or to randomly test the virtue of individuals": *Mack*, above note 262 at 941; see also 956–57.

chase tobacco from a retailer, without any reasonable suspicion that the retailer is not in compliance with provincial smoking laws. The court held that where a violation is discovered through the use of a random test shopper, prosecution of the retailer is not an abuse of process; in other words, in this context, the absence of reasonable suspicion does not result in a finding of entrapment.[271] The court reasoned that the first rationale underlying the doctrine of entrapment—the avoidance of random virtue testing and protection of individual privacy—did not apply where the government was testing compliance in a heavily regulated commercial activity such as selling tobacco.[272] The second rationale—preventing those who would otherwise not be involved in criminal activity from committing offences—also had no application in the context of this regulated activity.[273] These considerations are compelling and will likely apply to strict and absolute liability offences committed in the context of other regulated activities.

6) Procedural Fairness in Sentencing

Sentencing proceedings, like any other criminal proceedings, must be procedurally fair. The provisions of the *Criminal Code* governing sentencing hearings, together with the cases interpreting and applying them, generally provide the required guarantees of procedural fairness, including the opportunity for both parties to lead evidence and to make submissions on the issue of the fit sentence.[274] It is unlikely that section 7 requires any degree of procedural fairness beyond that already provided by the Code, though a generous interpretation of certain provisions may be required to ensure that the section 7 standard of fairness is met. In *R v W(V)*,[275] for example, the Ontario Court of Appeal considered whether a sentencing judge was required to permit the accused to cross-examine the maker of a victim impact statement. The court noted that there was nothing in section 724(3) of the Code, which gives a general right of cross-examination, that excluded cross-examination on victim impact statements; on the other hand, reading section 724(3) as "[c]onferring an automatic or unconstrained right to cross-examine would risk undermining the very purpose of victim impact statements, namely, to give victims a voice in the criminal justice process, to provide a way for victims to confront offenders with the

271 *R v Clothier*, 2011 ONCA 27.
272 *Ibid* at paras 34–40.
273 *Ibid* at para 42.
274 *Criminal Code*, above note 66, ss 720–726.2, and particularly s 723.
275 *R v W(V)*, 2008 ONCA 55.

harm they have caused, and to ensure that courts are informed of the full consequences of the crime."[276] The competing demands of this purposive understanding of victim impact statements and the accused's section 7 right to procedural fairness were reconciled by recognizing a sentencing judge's discretionary power to permit the cross-examination "when satisfied that there is an air of reality to the claim that the facts are in dispute and that the offender's request to cross-examine is not specious or empty."[277]

C. PROCEDURAL FAIRNESS IN EXTRADITION, DEPORTATION, AND REFUGEE PROCEEDINGS

1) Extradition

a) Overview of the Extradition Process

The extradition process begins with a request from an extradition partner (the requesting state) to the Minister of Justice, usually pursuant to the provisions of a treaty between Canada and the extradition partner, that Canada surrender a person (the person sought) to be prosecuted or to serve a sentence in the requesting state. If the Minister is satisfied that the conditions for extradition exist, she may issue an "authority to proceed" that authorizes the Attorney General to seek an order for committal;[278] the Minister may also issue an arrest warrant or a summons.[279]

The extradition process, once set in motion by the authority to proceed, has two phases: the judicial phase and the ministerial phase. The judicial phase requires an extradition hearing before a superior court judge. The judge must decide whether there is "evidence admissible under this Act of conduct that, had it occurred in Canada, would justify committal for trial in Canada"; if so, the judge "shall order the committal of the person into custody to await surrender."[280] The ministerial phase involves the Minister of Justice's decision whether to surrender the person sought, with or without assurances from the requesting state regarding the person's treatment.[281] The Act provides the Min-

---

276 *Ibid* at para 28.
277 *Ibid* at para 30.
278 *Extradition Act*, SC 1999, c 18, s 15(1).
279 *Ibid*, s 16.
280 *Ibid*, s 29(1)(*a*).
281 *Ibid*, s 40.

ister with a number of grounds on which surrender may or must be refused,[282] though some of these grounds are subordinated to certain multilateral agreements.[283]

The judicial committal order is subject to appeal and the ministerial surrender order is subject to judicial review, both in the provincial court of appeal,[284] and the appeal and application are frequently heard together. The grounds of review of the surrender order are imported from section 18.1(4) of the *Federal Courts Act*.[285]

The current *Extradition Act* came into force in 1999; thus, some of the cases discussed below were decided under predecessor statutes that were different in certain respects, notably in respect of the procedures for obtaining review of the committal or the surrender decision. I refer to these predecessor statutes to the extent necessary to make sense of the point under discussion.

As noted in Chapter 2, Section D(3)(c), it was established early in the *Charter* era that section 7 applies throughout the extradition process. Although the *Charter* does not apply to the actions of foreign states, it does apply to the actions of the Canadian government in acting on an extradition request.[286] Indeed, it has been said that "Section 7 permeates the entire extradition process . . . ."[287] The liberty of the person sought is at stake, both in Canada (as he may be detained during the proceedings in Canada) and in the requesting state (as he may be imprisoned if convicted). So the principles of fundamental justice demand a very high level of procedural fairness in extradition proceedings, at both the committal stage and the surrender stage.[288]

b)   The Committal Hearing

The standard for committal for extradition is stated in section 29(1)(*a*) of the *Extradition Act* as follows: the "judge shall order the committal of the person into custody to await surrender if . . . there is evidence admissible under this Act of conduct that, had it occurred in Canada, would justify committal for trial in Canada." The test for committal for trial at a preliminary inquiry in Canada is "whether or not there is any evidence upon which a reasonable jury properly instructed could

---

282 *Ibid*, ss 44, 46, 47.
283 *Ibid*, ss 45, 47.1.
284 *Ibid*, ss 49–57.
285 RSC 1985, c F-7.
286 *Canada v Schmidt*, [1987] 1 SCR 500 at 518–22 [*Schmidt*].
287 *United States v Cobb*, 2001 SCC 19 at para 34 [*Cobb*].
288 *United States v Shulman*, 2001 SCC 21 at para 29 [*Shulman*].

return a verdict of guilty."[289] This test had long been interpreted as preventing an extradition judge (or a judge at a preliminary inquiry) from assessing the reliability of the evidence in any way; the judge's task was simply to decide whether the evidence, if accepted by the trier of fact, would support a conviction. So in a case where there was direct evidence of every element of the offence, no matter how frail, the accused had to be committed for trial or for extradition. In a case where proof of an element rested on circumstantial evidence, the judge should "engage in a limited weighing of the evidence because, with circumstantial evidence, there is, by definition, an inferential gap between the evidence and the matter to be established." This weighing was limited to the question of whether the circumstantial evidence, if believed, could "reasonably support an inference of guilt."[290] But in *United States v Ferras* (*Ferras*),[291] the Supreme Court of Canada held that the principles of fundamental justice required a higher standard in extradition proceedings.

The *Extradition Act* provides a number of methods for putting evidence before the extradition judge. In *Ferras*, the requesting state relied on the "record of the case" method established in sections 32 and 33. The record of the case includes "a document summarizing the evidence available . . . for use in the prosecution."[292] If the requesting state certifies that the evidence "is available for trial," "is sufficient under the law of the [requesting state] to justify prosecution," and "was gathered according to the law of the [requesting state],"[293] then the record of the case is admissible at the extradition hearing.[294] The person sought may also lead evidence that is relevant to the test for committal "if the judge considers it reliable."[295]

McLachlin CJC, speaking for the Court, held that before a person could be extradited from Canada to face trial, there had to be a "meaningful judicial process;" that is, "a judicial determination that the requesting state has established a *prima facie* case that the person sought committed the crime alleged and should stand trial for it."[296] This process in turn required a "separate and independent judicial phase; an impartial judge or magistrate; and a fair and meaningful hearing."[297] So

---

289 *United States v Shephard*, [1977] 2 SCR 1067 at 1080.
290 *R v Arcuri*, 2001 SCC 54 at para 23.
291 *Ferras*, above note 10.
292 *Extradition Act*, above note 278, s 33(1)(*a*).
293 *Ibid*, s 33(3).
294 *Ibid*, s 32(1)(*a*).
295 *Ibid*, s 32(1)(*c*).
296 *Ferras*, above note 10 at para 20.
297 *Ibid* at para 22.

the question was whether the "record of the case" method met these requirements. McLachlin CJC held that it did, but only because she interpreted the *Shephard* test[298] for committal somewhat more rigorously than previously. *United States v Shephard* had been interpreted as requiring the requesting state merely to lead evidence which, if accepted by the trier-of-fact, would support a conviction. On this interpretation, the extradition judge was not permitted to assess the credibility or reliability of the evidence in deciding whether it was sufficient for committal. But this interpretation would violate section 7 of the *Charter*, as it would reduce the extradition judge to a "rubber stamp" and require committal for extradition even where the evidence was so manifestly unreliable that it could not support conviction. The words "justify committal" in section 29(1) could and should be read as incorporating the extradition judge's power to weigh the evidence to a limited degree.[299] Section 29(1) "grant[s] the extradition judge discretion to refuse to extradite on insufficient evidence such as where the reliability of the evidence certified is successfully impeached or where there is no evidence, by certification or otherwise, that the evidence is available for trial."[300]

To meet the requirements of procedural fairness, the judicial phase of the extradition process must also enable the person sought to know the case she has to meet. The person sought is therefore entitled to disclosure of the case made by the requesting state. But the scope of disclosure is limited by the scope of the extradition hearing: the person sought is entitled to disclosure only of (1) the materials relied upon by the requesting state to make its *prima facie* case against him and (2) materials relevant to a *Charter* issue that is properly before the extradition judge and that has an air of reality.[301] This threshold for disclosure is higher than the threshold applicable in criminal proceedings.[302]

The Supreme Court of Canada's leading cases on disclosure in extradition proceedings were decided before *Ferras*; but the British Columbia Court of Appeal has held that the elevated *Ferras* standard

---

298 Above note 289.

299 *Ferras*, above note 10 at para 46.

300 *Ibid* at para 50.

301 *United States v Dynar*, [1997] 2 SCR 462 at 517–19; *United States v Kwok*, 2001 SCC 18 at paras 97–101; *R v Larosa* (2002), 166 CCC (3d) 449 at para 76 (Ont CA).

302 See Section B(4)(a), above in this chapter. For some cases where applications for disclosure were dismissed, see *United States v McAmmond* (2004), 192 CCC (3d) 149 (Ont CA); *United States v Gramah*, 2004 BCSC 1603; *Australia (Commonwealth) v Lau*, 2006 BCCA 484, leave to appeal to SCC refused, [2007] SCCA No 13.

for committal does not enhance the requirements for disclosure.[303] In the court's view, the *Ferras* standard "has more to do with weighing inferences that might be drawn from circumstantial evidence than the weighing of direct evidence."[304] Under the earlier cases, challenges to committal on the ground of inferences drawn from the evidence considered at the committal hearing can be made on the basis of the material already subject to disclosure; consequently, there is no need to expand the duty of disclosure in extradition proceedings. This holding seems inconsistent with the clear intent in *Ferras* to give the extradition judge authority to refuse committal "where the reliability of the evidence certified is successfully impeached."[305] If the extradition judge has this power, the person sought should be able to obtain disclosure of information relevant to the reliability of a case certified under sections 32 and 33 of the *Extradition Act*.

c) The Surrender Decision

The Minister's decision to surrender the person sought, a highly discretionary executive act, is subject to *Charter* scrutiny.[306] Section 44(1) of the *Extradition Act* provides that the Minister must not surrender the person sought when "(a) the surrender would be unjust or oppressive having regard to all the relevant circumstances; or (b) [when] the request for extradition is made for the purpose of prosecuting or punishing the person by reason of their race, religion, nationality, ethnic origin, language, colour, political opinion, sex, sexual orientation, age, mental or physical disability or status or that the person's position may be prejudiced for any of those reasons." At the same time, since the surrender decision is subject to section 7, it must comply with the principles of fundamental justice. Surrender fails to do so where extradition would "shock the conscience"[307] or would expose the person sought to a situation that is "simply unacceptable."[308] Surrender in the circum-

---

303 *United States v Rosenau*, 2010 BCCA 461.

304 *Ibid* at para 53.

305 *Ferras*, above note 10 at para 50.

306 *Schmidt*, above note 286 at 521–22; *Lake v Canada (Minister of Justice)*, 2008 SCC 23 [*Lake*].

307 *Lake*, *ibid* at para 31; *Schmidt*, *ibid* at 522. In *United States v Burns*, 2001 SCC 7, it was held that shocking the conscience was not the test for a violation of s 7 but a way of describing a situation that violated s 7 on other grounds: "An extradition that violates the principles of fundamental justice will *always* shock the conscience" (para 68 [emphasis added]). However, *Lake* appears to have restored the earlier holding that the test for a violation is whether extradition would shock the conscience.

308 *United States v Allard*, [1987] 1 SCR 564 at 572.

stances mentioned in section 44(1) would be contrary to the principles of fundamental justice, and to that extent the provisions of the *Extradition Act* overlap with the requirements of section 7.[309] Given the broad language of section 44(1) and the principle that statutes should be interpreted in a manner that respects *Charter* values, most of the cases in which the principles of fundamental justice would require the Minister to refuse surrender are captured by section 44(1); but if any such cases did not fall under section 44(1), surrender would have to be refused under section 7.

Although the surrender decision engages the *Charter* rights of the person sought, the Minister's surrender decision is reviewable not on the standard of correctness but on the standard of reasonableness. This deferential standard of review is supported by the Minister's expertise in matters of international relations and by the discretionary nature of the surrender decision.[310] Thus, regardless of whether the Minister is applying the statutory "unjust or oppressive" standard or the constitutional "shock the conscience" standard, her decision will stand provided that it "falls within a range of reasonable outcomes" or amounts to "a defensible conclusion" based on the facts of the case.[311]

Although the person sought is not entitled to an oral hearing before the Minister, he is entitled to a fair process, which in this context requires that he have an opportunity to make written submissions to the Minister, and requires the Minister to respond to these submissions, to explain why she disagrees with them, and to give the person sought reasons for her decision.[312]

Under the current *Extradition Act* and its predecessors, the Minister of Justice plays several roles in the extradition process. She receives the extradition request from the foreign state, authorizes the proceedings in Canada, and (in her capacity as Attorney General) has carriage of the requesting state's case in the committal hearing. If the person sought is committed for extradition, the Minister then decides whether to order surrender. In *Idziak v Canada (Minister of Justice)* (*Idziak*),[313]

---

309 *Lake*, above note 306 at para 24; *Németh v Canada (Justice)*, 2010 SCC 56 at para 71 [*Németh*]. Compare *United States of Mexico v Hurley* (1997), 35 OR (3d) 481 (CA).

310 *Lake*, ibid at paras 34–38.

311 *Ibid* at para 41.

312 *Ibid* at para 25; *United States v Taylor*, 2003 BCCA 250 (Minister required to respond to submissions of person sought). The requirement to give reasons is an instance of the general administrative law duty to give reasons established in *Baker*, above note 5, where no *Charter* claim was raised.

313 *Idziak v Canada (Minister of Justice)*, [1992] 3 SCR 631.

the Supreme Court of Canada held that these multiple roles created no institutional bias and did not render the extradition process unfair. Cory J commented:

> . . . the decision to issue a warrant of surrender involves completely different considerations from those reached by a court in an extradition hearing. The extradition hearing is clearly judicial in its nature while the actions of the Minister of Justice in considering whether to issue a warrant of surrender are primarily political in nature. This is certainly not a case of a single official's acting as both judge and prosecutor in the same case. At the judicial phase the fugitive possesses the full panoply of procedural protection available in a court of law. At the ministerial phase, there is no longer a *lis* in existence. The fugitive has by then been judicially committed for extradition. The Act simply grants to the Minister a discretion as to whether to execute the judicially approved extradition by issuing a warrant of surrender.[314]

The Minister's exercise of discretion must, however, comply with the principles of fundamental justice, and in particular must be procedurally fair.

On the facts of *Idziak* itself, the Minister had made his decision based in part on a confidential memorandum "prepared by staff counsel." The person sought did not learn of the existence of this memorandum until after the surrender decision had been made. The Supreme Court held that the failure to disclose the memorandum was not contrary to the Minister's duty of procedural fairness because the memorandum was protected by solicitor-client privilege.[315] This holding is consistent with subsequent authority from the Supreme Court of Canada holding that a government actor's duty of fairness does not require disclosure of material protected by solicitor-client privilege[316] and with the more general proposition that solicitor-client privilege is itself probably a principle of fundamental justice (see Section A(3), above in this chapter).

Where the person sought has been granted refugee status in Canada, section 7 requires the Minister of Justice to consult with the Minister of Citizenship and Immigration.[317] Where the person sought has claimed but not been granted refugee status, section 40(2) of the *Extradition Act* requires the Minister of Justice to consult with the Minister of Citizenship and Immigration; it is likely that this consultation would in any event be required by the Minister of Justice's duty of fair-

---

314 *Ibid* at 659–60.
315 *Ibid* at 663.
316 *Pritchard*, above note 39.
317 *Németh*, above note 309 at para 66.

ness in the surrender decision.[318] The purpose of such a consultation is for the Minister of Justice to be informed of the nature of the refugee claim and to take that claim into account when balancing the section 7 interests of the person sought against the reasons supporting surrender.

d) Abuse of Process in Extradition Proceedings

Extradition proceedings that amount to an abuse of process, on the standard discussed in Section B(5), above in this chapter, are contrary to the principles of fundamental justice. The focus will often be on the conduct of the requesting state, rather than the conduct of Canadian authorities. As in criminal proceedings, the remedy of a stay of proceedings is available only in the clearest of cases when there is no other way to cure the abuse.

The Supreme Court of Canada recognized the possibility of a stay of proceedings for abuse of process, and indeed granted a stay, in *United States v Cobb*.[319] The United States sought the extradition of two persons for fraud-related offences. They argued that American authorities had threatened them if they did not voluntarily submit to extradition and otherwise co-operate with the investigation of the fraud. Specifically, the trial judge sentencing another person involved in the scheme had stated that anyone who did not co-operate and submit to extradition was "going to get the absolute maximum jail sentence that the law permits me to give,"[320] and the prosecutor who was the principal affiant in the extradition proceedings had stated in a television interview shortly before the committal hearing that the accused would "be the boyfriend of a very bad man if you wait out your extradition."[321] The extradition judge stayed the proceedings on the ground that these threats from a judge and a prosecutor shocked the conscience of Canadians and were "simply not acceptable."[322] The Supreme Court of Canada upheld the stay. The Court commented on the behaviour of the requesting state as follows:

> Both statements, or at the very least the prosecutor's statement, were an attempt to influence the unfolding of the Canadian judicial proceedings by putting undue pressure on the [persons sought] to desist from their objections to the extradition request. The pressure were not only inappropriate but also, in the case of the statements made

---

318 Compare *ibid* at para 70.

319 *Cobb*, above note 287.

320 Quoted *ibid* at para 7 [emphasis removed].

321 *Ibid* at para 8.

322 *Ibid* at para 14.

by the prosecutor on the eve of the opening of the judicial proceeding in Canada, unequivocally amounted to an abuse of the process of the court. We do not condone the treat of sexual violence as a means for one party before the court to persuade any opponent to abandon his or her right to a hearing. Nor should we expect litigants to overcome well-founded fears of violent reprisals in order to be participants in a judicial process.[323]

In *United States v Khadr*,[324] the person sought, a Canadian citizen, had been secretly and illegally detained in Pakistan for fourteen months and mistreated by Pakistani authorities. The requesting state, the United States of America, encouraged Pakistan to deny the person sought his consular right and to delay his repatriation to Canada, so that he could be interrogated by American intelligence officials. The extradition judge found that the requesting state had committed "serious misconduct"[325] to obtain the evidence that it offered at the committal hearing, and that the court had to dissociate itself from this "gross misconduct" by means of a stay of proceedings.[326]

In cases such as these, the conduct of the government of Canada is not at issue, except to the extent that lawyers from the federal Department of Justice represent the requesting state; rather, it is the conduct of the requesting state, as a party to the extradition proceedings, that is examined. If the conduct of the requesting state meets the high standard necessary to make the proceedings an abuse of process, then the proceedings will be stayed so that the Canadian justice system does not contribute to the perpetuation of the abuse.

2) Deportation

The Supreme Court of Canada has held that deportation in itself does not engage life, liberty, and security of the person; consequently, deportation as such does not have to comply with the principles of fun-

---

323 *Ibid* at para 43. See also *United States v Tsioubris*, 2001 SCC 20; *Shulman*, above note 288. In *Shulman*, on a slightly different factual record, the court held that the judge's comments would not by themselves have justified a stay of proceedings.

324 *United States v Khadr*, 2010 ONSC 4338, aff'd 2011 ONCA 358, leave to appeal to SCC refused, 2011 CanLII 69662 [*Khadr*].

325 *Ibid* at para 133.

326 *Ibid* at paras 150–51. Compare *United States v Tollman* (2006), 212 CCC (3d) 511 (Ont SCJ), where the requesting state sought to avoid Canadian extradition proceedings entirely by arranging for the deportation of the person sought from Canada. Though less egregious than in *Khadr*, this conduct justified a stay of the extradition proceedings.

damental justice.[327] But aspects of deportation proceedings, such as detention incidental to deportation, do engage section 7, and if so, the process must be procedurally fair. *Charkaoui*, discussed in Section A(2), above in this chapter, provides an example. *Chiarelli v Canada (Minister of Employment and Immigration)* (*Chiarelli*),[328] where the Court assumed without deciding that deportation did engage section 7, provides another. An immigration adjudicator made a deportation order against the applicant, who was a permanent resident, on the ground of serious criminality. The applicant appealed to the Immigration Appeal Board; his appeal was adjourned after the Solicitor General and the Minister of Employment and Immigration reported to the Security Intelligence Review Committee that there were reasonable grounds to believe that the applicant would be involved in organized crime. The committee then held a hearing. On the first day, the committee heard evidence *in camera* from two RCMP officers. The applicant received a summary of this evidence and an opportunity to cross-examine the officers. He did not cross-examine or lead any other evidence, but did make written submissions. The committee then reported to the Cabinet that the applicant was indeed a person whom there were reasonable grounds to believe would be involved in organized crime, and the Cabinet directed the Minister to issue a certificate to that effect. The effect of this certificate was that the applicant was deprived of the possibility of a successful appeal under the very open-ended and discretionary section 72(1)(*b*) of the *Immigration Act* as it then read; however, he retained the usual right of appeal on grounds of fact and law under section 72(1)(*a*).[329] The Supreme Court found no denial of the right to procedural fairness in this process. Assuming without deciding that the principles of fundamental justice required the usual right of appeal under section 72(1)(*b*), there was no principle of fundamental justice requiring "a compassionate appeal" or "an appeal on wider grounds."[330] The proceedings before the review committee were sufficiently fair because the applicant knew "the substance of the allegations against him" even if he did not know all the "details of the criminal intelligence investigation techniques or the police sources used to acquire that information."[331]

Charkaoui may suggest that the procedure sanctioned in *Chiarelli* is no longer adequate to comply with the principles of fundamental

---

327   *Medovarski v Canada (Minister of Citizenship and Immigration)*, 2005 SCC 51; see also Chapter 2, Section D(3)(g)(i).

328   *Chiarelli v Canada (Minister of Employment and Immigration)*, [1992] 1 SCR 711.

329   *Ibid* at 723–26.

330   *Ibid* at 739 and 742.

331   *Ibid* at 746.

justice, and in particular that providing the applicant with a summary of the evidence does not satisfy the requirements of a fair hearing as outlined in *Charkaoui*: perhaps a special advocate, or some equivalent procedure, is now required. It must be borne in mind that the Court has subsequently held that section 7 does not even apply in a case like *Chiarelli*, where the government seeks merely to deport the applicant without first detaining him. However, if the interest at stake both engaged section 7 and was as compelling as in *Charkaoui*, it does appear that the procedure found in *Chiarelli* to be fair enough for constitutional purposes might no longer be so.

3) Determination of Refugee Claims

a) Procedural Fairness
Singh v Canada (Minister of Employment and Immigration) (*Singh*),[332] one of the foundational section 7 cases, concerned the process for determining claims for refugee status by persons who would otherwise be removable from Canada. In accordance with the Refugee Convention,[333] federal law defines a "Convention refugee" as a person who, "by reason of a well-founded fear of persecution" on stated grounds was unable to return to her country of nationality or of habitual residence.[334] The procedure for determining whether a person was a Convention refugee was as follows. A person asserting that he was a refugee was examined under oath by a senior immigration officer. The transcript of the examination was sent to the Minister of Employment and Immigration, who in turn referred it to the Refugee Status Advisory Committee. The Minister, having received the advice of the committee, then decided whether the claimant was a refugee.[335] The Supreme Court commented that the committee "acts as a decision-making body isolated from the persons whose status it is adjudicating and it applies policies and makes use of information to which the refugee claimants themselves have no access."[336] The claimant could apply within fifteen days to the Immigration Appeal Board for a redetermination of the Minister's decision; however, the board would consider the application only if there were reasonable grounds to believe that the claim could succeed. If so, the Minister was entitled to notice of the hearing and to an opportun-

---

332 *Singh*, above note 1.

333 *Convention Relating to the Status of Refugees*, Can TS 1969 No 6.

334 *Immigration Act, 1976*, SC 1976-77, c 52, s 2(1), definition of "Convention refugee"; compare *IRPA*, above note 12, s 96.

335 *Immigration Act, 1976*, ibid, s 45.

336 *Singh*, above note 1 at 197.

ity to be heard.[337] As a result, the refugee claimant had to make her submissions to the board "without any knowledge of the Minister's case beyond the rudimentary reasons which the Minister has decided to give him in rejecting his claim."[338]

The Supreme Court held that these procedures did not comply with the principles of fundamental justice. In particular, the inability of the claimant to know and to challenge the Minister's reasons for rejecting his claim infringed section 7. The board was required to apply a high standard in deciding whether to hold a redetermination hearing at all, and even if a hearing was held, the claimant had to present his or her case with minimal knowledge of the reasons for the Minister's decision. Thus, "an application will usually be rejected before the refugee claimant has had an opportunity to discover the Minister's case against him in the context of a hearing. Indeed . . . , I find it difficult to see how a successful challenge to the accuracy of the undisclosed information upon which the Minister's decision is based could ever be launched."[339] In short, the procedures leading up to a possible hearing fell well short of the requirements of a fair hearing discussed above. In particular, the requirement that the person affected be informed of the case against him was not met.

After *Singh*, the *Immigration Act* was substantially amended to provide for the kind of hearing that the Court had found lacking. However, while the *Immigration and Refugee Protection Act* continues to provide that the Refugee Protection Division must hold a hearing to determine a refugee claim from an eligible claimant,[340] it also identifies a number of circumstances in which a refugee claimant is not eligible for a hearing before that division.[341] To the extent that they have been challenged, these aspects of *IRPA* have survived constitutional scrutiny.[342]

Recent amendments to the statute may raise an issue as to the independence of the Refugee Protection Division's members, one of the requirements of a fair process according to *Charkaoui*. Under section 153(1) of *IRPA* as it stands, members of the Refugee Protection Division

---

337   *Immigration Act, 1976*, above note 334 at s 71.

338   *Singh*, above note 1 at 215.

339   *Ibid* at 216.

340   *IRPA*, above note 12, s 170(*b*); the only exception is where the Minister has not indicated an intention to intervene, in which case the claim may be allowed without a hearing: s 170(*f*).

341   *Ibid*, ss 100 & 101.

342   See, for example, *Canadian Council for Refugees v Canada*, 2008 FCA 229 where the court did not reach the merits of the applicant's claim that the designation of the United States of America as a "safe third country" from which a refugee claim could not be made violated s 7 of the *Charter*.

and the two appeal divisions are appointed "during good behaviour" for seven years and can only be removed for cause. However, under amendments to come into force in 2012, members of the division will be appointed "in accordance with the *Public Service Employment Act*;"[343] that is, they will be federal civil servants and will be removable for whatever reasons and according to whatever procedure a civil servant can be removed. The constitutional question will be whether this change, which undoubtedly reduces the security of tenure of members of the division, will make those members insufficiently independent of the government to provide a fair hearing where the section 7 interests of the refugee claimant are at stake.

b) Deportation to Torture

As noted in Chapter 2, Section B(3), in *Suresh*, the Supreme Court of Canada has left open the possibility that Canada might deport (refoule) a refugee to face torture in his home country. The applicant Suresh was a Sri Lankan national who had been granted refugee status in Canada. The Minister of Citizenship and Immigration sought to deport him on grounds of terrorism and danger to the security of Canada. In the resulting deportation proceedings, the applicant argued that he would face a risk of death or torture if he were returned to Sri Lanka; in effect, he reiterated the grounds on which he had been found to be a refugee. The Minister issued a "danger opinion,"[344] which meant that the applicant was deemed to be a danger to the security of Canada and could be removed to Sri Lanka even though he had been determined to be a refugee; that is, even if his "life or freedom would be threatened" on his return.

The applicant sought judicial review of the Minister's decision to issue the danger opinion. He argued that the Act was unconstitutional to the extent that it permitted deportation to torture. The Court rejected the argument on the ground that the statute did not authorize violations of the relevant constitutional principles, and described the applicable constitutional norm as follows:

> . . . torture is so abhorrent that it will almost always be disproportionate to interests on the other side of the balance, even security interests. This suggests that, barring extraordinary circumstances,

---

343 *Balanced Refugee Reform Act*, SC 2010, c 8, s 26, adding s 169.1 to *IRPA*; this amendment will come into force on 9 June 2012, or earlier: *Balanced Refugee Reform Act*, s 42.

344 Pursuant to s 53(1)(*b*) of the then *Immigration Act*, RSC 1985, c I-2.

deportation to torture will generally violate the principles of fundamental justice protected by s. 7 of the *Charter*.[345]

In making the decision under section 53(1)(b), the Minister was required to choose procedures that met the following criteria: the person
facing deportation had to be informed of the case to meet[346] and had
to be given an opportunity to respond to that case (including an opportunity to challenge the information available to the Minister and
to challenge any assurances provided by the state to which the person
would be deported),[347] and the Minister had to provide written reasons
for the decision.[348] In short:

> If the refugee establishes that torture is a real possibility, the Minister
> must provide the refugee with all the relevant information and advice
> she intends to rely on, provide the refugee an opportunity to address
> that evidence in writing, and after considering all the relevant infor-
> mation, issue responsive written reasons.[349]

None of these procedures was expressly required by the *Immigration
Act* itself; they were imposed by the Court to ensure that the Minister's
decision would respect the principles of fundamental justice both substantively and procedurally.

What is troubling about *Suresh* is not the content of the duty of fairness imposed by the Court; it is whether it can ever be fundamentally
just to deport someone to face torture. Moreover, as the Court recognized in the *Motor Vehicle Reference*,[350] the principles of fundamental
justice are not exhausted by principles of procedural fairness: they include substantive principles as well. In other words, the problem in
Suresh is one of substantive rather than procedural justice. As argued in
Chapter 3, Section B(4)(b)(i), the Court should recognize a right against
deportation to torture under section 7 of the *Charter*, either as a principle of fundamental justice in its own right, or through the doctrine of
per se gross disproportionality.[351] Torture has such a severe impact on
security of the person that no state interest could be proportionate to it.

---

345   *Suresh*, above note 6 at para 76; compare para 78.
346   *Ibid* at para 122.
347   *Ibid* at paras 124–25.
348   *Ibid* at para 126.
349   *Ibid* at para 127.
350   *Re BC Motor Vehicle Act*, [1985] 2 SCR 486 (more commonly known as the *Mo-
      tor Vehicle Reference*): for further discussion, see Chapter 3, Section B(1).
351   See Chapter 4, Section B(4).

D. OTHER PROCEEDINGS

As discussed in Chapter 2, section 7 applies whenever state action affects an individual's life, liberty, or security; consequently, it applies to any proceedings where those interests are at stake. Most tribunals making decisions that affect life, liberty, and security of the person are in any event required to adhere to the principles of natural justice by virtue of either their enabling statutes or administrative law (or both), and outside penal and refugee law, situations where section 7 has added anything to the common law duty of procedural fairness are fairly rare. However, one such case should be noted here.

In *New Brunswick (Minister of Health and Community Services) v G(J)* (*G(J)*),[352] the Supreme Court of Canada somewhat surprisingly recognized a section 7 right to state-funded counsel in a non-penal context. The applicant, a mother of three children, was refused funding from a provincial legal aid plan to contest an application by the province to extend an order removing the children from her custody. Having found that the proceedings engaged her security of the person, the Court said that the principles of fundamental justice required her to have counsel in light of three factors specific to the circumstances: "the seriousness of the interests at stake, the complexity of the proceedings, and the capacities of the [applicant]."[353] Thus, *G(J)* does not support a right to state-funded counsel in all child-protection proceedings, or in all proceedings where the section 7 interests are engaged;[354] like the right to state-funded counsel in criminal matters,[355] the right to state-funded counsel in child protection proceedings is case-specific, arising where necessary to ensure procedural fairness.

---

352   *New Brunswick (Minister of Health and Community Services) v G(J)*, [1999] 3 SCR 46, 177 DLR (4th) 124.
353   *Ibid* at para 75.
354   See *Canadian Bar Association v British Columbia*, 2008 BCCA 92 at para 49.
355   See Section B(1), above in this chapter.

FURTHER READINGS

CAMERON, JAMIE, ED. *The Charter's Impact on the Criminal Justice System* (Scarborough, ON: Carswell, 1996).

CARTIER, GENEVIÈVE ."The *Baker* Effect: A New Interface between the *Canadian Charter of Rights and Freedoms* and Administrative Law: The Case of Discretion" in David Dyzenhaus, ed, *The Unity of Public Law* (Oxford: Hart, 2004) 61.

CODE, MICHAEL. "Problems of Process in Litigating Claims of Privilege under the Flexible Wigmore Model" in The Law Society of Upper Canada, *Special Lectures 2003: The Law of Evidence* (Toronto: Irwin Law, 2004) 251.

HUDSON, GRAHAM. "The Administration of Justice? Certificate Proceedings, *Charkaoui II*, and the Value of Disclosure" (2010) 48 Alta L Rev 195.

JENKINS, DAVID. "Rethinking *Suresh*: Refoulement to Torture under Canada's *Canadian Charter of Rights and Freedoms*" (2009) 47 Alta L Rev 125.

MULLAN, DAVID. "Deference from *Baker* to *Suresh* and Beyond: Interpreting the Conflicting Signals" in David Dyzenhaus, ed, *The Unity of Public Law* (Oxford: Hart, 2004) 21.

ROACH, KENT. "The Protection of Innocence under Section 7 of the *Charter*" (2006) 34 Sup Ct L Rev (2d) 249.

———. "Must We Trade Rights for Security? The Choice between Smart, Harsh, or Proportionate Security Strategies in Canada and Britain" (2006) 27 Cardozo L Rev 2151.

———. "Unreliable Evidence and Wrongful Convictions: The Case for Excluding Tainted Identification Evidence and Jailhouse and Coerced Confessions" (2007) 52 Crim LQ 210.

STEWART, HAMISH. "Section 7 of the *Charter* and the Common Law Rules of Evidence" (2008) 40 Sup Ct L Rev (2d) 415.

STUART, DON. *Charter Justice in Canadian Criminal Law*, 4th ed (Toronto: Thomson Carswell, 2005) ch 2.

STRATAS, DAVID. "The Law of Evidence and the *Charter*" in The Law Society of Upper Canada, *Special Lectures 2003: The Law of Evidence* (Toronto: Irwin Law, 2004) 277.

CHAPTER 6

JUSTIFYING INFRINGEMENTS OF SECTION 7

A. INTRODUCTION

Section 1 of the *Canadian Charter of Rights and Freedoms* reads as follows:

> The *Canadian Charter of Rights and Freedoms* guarantees the rights and freedoms set out in it subject only to such reasonable limits prescribed by law as can be demonstrably justified in a free and democratic society.[1]

The double character of section 1 has often been noted: it guarantees *Charter* rights and it provides a criterion for limiting them.[2]

Section 1 refers to "limits" on *Charter* rights. This language might suggest that some violations of *Charter* rights could not be justified because they went beyond merely "limiting" a given right to denying it altogether.[3] Or it might suggest that section 1 helps to define rights by specifying their "limits."[4] But the Supreme Court of Canada has not adopted either of these approaches. The Court has never rejected

---

1 Canadian Charter of Rights and Freedoms, Part I of the Constitution Act, 1982, being Schedule B to the Canada Act 1982 (UK), 1982, c 11, s 1 [Charter].

2 *R v Oakes*, [1986] 1 SCR 103 at 135 [*Oakes*].

3 See, for instance, *R v Morgentaler*, [1988] 1 SCR 30 at 183 [*Morgentaler*], Wilson J; *R v Sharpe*, 1999 BCCA 416 at paras 93–94 (BCCA), Southin JA, rev'd 2001 SCC 2.

4 Grégoire Webber, « La disposition limitative de la Charte canadienne : une invitation à définir les droits et libertés aux contours indéterminés » in LB Trem-

a section 1 argument on the ground that the violation of the right in question was so severe that it did not count as a limit. And, although the effect of a successful section 1 justification is in effect to redraw the boundaries of a right, the Court has consistently treated section 1 arguments as justifications for infringements of rights rather than as definitions of the boundaries of rights. Rather than drawing a linguistic distinction between justifiable or definitional "limits" and unjustifiable "violations," the Court has considered how the criteria for justification under section 1 apply to each infringement of a *Charter* right. An egregious infringement of a *Charter* right is and should be very difficult to justify under section 1, but that is because of the way the criteria for justification apply to the infringement, not because of its description as an "infringement" rather than as a "limit" or "boundary."

B. THE TEST FOR JUSTIFICATION UNDER SECTION 1

The test for whether a legal limit on a *Charter* right is "reasonable" and "demonstrably justified in a free and democratic society" is laid out in several steps by the well-known *Oakes* test.[5] The limit on a right must:

- be "prescribed by law";[6]
- have an objective relating to "concerns which are pressing and substantial in a free and democratic society";[7] and
- meet a three-part test for proportionality requiring that the limit
  - "be rationally connected to the objective";[8]
  - impair the right as little as reasonably possible;[9] and
  - have a salutary effect on the objective that is not outweighed by its deleterious effects on the right.[10]

Every element of this test has been considerably elaborated in the cases following *Oakes*. In this chapter, I make no attempt to trace these developments in detail; instead, I discuss each element of the *Oakes* test

---

blay & Grégoire Webber, eds, *The Limitation of Charter Rights: Critical Essays on R v Oakes* (Montréal: Thémis, 2009).

5   *Oakes*, above note 2.

6   *Charter*, above note 1, s 1; *Alberta v Hutterian Brethren of Wilson Colony*, 2009 SCC 37 at paras 39–40 [*Hutterian Brethren*].

7   *Oakes*, above note 2 at 138–39.

8   *Ibid* at 139.

9   *Ibid*.

10   *Ibid* at 139–40.

with reference to a number of efforts to justify a limit on the section 7 right.

C. SECTION 7 AND SECTION 1

1) The Threshold for Limiting a Section 7 Right

To show a violation of section 7, the *Charter* applicant has to demonstrate that his most basic interests (life, liberty, and security of the person) have been affected in a manner that is not fundamentally just. This is a significant burden, so when it is met, a significant violation of a person's rights has been established. For this reason, Wilson J took the view that a violation of the right to life, liberty, and security of the person that was not in accordance with the principles of fundamental justice could never be justified under section 1:

> If . . . the limit on the s. 7 right [to life, liberty, and security of the person] has been effected through a violation of the principles of fundamental justice, . . . the limit cannot be sustained under s. 1. I say this because I do not believe that a limit on the s. 7 right which has been imposed in violation of the principles of fundamental justice can be either "reasonable" or "demonstrably justified in a free and democratic society."[11]

Wilson J's view has never been accepted by a majority of the Court: the rights guaranteed by section 7 of the *Charter*, like all *Charter* rights, are in principle subject to limitation under section 1. But, remarkably, a majority of the Supreme Court of Canada has never found an infringement of the section 7 right to be justified under section 1.[12] The Court has often expressly stated that infringements of section 7 rights are very difficult to justify under section 1. This position, though less extreme than Wilson J's view, reflects the same underlying considerations.

---

11   *Re BC Motor Vehicle Act*, [1985] 2 SCR 486 at 523 [*Motor Vehicle Reference*].

12   There are only two cases in which individual judges of the Supreme Court of Canada have found clear violations of s 7 but would have upheld those violations under s 1: *R v Penno*, [1990] 2 SCR 865 at 881–85 [*Penno*], Lamer CJC concurring in the result; *R v Hess; R v Nguyen*, [1990] 2 SCR 906 at 950–51 [*Hess; Nguyen*], McLachlin J dissenting. There are also cases where judges have found no s 7 violation but would, in the alternative, have upheld the violation under s 1: see, for example, *R v Seaboyer; R v Gayme*, [1991] 2 SCR 577 at 702–12 [*Seaboyer*], L'Heureux-Dubé J dissenting.

As Lamer CJC put it, there are two reasons why a limit on the section 7 right is very difficult to justify:

> First, the rights protected by s. 7 — life, liberty, and security of the person — are very significant and cannot ordinarily be overridden by competing social interests. Second, rarely will a violation of the principles of fundamental justice, specifically the right to a fair hearing, be upheld as a reasonable limit demonstrably justified in a free and democratic society.[13]

Thus, the threshold for justifiably limiting a section 7 right is higher than the threshold for justifiably limiting other *Charter* rights, in the sense that some special or unusual circumstances would be required. In *Re BC Motor Vehicle Act* (*Motor Vehicle Reference*), Lamer J commented that "administrative expediency" as a justification for a violation of section 7 might succeed, "but only in cases arising out of exceptional conditions, such as natural disasters, the outbreak of war, epidemics and the like."[14] Similarly, in *R v Ruzic* (*Ruzic*), a unanimous Court commented that "exceptional circumstances, such as the outbreak of war or a national emergency, are necessary before such an infringement may be justified."[15]

R v Mills (*Mills*)[16] is sometimes read as retreating from the stringent threshold in the *Motor Vehicle Reference*. The majority in *Mills*, after drawing the familiar contrast between the section 7 definition of a *Charter* right and the section 1 justification of a limit on that right, commented that the "interests to be balanced" in the justification of a limit under section 1 were "broader in nature" than the interests balanced in the definition of the right under section 7.[17] The section 1 interests could include "respect for the inherent dignity of the human person, commitment to social justice and equality, accommodation of a wide variety of beliefs, respect for cultural and group identity, and faith in social and political institutions which enhance the participation of individuals and groups in society,"[18] and went beyond "the guarantees enumerated in the *Charter*."[19] These comments suggest that a wide range of considerations, falling well short of war or national emer-

---

13 *New Brunswick* (*Minister of Health and Community Services*) *v G(J)*, [1999] 3 SCR 46 at para 99.

14 *Motor Vehicle Reference*, above note 11 at 518.

15 *R v Ruzic*, 2001 SCC 24 at para 92 [*Ruzic*].

16 *R v Mills*, [1999] 3 SCR 668.

17 *Ibid* at para 67.

18 *Ibid*, quoting from *Oakes*, above note 2 at 136.

19 *Ibid*, quoting from *R v Keegstra*, [1990] 3 SCR 697 at 737.

gency, might justify an infringement of section 1.[20] However, in *Mills* the Court found that the statute at issue did not violate section 7 and so did not have to consider a proposed section 1 justification,[21] whereas in the *Motor Vehicle Reference* and *Ruzic* the section 1 justification was in issue. For that reason, it would be unwise to read too much into these comments from *Mills*.

Regardless of precisely how *Mills* is read in relation to the *Motor Vehicle Reference* and *Ruzic*, the Court's general reluctance to find justifications for violations of section 7 probably does indicate that some special or unusual circumstances would be required as a threshold matter. Thus in *Re Charkaoui* (*Charkaoui*),[22] McLachlin CJC, speaking for a unanimous Court, commented on the relationship between section 7 and section 1 as follows:

> The rights protected by s. 7—life, liberty and security of the person—are basic to our conception of a free and democratic society, and hence are not easily overridden by competing social interest. It follows that violations of the principles of fundamental justice . . . are difficult to justify under s. 1 . . . . Nevertheless, the task may not be impossible, particularly in extraordinary circumstances where concerns are grave and the challenges complex.[23]

In *Charkaoui* itself, the government's heightened concerns about international terrorism that followed the terrorist attacks of 11 September 2001 did not move the Court to find a section 1 justification for violations of procedural fairness in dealing with non-citizens suspected of involvement in terrorism.

The difficulty of justifying a limit on the section 7 right under section 1 means that in most section 7 cases, the parties must direct most of their argument and evidence at the questions addressed in Chapters 2 through 5: whether the *Charter* applies; whether life, liberty, or security of the person is engaged; and whether the principles of fundamental justice are violated. Indeed, there are cases where the government has directed all of its arguments to these questions and has made no sub-

---

20   This view may have been anticipated by Lamer CJC's concurrence in *Penno*, above note 12.

21   Lamer CJC, dissenting in part, found that one aspect of the statutory scheme did violate s 7 and was not justified under s 1 because it was not minimally impairing: *ibid* at para 11. He did not say that a war or a national emergency would be required for justification. *Mills* is discussed in more detail in Chapter 5, Section B(4)(b).

22   *Charkaoui v Canada* (*Citizenship and Immigration*), 2007 SCC 9 [*Charkaoui*].

23   *Ibid* at para 66.

missions on the question of whether a violation of section 7, if there is one, is justified.[24]

2) A Limit Prescribed by Law

The requirement that a section 1 limit on a *Charter* right be "prescribed by law" flows not only from the express wording of section 1 itself but also from the general constitutional principle of the rule of law, mentioned in the preamble to the *Charter* and identified as one of the principal or structural principles underlying the Canadian Constitution.[25] Since state officials have only the powers granted to them by law, a limit on a *Charter* right imposed by a state official acting outside her powers cannot be "prescribed by law" for section 1 purposes. Put another way, the infringement of an individual's section 7 rights by a state agent acting without legal authorization cannot be justified *ex post*.

A limit is "prescribed by law" where "it is expressly provided for by statute or regulation, or results by necessary implication from the terms of a statute or regulation or from its operating requirements . . . [or] from the application of a common law rule."[26]

Where a statute, regulation, or bylaw, or a common law rule, violates section 7, the limit on the section 7 right is generally "prescribed by law" for section 1 purposes.[27] But if the law is excessively vague, it does not constitute a limit "prescribed by law" because no-one can govern his conduct with reference to it. The Supreme Court has recognized this possibility, but has never found a law infringing a *Charter* right so vague that it fails to be prescribed by law.[28]

Where state action is not authorized by any statute, subordinate legislation, or common law rule, it is not "prescribed by law" and cannot be justified under section 1. For example, where the applicable statute requires a hearing, and the failure to hold a hearing would violate the principles of fundamental justice, the failure cannot be justified under section 1: since the statute does not permit the tribunal to dis-

---

24   See, for example, *Ruzic*, above note 15 at para 91.

25   *Reference re Secession of Quebec*, [1998] 2 SCR 217 at paras 49–51, 71.

26   *R v Therens*, [1985] 1 SCR 613 at 645; see also *R v Orbanski; R v Elias*, 2005 SCC 37 at paras 34–39 [*Orbanski*].

27   See, among many other cases, *Charkaoui*, above note 22 (statutory scheme violating applicant's s 7 right to procedural fairness); *Irwin Toy Ltd v Quebec (AG)*, [1989] 1 SCR 927 [*Irwin Toy*] (Quebec regulation affecting freedom of expression); *R v Swain*, [1991] 1 SCR 933 [*Swain*] (common law rule infringing applicant's s 7 right to control the conduct of his defence).

28   See, for instance, *Irwin Toy, ibid* at 980–83; *Osborne v Canada (Treasury Board)*, [1991] 2 SCR 69 at 94–96.

pense with the hearing, the failure to hold one is not prescribed by law.[29] This principle is of considerable importance in criminal investigations, where the section 7 interests of accused persons are always engaged because of the potential loss of liberty flowing from a criminal conviction. An investigative technique that infringes section 7 and is not authorized by law cannot be justified under section 1, and any evidence derived from that technique is potentially inadmissible at the accused's trial. For example, it is a principle of fundamental justice that accused persons have a pre-trial right to silence.[30] Where the police infringe this right, by using agents or undercover officers to improperly elicit statements from persons in custody[31] or depriving the accused of an effective choice about speaking to them during an interrogation,[32] the infringement is not authorized by any statute or common law rule and cannot be justified under section 1.[33] Any evidence obtained from the violation, such as a statement or real evidence deriving from the statement, is subject to exclusion at trial under section 24(2) of the *Charter*.[34] However, the law does not have to authorize the state action expressly; there may be cases where a statute can be creatively interpreted so as to authorize a *Charter* violation by necessary implication.[35]

Where a statute grants a state agent a discretion to do something that affects the interests protected by section 7 of the *Charter*, and where the discretion itself is constitutionally valid, the state agent's particular decision or act is not usually considered to be a limit on the section 7 right that is "prescribed by law" and subject to section 1 justification. Rather, the question to be asked is whether the discretion was exercised in accordance with section 7;[36] if not, the decision or act violates section 7 and cannot be justified under section 1.

However, there are cases where courts have considered whether particular discretionary acts that infringe *Charter* rights can be justi-

---

29   *Re T(R)*, 2004 SKQB 503 at para 100.

30   See Chapter 4, Section E(1).

31   As in *R v Hebert*, [1990] 2 SCR 151 [*Hebert*], or *R v Broyles*, [1991] 3 SCR 595.

32   As in *R v Otis* (2000), 151 CCC (3d) 416 (Que CA).

33   *Hebert*, above note 31 at 187.

34   The test for exclusion in s 24(2) is whether "having regard to all the circumstances, the admission of [the evidence] in the proceedings would bring the administration of justice into disrepute." The test was recently reinterpreted in *R v Grant*, 2009 SCC 32.

35   See, for example, *Orbanski*, above note 26, where a highway traffic statute was interpreted as impliedly authorizing a violation of the s 10(*b*) right to counsel when the police administered roadside sobriety tests.

36   See Chapter 2, Section B(3) for further discussion of the Supreme Court's approaches to review of administrative decision making under the *Charter*.

fied under section 1. In *Slaight Communications Inc v Davidson*,[37] for example, a labor arbitrator ordered an employer to write a letter of recommendation, with specified content, for a former employee who had been improperly dismissed, and forbad the employer from responding to requests about the former employee except by sending a copy of the letter. The Supreme Court held that the order limited the employer's freedom of expression. The law empowering the arbitrator to make such an order gave him "an imprecise discretion."[38] One might have thought that a decision made under such a discretion that violated *Charter* rights could not be justified under section 1 on the straightforward basis that the statute did not authorize the decision; however, the Court held that it was necessary to consider whether the particular decision could be justified under section 1. If so, the decision would be upheld because "the [decision maker] had the power to make an order reasonably and justifiably limiting a right or freedom mentioned in the *Charter*"; if not, the decision maker would exceed her jurisdiction.[39] The Court found that the arbitrator's order was justified under section 1. It is difficult to understand how the Court's holding that a statute which "does not confer, either expressly or by necessary implication, the power to limit the rights guaranteed by the *Charter*" can nonetheless give rise to a decision limiting rights that can be justified under section 1.[40]

3) A Pressing and Substantial Objective

To be justifiable under section 1, a limit on a *Charter* right must have an objective that is pressing and substantial in a free and democratic society.

In the vast majority of cases where a *Charter* right is infringed, it is not difficult to identify a pressing and substantial objective. However, it may be the case that some objectives, regardless of how pressing and substantial they appear to the legislature or to the government of the day, are not suitable for a free and democratic society and so cannot justify a limit on a *Charter* right. This may have occurred in *Vriend v Alberta (Vriend)*.[41] The Supreme Court of Canada found that the omission of sexual orientation as a ground of discrimination from Alberta's

---

37   *Slaight Communications Inc v Davidson*, [1989] 1 SCR 1038.
38   *Ibid* at 1080.
39   *Ibid* at 1081.
40   *Ibid* at 1080.
41   *Vriend v Alberta*, [1998] 1 SCR 493, rev'g (1996), 132 DLR (4th) 595 (Alta CA) [*Vriend*].

Individual Rights Protection Act violated section 15(1) of the *Charter*. At the section 1 stage, the Court was unable to identify anything in the province's submissions that established that the omission had a pressing and substantial objective.[42] The section 1 justification therefore failed, and the phrase "sexual orientation" was read into the Act. There were indications in the record that the legislature omitted sexual orientation simply because it did not wish to extend statutory human rights protection to gay and lesbian people; doing so would have required it to take a position on a controversial moral debate.[43] There was, presumably, significant public support for the proposition that homosexual behaviour was immoral, and gay and lesbian people were therefore not entitled to the protection of human rights legislation. The Court would surely not have accepted such a blatantly unconstitutional objective as "pressing and substantial."[44] An objective of this kind could be pursued only by invoking the override or "notwithstanding" clause in section 33 of the *Charter* (see Chapter 1, Section C(4)) — as the Alberta legislature was urged, but decided not, to do after *Vriend* was released.[45]

While it is generally easy to identify a pressing and substantial objective, as Hogg has pointed out that objective can be specified at "various levels of generality":[46] usually, the higher the level of generality, the easier it will be to find that the other elements of the *Oakes* test[47] are satisfied. In light of the purpose of section 1 and its relationship with the rest of the *Charter*, the best way to find an appropriate level of generality is to focus on the objective of the limitation, not on the objective of the statutory scheme in which the limitation figures. It will be rare indeed to find a statute that does not have a pressing and substantial objective; but the need for the state to limit *Charter* rights in pursuit of that objective is best assessed not by asking about the purposes of the statute as a whole but about the purpose of the limitation itself, within the scheme. It is the limit on the right, not the statute as a

---

42   *Ibid* at paras 113–16 (SCC).

43   See *Vriend*, above note 41 at 652 (CA), Hunt JA dissenting and at 601–10, McClung JA.

44   Compare *Vriend*, above note 41 at para 115 (SCC), expressing doubts as to whether "'moral "considerations' . . . could be said to amount to a pressing and substantial objective . . . in this case."

45   See Tsvi Kahana, "The Notwithstanding Mechanism and Public Discussion: Lessons from the Ignored Practice of Section 33 of the *Charter*" (2001) 44 Can Pub Admin 255 at 273.

46   Peter W Hogg, *Constitutional Law of Canada*, 5th ed (Scarborough, ON: Thomson Carswell, 2007) §35.9(a). Compare *Vriend*, above note 41 at paras 109–11 (SCC).

47   See Section B, above in this chapter.

whole, that needs to be justified. *Oakes* itself furnishes a good example of this method. The limit on the right in that case was a statutory reverse onus provision requiring those accused of possessing narcotics to prove on a balance of probabilities that they were in possession for a purpose other than trafficking.[48] The Court considered the purpose of this limitation in the context of a statute directed at drug trafficking. It would not have been helpful to hold that the pressing and substantial objective was to combat drug trafficking; that was the general purpose of the statute as a whole. The purpose of the limit on the right—the reverse onus—considered in light of the more general purpose of combating drug trafficking, was "facilitating the conviction of drug traffickers." This more specific objective was "pressing and substantial."[49] But the Supreme Court has not consistently adopted this approach. In *Egan v Canada*,[50] the Supreme Court considered a pension scheme that treated same-sex couples differently from opposite-sex couples. Sopinka J, who furnished the pivotal vote upholding the scheme, held that it violated section 15(1) of the *Charter* by excluding same-sex couples but found a pressing and substantial objective in the scheme as a whole. By understanding the objective of the scheme as the "alleviation of poverty of elderly spouses" against a background of limited resources,[51] he avoided the question whether the limit on the right—the exclusion of same-sex couples—itself had a pressing and substantial objective.

In cases where section 7 is infringed, Canadian courts have generally held that the limit on the right has a pressing and substantial objective. It will be sufficient to cite five examples from the Supreme Court of Canada. In *R v Morgentaler* (*Morgentaler*), a provision of the *Criminal Code* criminalizing abortion had the objective of protecting the foetus.[52] In *R v Hess; R v Nguyen* (*Hess; Nguyen*), the absolute liability offence of having sexual intercourse with a girl under fourteen was "designed to protect female children from premature sexual intercourse."[53] In *R v Seaboyer* (*Seaboyer*), a restriction on the admissibility of evidence concerning the sexual history of the complainant in a sexual assault

---

48 Without that provision, the Crown would have to prove the accused's purpose of trafficking beyond a reasonable doubt.

49 *Oakes*, above note 2 at 140–41. The s 1 justification failed at a later stage.

50 *Egan v Canada*, [1995] 2 SCR 513.

51 *Ibid* at para 106.

52 *Morgentaler*, above note 3 at 122–24, Beetz J; and at 181, Wilson J. Dickson CJC understood the objective to be the balancing of the interest of the foetus with the interests of pregnant women: at 74–75.

53 *Hess; Nguyen*, above note 12 at 920, Wilson J; compare *ibid* at 948–49, McLachlin J.

case was intended to promote procedural fairness by removing the influence of myths and stereotypes about sexual behaviour from the fact-finding process.[54] In *Chaoulli v Quebec (AG)* (*Chaoulli*), a restriction on private health insurance had the objective of "protecting the public health regime."[55] In *Charkaoui*, the secrecy requirements of the security-certificate procedure had a pressing and substantial objective; namely, protecting "Canada's national security and related intelligence sources."[56] In each case, it is the objective of the limit on the right, considered in the context of the legislative scheme as a whole, that is found to be pressing and substantial. The Court had no difficulty in accepting that all of these various objectives were sufficiently important to justify a limit on a *Charter* right; in each case, the proposed section 1 justification failed at a later stage.

4) Proportionality

a) Rational Connection

A limit on a *Charter* right must be rationally connected to the pressing and substantial objective that it is meant to promote.

The reason for requiring a rational connection is straightforward. If the limit on the right is not rationally connected to the objective, and does not promote it, the right has been limited for no good reason.

It is less straightforward to determine whether a connection is rational. Since the state bears the burden of establishing the elements of a justification under section 1, it might be thought that the government should be required to prove, using social-science evidence, that the limit in fact promotes the objective. But social-science evidence is often inconclusive in the sense that different social scientists, acting in good faith and in accordance with the methodological norms of their discipline, may reach inconsistent or opposed conclusions; moreover, social-science evidence sometimes does not speak to the precise empirical issue that the court is concerned with, or is based on data from other jurisdictions. Suppose, for example, a Canadian court was required to decide whether the imposition of the death penalty was a reasonable limit on the right to be free from cruel and unusual punishment.[57] The government would probably argue that the objective of the

---

54 *Seaboyer*, above note 12 at 626 and compare 606.

55 *Chaoulli v Quebec (AG)*, 2005 SCC 35 at para 155 [*Chaoulli*].

56 *Charkaoui*, above note 22 at para 68.

57 This issue could not arise in domestic Canadian law as it now stands because the death penalty has been abolished: see Chapter 2, Section D(2). It could arise under extradition law, if a court was asked to consider the constitutionality of

limit on the right was to deter potential murderers; the rational connection argument might then turn on whether the death penalty does
in fact deter. This empirical issue has been intensively studied in the
United States, but it is difficult to identify a consensus view, and the
data used are of course mostly American.[58] So a Canadian court might
hesitate to make a definitive finding one way or the other. Since the
burden of proof is on the government, the *Charter* applicant might then
argue that the court should find that the government has not established a rational connection. Rather than accepting this argument, the
Supreme Court of Canada has usually held that where social-science
evidence is inconclusive, the government may establish a rational connection by pointing to a "reasoned apprehension" that the limit on the
right will promote the objective in question.[59]

In *R v Butler*,[60] the Court considered the criminal prohibitions in
section 163 of the *Criminal Code*, relating to "obscene" materials. These
prohibitions infringed the right to freedom of expression in section
2(*b*) of the *Charter*. This limit was said to be justified by the prevention
of harm, particularly harm to women's equality. Social-scientific evidence concerning the link between exposure to pornographic materials and harmful attitudes was inconclusive. But the Court did not reject
the claim that there was a rational connection between the prohibition
and its objective; instead, the Court held that the material before it, including the inconclusive social-science evidence, showed a "reasoned
apprehension of harm" sufficient to establish a rational connection.[61]
Similarly, in *R v Bryan*,[62] the Court considered a statutory ban on the
publication of election results before the polls in that part of the coun-

---

extraditing someone to face the death penalty where the relevant extradition
treaty, or the law of the requesting state, did not permit Canada to seek assurances that the death penalty would not be imposed.

58 What follows is a small sample from the large social-scientific literature on this
topic: Isaac Ehrlich, "The Deterrent Effect of Capital Punishment: A Question
of Life and Death" (1975) 65 American Economic Review 397; William C Bailey
& Ruth D Peterson, "Murder and Capital Punishment: A Monthly Time-Series
Analysis of Execution Publicity" (1989) 54 American Sociological Review 722;
Joanna M Shepherd, "Murders of Passion, Execution Delays, and the Deterrence
of Capital Punishment" (2004) 33 J Leg Stud 283; Bijou Yang & David Lester,
"The Deterrent Effect of Execution: A Meta-analysis Thirty Years after Ehrlich"
(2008) 36 Journal of Criminal Justice 453.

59 *R v Butler*, [1992] 1 SCR 452 at 494–99.

60 *Ibid*.

61 *Ibid* at 501–4.

62 *R v Bryan*, 2007 SCC 12 [*Bryan*]. The majority consisted of separate reasons by
Bastarache J and Fish J; Deschamps, Charron, and Rothstein JJ concurred with
both.

try had closed. The ban infringed the right to freedom of expression in section 2(*b*) of the *Charter*, and its purpose was held to be "to ensure informational equality by adopting reasonable measures to deal with the perception of unfairness created when some voters have general access to information that is denied to others, and the further possibility that access to that information will affect voter participation or choices."[63] But these objectives depended on the ban's effectiveness in promoting public confidence by preventing certain effects associated with allowing voters in western Canada to learn of the results in eastern Canada before voting. Two effects were of particular concern: since it would often be possible to anticipate the overall result of the election based on the results from eastern Canada, voters in western Canada might decide not to vote at all (the turnout effect) or to vote for the winning party regardless of their true preference (the bandwagon effect). The social-science evidence concerning these effects was inconclusive and was based largely on American data. Nonetheless, the Court agreed that the material before it gave Parliament a reasonable basis for enacting the ban.[64]

Whether a limit on a section 7 right is rationally connected to its objective depends in part on the nature of the infringement of section 7. If the law in question is arbitrary, it cannot be rationally connected. To show that a law is arbitrary, a *Charter* applicant must demonstrate that "it bears no relation to, or is inconsistent with" the objective of the legislation in question.[65] When this stringent test for arbitrariness is met, the law cannot be rationally connected to its objective. As Beetz J stated in *Morgentaler*, "A rule which is unnecessary in terms of Parliament's objectives cannot be said to be 'rationally connected' thereto or to be 'carefully designed to achieve the objective in question.'"[66] In *Chaoulli*, for example, the same facts that led the majority to find the law in question arbitrary also led it to find that the rational connection branch of the *Oakes* test was not satisfied.[67] If a law passes the test for arbitrariness, it does bear some relation to and is consistent with its objective, and it is therefore very likely that the limit imposed by the law on the section 7 right will be rationally connected to the objective of the limit.

---

63   *Ibid* at para 14, Bastarache J.

64   *Ibid* at paras 16–23, Bastarache J and at para 64, Fish J, and at para 105, Abella J dissenting on other grounds.

65   *Rodriguez v British Columbia (AG)*, [1993] 3 SCR 519 at 620–21.

66   *Morgentaler*, above note 3 at 125.

67   *Chaoulli*, above note 55 at para 155.

Where the section 7 defect in the law is not a matter of arbitrariness, the court will usually find that the limit on the section 7 right is rationally connected to its objective. In *Hess; Nguyen*, an absolute liability offence was rationally connected to the offence's deterrence objectives.[68] In *Charkaoui*, the unfair aspects of the procedure for determining the reasonableness of a security certificate were rationally connected to the objectives of protecting national security and intelligence sources, particularly in light of Canada's position as "a net importer of security information."[69]

However, on occasion a law that is not arbitrary but that violates some other principles of fundamental justice will not be rationally connected to its objective. In *R v B(D)* (*B(D)*),[70] the Supreme Court of Canada held that the provisions of the *Youth Criminal Justice Act*,[71] imposing in certain cases an onus on a young person to show why an adult sentence was not warranted, violated the principle of fundamental justice entitling young persons to a presumption of diminished moral capacity. The objective of the imposition of an adult sentence on a young offender was to serve "accountability, public protection and public confidence"; but the violation was not rationally connected because "it is the availability of a more serious outcome (that is, the adult sentence and the lifted publication ban), rather than the placement of the onus on the young person to escape such an outcome, that serves these objectives."[72]

b) Minimal Impairment

A limit on a *Charter* right must impair the right as little as is reasonably possible to promote the pressing and substantial objective that it is meant to forward.

Like the rational connection branch, the minimal impairment branch is intended to ensure that the right is not limited more than necessary to achieve the state's objective. If the state's objective can be promoted in a way that impairs the right less than the limit sought to be justified, then the impairment of the right is to that extent unnecessary. In practice, it is very difficult to know whether a limit is minimally impairing. It is always possible to imagine a hypothetical law that would impair the right less than the impugned law, but it rarely clear that the hypothetical law will promote the objective as effectively.

---

68 See, for instance, *Hess; Nguyen*, above note 12 at 920–21.
69 *Charkaoui*, above note 22 at para 68.
70 *R v B(D)*, 2008 SCC 25 [*B(D)*].
71 *Youth Criminal Justice Act*, SC 2002, c 1.
72 *B(D)*, above note 70 at para 91, quoting with approval from the decision of the court below (2006), 206 CCC (3d) 289 at para 86 (Ont CA).

Similarly, among possible laws that are arguably equally effective in promoting the objective, it is not always clear which is in fact least impairing of the right. For these reasons, the Supreme Court of Canada has been prepared to grant the state a "margin of appreciation" in its choice among the different ways of pursuing its objective,[73] and the Court does not insist that the proposed less drastic means achieves the government's objectives to precisely the same degree as the impugned law.[74] These considerations are reflected in the reformulations of the minimal impairment test as whether the limit impairs the right as little as reasonably possible, or whether the limit is reasonably necessary,[75] particularly where the law in question can be characterized as "mediating between the claims of competing groups."[76]

But regardless of the precise formulation of the minimal impairment branch, the limit on the section 7 right imposed by a law that is vague, overbroad, arbitrary, or grossly disproportionate (see Chapter 4, Section B) cannot be a minimal impairment of the right because it will always be possible to imagine a more carefully tailored law that impairs the right less. As Cory J put it in R v Heywood (Heywood), "Overbroad legislation which infringes s. 7 of the Charter would appear to be incapable of passing the minimal impairment breach of the s. 1 analysis."[77] An overbroad law is substantively defective because it affects life, liberty, and security of the person more than necessary to achieve the state's objective; it is therefore always possible to envision a more carefully drafted or more narrowly tailored law, and this possibility means that the overbroad law cannot be justified under section 1.[78] In Heywood itself, a law restricting the liberty of sexual offenders violated section 7 because it was broader than it needed to be to achieve its purposes and could therefore not be a minimal impairment of the section 7 right.

Even where the section 7 violation arises in some other way, it is difficult to demonstrate that a limit on a section 7 right is a minimal impairment of the right because it is generally possible to imagine an

---

73   Irwin Toy, above note 27 at 993; Newfoundland (Treasury Board) v Newfoundland and Labrador Association of Public and Private Employees, 2004 SCC 66 at para 84.

74   Hutterian Brethren, above note 6 at para 55.

75   For a sample of many similar statements of this idea, which is in principle applicable even where s 7 is violated, see R v Chaulk, [1990] 3 SCR 1303 at 1343; Eldridge v British Columbia (AG), [1997] 3 SCR 624 at para 86; Charkaoui, above note 22 at para 85; Hutterian Brethren, ibid at para 53.

76   Irwin Toy, above note 27 at 993.

77   R v Heywood, [1994] 3 SCR 761 at 802–3.

78   Compare R v Demers, 2004 SCC 46 at para 46; Swain, above note 27 at 1018–20.

alternative to the impugned law that would impair the right less without interfering with the objectives of the legislation.

In cases where the statute in question violates the principles of fundamental justice because of procedural unfairness, the section 1 justification will usually fail because it will be possible to design a statutory scheme that achieves the state's objectives but is procedurally fair. In *Seaboyer*, for example, the challenged provisions of the *Criminal Code* were procedurally unfair because they had the effect of excluding evidence that was relevant and probative of an accused person's defence and that was not excessively prejudicial. This limit on the section 7 right was not justified because it was "overbroad" in terms of its objective of excluding excessively prejudicial evidence.[79]

In *Charkaoui*, the Supreme Court held that the procedure for determining the reasonableness of a security certificate under the *Immigration and Refugee Protection Act*[80] was inconsistent with the principle of fundamental justice requiring a fair hearing, in particular because the procedure was designed to ensure that the person named in the certificate would not be able to know and to respond to the case against him.[81] The procedure, though directed at and rationally connected to the pressing and substantial objective of protecting Canada's security and intelligence sources, was not the minimal impairment of the right to a fair hearing because there were other ways "to protect sensitive information while treating individuals fairly."[82] In proceedings before the Security Intelligence Review Committee (SIRC), for example, independent and security-cleared counsel were used during closed portions of hearings to challenge the information put before the committee by the Canadian Intelligence Security Service (CSIS), though the information was not disclosed to the person affected.[83] The system of "special advocates" used in the UK by the Special Immigration Appeals Commission (SIAC) is somewhat similar. The special advocate represents the interests of a person appealing to SIAC and is allowed to see any protected information that is put before SIAC, but she is not permitted to communicate with the appellant once she has seen the protected information.[84] These procedures enable sensitive information to

---

79   *Seaboyer*, above note 12 at 626.
80   *Immigration and Refugee Protection Act*, SC 2001, c 27 [*IRPA*].
81   *Charkaoui*, above note 22 at paras 19–65, and see Chapter 5, Section A(2).
82   *Ibid* at para 70, and see also para 87.
83   *Ibid* at paras 71–74.
84   *Ibid* at paras 80–84.

be effectively challenged in an adversarial setting, though not disclosed to the person affected by the decision.[85]

Where the principle of fundamental justice in issue cannot be clearly characterized as procedural or substantive, it will often be the case that a reformulated rule will achieve the state's objective without violating the individual's rights; thus, the impugned rule will not be minimally impairing. In *R v Swain*,[86] for example, the Court held that the common law rule permitting the Crown to allege the accused's insanity infringed the principle of fundamental justice giving the accused the right to control his own defence.[87] A less minimally impairing alternative was readily envisaged: "a rule which would allow the Crown to raise independently the issue of insanity only after the trier of fact had concluded that the accused was otherwise guilty of the offence charged" or where "the accused's own defence has somehow put his or her mental capacity for criminal intent in issue."[88] Similarly, in *B(D)*, the Court held that a reverse onus on a young person to establish the conditions for a youth sentence violated the principles of fundamental justice.[89] This infringement was not justified under section 1 because placing the onus on the Crown would achieve the state's objectives without infringing the accused's rights.[90]

In cases where the principle of fundamental justice at stake is related to the fault element of criminal offences, the Court will generally hold that redefining the offence with a constitutionally sufficient fault element, or creating a new offence that more directly achieves the objective of the legislation, is a less impairing alternative.[91] Consider, for example, *Hess; Nguyen*. The two accused challenged a provision of the *Criminal Code* creating the offence of having sexual intercourse with a female under fourteen "whether or not [the accused] believes she is fourteen years of age or more," with a possible penalty of life imprisonment.[92] This absolute liability offence offended the principle of fundamental justice requiring a minimum level of fault for penal offences (see Chapter 4, Section C(2)). Wilson J, for the majority, found that it served the pressing and substantial objective of protecting young girls

---

85   In response to *Charkaoui*, Parliament amended *IRPA* to create a system of special advocates for security certificate proceedings.

86   Above note 27.

87   See Chapter 4, Section D(3).

88   *Swain*, above note 27 at 986–87.

89   See Chapter 4, Section D(4).

90   *B(D)*, above note 70 at para 91.

91   Indeed, these alternatives typically do not infringe s 7 at all.

92   *Criminal Code*, RSC 1970, c C-34, s 146(1).

from premature sexual intercourse and that it was rationally connected to that objective. McLachlin J, dissenting, would have found that the provision for absolute liability enhanced the deterrent associated with the offence because "it effectively puts men who are contemplating intercourse with a girl who might be under fourteen years of age on guard. They know that if they have intercourse without being certain of the girl's age, they run the risk of conviction, and many conclude that they will not take the chance."[93] Thus, in her view there was no way of achieving the objective that was less impairing of the right.[94] But Wilson J, for the majority, rejected this analysis. In her view, the law failed the minimal impairment branch because there was no reason to think that the deterrent effect of an absolute liability offence was any greater than the deterrent effect of an offence with a negligence-based fault element, and certainly the Crown had not led any evidence to support that proposition.[95] As she noted, McLachlin J's analysis "begs the question: what if [the accused] is sure that [the complainant] is over fourteen but turns out to be wrong?"[96] There is no reason to think that absolute liability has any deterrent effect that is additional to what would be provided by a requirement that the accused use reasonable care to ensure that the complainant is over fourteen.

In *R v Martineau*,[97] the Supreme Court held that the constructive murder provisions of the *Criminal Code* violated section 7 because they violated the principle of fundamental justice requiring subjective foresight of death to be an element of the offence of murder (see Chapter 4, Section C(4)). Once again, the section 1 argument in favour of the provision was deterrent-based: a person contemplating the commission of one of the predicate offences might be deterred by the thought that if she unintentionally killed someone while committing the predicate offence, she would be liable for the much more serious offence of murder.[98] The Court accepted that "the objective of deterring the infliction of bodily harm during the commission of certain offences" was a pressing and substantial objective and that the imposition of constructive

---

93   *Hess; Nguyen*, above note 12 at 950.
94   *Ibid* at 951, McLachlin J dissenting.
95   *Ibid* at 922–23, Wilson J.
96   *Ibid* at 923.
97   *R v Martineau*, [1990] 2 SCR 633 [*Martineau*].
98   *Martineau* was concerned specifically with predicate offences that involved the infliction of bodily harm; in R v Vaillancourt, [1987] 2 SCR 636, the Court had previously struck down a form of constructive murder for which the predicate offences involved the carrying of weapons rather than the infliction of harm. But in either case, the argument in favour of the law was that it would deter the commission of the predicate offence.

liability for murder was rationally connected to the objective.[99] But constructive liability was not a minimal impairment of the section 7 right because "it is not necessary in order to achieve this objective to convict of murder persons who do not intend or foresee death" because Parliament could deter the infliction of bodily harm simply by "punish[ing] persons for causing the bodily harm."[100]

c) Balancing Salutary and Deleterious Effects

The salutary effects of a limit on a *Charter* right on the objective it is meant to forward must not be disproportionate to the deleterious effects.

The "effects-balancing" branch of the proportionality test is somewhat different from the first two branches. The rational connection test and the minimal impairment test both require, in principle, that the law be instrumentally rational; that is, that it promotes its purpose and that it goes no farther than necessary to achieve its purpose. But the effects-balancing branch is, even in principle, more complex, because it asks whether the law is justified even if it is rationally connected to a pressing and substantial objective and minimally impairing of the right. Put another way, there is no need to consider the effects-balancing branch unless the law is rationally connected and minimally impairing; the effects-balancing branch asks whether the cost of achieving the objective is simply too great.[101]

The effects-balancing branch played a minor role in the early section 1 cases, and has recently begun to assume more importance.[102] Nonetheless, the Supreme Court has never found that a limit on a right passes the rational connection and minimal impairment branch but fails the effects-balancing branch.[103] There are a number of cases involving section 7 violations in which the Court, having found that the section 1 justification failed at an earlier stage, has commented that the deleterious effects of the limit outweighed the salutary effects.[104]

---

99 *Martineau*, above note 97 at 647.

100 *Ibid*.

101 *Hutterian Brethren*, above note 6 at paras 76–78.

102 It was critical to LeBel J dissenting in *Hutterian Brethren*, *ibid*.

103 The dissenting minority in *Bryan*, above note 62, would have done so.

104 See, for example, *Morgentaler*, above note 3 at 126, Beetz J; *Seaboyer*, above note 12 at 627.

FURTHER READINGS

CHOUDHRY, SUJIT. "So What is the Real Legacy of *Oakes*? Two Decades of Proportionality Analysis under the Canadian *Charter*'s Section 1" (2006) 34 Sup Ct L Rev (2d) 501.

HOGG, PETER W. "Section 1 Revisited" (1991–92) 1 NJCL 1.

JACKMAN, MARTHA. "Protecting Rights and Promoting Democracy: Judicial Review under Section 1 of the *Charter*" (1996) 34 Osgoode Hall LJ 661.

PACIOCCO, DAVID. "*Charter* Vertigo: Losing Constitutional Balance in Criminal Cases" in Joseph E Magnet & Bernie Adell, eds, *The Canadian Charter of Rights and Freedoms after Twenty-Five Years* (Markam, ON: LexisNexis Canada, 2009) 163.

SHARPE, ROBERT J, & KENT ROACH. *The Canadian Charter of Rights and Freedoms*, 4th ed (Toronto: Irwin Law, 2009) ch 4.

TREMBLAY, LUC B, & GRÉGOIRE WEBBER, EDS. *The Limitation of Charter Rights: Critical Essays on* R v Oakes (Montréal: Thémis, 2009).

WEINRIB, LORRAINE. "The Supreme Court of Canada and Section One of the *Charter*" (1988) 10 Sup Ct L Rev 469.

CHAPTER 7

THE SIGNIFICANCE OF SECTION 7

Section 7 has proved to be one of the most fertile, even protean, sections of the *Charter*, as its very general language has made it the source for numerous constitutional claims that might be difficult to assert under other sections of the *Charter*. The Supreme Court of Canada's early determination that the principles of fundamental justice included both principles of procedural fairness and principles of substantive justice[1] opened up grounds for challenging state action that would otherwise have been immune to review on constitutional or administrative law grounds. Some of the Court's most dramatic interventions in Canadian law — its invalidation of the abortion prohibition in the *Criminal Code*,[2] its constitutionalization of basic principles in criminal law,[3] its foray into health care policy[4] — were made possible by the power to review laws for compliance with substantive principles of justice. Given the unwillingness of the Court to recognize a section 1 limit on a section 7 right and the reluctance of legislatures to use the section 33 override to immunize legislation from *Charter* review, the stakes in a section 7 challenge are high indeed. A successful claim that a statute violates section 7 generally leads to the invalidation of the statute; the legislative

---

1   *Re BC Motor Vehicle Act*, [1985] 2 SCR 486 [*Motor Vehicle Reference*], and see Chapter 3.
2   *R v Morgentaler*, [1988] 1 SCR 30 [*Morgentaler*].
3   *Motor Vehicle Reference*, above note 1; *R v Martineau*, [1990] 2 SCR 633; *R v Ruzic*, 2001 SCC 24.
4   *Chaoulli v Quebec (AG)*, 2005 SCC 35.

response (if any) is usually intended to be consistent with section 7.[5] Thus, perhaps more than any other section of the *Charter*, section 7 has increased the law-making power of the courts and particularly of the Supreme Court of Canada. For some commentators, review under section 7 is only the most egregious instance of the power to make law being transferred from popularly elected and democratically accountable legislative institutions to unelected and unaccountable judicial elites.[6] Even those who generally support judicial review of legislation as a means of ensuring compliance of the law with basic norms of justice have been critical of some of the Supreme Court's decisions under section 7.[7]

This brief concluding chapter is not the place to provide a new justification for judicial review of statutes on rights-based grounds, or even to choose among the many existing accounts.[8] But I would like to

---

5   Parliament has occasionally challenged the Court's constitutional reasoning, by enacting statutes that appear inconsistent with s 7: see *Criminal Code*, RSC 1985, c C-46, ss 278.1–278.91, responding to *R v O'Connor*, [1995] 4 SCR 411 [*O'Connor*], and upheld in *R v Mills*, [1999] 3 SCR 668 [*Mills*]; *Criminal Code*, ibid, s 33.1, responding to *R v Daviault*, [1994] 3 SCR 63 [*Daviault*]. But *O'Connor* and *Daviault* did not invalidate any statutes; they were essentially decisions that modified the common law on constitutional grounds.

6   This theme has appeared in critiques of the *Charter* from commentators across the political spectrum: Michael Mandel, *The Charter of Rights and the Legalization of Politics in Canada* (Toronto: Wall & Thomson, 1989); Allan Hutchinson, *Waiting for Coraf: A Critique of Law and Rights* (Toronto: University of Toronto Press, 1995); Andrew Petter, *The Politics of the Charter: The Illusive Promise of Constitutional Rights* (Toronto: University of Toronto Press, 2010); Patrick J Monahan, *Politics and the Constitution: The Charter, Federalism and the Supreme Court of Canada* (Toronto: Carswell, 1987); Christopher P Manfredi, *Judicial Power and the Charter*, 2d ed (Don Mills, ON: Oxford University Press, 2001); FL Morton & Rainer Knopff, *The Charter Revolution and the Court Party* (Peterborough, ON: Broadview, 2000). For a critique of judicial review not tied to any particular positive legal order, see Jeremy Waldron, "The Core of the Case Against Judicial Review" (2006) 115 Yale LJ 1346.

7   See, for instance, Sujit Choudhry, "Worse than *Lochner*?" in Colleen Flood, Kent Roach, & Lorne Sossin, eds, *Access to Care, Access to Justice* (Toronto: University of Toronto Press, 2005) 76.

8   Which include, among many others, Alexander Bickel, *The Least Dangerous Branch*, 2d ed (New Haven: Yale University Press, 1986); John Hart Ely, *Democracy and Distrust* (Cambridge, MA: Harvard University Press, 1980); Ronald Dworkin, *Law's Empire* (Cambridge, MA: Belknap Press of Harvard University Press, 1986), ch 10; Kent Roach, *The Supreme Court on Trial* (Toronto: Irwin Law, 2001); David Beatty, *The Ultimate Rule of Law* (Oxford: Oxford University Press, 2004); WJ Waluchow, *A Common Law Theory of Judicial Review* (Cambridge: Cambridge University Press, 2007); Richard Fallon, "The Core of an Uneasy Case for Judicial Review" (2008) 121 Harv L Rev 1693.

sketch a liberal-democratic defence of the Supreme Court of Canada's broad interpretation of section 7; without such a defence, many of the doctrines discussed in this book would amount to an unjustified arrogation of power by an elite, unelected group of state officials.

In a contemporary liberal-democratic state—a "free and democratic society," in the words of the *Charter*—individual citizens must be able to be, and to see themselves as, more than mere means or resources for the state to use in its pursuit of public objectives, but as the persons whose interests those objectives and the means used to pursue them must ultimately serve and to whom those objectives and means must ultimately be justified. Elements of this vision of liberal democracy appear in the work of both critics and supporters of judicial review. There are many disagreements about what counts as using the citizen merely as a means to an end; about the objectives that the state may legitimately pursue; and about who should decide these questions. Yet at a sufficiently high level of abstraction, both critics and supporters of judicial review share the view that the state should be both democratic—responsive to the people's views about what the law should be—and liberal—committed to the "liberal confidence . . . in the worth of the individual"[9] and therefore to some conception of individual rights and civil liberties.[10] Many of the rights in the *Charter* can be understood as contributing to the liberal-democratic project so understood—the requirement for periodic Parliaments, the guarantees of voting and mobility rights, the expansive protection for freedom of conscience, expression, and peaceful assembly all play a role in ensuring that the individual citizen is treated both as an end in herself and as a participant in the process of explaining and justifying uses of public power. And the individual rights guaranteed by section 7 of the *Charter* are also central to the proper operation of a free and democratic society in this sense. When state action affects the most basic interests of individuals—their life, liberty, and security—section 7 requires state action to be both procedurally and substantively fair, thus in principle ensuring that individuals are treated not merely as means to the governmental or social purposes that the state action is aimed at,

---

9   Alan Brudner, *Constitutional Goods* (Oxford: Oxford University Press, 2004) at 13.

10   Critics of judicial review who share this "liberal confidence" include Petter, above note 6 at 226–27; Morton & Knopff, above note 6 at 149; Manfredi, above note 6 at 199 (characterizing the Constitution as "both limiting and limited;" that is, as both constraining the exercise of state power and enabling deliberation about what powers the state should have). Waldron, above note 6 at 1364–65, strongly endorses a version of the liberal confidence.

but as individuals in their own right. Indeed, while the traditional civil liberties protected by sections 2 and 3 are undoubtedly fundamental to a free and democratic society, the interests protected by section 7 are no less fundamental. The right to vote or to express oneself freely is of little value to a person deprived of liberty or security following an unfair hearing, on the basis of a fundamentally unjust law, or by means of arbitrary state action.

Consider criticisms of the *Motor Vehicle Reference* in this light. In the *Motor Vehicle Reference*, the Supreme Court of Canada held that the principles of fundamental justice were not limited to principles of procedural fairness, but might include substantive principles of justice as well. The standard critique of this holding runs as follows: in choosing the phrase "fundamental justice" the drafters of the *Charter* were obviously referring to procedural fairness, and by choosing to assign the phrase a broader meaning, the Court imposed its own views on a reasonably clear text and thus arrogated to itself much more power than had been intended.[11] The claim that section 7 was obviously about procedural fairness rather than substantive judgments depends on the persuasive evidence that the Department of Justice officials who drafted section 7 of the *Charter*, as well as other political actors, thought so; the claim that the Court imposed its own view depends on the Court's conscious decision to give this evidence little weight in determining the meaning of section 7. As Manfredi puts it, "The Court's power to declare absolute liability offences contrary to substantive fundamental justice and in violation of the *Charter* (when such offences are enforced by imprisonment) had no source other than judicial will."[12]

The standard critique is at best incomplete. The question before the Court in the *Motor Vehicle Reference* was the proper legal meaning of the phrase "principles of fundamental justice." But any answer the Court gave would have been an answer chosen by the Court; to have adopted the interpretation proposed by the civil servants who drafted the *Charter* would have been just as much an act of judicial will as was the rejection of that interpretation.[13] The task of the Court, at the most

---

11   Manfredi, *ibid* at 35–38; Robert E Hawkins, "Intepretivism and Sections 7 & 15 of the *Canadian Charter of Rights and Freedoms*" (1990) 22 Ottawa L Rev 275 at 285–93.

12   Manfredi, *ibid* at 38.

13   Compare the "realist" theory of statutory interpretation offered by Michel Troper, *La théorie du droit, le droit, l'état* (Paris: Presses universitaires de France, 2001) at 69–84 (though, as a strict positivist, Troper would confine himself to identifying the norm established by the *Motor Vehicle Reference*, above note 1, and would not engage in any criticism or defence of the decision), and the

abstract level, is to enforce the law; when interpreting a statute or a constitution, that task is not to defer to some other institution's conception of what the law should mean, but to give the statute or constitution its best legal meaning. Thus, a persuasive criticism of the *Motor Vehicle Reference* must go beyond showing that the Court gave section 7 the meaning it thought the section should have; of course it did that. Rather, critics of the decision must show that there are legal reasons, appropriate to a liberal-democratic state, that justify restricting the principles of fundamental justice to procedural fairness. Most critics of judicial review under the *Charter* have avoided this challenge, preferring instead to argue that it is undesirable to put so much law-making power in the hands of the judiciary.[14] But this critique, too, is incomplete; even without the power of judicial review, courts have a critical role to play in the interpretation and application of statutes and in the review of administrative decision making, in which all the constitutional questions about the appropriate role of judges in a democracy replicate themselves in a different guise. The task of judges under the *Charter* is not fundamentally different from their task in non-*Charter* cases: it is to give the best legal answer to the questions that they are asked to decide.[15]

Supporters of the decision must, on the other hand, show that there are good legal reasons justifying the broader interpretation of section 7 that the Court ultimately chose. Here I would suggest that even though relatively few statutes have been invalidated on section 7 grounds (especially outside the *Criminal Code*), the generous interpretation of s 7 in the *Motor Vehicle Reference* has had a beneficial effect on Canadian legal culture. Section 7 has not only enabled courts to intervene to remedy some of the more egregiously unfair applications of state power to individuals,[16] it has encouraged governments to ensure that the draft

---

similar emphasis on the role of judicial choice and acts of will in Richard A Posner, *The Problems of Jurisprudence* (Cambridge, MA: Harvard University Press, 1990) at 262–311 and in Stanley Fish, *Doing What Comes Naturally* (Durham, NC: Duke University Press, 1989) at 103–40. See also Morton & Knopff, above note 6 at 40–53.

14   See especially Mandel, above note 6; Hutchinson, above note 6; Morton & Knopff, above note 6. An exception is Petter, above note 6 at 66, who offers an argument as to why the imposition of absolute liability was not unfair in the context of the statute at issue. Contrast Manfredi, above note 6 at 35–38, who expresses no opinion on this substantive issue.

15   On these matters, see especially David Dyzenhaus, *The Constitution of Law* (Cambridge: Cambridge University Press, 2006).

16   In addition to the *Motor Vehicle Reference*, above note 1 (holding absolute liability to be inconsistent with the principles of fundamental justice); *Morgentaler*, above note 2 (requiring the procedures for obtaining a lawful

legislation they bring to the legislative process respects the basic norms protected by section 7.[17] It has been argued that this sort of "*Charter*-proofing" is undesirable because it encourages legislators and the public to think that constitutionally valid legislation is good legislation.[18] It is certainly the case that mere compliance with the *Charter* is no guarantee that legislation will be effective or wise. But there is reason to think that Bill C-36, the legislative response to the terrorist attacks of 11 September 2011, was more respectful of civil liberties than it would have been without the *Charter*, and in particular without the substantive guarantees of section 7.[19] It may be that some of the new terrorism offences created by Bill C-36 were unnecessary, but at least they are all full *mens rea* offences, no doubt reflecting the fears of its drafters that guilt imposed on a lesser standard would violate section 7. Moreover, the interplay between *Charter* values and the principles of statutory interpretation has enabled the Supreme Court of Canada to interpret some of the provisions of Bill C-36 so as to provide substantial protection for persons affected by some of its new procedures.[20] That is not to say, of course, that the courts are always correct in their interpretation and application of these rights. *R v Chaoulli* (*Chaoulli*), in particular, has been roundly criticized by both supporters and critics of judicial review under the *Charter*. But, as argued above, the central flaw in *Chaoulli* was the Court's misapprehension of the facts. If, as the majority of the Court was persuaded, it really was the case that people were dying (for no reason) because the government was preventing them from getting health care, there would be every reason for the Court to do what it could to encourage the government to remedy the situation.

---

abortion to be fair and non-arbitrary); *United States v Burns*, 2001 SCC 7 (requiring the Minister of Justice to obtain assurances that another state will not execute a person extradited from Canada to face a death sentence); and *Charkaoui v Canada* (*Citizenship and Immigration*), 2007 SCC 9 (requiring a fair hearing for determining whether a permanent resident or foreign national is a threat to the security of Canada).

17   Compare Janet Hiebert, *Charter Conflicts: What is Parliament's Role?* (Montreal: McGill-Queen's University Press, 2002).

18   See, for instance, Kent Roach, "The Dangers of a *Charter*-Proof and Crime-Based Response to Terrorism" in Ronald J Daniels, Patrick Macklem, & Kent Roach, eds, *The Security of Freedom: Essays on Canada's Anti-Terrorism Bill* (Toronto: University of Toronto Press, 2001) 151.

19   Contrast the response to the October Crisis: *Public Order* (*Temporary Measures*) *Act*, SC 1970-71-72, c 2. For a comparative discussion of counter-terrorism legislation and policy since 2001, see Kent Roach, *The 9/11 Effect* (Cambridge: Cambridge University Press, 2011).

20   See *Re Application under s 83.28 of the Criminal Code*, 2004 SCC 42; *R v Ahmad*, 2011 SCC 6.

Moreover, the Court sometimes responds to criticisms of its decisions by backing away from a controversial intervention. On at least one occasion, the Supreme Court has reconsidered the content of section 7 in the face of a legislative response inconsistent with its clearly expressed views on the question at issue.[21] Finally, the section 33 override is in principle available to the legislature in case of an egregious error by the courts, or in case of a sufficiently sharp disagreement between the Court and the legislature about the proper application of section 7. But in response to declarations of invalidity, Canadian legislatures generally prefer to amend statutes so that they comply with the *Charter* rather than to use the override. These trends suggest that the values underlying the *Charter*, and section 7 in particular, have come to permeate both the legislative and the judicial process. Section 7 forwards the liberal-democratic project of requiring exercises of state power to be justifiable to individual persons in their capacity as subjects of the law, without unduly interfering with their capacity as makers of the law through democratic institutions.

---

21   In *O'Connor*, above note 5, a majority of the Supreme Court fashioned a common law procedure for dealing with a conflict between an accused person's right to make full answer and defence and a witness's right to privacy and equality; the minority proposed a procedure that offered more protection to the witness. Parliament responded to *O'Connor* by amending the *Criminal Code* so that a version of the minority's proposal would apply in sexual cases. In light of *O'Connor*, this legislative response seemed plainly to violate s 7; but in *Mills*, above note 5, the Court upheld the legislation. (For further discussion, see Chapter 5, Section B(4)(b)). Similarly, in s 33.1 of the *Criminal Code*, above note 5, Parliament adopted a version of the minority position in *Daviault*, above note 5. The Supreme Court of Canada has yet to consider the constitutionality of this response.

FURTHER READINGS

BEATTY, DAVID. *The Ultimate Rule of Law* (Oxford: Oxford University Press, 2004).

BICKEL, ALEXANDER. *The Least Dangerous Branch*, 2d ed (New Haven: Yale University Press, 1986).

BRUDNER, ALAN. *Constitutional Goods* (Oxford: Oxford University Press, 2004).

DYZENHAUS, DAVID. *The Constitution of Law* (Cambridge: Cambridge University Press, 2006).

ELY, JOHN HART. *Democracy and Distrust* (Cambridge, MA: Harvard University Press, 1980).

FALLON, RICHARD. "The Core of an Uneasy Case for Judicial Review" (2008) 121 Harv L Rev 1693.

HIEBERT, JANET. *Charter Conflicts: What is Parliament's Role?* (Montreal: McGill-Queen's University Press, 2002).

HUTCHINSON, ALLAN. *Waiting for Coraf: A Critique of Law and Rights* (Toronto: University of Toronto Press, 1995).

MANDEL, MICHAEL. *The Charter of Rights and the Legalization of Politics in Canada* (Toronto: Wall & Thomson, 1989).

MANFREDI, CHRISTOPHER P. *Judicial Power and the Charter*, 2d ed (Don Mills, ON: Oxford University Press, 2001).

MONAHAN, PATRICK J. *Politics and the Constitution: The Charter, Federalism and the Supreme Court of Canada* (Toronto: Carswell, 1987).

MORTON, FREDERIK LEE, & RAINER KNOPFF. *The Charter Revolution and the Court Party* (Peterborough, ON: Broadview, 2000).

PETTER, ANDREW. *The Politics of the Charter: The Illusive Promise of Constitutional Rights* (Toronto: University of Toronto Press, 2010).

ROACH, KENT. *The Supreme Court on Trial* (Toronto: Irwin Law, 2001).

WALDRON, JEREMY. "The Core of the Case Against Judicial Review" (2006) 115 Yale LJ 1346.

WALUCHOW, WJ. *A Common Law Theory of Judicial Review* (Cambridge: Cambridge University Press, 2007).

TABLE OF CASES

INDEX

disposition hearing, 206, 207
Miscarriage of justice. *See* Trials and
hearings, miscarriage of justice
Mistake of fact, 162, 164, 191, 192
Mistake of law, 164
Mobility rights, 10, 30, 80, 309
Money laundering, 48
Murder, 46, 50, 105–6, 118, 166–72, 179,
252, 263, 264. *See also* Stigma
offences; "Subjective foresight of
death"
constructive murder, 105, 168, 304
felony murder, 106
wrongful conviction, 117

Narcotics, 147, 199, 269, 296. *See also*
Marijuana; Safe injection sites
Negligence, 40, 44, 45, 163
contributory, 42
criminal, 166
Notice, 104, 111, 124, 127, 161, 163, 164,
220, 229, 253, 257, 260. *See also*
Notification
hearing, of, 93, 254, 281–82
periods, 24
Notification, 99, 134, 164, 219, 284. *See
also* Notice
"Notwithstanding clause." *See* Legislative
override

Occupation, choice of, 92
Occupational health and safety, 233
Offenders. *See also* Medical procedures and treatments, persons in
custody
dangerous, 222
in custody, 94
Organized crime, 280
Overbreadth, 112, 151–56, 206, 208, 301,
302
test for, 135–36

Panhandling, 64
Parental obligations, 76. *See also* Cor-
poral punishment
Parole, 74, 111–12
Party liability, 177–78, 186
Patriation, 2–3
Peace bonds, 78, 115
Pecuniary interest, 230

Penal liability, 100, 101, 103, 158, 161,
193, 201, 217
Permanent residency, 10, 77, 80, 227,
229, 280. *See also* Citizenship
Picketing, 33
Police officers, 37–39, 44–45, 157, 211,
212, 213, 216, 247, 267, 293
disclosure and, 78, 251, 259
operating abroad, 47, 48
powers of arrest, 128
Pornography, 298
Prejudice. *See* Trials and hearings, preju-
dice
Presumptive offences, 79, 209, 218
Probation, 69
Prosecutorial discretion, 123–24, 130,
219–20
Prostitution, 92, 119, 147–48, 150
Provocation, 197
Psychological integrity, 88, 95
Public officials, 40. *See also* Tax officials
operating abroad, 46–50
Canadian Forces personnel, 52
Public safety, 135, 143, 154, 206, 207,
208, 231. *See also* Disclosure; Ter-
rorism
Publication bans, 36, 79

Quebec *Charter. See Charter of Human
Rights and Freedoms* (Quebec)

"Reasonable steps," 181–82
Refugees, 29, 58, 86, 115, 277–78,
281–84. *See also* Extradition and
deportation
disclosure and, 281–82
Religion, freedom of, 27
Right to counsel. *See* Counsel, right to
Right to trial within a reasonable time, 9
"*Rowbotham* order." *See* Counsel, funding
of

Safe injection sites, 28, 64, 142, 147. *See
also* Narcotics
School boards, 27
Search and seizure
bodily samples, 6–7, 83
reasonableness of, 6, 8, 156
vehicle search, 7
warrants, 8, 48–49, 132, 217

ABOUT THE AUTHOR

Hamish Stewart is a professor of law at the University of Toronto, where he has taught criminal law, the law of evidence, and legal theory since 1993. Before attending law school, he studied economics, receiving his BA from the University of Toronto in 1983 and his PhD from Harvard University in 1989. He received his LLB from the University of Toronto in 1992, clerked at the Ontario Court of Appeal in 1992–93, and was called to the Ontario Bar in 1998. He is the principal author of *Sexual Offences in Canadian Law* (2004) and has published more than fifty scholarly papers in criminal law, evidence, legal theory, and economics. He recently contributed the *Evidence* title to *Halsbury's Laws of Canada* (2010). He is the general editor of *Evidence: A Canadian Casebook*, 3d ed (2011) and an associate editor of the *Canadian Criminal Cases*.